MAIMONIDES AS BIBLICAL INTERPRETER

Sara Klein-Braslavy

Emunot: Jewish Philosophy and Kabbalah

MAIMONIDES AS BIBLICAL INTERPRETER

Sara Klein-Braslavy

Boston
2011

Library of Congress Cataloging-in-Publication Data

Klein-Braslavy, Sara.

Maimonides as biblical interpreter / Sara Klein-Braslavy.

p. cm. -- (Emunot : Jewish philosophy and Kabbalah)

Some of the articles in this volume are based on portions of Perush ha-Rambam le-sipur Beri'at ha-'olam, Perush ha-Rambam la-sipurim 'al Adam be-farashat Be-reshit, and Shelomoh ha-Melekh veha-ezoterizm ha-filosofi be-mishnat ha-Rambam, works by the same author.

Essays in English and English translations of Hebrew essays.

Includes bibliographical references and index.

ISBN 978-1-936235-28-5 (hardback)

1. Maimonides, Moses, 1135-1204. 2. Bible. O.T.--Criticism, interpretation, etc., Jewish. 3. Bible. O.T.--Hermeneutics. 4. Maimonides, Moses, 1135-1204. Dalalat al-ha'irin. I. Klein-Braslavy, Sara. Perush ha-Rambam le-sipur Beri'at ha-'olam. II. Klein-Braslavy, Sara. Perush ha-Rambam la-sipurim 'al Adam be-farashat Be-reshit. III. Klein-Braslavy, Sara. Shelomoh ha-Melekh veha-ezoterizm ha-filosofi be-mishnat ha-Rambam. IV. Title.

BS1186.K58 2011

221.6'092--dc22

2011015459

Book design by Adell Medovoy

On the cover:
Maimonides, *Moreh Nevukhim*, manuscript, Spain, 14th century.
From the collection of The Royal Library, Copenhagen.

Published by Academic Studies Press in 2011
28 Montfern Avenue
Brighton, MA 02135, USA
press@academicstudiespress.com
www.academicstudiespress.com

Contents

Introduction 7

Part One: The Creation of the World and the Story of the Garden of Eden 19

A Chapter in Maimonides' Biblical Exegesis: The Interpretation of the Story of the Second Day of Creation 21

On Maimonides' Interpretation of the Story of the Garden of Eden in the *Guide of the Perplexed* I.2 51

The Creation of the World and Maimonides' Interpretation of Genesis 1-5 71

Part Two: Maimonides' Methods of Interpreting the Bible 87

Maimonides' Interpretation of Jacob's Dream of the Ladder 89

Maimonides' Strategy for Interpreting "Woman" in the *Guide of the Perplexed* 125

Interpretative Riddles in Maimonides' *Guide of the Perplexed* 145

Part Three: Maimonides and Esotericism 161

King Solomon and Metaphysical Esotericism According to Maimonides 163

Maimonides' Exoteric and Esoteric Biblical Interpretations in the *Guide of the Perplexed* 195

Appendix: Abraham Bar Ḥiyya's Interpretation of the Story of the Creation of Man and the Story of the Garden of Eden 221

Bibliography 273

Index of Topics and Names 283

Index of Sources and Citations 293

Introduction

Maimonides' interpretation of the Bible has interested me for many years. I realized that, although Maimonides, unlike R. Saʿadiah Gaon and R. Abraham Ibn Ezra before him and Gersonides after him, did not write a running commentary on any of the books of the Bible, biblical exegesis occupies a central place in his writings, particularly in the *Guide of the Perplexed*. In fact, the *Guide of the Perplexed* is mostly an exegetical work.

In the Introduction to the *Guide*, Maimonides describes the book as an exegetical work:

> The first purpose of this treatise is to explain the meaning of certain terms occurring in books of prophecy. Some of these terms are equivocal... Others are derivative terms... Others are amphibolous terms... This Treatise also has a second purpose: namely, the explanation of very obscure parables occurring in the books of the prophets, but not explicitly identified there as such... (p. 2 / pp. 5-6)

Maimonides emphasizes this point in the Introduction to *Guide* II.2, where he explicitly states that his book is not a philosophical book concerned with physics and metaphysics, but rather an exegetical work:

> Know that my purpose in this Treatise of mine was not to compose something on natural science, or to make an epitome of notions pertaining to the divine science according to some doctrines, or to demonstrate what has been demonstrated in them. Nor was my purpose in this Treatise to give a summary and epitomized description of the spheres, or to make known their number. For the books composed concerning these matters are adequate... My purpose in this Treatise, as I have informed

> you in its introduction is only to elucidate the difficult points of the Law and to make manifest the true realities of its hidden meanings, which the multitude cannot be made to understand because of these matters being too high for it. (p. 176/ p. 253)

The subjects he aims to treat are the Account of the Beginning (*Maʿaseh Bereshit*) and the Account of the Chariot (*Maʿaseh Merkavah*) as he explains clearly in the Introduction to Part Three of the *Guide*:

> [T]he chief aim of this Treatise is to explain what can be explained of the *Account of the Beginning* and the *Account of the Chariot*... We have already made it clear that these matters belong to *the mysteries of the Torah*... (p. 297/ p. 415)

I argue that Maimonides has a consistent theory of biblical interpretation that he applies to biblical texts and that he elaborates various methods for interpreting them. The theory of biblical interpretation and the methods of interpretation used in the *Guide* take into account two basic presuppositions: first, Maimonides accepts Alfarabi's political theory according to which the ideal state is one whose beliefs are based on philosophy. Religion comes after philosophy and offers educational myths that imitate philosophical truths by images that can be understood by the masses. Hence, Maimonides assumes that the biblical text professes philosophical ideas—those elaborated in the Aristotelian school, mainly by the Arabic philosophers Alfarabi, Avicenna and Ibn Bajja. Second, the Bible belongs to a literary genre that might be called "esoteric literature." It does not profess philosophical truths in a direct way, but conceals them from the masses and only reveals them to those who have the requisite degree of knowledge and the capacity to comprehend them. The Bible uses diverse techniques of hiding/revealing the philosophical notions; hence, it is the interpreter's task to decipher the texts and to understand them. Maimonides takes up this task.

On the one hand, Maimonides addresses the *Guide* to the "perplexed" reader, a believing Jew who observes the commandments and accepts the Bible as authoritative, but has read Aristotelian philosophy and accepts it as well. Discovering contradictions between his understanding of the biblical text and Aristotelian philosophy, he becomes perplexed. Maimonides' aim in writing the *Guide* is to free such a reader from his perplexity by means of his biblical exegesis. This exegesis is intended to show that the biblical truth is in fact identical with Aristotelian philosophy, so that the "perplexed" can be Jew and philosopher at the same time.

On the other hand, following the Sages in the Talmudic literature (Ḥagigah 2.1 and in B. Ḥagigah 13a), Maimonides considers the main subjects of his book — the Account of the Beginning and the Account of the Chariot — to be esoteric, and hence subjects that ought not to be divulged. He is obedient to the halakhic prescription, "'*Arayot* may not be expounded to three, nor *Maʿaseh Bereshit* to two, nor *Merkavah* to an individual, unless he is wise and understands on his own," coupled with R. Ḥiyya's saying in B. Ḥagigah 13a "one conveys to him chapter headings." Identifying the Account of the Beginning and the Account of the Chariot with Aristotelian physics and metaphysics respectively, Maimonides uses esoteric methods of transmission, whereby he simultaneously hides and reveals a part of his biblical exegesis—hiding it from the broad masses, and revealing it to one who is capable of understanding. The *Guide* itself belongs, at least partially, to the same literary genre as the Bible: namely, that of esoteric literature. It is the task of his reader to decipher it. His acceptance of the formal guidelines of the Sages regarding the transmission of the Account of the Chariot to others enables Maimonides to use Jewish tradition to justify his own way of writing about *Ma'aseh Bereshit* and *Ma'aseh Merkavah*, and to argue that, in writing in a concealing and allusive manner, he is continuing an existing tradition as to how to convey "the mysteries of Torah."

The present volume is the fruit of an initiative of Professor Dov Schwartz, editor of the series "Emunot." It consists of a collection of essays that I wrote in English together with translations of some of my Hebrew articles on Maimonides' biblical exegesis; these were written between the years 1982 and 2008, and deal with some of the most interesting of Maimonides' biblical interpretations.

The book is divided into three parts. The first part, "The Creation of the World and the Story of the Garden of Eden," encompasses articles dealing with *Maʿaseh Bereshit* - Maimonides' interpretation of the stories of the Creation of the world and that of the Garden of Eden:

"A Chapter in Maimonides' Biblical Interpretation – The Interpretation of the Story of the Second Day of Creation" is focused on one of the most interesting parts of Maimonides' interpretation of the story of creation in *Guide* II.30 and deals with various aspects of his methods of interpretation. I included in this translation only a part of the original article – that dealing with the interpretation of the second day of Creation – and omitted the introductory sections, whose contents I later elaborated in my Hebrew book *Maimonides' Interpretation of the Story of Creation*, pp. 17-46; 63-69. This paper deals with two issues: Maimonides' philosophical interpretation of *shamayim* (heaven), *mayim* (waters) *raqiʿa* (firmament) *mayim ʾasher meʿal la-raqiʿa* (the waters which were above the firmament) *mayim ʾasher mitaḥat la-raqiʿa* (the waters which were under the firmament), and Maimonides' answer to the question as to why the phrase *ki tov* ("it was good") does not appear at the end of the second day of Creation.

Though Maimonides interprets the story of Creation in *Guide* II.30, one needs to follow his guideline in the "Instruction with Respect to this Treatise": "connect its chapters one with another" (p. 9/ p. 15), supplementing his statements in one chapter with what he says in other chapters of the *Guide*. My reading of his interpretation of the words *shamayim* (heaven) and *tov* (good) follows this counsel.

Maimonides considers the interpretation of *mayim ʾasher meʿal la-raqiʿa* (the waters which were above the firmament) *mayim ʾasher mitaḥat la-raqiʿa* (the waters which were under the firmament) to be esoteric. Hence he does not explain them fully, but only alludes to their meaning by stating that the clue for their understanding is to be found in Aristotle's *Meteorology*, leaving it to the reader to interpret these two expressions by his knowledge of the *Meteorology*. It should be emphasized that Maimonides was the first Jewish philosopher to use the *Meteorology* for interpreting the story of Creation. In my article I cite the various explanations proposed for this hint by the medieval commentators of the *Guide*.

As for Maimonides' explanation of biblical words: this article shows that he does not think that the Bible uses only equivocal words, as one might think from the Introduction to the *Guide*, but also includes words that serve as a metalanguage and help its readers to understand its meaning. Maimonides considers the verbs *hivdil* and *va-yiqraʾ* to be such words. The article explains their meaning and their role in the biblical description of the second day of Creation, according to Maimonides.

"On Maimonides' Interpretation of the Story of the Garden of Eden in *Guide of the Perplexed* I.2" deals with the first step of Maimonides' allegorical interpretation of the story of the Garden of Eden that culminates in *Guide* II.30. Maimonides presents it in a particular way, as a dialogue or rather a debate on the meaning of the story of the Garden of Eden conducted between himself and "a man busy with sciences." The article is centered on four main topics: (a) the structure of the chapter; (b) the place and the importance of this interpretation within the framework of the *Guide* and within the framework of Maimonides' full interpretation of the story of the Garden of Eden therein; (c) the figure of the "man busy with sciences" and its role in the interpretation of the story; (d) the address of the interpretation. I argue that the chapter has a twofold address: the "disciple" whom Maimonides tells about the objections put forward by "the man busy with sciences" and the answer he gave him, and "the man busy with sciences" himself, to whom this answer was initially addressed. Parts of Maimonides' interpretation are only addressed to the ideal reader.

"The Creation of the World and Maimonides' Interpretation of Genesis 1-5" deals with the problem of Maimonides' position on the Creation of the world from the point of view of his biblical exegesis. I examine two central topics: (1) Maimonides' interpretation of the verb *bara*ʾ in Gen. 1:1; (2) the question as to whether or not Maimonides interpreted the stories about Adam historically. I show that the analysis of these two themes may lead us to a new solution of the problem of Creation in Maimonides' thought: namely, that Maimonides behaved in this issue as a skeptic who maintained epochē and abstained from judging a matter which he was unable to decide logically or philosophically. He did not decide among the three views on the Creation of the world that he presented in *Guide* II.13 nor did he hold any firm opinion on this issue: namely *creatio ex-nihilo*; the Platonic position of the creation of the world from an antemundane matter at some defined point in the past; and the Aristotelian position of the eternity of the world.

The second part of the book deals with Maimonides' methods of interpreting the Bible. In all my articles I pay attention to Maimonides' methods of interpretation. I realized that his biblical exegesis is much more complicated and rich than one might surmise from reading only his Introduction to the *Guide*. The articles included in this section pay special attention to various aspects of his biblical exegesis.

"Maimonides' Interpretation of the Dream of Jacob's Ladder" deals with three types of interpretation of biblical parables by means of midrashim, all of which rely on aggadic expansions. These are exemplified by three different interpretations of Jacob's dream of the ladder (Gen. 28:12–13) offered by Maimonides in his writings: *Hilkhot Yesodei ha-Torah* 7.3, *Guide of the Perplexed* II.10 and *Guide of the Perplexed* I.15. According to *Hilkhot Yesodei ha-Torah* 7.3, it is a prophecy of future events. According to the *Guide of the Perplexed* it is concerned with "mysteries of the Torah" (i.e., esoteric teachings). According to *Guide* I.15 it represents the structure of the physics of the sublunary world, the apprehension of God as the prime mover of the spheres, and the imitation of God by the prophet (who is also a political leader), while according to *Guide* II.10 it has only one subject: the vision of the physics of the sublunary world.

From the methodological viewpoint, this article deals not only with the use of midrashim in the interpretation of biblical texts, but also with Maimonides' theory of the parable and the manner in which he explains equivocal terms in the biblical texts.

"Maimonides' Strategy for Interpreting 'Woman' in the *Guide of the Perplexed*" deals with the motif of "woman" in the *Guide*. It shows that Maimonides interprets three types of biblical literary units that are concerned with "woman": the word "woman"; the metaphor – "married harlot"; and the allegory – the allegory of the "married harlot" and the allegory of "a woman of virtue." I focus on his strategy in interpreting each one of these. I argue that the main strategy employed here is a "structure of relation"— the types of relations that "woman" has with other objects, mostly "man." These relations are, according to Maimonides, the key for understanding the meaning of "woman" in the biblical texts.

"Interpretative Riddles in Maimonides' *Guide of the Perplexed*" is another example of Maimonides' use of midrashim in his biblical exegesis. The article deals with one of Maimonides' methods of esoteric biblical interpretation in the *Guide*—the method I call "interpretative riddle." I maintain that this method has much in common with the riddle, especially the literary riddle, and that the theory of the literary riddle can help us understand its application in the *Guide*. I exemplify this contention by analyzing two related allegories interpreted in *Guide* II.30: the creation of Adam and Eve and the character of the serpent in the story of the Garden of Eden. The interpretative riddles answer the questions: Who are Adam and Eve? And: Who is the serpent that seduced Eve in the story of the Garden of Eden? I point out that Maimonides uses the aggadic expansions in the midrashim *Genesis Rabbah* (8.1.) and *Pirqei de-Rabbi Eliezer* (ch. 13), respectively, as comments of the interpretative riddles.

In this article I point out that, according to Maimonides, the Bible does not only use equivocal terms dealt with by Aristotelian logic, as he states in the Introduction to the *Guide*, but also equivocal terms based on their etymology, or what is in fact pseudo-etymology, as a literary device to transmit esoteric meaning. Maimonides does not explain these words but only alludes to their meaning, claiming that their significance is indicated by their etymology. This is the case of the words *naḥash* (serpent) in the Bible and Sammael in the Midrash. The reader needs to understand the allusion by himself and to interpret the names within their context using the principles of Aristotelian philosophy. I suggest an interpretation of these two words.

As for its contents: the article also sheds light on a part of Maimonides' second step of the interpretation of the story of the Garden of Eden – its full interpretation as a philosophical allegory in *Guide* II.30.

The third part of the book deals with some aspects of esotericism in Maimonides' *Guide*.

"King Solomon and Metaphysical Esotericism According to Maimonides" shows that Maimonides not only interprets the Bible as a text professing philosophical notions, but that he is also interested in the Bible as an historical account. Hence he not only interprets words and parables, but also certain historical biblical figures, such as the patriarchs (especially Abraham), Moses, Solomon, and other prophets and their deeds. These interpretations are based on his theory of prophecy, his theory of Providence, and other philosophical and philosophical-theological ideas that, according to his view, are maintained by the Bible, as well as his theory of the biblical philosophical esoterism. The article deals with one aspect of Maimonides' interpretation of the character of King Solomon – King Solomon as an esoteric philosopher who warns against the public teaching of esoteric doctrines and gives his audience instruction in the apprehension of God. He cautions his readers against attempting to go beyond the limits of human capability in their effort to apprehend God, and guides and instructs them toward a proper understanding of God within their mortal limitations.

I argue that Maimonides' interpretation of the character of Solomon is a continuation and explication of an existing tradition in Judaism, which he invests with philosophical meaning.

"Maimonides' Exoteric and Esoteric Biblical Interpretations in the *Guide of the Perplexed*": In this article I argue that not all of Maimonides' philosophical biblical exegesis is esoteric, but that he engaged in exoteric philosophic interpretations as well. Some of these are addressed to the masses as well as to the "perplexed" and the intellectual elite. These include the interpretations of equivocal terms in the Bible that are likely to corporealize God, and some of the divine revelations. There are also exoteric philosophical interpretations meant exclusively for the intellectual elite, such as his interpretation of the metaphor of the "married harlot" and the parable (allegory) constructed around it in Proverbs 7:6–21; the interpretation of God's promise to reveal Himself to Moses in the Cleft of the Rock (Exod. 33:21–23); the interpretations of Moses' requests, God's answers, and His actual revelation (Exod. 33:13–20 and 34:6–7) in *Guide* I.54; as well as part of his interpretation of the story of Creation in *Guide* II.30.

I argue that, when the interpretation of a biblical revelation is scattered in several chapters of the *Guide*, this scattering is not necessarily an esoteric device used by Maimonides to convey esoteric content. Scattering the interpretation may also be the result of the structure of the *Guide*. Such is the case in Maimonides' interpretation of the revelation in the Cleft of the Rock.

Esoteric interpretations are those interpretations that must be concealed from the masses because they are liable to damage their faith. Maimonides uses two kinds of esoteric methodology, "soft" and "hard," which differ in the type of allusions they use; "Soft" esoteric interpretations tell readers which Aristotelian text can assist them to identify the objects intended by the Bible. "Hard" esoteric interpretations, which are more common in the *Guide*, employ various allusive methods. Maimonides provides "soft" esoteric interpretations to "the firmament" and "the water above the firmament" (Gen. 1:7) and a "hard" esoteric interpretation to the word *bereshit* ("in the beginning") (Gen. 1:1), using the method I call "interpretative riddle."

Following the recommendation of Professor Dov Schwartz, I have included as an appendix a translation of the article "The Creation of Man and the Story of the Garden of Eden in the Thought of Abraham Bar

Ḥiyya." This article, concerning one of the most interesting topics dealt with by Maimonides in his biblical exegesis – namely, the interpretation of the story of the Garden of Eden – acquaints the reader with one of the earliest stages of philosophical interpretation of this subject in biblical exegesis of Jewish medieval philosophy. Bar Ḥiyya's exegesis is very different from the Aristotelian exegesis of Maimonides and his school, both in the meaning he ascribes to the stories of the creation of man and that of the Garden of Eden, as well as by its methods of interpretation, although some of them do precede those of Maimonides.

Like Maimonides, Bar Ḥiyya did not write a consecutive commentary on the Bible. He interprets the story of the creation of man and that of the Garden of Eden in his eschatological book *Scroll of the Revealer* (*Megillat ha-Megalleh*) (1120-1129) in order to support his view concerning the Resurrection of the Dead. He asserts that at the beginning of history the first human beings were immortal and that they will return to the state at the End of days. The story of the Garden of Eden explains why human beings lost their immortality.

According to Bar Ḥiyya, a correct interpretation of the Bible should conform to contemporary philosophical and scientific doctrines as well as to Hebrew grammar. The most important scientific doctrine he relies on here is Galen's physiological theory on the causes of human death.

I demonstrate that Bar Ḥiyya is more sensitive than Maimonides to the wording of the biblical text and that he interprets more elements in the story than does Maimonides. His interpretation of the stories is very elaborate and resolves many exegetical problems raised by ancient and modern commentators.

***

Some of the articles in this volume were written before I wrote my Hebrew books and were later integrated within them, with certain modifications and elaborations. Thus, "A Chapter in Maimonides' Biblical Interpretation – The Interpretation of the Story of the Second Day of Creation" was incorporated within *Maimonides' Interpretation of the Story of Creation* (Jerusalem, 1978, repr. Jerusalem 1987); "On Maimonides' Interpretation of the Story of the Garden of Eden in the *Guide of the Perplexed* I.2" was integrated into *Maimonides' Interpretation of the Adam Stories in Genesis - A Study in Maimonides' Anthropology* (Jerusalem,

1986); and "King Solomon and Metaphysical Esotericism According to Maimonides" was included in my book *King Solomon and Philosophical Esotericism in the Thought of Maimonides* (Jerusalem, 1996 repr. 2008). The articles "The Creation of the World and Maimonides' Interpretation of Gen. 1-5"; "Maimonides' Strategy for Interpreting 'Woman' in the *Guide of the Perplexed*"; "Maimonides' Exoteric and Esoteric Biblical Interpretations in the *Guide of the Perplexed;*" and "Interpretative Riddles in Maimonides' *Guide of the Perplexed*" were written after I wrote the above-mentioned Hebrew books and they complement them. "Maimonides' Interpretation of the Dream of Jacob's Ladder" deals with a subject not treated in any of my books.

The articles have been revised for publication in this volume. I have added references to English translations of the texts cited when such translations exist, updated some of the references, added cross references to other articles in the book to enable the reader to receive a wider picture of the issues and the methods dealt with in the articles. On occasion, I also emended some of them.

Forms of Reference and Abbreviations

Page references to the *Guide of the Perplexed* are first to the Arabic text *Dalālat al- Ḥāʾirīn* redacted by S. Munk and edited with variant readings by Y. Joel (Jerusalem, 1930-31), then following a slash to Pines' English translation of the *Guide of the Perplexed*: Moses Maimonides, *The Guide of the Perplexed*, trans. by Shlomo Pines (Chicago, 1963). In some articles the page references are to Pines' English translation only. The words in italics in the citations from the *Guide* are those that appear in Hebrew in the Arabic text.

Page references to Efodi, Shem Tov, Crescas and Abravanel's commentaries on the *Guide* are to: *Sefer Moreh Nevukhim* ... translated into Hebrew by Samuel Ibn-Tibbon... with four commentaries: *Efodi, Shem Tov, Crescas* and *Abravanel*, edited by I. Goldman (Warsaw 1861, repr. Jerusalem 1960).

Page references to Narboni's commentary on the *Guide* are to: *Beʾur le sefer Moreh Nevukhim*, edited by J. Goldenthal (Wien 1852).

I refer to my book *Maimonides' Interpretation of the Story of Creation*

(2end edition with corrections and additions, Jerusalem: Reuben Mass, 1987 [Hebrew]) as Klein-Braslavy, *Creation*. To my book *Maimonides' Interpretation of the Adam Stories in Genesis - A Study in Maimonides' Anthropology* (Jerusalem: Reuben Mass, 1986 [Hebrew]) as: Klein-Braslavy, *Adam Stories*, and to my book *King Solomon and Philosophical Esotericism in the Thought of Maimonides* (Jerusalem: Magnes 1996, repr. 2008 [Hebrew]) as Klein-Braslavy, *Esotericism* .

ACKNOWLEDGMENTS

I gratefully acknowledge permission granted by the original publishers and editors of these articles to publish them here. The original places of publication are as follows:

"The Creation of Man and the Story of the Garden of Eden in the Thought of Abraham Bar Ḥiyya," *Professor Israel Efros - Poet and Philosopher*, I. Orpaz, N. Govrin, A. Kasher B.Y. Michali, Z. Malachi (eds.), (The Chaim Rosenberg School of Jewish Studies, Tel-Aviv University: Tel Aviv, 1981), pp. 203-229 (Hebrew)

"A Chapter in Maimonides' Biblical Interpretation – The Interpretation of the Account of the Second Day of Creation," *Sefer Yeshayahu Leibowitz*, A. Kasher and J. Levinger (eds.), (Papyrus, Tel Aviv University: Tel Aviv, 1982), pp. 192-221 (Hebrew)

"Maimonides' Interpretation of the Story of the Garden of Eden in the *Guide of the Perplex*ed I. 2" - a lecture presented at the conference on "Maimonides in Egypt" held in Tel Aviv University in June 28-30, 1982 (not published before).

"The Creation of the World and Maimonides' Interpretation of Gen. i-v," *Maimonides and Philosophy*, S. Pines and Y. Yovel (eds.), (Nijhoff--Dordrecht, 1986), pp. 65-78.

"Maimonides' Interpretation of Jacob's Dream of the Ladder," *Annual of Bar-Ilan University, Studies in Judaica and Humanities, Moshe Schwarcz Memorial Volume*, XXII-XXIII (1987), pp. 329-349 (Hebrew)

"King Solomon and Metaphysical Esotericism According to Maimonides," *Maimonidean Studies*, 1 (1990), pp. 57-86.

"Maimonides' Strategy for Interpreting 'Woman' in *the Guide of the Perplexed," Ecriture et réécriture des textes philosophiques médiévaux, Volume d'hommage offert à Colette Sirat,* J. Hamesse et O. Weijers (eds.), (Turnhout Belgium: Brepols, 2006), pp. 291-310.

"Maimonides' Exoteric and Esoteric Biblical Interpretations in the *Guide of the Perplexed," Study and Knowledge in Jewish Thought*, H. Kreisel (ed.) (Ben-Gurion University of the Negev, 2006), pp. 137-164.

"Interpretative Riddles in Maimonides' *Guide of the Perplexed," Maimonidean Studies* 5 (2008), pp. 141-158.

The articles: "The Creation of Man and the Story of the Garden of Eden in the Thought of Abraham Bar Ḥiyya," "A Chapter in Maimonides' Biblical Interpretation – The Interpretation of the Story of the Second Day of Creation," "Maimonides' Interpretation of Jacob's Dream of the Ladder," "King Solomon and Metaphysical Esotericism According to Maimonides" were translated from the Hebrew by Rabbi Yehonatan Chipman.

"Maimonides' Interpretation of the Story of the Garden of Eden in the *Guide of the Perplexed* I.2" was translated from the Hebrew by Professor Michael Schwarz.

Part One

The Creation of the World
And the Story of the Garden of Eden

A Chapter in Maimonides' Biblical Exegesis: The Interpretation of the Story of the Second Day of Creation*

Maimonides devoted an entire chapter of the *Guide* (II.30) to the interpretation of the Story of Creation which, in his interpretation, includes the narrative of the Creation of the World in Genesis 1:1-2:3; that of the Creation of Man in Genesis 1:26-27 and 2:7; that of the Garden of Eden in Genesis 2:4-3:24; and that of the sons of Adam, Cain and Abel, in Genesis 4:1-15. In addition, individual verses, fragments of verses, and isolated words from these stories are also explained in other chapters of the *Guide*. In order to understand his interpretation, one must use the method which he recommends in the "Instruction with respect to this treatise"—namely, to "connect its chapters one with another" (p. 15), complementing his interpretation in *Guide* II.30 by means of these interpretations.[1]

There is a definite literary structure to the Creation story in Genesis: it begins with two verses which serve as an introduction to the narrative as a whole—Genesis 1:1-2; followed by six narrative units—the six days of Creation—characterized stylistically by identical openings and closings: each one opens with the words, "and God said" and (with the exception of the story of the second day) concludes with the words

---

* After writing the original version of this paper, I wrote my book, *Maimonides' Interpretation of the Story of Creation* (Hebrew), in which I analyzed Maimonides' interpretation of Genesis 1:1-2:3. The present paper is an edited and revised version of the earlier Hebrew paper, sections of which were included in the above volume. The version of the paper brought here focuses exclusively upon the interpretation of the second day of Creation. I have deleted the introduction to the analysis of this interpretation found in the original article, which was greatly expanded in pp. 17-35 and 63-69 of my book, as well as the analysis of the interpretation of the verb va-yo'mar ("and He said"), which does not contribute directly to understanding the interpretation of the second day of Creation.

1 As opposed to what I thought in the past, today I do not think that he necessarily applies the "method of scattering" to which he refers in the Introduction to the Guide as intended to conceal his esoteric interpretations of the biblical texts, in all those cases in which Maimonides interprets words and fragments of verses that are likely to illuminate the understanding of a biblical text that he interprets in the other chapters of the *Guide*. See on this my paper (in this volume), "Maimonides' Exoteric and Esoteric Biblical Interpretations."

"and God saw that it was good; and it was evening, and it was morning, the (such-and-such) day."[2] The narrative as a whole concludes with an additional narrative unit corresponding to the Shabbat (Gen. 2:1-3).

The present paper is devoted to Maimonides' interpretation of the second unit in the story of the Creation—the story of the second day of Creation, found in Genesis 1:6-8. The exegetical problems that emerge from this text and the solutions suggested by Maimonides are among the most interesting in his interpretation of the Creation story, and are thus deserving of special attention. An analysis of this interpretation will enable me to exemplify several of the methods used by Maimonides in interpreting the Bible, and particularly one of those he used for the esoteric interpretation of biblical texts.

The Interpretation of the Second Day of Creation

1. The Exegetical Problem

The world as a whole was created, according to Maimonides, by a single act of creation, indicated by the verb *baro*ʾ, "to create," through which the heaven and the earth and everything therein were created. For our purposes, it is of particular importance to note Maimonides' interpretation of the word *shamayim* ("Heaven"). At the beginning of *Guide* II.30, Maimonides translates Genesis 1:1 into Arabic as *fī biʾati khalqi allāh al-ʿulūwa wa-l-sufl*. Ibn Tibbon translates his words into Hebrew, as follows: "At the beginning, God created the upper and the lower realms" (*ba-hatḥalah bara*ʾ *ha-shem ha-*ʿ*elyonim ve-ha-taḥtonim)*. Qāfiḥ, instead of "the upper and the lower realms," suggests translating this as "above and below" (*ma*ʿ*la va-matah*) (p. 380);[3] it was similarly translated into French and English, respectively, by S. Munk and S. Pines. Munk translates, "le haut et le bas" (*Le Guide des Égarés,* II, p. 232), while Pines renders it as, "what is high and what is low" (p. 349). The heaven is thus "that which is above." Hence, one might ask the question: what is meant by "above" according to Maimonides? Does this refer both to the separate intellects and the spheres—or perhaps to the spheres alone?

2 The description of the first day of Creation does not conclude with the formula, "and God saw that it was good." Rather, this formula appears in the middle of the description of the creation of that day. For an explanation of this stylistic deviation, see Klein-Braslavy, *Creation,* p. 156.

3 See also n. 10 there.

From the continuation of his interpretation of the story of Creation, the impression gained is that *shamayim* ("heaven") refers to the spheres alone. Thus, in interpreting Genesis 1:17, "and God set them in the firmament of the heaven," Maimonides comments: "that all the stars as well as the sun and the moon are situated within the sphere—as there is no vacuum in the world—and that they are not located upon the surface of a sphere, as the vulgar imagine" (p. 352). That is, the phrase *raqiʿa ha-shamayim* ("the firmament of the heaven") is interpreted here as "sphere" or "spheres." Similarly, in *Guide* I.70, where he deals with the interpretation of the equivocal term *rakhob* ("to ride"), the meaning of the term *shamayim* is "the spheres," and particularly the highest sphere. "The rider of the heavens is helping you" (Deut. 33:26) is interpreted by Maimonides by saying, "He who dominates the heavens" (p. 171). Towards the end of the chapter he writes: "The dictum, *the rider of the heavens*, signifies: He who makes the encompassing heaven revolve and who moves it in virtue of His power and His will"[4] (p. 175). This likewise follows from his interpretation of *shamayim* ("heavens") in the verses, "who is enthroned in the heavens" (Ps. 123:1) and "He who sits in the heavens" (Ps. 2:4);[5] from *Guide* I.11, a chapter dealing with the interpretation of the equivocal term *yeshivah* ("sitting"); and from his interpretations of the verse "The heaven is My throne" (Isa. 66:1) in *Guide* I.9, which deals with the interpretation of the equivocal noun *kisei* ("throne" or "chair").[6] Likewise, in explaining the Arabic terms *al-samawāt* and *al-samāʾ*, Maimonides explicitly states that they are to be understood as referring to spheres. In *Guide* III.4, he writes, "Hence the heavens [Arabic: *al-samawāt*] were called *galgallim* because of their being round—I mean, because of their being spherical" (p. 424), while in *Guide* I.58 he writes "Now you who read this Treatise with speculative intent, know that whereas this heaven [*al-samāʾ*] is a moving body..." (p. 136).

However, the ambiguity of the translation of *shamayim* ("heaven") as *al- ʿulūwa* also leaves room for one to think, as did Narboni: "There by a cause God created the upper and lower realms and it [the verse] alluded to the separate [intellects] and elucidating spoke explicitly of the

---

4 For a more extensive interpretation of Maimonides' view of "heavens" in *Guide* I.70, see also (in this volume), "Maimonides' Interpretation of Jacob's Dream of the Ladder" p. 108-110.

5 See p. 38.

6 See p. 34.

spheres and the lower existents [the existents in the sublunary world]" (*Be'ur le-Sefer Moreh Nevukhim*, 39a). That is: the term "heaven" alludes not only to the spheres, but also to the separate intellects. This sort of interpretation resolves a question that almost inevitably emerges upon reading Maimonides' interpretation of the biblical story of Creation: namely, where does the Creation narrative in Genesis 1 refer to the creation of separate intellects or the angels?

It seems to me that one need not interpret this passage as does Narboni, for Maimonides explicitly states that the subject of Genesis 1 is "the Account of Creation"—that is, physics—whereas the creation of the angels, the separate intellects, is a concern of metaphysics. In similar fashion, his interpretation of the word *shamayim* ["heaven"] in all those places that I have examined in the *Guide of the Perplexed* leads one to think that Maimonides did not interpret "heaven" in Genesis 1:1 any differently than he did elsewhere.

The identification of "Heaven" with the spheres presents Maimonides with a difficult exegetical problem: how is one to interpret Genesis 1:6-8? According to Aristotelian physics, there is nothing beyond the highest sphere, whereas the biblical narrative speaks of "the waters which were above the firmament." If one identifies "Heaven" with "the firmament" (*raqiʿa*), as he does in a number of places in the *Guide*,[7] one is forced to the conclusion, absurd within the framework of Aristotelian physics, that there is something beyond the spheres. If, on the other hand, one does not identify the Heaven with the firmament, one confronts two exegetical problems: first, to find a structure within the physical world which answers the requirement of being a body located between the spheres and the earth beneath it, while above it there are other bodies which may justifiably be described as "water" (*mayim*). The second difficulty is how to interpret the idiom *raqiʿa ha-shamayim* (which we have translated, "the firmament of the heaven") in Genesis 1:14, 15, 17, and 20, and how one ought to interpret v. 8, "and God called the firmament Heaven."

7 See *Guide* III. 2, 7: the interpretation of Ezekiel's vision of the chariot. This is also implied by Maimonides' interpretation in *Guide* II.5 of Ps. 19:2: "The Heavens tell the glory of God and the firmament proclaims His handiwork."

2. *The Interpretation of the Verbs Va-ya'aś ("and He made"), Va-yavdel ("And He separated") and Va-yiqra' ("and He called")*

The key to the interpretation of the phrases *raqi'a* ("firmament"), *mayim asher mi-taḥat la-raqi'a* ("the waters which were under the firmament") and *mayim asher me-'al la-raqi'a* ("the waters which were above the firmament") is to be found, according to Maimonides, in the interpretation of the verbs *va-yavdel* ("and He separated") and *va- yiqra'* ("And He called") in Genesis 1:6-8. To these one might add the verb *va-ya'aś* ("and He made"), although Maimonides does not explicitly relate to it in this context explicitly.

At this point we need to say a number of things about Maimonides' manner of interpretation of the verbs and nouns used in the Creation story. In interpreting the narrative of the Creation in *Guide* II.30, Maimonides draws a distinction between the discussion of the nouns used in the story and those verbs relating to God which are brought in order to clarify the significance of these nouns, and the discussion of those verbs relating to God which indicate the *origin* of the physical world. Those verbs relating to God used to clarify the significance of the nouns in the Creation story are *va-yavdel* ("and He separated") and *va yiqra'* ("and He called"), which Maimonides explicates during the course of explaining the nouns. By contrast, the verbs *bara'* ("He created"), *'aśah* ("He made"), and *va-yo'mer* ("and He said"), are not explicated by Maimonides in his exegesis of the text of the Creation story. Rather, the verbs *bara'* and *'aśah* are explained at the end of Chapter 30, in a kind of aside to his interpretation of the Creation story, along with other words indicating the relation between God and the Heaven. The verb *va-yo'mer* ("and He said") is not interpreted at all in the context of the chapter devoted to the Creation story, but rather in *Guide* I.65-67.[8]

a. The Interpretation of the Verb "to make"(*'Aśoh*)

The verb *'Aśoh* ("to make") is interpreted by Maimonides in *Guide* II.30, following his interpretation of the verb *baro'* ("to create"): "It also says *'aśoh* ("to make"), which is applied to the specific forms that were given them [i.e., heaven and earth]—I mean their natures" (p. 358). His remarks in *Guide* I.66 complement his words here: "for all natural things are called 'the work of the Lord': [as in] "'These saw the works of the

8 For the interpretation of the verb "say" (*'amor*) in the *Guide*, see Klein-Braslavy, *Creation*, pp. 91-96.

Lord' [Ps. 107:24]" (p. 160). That is to say: this verb, when attributed to God, indicates the fact that objects in the physical world were given their natural forms by God.

One of the problems occupying modern biblical commentators is that two completely different verbs appear in the Creation story to signify the activity of creation: the verb *va-yo'mer* ("and He said"), and that of *va-ya'aś* or *'aśoh* ("He made"/to make). The verb "He said" indicates that Creation was accomplished by means of speech, while the verb "He made" signifies actual physical forming or making, a physical activity such as that performed by a craftsman in fashioning raw material. From this, modern commentators reached the conclusion that there were two separate versions of the Creation narrative, the *Wortbericht* and the *Tatbericht*, that were later united into a single story.[9] In his interpretation of the various verbs used in the Creation story, Maimonides overcomes this problem by asserting that each of these verbs indicates a different aspect of the selfsame activity of Creation. *Va-yomer,* "and He said," indicates the relationship between God and the created things, the manner of Creation itself; it thereby indicates that the Creation was performed as an act of will.[10] By contrast, *va-ya'aś*, "and He made," refers to the act of Creation from the viewpoint of the things created, explaining precisely what was done with will: by means of will, those things in the physical world were given their natural, substantive forms. Maimonides finds support for this interpretation in Psalm 33:6: "By the word of the Lord, the heavens were made." In this verse there appear alongside one another the word *davar* ("speech / word")—which is an equivocal word and a synonym of *'amirah* (saying) (a gerund based on the root *'amor*) whose meaning in this verse, according to Maimonides, is "will"—and *na'aśu* ("were made"). Maimonides' conclusion is:

> Its saying "with the finger of God" (Exod. 31:18) is analogous to its saying, with reference to the heavens, "the work of Thy fingers" (Ps. 8:4). For Scripture has

9 This distinction is made by W. H. Schmildt, Die Schöpfungsgeschichte der Priesterschrift: zuh Überlieferungsgeschichte von Genesis, 1,1-2,4a (WMANT, 17; Neukirchen Vluyn, 1964). P. Ricœur relies upon him in two of his papers dealing with the interpretation of the Creation story: "Qu'est-ce qu'un Texte." In *Hermeneutik und Dialektik*, II, ed. R. Bubner (Tübingen, 1970), pp. 197-199; "Sur l'exégèse de Genèse 1,1-2,4a." In *Exégèse et Herméneutique* (Paris, 1971), pp. 67-84.

10 See note 8 above.

> made clear with regard to the heavens that they have been made by "saying": "By the word of the Lord were the heavens made" (Ps. 33:6). It has then become clear to you that, with regard to the coming into being of a thing, the texts "figuratively use the terms *ʾamira* ("saying") and *dibur* ("speaking") and that it is one and the same thing of which it is said that it was "made by speech" and of which it is said that it is the "work of a finger" (*Guide*, I. 66, p. 160).

b. The Interpretation of the Verb *Va-yavdel* ("and He Separated")

The verb, *va-yavdel* ("and He separated") appears twice in the Creation story: "And God separated between the light and the darkness" (Gen. 1:4) and "He separated between the waters which were beneath the firmament and the waters which were above the firmament" (Gen. 1:7).[11] In its meaning this verb is similar to the verb *ʿaśoh,* "to make," it too indicates the giving of a natural form to things. When a particular thing is given form, it makes it into what it is, but it also distinguishes it from other things, it particularizes it. The verb, "to make," emphasizes the former aspect: the giving of the specific form to things, their being made into what they are; whereas the verb *hivdil* ("separated") emphasizes the second aspect: it indicates that the giving of the natural form to a certain thing distinguishes it from others, evidently one with whom it shares a common matter.

c. The Interpretation of the Verb *Va-yiqra*ʾ ("and He Called")

In the Introduction to the *Guide of the Perplexed*, in the course of explaining the nature of the complete parable by means of a metaphor taken from the Book of Proverbs, "Like apples of gold in a silver setting, is a word fitly spoken" (Prov. 25:11), Maimonides states that the apparent, external, level of the parable is comparable to "settings of silver"—that is, to a piece of jewelry made of silver having different facets enabling one to look beyond it to the inside of the jewelry, to the apples of gold which represent the inner, the hidden, level of the parable. This explanation teaches that the apparent level contains allusions leading us to

11 The verb *hivdil* ("separated") appears in various different forms three more times in the Creation story (Gen. 1:6; 14, 18); however, Maimonides does not interpret those appearances thereof.

the hidden level, so that we do not have here simply a narrative with two different levels of meaning. It may be that one of these alludes to the contradiction between the literal meaning of things and Aristotelian philosophy. The existence of such a contradiction suggests that we must not understand a given text on the basis of its straightforward, literal meaning alone but that one must seek its hidden level by means of a suitable interpretation: that is, that meaning which is appropriate to the reader's knowledge of philosophy. And indeed, the interpretation of the Creation story indicates that the apparent level of the narrative incorporates a number of hints that lead the reader directly to the correct interpretation. One example of such is that, according to Maimonides' interpretation, the significance of the verb *va-yiqra'* ("He called") is not to be sought on the level to which the text refers, on the level of those things of which the text speaks, but rather on the level of the language of the text: that is, this word does not designate any Divine action, but rather serves as a meta linguistic key,—that is, a hint or indication provided by the text itself as to the manner in which it ought to be read and understood. Regarding this verb Maimonides says: "That also is a great secret among the secrets; namely, wherever you find him saying, 'God named something thus,' he does this in order to differentiate between the particular notion envisaged and the other notion equally signified by the term" (*Guide* II.30, p. 351). The word "and He called" thus indicates that the word appearing alongside it in the biblical text is an equivocal noun, whose meaning when alongside *va-yiqra'* is different from its meanings earlier in the narrative.[12]

3. *The Interpretation of "Waters," "Firmament," "the Waters Which were Above the Firmament," and "the Waters Which were Under the Firmament"*

In his interpretation of "water," "firmament," "the waters which were above the firmament," and "the waters which were under the firmament," Maimonides follows the method announced in the Introduction to the *Guide:* "A sensible man thus should not demand of me or hope that when we mention a subject, we shall make a complete exposition of it, or that when we engage in the explanation of the meaning of one of

12 The verb *qara'* ("He called") appears five times in the Creation story (Gen. 1:5, 8, 10). The equivocal nouns to which it relates are: *or* (light); *Ḥosekh* (darkness); *shamayim* (heaven); *'ereṣ* (earth) and *mayim* (water).

the parables, we shall set forth exhaustively all that is expressed in that parable" (p. 6). Here he uses a method of writing which he described at the beginning of his commentary on the story of Creation at the end of *Guide* II.29: "...you will find that with regard to these *mysteries*, I always mention the single saying on which the matter is based, while I leave the rest to those whom it befits that this should be left to them" (p. 347). Maimonides does not explain these words fully, but merely alludes to the correct interpretation they ought to be given—among other things by the argument that they ought to be interpreted on the basis of Aristotle's *Meteorology*.[13] He expects the reader with philosophical training to complete the interpretation by himself and to identify "water," "firmament," "the waters which were above the firmament" and "the waters which were under the firmament" with the appropriate phenomena in the world of physics about which the *Meteorology* speaks.[14]

The word "waters" *(mayim)* is mentioned for the first time in Genesis 1:2—"and the spirit of God was moving over the face of the waters." Maimonides interprets this word there as indicating one of the four elements, the element of water. In verse 7, the Torah uses the verb *va-yavdel* ("and He separated") in relation to "the waters which were under the firmament" and "the waters which were above the firmament." As we have seen, the verb "separate" indicates the giving of form to matter such that it distinguishes a thing from another thing. The verse, "and God separated the waters which were under the firmament from the waters which were above the firmament," is thus interpreted by Maimonides as meaning that He gave form to the waters above the firmament and to

---

13 Maimonides was evidently familiar with Yaḥyā ibn al-Biṭriq (d. c. 830) inexact translation of the *Meteorologica*. See M. Steinschneider, *Die hebräischen Übsersetzungen des Mittelalters* (Berlin, 1893; repr. 1956) §61, pp. 132-133. This translation was published in Arabic by C. Petraitis, *The Arabic Version of Aristotle's Meteorology*, a critical edition with introduction and Greek-Arabic glossaries (Beyrouth, 1967), and see there on Maimonides, pp. 54 and 56. On this translation cf. Paul Lettinck, *Aristotle's Meteorology and its Reception in the Arabic World* (Leiden–Boston: Brill, 1999), pp. 7-8. However, one should not completely dismiss the possibility that Maimonides also knew interpretations of this text and passages in the writings of Avicenna parallel to the *Meteorology* and was influenced by them. Aristotle's *Meteorology* is known in Arabic as *al-āthār al-ʿalawiyya*. Ibn Tibbon, as well as modern translators of the *Guide*, such as Munk *(Guide*, I, p 241 and n. 1), Pines (p. 353 and n. 49) and Schwarz (p. 365), think that by the word *fī l-āthār* Maimonides alludes to Aristotle's *Meteorology*. Qāfiḥ, (*Moreh Nevukhim* [Jerusalem, 1972], p. 384 and n. 53 there) objects to this translation and thinks that *fī l- āthār* means "in the tradition," translating it as *be-divrei ḥakhamim* ("in the words of the Sages"). I have here accepted the opinion of the former group.

14 On the nature of the esotericism in this interpretation, see my paper (in this volume) "Maimonides' Exoteric and Esoteric Biblical Interpretations", p. 214-215.

those which were below the firmament, in such a way as to distinguish them from one another.

> Among the things you ought to know is that the words, 'And He divided between the waters," and so on (Gen. 1:7), do not refer merely to a division in place in which one part is located above and one below, while both have the same nature. The correct interpretation of these words is that He made a natural division between both of them—I mean with regard to their form—making one part, that which He first calls water [i.e. the element of water], into one particular thing by means of the natural form with which He invested it, and bestowing upon the other part a different form, that latter part being water proper [i.e. the waters which are in the seas]. (p. 352)

Maimonides thus explains that the giving of form meant the giving of form to the elemental waters. The elemental waters received two different forms, by means of which they became two distinct entities: "the waters which were under the firmament" and "the waters which were above the firmament." They therefore shared a common matter—that of the element water—but differed from one another in the form given to this matter.

Maimonides finds this interpretation confirmed by the use of the verb *qara'* ("He called") in verse 10, in the story of the third day of Creation: "and the waters that were gathered together He called Seas"—an act which, in his opinion, completed the second day of Creation, as we shall see below. As noted earlier, the word "He called" indicates that the word that appears alongside it is an equivocal term, whose meaning is different from that which it previously had in the biblical text. The word "waters" (*mayim*) appears in the expression "the waters that were gathered together." Maimonides explains that the word, "He called," is used to indicate the equivocality of this noun, and to indicate the difference between the meaning of the word "waters" in verse 2 and that in verse 10. In verse 2, "and the spirit of God was moving over the face of the waters," its meaning is as already noted—namely, the element of water. It follows from this that in verse 10 it must have some other meaning. Thus, "waters" in the expression "the waters that were gathered together" does not mean the element of water, but rather something else: "In this way it makes it clear to you that first *water* of which it is said, 'over the face of the waters' (*ibid.*, 4) is not the water that is in the *seas*" (p. 352). In verse 10, "and the waters that were gathered together He called Seas," the meaning of the word *mayim* (water) is the water of the seas. It follows from Maimonides' interpretation that the noun *mayim* ("waters") is an equivocal noun, in the same way as the noun *ʾereṣ* ("earth"). It is a noun that is used both "in general and in particular": it is used "in general" to refer to the element of water, and "in particular" to refer to the specific form assumed by these waters: namely, "the waters of the sea" and, as we shall see thereafter, also "the waters that were above the firmament."[15]

Maimonides' interpretation fits the explanation in Aristotle's *Meteorology* for the creation of the sea, whose waters are salty. The sea is the "remnant" of the element of water, whose natural place is in the place where the sea is located. When the sweeter and lighter portion of this element evaporated through the warming activities of the sun and it became a moist exhalation, the salty and heavier portions of the water remained, constituting the salty waters of the sea.[16] There is thus a certain justification for Maimonides' assertion that the waters of the sea are different in form from the elemental waters.

However, the real exegetical problem in the present text is the interpretation of the words "firmament" and "the waters that were above the firmament." The meaning of these words may only be established in their mutual context: the interpretation of the word "firmament" will determine that of "the waters which were above the firmament" and vice versa—the determination of the meaning of "the waters which were above the firmament" will facilitate our determination of the meaning of the word "firmament."

Maimonides thinks that the firmament, that was made "within" the elemental waters, was made "from" these waters by giving a form to the elemental waters. "Let there be a firmament in the midst of the waters" (Gen. 1:6) means that there shall be a firmament within the elemental waters. The word "waters" in verse 6 thus refers to the elemental waters.

---

15 This is likewise the opinion of Abravanel regarding this noun, although his interpretation of the subject itself is different: "'*ha-mayim*' (waters)—this noun ought to be interpreted as is said in general and in particular like the noun *ʾereṣ* (earth)"—*Perush ha-Torah* (Jerusalem, 1964), p. 26.

16 See *Meteorology* II.2, 354b, 24-32; II.2-3, 354b 32–355b 20; II. 3, 357 b17—21; 358a 5-27.

In support of this interpretation, Maimonides cites the words of the Sages in *Genesis Rabbah* 4.1: "the middle group congealed," from which he infers that "the *firmament* itself was produced from water" (p. 352). To these explicit words one might also add that which is implied by his interpretation of the verb "He made": as we have seen, the verb "to make" (*'aśoh*) indicates the giving of the specific form to a given thing. "And God made the firmament" (Gen. 1:7) means: He gave the elemental waters a natural form. However, Maimonides does not explain what that natural form was, nor what phenomenon in the world of nature is to be identified with the firmament.

Maimonides' comments regarding "the waters which were above the firmament" are not much clearer. In addition to his statement that the place of these waters is above the firmament, Maimonides adds that their place is above the *firmament*: "some part of it turned into a thing that is above the firmament" (p. 352). To this statement Maimonides adds a quotation from the words of R. Akiva in the narrative of the four Sages who "entered *Pardes*," i.e., who engaged in esoteric activities, as related in B. Ḥagigah 14b: "When you come to the stones of pure marble, do not say, 'Water, Water,' for it is written: 'He that speaks falsehood shall not be established before my eyes' [Ps. 101:7]" (p. 353). These words, says Maimonides, strengthen the assertion that "that which is above the *firmament* is called water in name only and that it is not the specific water known to us" (p. 353). According to the introductory sentence to the quotation from the words of R. Akiva, Maimonides thought that R. Akiva's words relate to the supernal waters, which are different in form from the waters of the sea. R. Akiva's words thus confirm Maimonides' thesis concerning the difference in form, as he did not agree that the supernal waters, which are "pure marble stones," should be called "water," as it would be a falsehood to call them thus: they are not literally water.

Maimonides does not elaborate further upon the words of R. Akiva, leaving their interpretation to the reader. He says:

> Reflect, if you are one of those who reflect, to what extent he [R. Akiva] has made clear and revealed the whole matter in this statement, provided that you consider it well, understand all that has been demonstrated in the

> *Meteorologica,*[17] and examine everything that people have said about every point mentioned in that work. (p. 353)

Maimonides claims that R. Akiva's words are the key to understanding "the thing as a whole"—that is, the entire issue of the water: "the waters which were above the firmament," "the firmament," and "the waters which were under the firmament." He then adds an additional hint: that the entire matter issue is to be understood according to Aristotle's *Meteorology*. The *Meteorology* is thus the key to understanding "the waters which were above the firmament" and the "firmament."[18]

One might well ask the question: with what phenomena of nature spoken of in the *Meteorology* ought one to identify "the waters which were above the firmament" and the "firmament"?

According to the *Meteorology*, the elements of air and that of fire come into being constantly by the transformation of the exhalations that rise from the earth and from the sea: steam, which is hot and dry exhalation, and the moist exhalation. In the region between the earth and the seas and the lunar sphere, there are thus to be found not only the elements of fire and air, but also matters mixed from these elements, from the exhalations which rise from the earth and from the seas. The region close to the earth is the hot–moist region. It is the region in which the air is mixed with the moist exhalation that ascends from the sea. This region is hot because it is warmed by the ray of the sun that strikes the earth and returns from it to the lower part of the air. Above it is found the cold-moist region, which consists of air mixed with the moist exhalation that ascends from the sea. This region is not hot, because it is warmed neither by the element of fire, which is warmed by the motion of the sphere, nor by the ray of the sun that refracts on the earth and returns from it to the air, because it is too far both from the element of fire and from that region upon which the reflected ray of the sun acts; hence, its warmth does not reach it. This is the intermediate region of the air. Above it is found the higher hot–moist region, composed of pure air,

---

17 See above, n. 13, concerning this translation.

18 This allusion may also hold true for the interpretation to be given according to Maimonides to "light" and its function in the Creation; to the uncovering of the dry land; to "but a mist went up from the earth," and to the interpretation of the order of Creation—all these aspects of the story of Creation are to be understood according to the hints found in Maimonides' commentary, on the basis of Aristotle's *Meteorology*.

and above that the hot–dry region which is identified with elemental fire. The majority of the hot–dry exhalations ascend to this region, albeit small quantities thereof are also mixed with the air in the regions beneath it.[19]

The "firmament" and the "waters which were above the firmament" are both to be sought in these regions. According to Maimonides' interpretation, both the firmament and the waters which were above the firmament are elemental waters that assumed different forms, and thereby became distinct substances from one another. It follows from this that they are to be sought in the lower hot–moist regions, the intermediary cold–moist region and the upper hot–moist region, in which are found the moist exhalations which ascended from the water, and not in the hot–dry region, in which the dry exhalations which ascend from the earth dominate. Their exact identification raises numerous difficulties, and Maimonides' commentators disagreed among themselves as to the manner in which Maimonides' intentions here are to be understood. A number of solutions were suggested for the identification of the "firmament" and the "waters which were above the firmament," and even offered an additional interpretation for "the waters which were under the firmament," which was determined anew on the basis of one of the interpretations of the "firmament." These interpretations are an interesting example of the "completion" which a person with a philosophical background and a good knowledge of Aristotle's *Meteorology* can make of Maimonides' interpretation.

(1) According to the first possible interpretation, the firmament is the hot-moist region while the supernal waters are the cold–moist region. This solution answers the requirement that the firmament and the supernal waters be made of elemental waters, which will contain, according to Maimonides, "one common matter which is called water," for it is in those regions that one finds the moist exhalation that ascended from the water and, upon evaporating, left the salty seas. It also meets the requirement that the supernal waters be above the firmament, being located above the moist–hot region closest to the earth, which is the lower portion of the air. The supernal waters are different from the specific water—that is, the waters of the seas—because they are water "in potential" and not in actuality. According to the *Meteorology*, the clouds

19 See especially *Meteorology* I.3.4.9.

come into existence in the cold–moist region, by means of a thickening of the moist exhalation that ascends thereto from the earth, due to the coldness that dominates this part of the air.[20] The cold, according to the *Meteorology*, is an active cause, whose influence on the water is their thickening.[21] One may therefore call "the waters that were above the firmament" water in the sense of a homonym, because they are waters only "in potential" and not "in actuality." This solution is likewise consistent with the words of R. Akiva: the pure marble stones suggest a solid (stone) and cold (marble) substance, a description that is suitable to cloud, the exhalation which has been thickened by the coldness in the cold–moist region.

This solution is one of two solutions mentioned by Narboni in his interpretation to *Guide* I.30,[22] and is also accepted by Shem Tov, who quotes it in the name of Narboni as the correct interpretation of Maimonides' words here.[23] Both of them see the distinction in form between the upper waters and the lower waters as that between water in potentiality and water in actuality. Similarly Abravanel, in his *Commentary on the Torah*, mentions it in the "fourth opinion" of the meaning of the term "firmament," seeing it as Maimonides' interpretation. However, according to his description of this opinion, R. Akiva's words refer, not to the supernal waters, but to the upper part of the hot–moist air, which is water neither in potential nor in actuality; therefore, one who calls them "water" is clearly speaking falsehood according to R. Akiva.

(2) According to the second possible interpretation of "firmament," and "the waters which were above the firmament," the firmament is the cold–moist region while the upper waters are the hot-moist region: that is, pure air. This interpretation is largely based upon the passage brought by Maimonides in support of his view from the words of the Sages in *Genesis Rabbah* 4.2—"the middle drop was congealed"—as an interpretation of the word "firmament." Those who understand Maimonides' words in light of this saying see the key to the identification of the firmament in the word "middle." As the firmament is the middle drop which froze over or congealed, it must be the middle section of the air—that is, the cold–moist region. It follows from this that the

20 *Ibid.*, I.9, 346b25-30.
21 *Ibid.*, IV.6, 383a 5-10.
22 See his *Be'ur le-Sefer Moreh Nevukhim*, p. 39b.
23 See his *Perush le-Moreh Nevukhim*, p. 60a.

waters which were above the firmament refer to that region above it, i.e., the region of pure air. In this region the moist exhalation turned into real air, and therefore it is made from the elemental waters, from the moist exhalation. But it is no longer water, neither in potential nor in actuality; hence it is justified to say that it is only "water" in the equivocal sense of the noun "water." The upper waters are "above the air"—that is, above the middle region of the air, the moist–cold region that constitutes the firmament. The problem with this solution is that it is difficult to reconcile it with the words of R. Akiva. It is difficult to see why the upper air, the hot–moist portion, should be called "pure marble stones."

This interpretation is cited by Shem Tov under the heading, "the commentators said..."[24] He adds an alternative interpretation of "the waters which were under the firmament," saying that this refers to that water which came into existence in the cold part of the air—namely, rain. However, according to Shem Tov's view, the advocates of this interpretation identify the "pure marble stones," not with the upper waters, as implied by *Guide* II.30, but rather with the firmament. This identification derives from the improbability of the identification of pure marble stones with the supernal hot-moist air, which according to these commentators are the upper waters. Hence they identify the "pure marble stones" with the cold–moist region.

The interpretation brought by Shem Tov in the name of "the commentators" is evidently the second interpretation mentioned by Narboni.[25] However, according to Narboni's interpretation the lower waters are not the rain, which is already water in actuality, but the potential water—that is, the moist exhalation before they once again become (i.e., condense into) water in actuality. Narboni also explicitly identifies the "pure marble stones" with the hot-moist region, therefore preserving the principle that "pure marble stones" must be parallel to "the waters which were above the firmament."

(3) According to the third possibility, the firmament refers to "the cold–moist place"—that is, the air to which the cold–moist exhalation ascends. The upper waters are the cold–moist exhalation from which water comes into existence and is water in potentiality, whereas those

24 See *Perush le-Moreh Nevukhim*, p. 59b.

25 See his *Be'ur le-Sefer Moreh Nevukhim*, 39b-40a.

waters that are below the firmament are "the specific waters which are found with us in actuality"—that is, the waters of the seas. This solution is proposed by Efodi in his interpretation of *Guide* II.30.[26]

This solution answers the requirement that the upper waters be found "above the firmament," for the middle air surrounds the moist-cold exhalation that ascends to it from all sides. The upper waters are "water" only in the equivocal sense of the word, being nothing but water "in potentiality." The upper waters may be identified with the "pure marble stones" because they are the thick exhalation of clouds in the cold region. This identification of the firmament with the middle region of the air is likewise appropriate to the words of the Sages in *Genesis Rabbah* 4.2: "the middle drop congealed."

The second exegetical problem that arises in explaining the story of the second day of Creation is how to explain the seeming identification of "firmament" (*raqiʿa*) with "heaven" (*shamayim*) in Genesis 1:8: "and God called the firmament heaven." However, according to Maimonides' interpretation of the verb "He called," *va-yiqraʾ*, this verse does not present any exegetical difficulty at all, as the verb "He called" indicates that the noun which appears alongside it is an equivocal noun, bearing a different meaning than that which it previously had in the text. In verse 8 the verb "He called" indicates that "heaven" is an equivocal noun, different in meaning from *shamayim* in verse 1. This "heaven" that is identical to the "firmament" is not the spheres, but rather the lower hot-moist region of the air, or the cold- moist region which is the middle air—depending upon the interpretation chosen among the three possible interpretations of the word "firmament" which we presented earlier.

> The words, "And God called the firmament Heaven," (Gen. 1:8) is intended, according to what I have explained to you, to make clear that the term is equivocal and that the *heaven* mentioned in the first place, in the words "the heaven and the earth" (Gen. 1:1): is not what is generally named "heaven." (Gen. 1:1) (p. 352)

However, the statement that the word "heaven" is an equivocal term

26 See his *Perush le-Moreh Nevukhim, ibid.*

does not completely solve the exegetical problem of the phrase "the firmament of the heaven" in the Creation story. Maimonides adds—this time without relying upon the verb "He called"—that the term "firmament" is also an equivocal term: "Because of this equivocality of the terms, the true 'heaven' is sometimes called 'firmament,' just as the true 'firmament' is sometimes called 'heaven'" (p. 352). It follows from this that the term "the firmament of the heaven" is composed of two separate equivocal terms whose meaning is identical in all their appearances to the term, "the firmament of the heaven." In verses 14, 15, and 17, both of them mean "spheres," while in verse 20 it refers to one of the sections of the air.

4. Why Doesn't it Say "It was Good" at the end of the description of the Second Day of Creation?

One of the issues that has engaged all biblical commentators, from the Rabbinic Sages on down, is that of the interpretation of the stylistic deviations in the story of Creation—i.e., the omission of the phrase "it was good" from the description of the second day of Creation. Maimonides raises this problem in *Guide* II.30, after explaining the terms "firmament," "the waters which were above the firmament," and "the waters which were under the firmament," resolving it in light of the meaning which he attributes to the term "good" (*tov*).

a. The Interpretation of the Adjective "Good" (*tov*).

The term "good" (*tov*) is explained by Maimonides in *Guide* II.30. However, he again interprets it in three other places in the Third Book of the *Guide of the Perplexed:* in Chapter 10, and in two of the chapters concerning the final end, namely, Chapters 13 and 25.

In *Guide* II.30, Maimonides explains that, "For whenever it mentions a thing among those that exist, having been produced in time and subsisting in durable, perpetual, and permanent fashion, it says with reference to it 'that it was good'" (p. 353). And slightly further on he states: "For the meaning of the words, 'that it was good,' is that the thing in question is of externally visible and manifest utility for the existence and permanence of that which exists" (p. 354). According to the former explanation, the term "and it was good" (*ki tov*) indicates something that is created, something that has a continuous, ongoing and unchanging reality or existence—that is, something eternal lasting into the future time. According to the second explanation, the nature of the thing created must both be visible to the eye and clear to all. Maimonides thereby tells us that the expression "and it was good" corresponds to the understanding of a person who looks at the creation and arrives at the judgment that a given thing created by God is beneficial for the existence and persistence of reality.

This understanding of the term, "it was good," is clearer in the chapters concerning the final end. Whereas in *Guide* II.30 Maimonides simply tells us that "it was good" is stated regarding things that are created, that are constant in their existence, and that are of an unchanging nature, in the chapters of the final end he explains to us *why* it states regarding them that they "are good." The clearest explanation of this appears in III. 13:

> "He only says that He brought every part of the world into existence and that its existence conforms to its purpose. This is the meaning of his saying, 'and God saw that it was good (*tov*).' For you know what we have explained with regard to their saying: 'the Torah speaks in the language of human beings.' And *good [tov]* is an expression applied by us to what conforms to our purpose" (p. 453).

Maimonides here develops the view that "it was good" is an expression that expresses and corresponds to human understanding, relying upon one of the most important assumptions underlying his interpretation of the Torah, which he received from the Rabbinic Sages: namely, that "the Torah speaks in the language of human beings."[27] He understands that by these words the Sages established the rule that, on its literal level, the Torah speaks according to the apprehension and the understanding of the multitude. The multitude attributes to God and to His activities terms that are analogous to those terms that may be attributed to himself and his own activities. Thus, the term "good" is used to indicate the correspondence between that which was intended and that which was done in practice: that is, when through our activities we in fact succeeded in realizing our intentions. Therefore, when Moses, the

27 B. Baba Meṣi'a 31b; B. Berakhot 31a; B. Kiddushin 17b; and on this matter see also my abovementioned article, n. 14, p. 193-195.

author of the Torah, set out to express the idea that the Divine activity, the creation of each one of the things described in the Creation story, corresponded to the Divine intention, he used the expression "good," corresponding to the popular understanding of this Divine activity.

Maimonides here suggests an explanation of the term "good," as attributed to the Divine activity, similar to that which he gave to the Thirteen Qualities in Exodus 34:6-7 in his discussion in *Guide* I.54, devoted to Moses' requests and to the epiphany in the Cleft of the Rock in Exodus 33 and 34.[28] According to Maimonides, the ethical realm is inferior to that of theoretical knowledge. The former is a realm of relative values, whereas the realm of the intelligibles is one of absolute judgments. Ethics is essentially the result of agreement among human beings within human society, and as such does not apply to God.[29] The ethical descriptions through which Moses expresses his apprehension in the Cleft of the Rock (Exod. 34:6-7) is the outcome of Moses' translation of his own apprehension to the perception of the masses. The Thirteen Qualities are thus attributes of relation that exist within the human intellect. It is man who attributes them to God upon observing God's activities in the world—that is, when he examines the structure of those things that exist, the mutual relations among them, and the events that were established in the world by the constant laws of nature. As there is a tendency to describe God on the basis of a human model, one observing nature draws an analogy between human activities and what appear to him to be similar activities of God; in the wake of this analogy, he attributes to God those same qualities which would be the source of similar actions on the part of a human being. Thus, the interpretation that ought to be given to the ethical terms is in reality cosmological; each of them expresses one of the manifestations of the natural law. The term "good," attributed to the Divine activity in the Creation story was created according to this selfsame model, except that, unlike the ethical terms, this term is not attributed to God Himself, but to the Divine activity.

The question is asked: What is meant by that "Divine intention" which

---

28 On Maimonides' interpretation of the revelation in the Cleft of the Rock, see (in this volume) "Maimonides' Exoteric and Esoteric Biblical Interpretations in the *Guide of the Perplexed,*" p. 202-205; (in this volume) "Maimonides' Interpretation of Jacob's Dream of the Ladder" p. 118-123; "Bible Commentary," pp. 253-254. For a full interpretation of the revelation in the Cleft of the Rock, see Hannah Kasher, "Maimonides' Interpretation of the story of the Cleft of the Rock" *Da'at* 35 (1995), pp. 29-66 (Hebrew).

29 See *Guide* I.2.

was realized in God's activities and which, once realized, was judged to be good on the basis of the analogy between the activity which realized them and similar human activity? According to the above-cited passage from *Guide* III.13, the Divine intention was to provide existence to every existing thing. This statement is repeated in Chapter 25, albeit there Maimonides attributes the activity of creation not only to the Divine will, but to Divine wisdom as well:[30] "that the entire purpose consists in bringing into existence the way you see it everything whose existence is possible" (p. 504). Slightly further down he says: "what is primarily intended—namely, the bringing into being of everything whose existence is possible, existence being indubitably a good" (p. 506). That is to say: the Divine intention was to create the world with all its plenitude—the heavens, the stars, various kinds of minerals and vegetation and animal life—all those things whose existence was possible according to the Divine wisdom and realized by the Divine will. In accordance with this explanation, Maimonides is able to identify existence with "good," and to say in Chapter 25: "existence being indubitably a good" (*ibid.*)

In Chapter 13 Maimonides emphasizes another aspect of the question of the final end of the existents, one that is important for understanding the phrase "for it was good" in the story of the Creation. Each one of the things created was "intended for itself," that is, is "a final end for itself": "It should not be believed that all the beings exist for the sake of the existence of man. On the contrary, all the other beings too have been intended for their own sakes and not for the sake of something else" (p. 452). One may then understand from this why it states "it was good" regarding each of the days of Creation, regarding the creation of each distinct thing, as it is possible to say regarding each thing in its own right that there was a Divine intention to create it and that this intention was realized by the Divine will.

If we now reexamine the explanations of the term "and it was good" in *Guide* II.30 and in *Guide* III.13 and 25, we will find that in II.30 the definition of those things to which the term "good" refers is more precise, and possibly more limited. According to Chapter 30, "it was good" does not refer to everything that was created, but only to those things

30 Maimonides' interpretation of the story of the Creation seems closer to *Guide* III.13, in which there is not mentioned the function of the Divine wisdom in Creation except for an incidental comment at the end.

which were created and whose existence is continuous, constant and unchanging. This means, in the context of Maimonides' views: in relation to the *individuals* of the spheres and the stars, but to the *species* of minerals, animals, and the human race but not to its individuals. Concerning the species in the sublunar world it says "it was good," but not regarding its concrete individuals who were created in the act of the Creation of the world.

This distinction between *Guide* II.30 and *Guide* III.13 may be explained by noting that in Chapter 13 Maimonides preserves the meaning of the constancy of the existents produced in time after not having existed for the term "very good." "Good" is only an indication of something being produced after not having existed in a manner suitable to the intention of the One who produced it, while the addition of the word "very" (*meʾod*) at the end of the story of the Creation comes to indicate the persistence of that "good" thing—that is of the Creation as a whole.

> About the whole, it says: "And God saw everything that He had made, and, behold, it was very good [*tov meʾod*]" [Gen. 1:31]. For the production in time of everything that was produced conformed to its purpose, and nothing went wrong. And that is the meaning of the expression: "very" [*meʾod*]; for sometimes a thing is *good* and conforms for a time to our purpose, whereas afterwards the goal is missed. Accordingly it gives the information that all the things made, conformed to His intention and purpose and that they continued without ceasing to correspond to what was intended with regard to them. (pp. 453-454)

Evidently, Maimonides does not draw a distinction between "good" and "very good" in the other chapters of the *Guide of the Perplexed*. In *Guide* III.25, Maimonides defines the good action by saying, "The good and excellent action is that accomplished by an agent aiming at a noble end, I mean one that is necessary or useful, and achieves that end" (p. 503). Further on in this chapter, he repeats his claim that God's activities are very good without explaining whether there is a difference between "good" and "very good," relying upon Genesis 1:31: "According to our opinion—that is, that of all of us who follow the Law of Moses, our master—all His actions are good and excellent. He says: 'And God saw everything that had made, and, behold, it was very good" (*ibid.*). He repeats this at the end of the chapter: "It is upon this opinion [i.e., that the actions of God are for a good end] that the whole of the Torah of Moses our Master is founded; it opens with it: 'And God saw every thing that He had made, and, behold, it was very good'; and it concludes with it: 'The Rock, His work is perfect,' and so on [Deut. 32:4]. Know this" (p. 506).

Likewise in *Guide* III.10, Maimonides does not distinguish between a good action and one that is very good. He begins by saying: "Rather all His acts, may He be exalted, are an absolute good; for He only produces being, and all being is a good" (p. 440). Somewhat further on, relying upon Genesis 1:31, he says: "Accordingly the true reality of the act of God in its entirety is the good, for the good is being. For this reason, the book that has illumined the darkness of the world has enunciated literally the following statement: 'And God saw everything that He had made, and, behold, it was very good'" (*ibid.*).[31]

This selfsame explanation is repeated in *Guide* I.54, when Maimonides interprets the revelation in the Cleft of the Rock: "I shall pass all my goodness before you" (Exod. 33:19): "This dictum—'All my goodness'—alludes to the display to him of all existing things of which it is said, 'And God saw every thing that He had made, and, behold, it was very good'" (p. 124). "All My goodness" thus refers to the Divine good, that is, the totality of all those things that exist, as related in the Creation story, Genesis 1.

The expressions "good" and "very good" as they appear in the Cre-

31 In this passage, Maimonides brings a different or possibly additional interpretation of "it was very good," based upon R. Meir's homily in *Genesis Rabbah* 9.5: "In the Torah [scroll] of R. Meir they found it written: 'and behold it was very good'—and, behold, death was good." He says: "Accordingly the true reality of the act of God in its entirety is the good, for the good is being. For this reason the book that has illumined the darkness of the world has enunciated literally the following statement: 'And God saw everything that He had made, and, behold, it was very good' [Gen. 1:31]. Even the existence of this inferior matter, whose manner of being it is to be a concomitant of privation entailing death and all evils, all this is also *good* in view of the perpetuity of generation and the permanence of being through succession. For this reason Rabbi Meir interpreted the words, 'And, behold, it was very [*me'od*] good—and, behold, death [*mavet*] was good,' according to the notion to which we have drawn attention." (*Guide* III.11, p. 440). The expression "very good" is intended to say that, in an overall view, everything that God created is good, including the matter of the sublunary world, which is always joined to privation of the form. The matter of the sublunary world is good because it benefits the perpetuation of existence; it enables the constant process of generation and corruption by which individuals are destroyed but the species perpetuate.

ation story are thus intended, according to Maimonides, to add to the explanation of the *structure of the created world* the explanation of its purpose: the Torah notes the creation of each one of the existing things as "good" and concludes the story of the Creation as a whole by saying "it was very good," in order to emphasize that the end of the world is its ongoing, continuous and unchanging existence, and that each of the things created in the world of the spheres, and each of the species of creatures in the sublunar world, is an end in its own right. The world as a whole does not have one final end such that all of its parts are the means for its realization.

b. The Meaning of the Omission of the Term "It was Good" in the Description of the Second Day of Creation

Maimonides' point of departure in interpreting the omission or deletion of the phrase, "it was good," from the description of the second day of Creation is his view of the literary nature of the biblical text. There are two separate levels of meaning in the biblical text: the external level (*ẓāhir*) is addressed to the vulgar, while the inner level (*bāṭin*) is addressed to the educated person.

As noted, the adjective "good" is used, in referring to the Divine activity of each of the other five days of Creation, as an expression of judgment, by which man evaluates the Divine activity using terms taken from the world of human activity. By recognizing that God created every thing in accordance with His intention, He refers to this activity as "good." It follows from this that "good" can only be said with regard to the visible Divine activities in the world as apprehended by the vulgar. It is only regarding them that the vulgar can understand why it says that "it was good."

In the story of the Creation, the "firmament" and "the waters which were above the firmament" also have two levels of meaning: the apparent level and the hidden level. If we examine the possible understandings of each of these two levels of significance, argues Maimonides, it would seem as if none of them allow one to say "it was good" regarding the creation of the "firmament" and of "the waters which were above the firmament."

As an interpreter of the apparent level of the biblical text, Maimonides does not have in mind the vulgar. In fact, he does not explain at all how such a person, entirely lacking in philosophical training or, to quote the language used in the *Introduction* to *Pereq Ḥeleq*, "the man of the first group," who understands the text according to its apparent level and believes everything written therein even if it contradicts common sense[32]—will understand the story of the second day of Creation. It is possible that such a person may think that the blue which he sees above him to which he refers by the name "firmament" is a body in the literal sense, and that above it are located actual waters, identical to the "storehouse of rain" from which God brings rain upon the earth according to His will.[33] It seems plausible that Maimonides does not present the interpretation that the vulgar would give to the biblical text because, according to the latter's interpretation, it might be possible to say "it was good" regarding the creation of the second day. In any event, as one attempting to interpret the literal meaning of the text, he represents the person addressed as one having only partial and superficial philosophical training. Maimonides describes such a person in somewhat different context in the *Introduction* to *Pereq Ḥeleq*,[34] where he portrays three types of readers who interpret the rabbinic aggadot. The "second type" is one who, on the one hand, has a certain degree of scientific education, albeit rather fragmentary (the outstanding figures from this group are, according to Maimonides, physicians and astrologers who consider themselves wise men and philosophers, but are not really so); on the other hand, he does not discern that the text at hand, containing the homilies or legends of the Sages, has an additional level of meaning beyond that apparent

32 On the member of the first group according to the *Introduction* to *Pereq Ḥelek*, see Klein-Braslavy, *Creation*, pp. 49-51

33 In the "fifth opinion" regarding the interpretation of the word "firmament" (*raqiʿa*), Abravanel mentions a similar opinion, that of R. Saʿadiah Gaon (which was presented in his lost *Commentary on the Book of Genesis*) and by a number of "wise men of the nations": "The fifth opinion is that the firmament mentioned here is a strong spherical body that was created on the second day within the element of water, and it is fixed in the middle of the space of the world, and water is fixed above it and other water below it, but human beings do not apprehend it by their senses" (*Commentary on the Torah*, [Jerusalem, 1964] p. 37). According to Abravanel, this view is the result of imagination and has no correspondence, to either the reality subject to sense apprehension or that subject to logical, intellectual proof.

34 *Introduction to Pereq Ḥeleq*, ed. M.D. Rabinowitz (Jerusalem, 1961), pp. 117-122. In the Introduction to the *Guide*, Maimonides suggests a somewhat different classification. He distinguishes between the approach of the "ignoramus among the multitude of the Rabbanites" and two possible approaches of the "perfect man"—the one who discerns that the text at hand contains a hidden level of meaning, and the one who does not discern this, therefore finding contradictions between the literal meaning and his philosophical education and rejecting the text as incorrect. His description of the reader of Gen. 1:6-8 is more suitable to the classification in the *Introduction to Pereq Ḥeleq*, in which the member of the second group is not a "perfect man," but rather one with only partial philosophic education.

to the eye, a hidden level. He therefore understands the text in the literal sense, finding that his partial knowledge of the sciences is not consistent with what is stated in the text. The problem that arises as a result of this is resolved by rejecting the text as so much nonsense and holding fast to his own views.

When such a person reads the story of the second day of Creation, he understands that "firmament" and "the waters which were above the firmament" both refer to physical bodies. But, upon attempting to reconcile his partial knowledge of Aristotelian physics with what he reads on the revealed level of the biblical text, he arrives at the conclusion that the "firmament" and the "waters which were above the firmament" do not exist at all: in other words, he rejects what is stated in the biblical text. According to Maimonides, he arrives at this conclusion in the following way: he first understands, as did Maimonides himself, that "heaven" in verse 1 refers to the "spheres," and that the "firmament" is not identical with the heaven, but must allude to some other body in addition to them.[35] At this point, there are two options available to him by which to explain the meaning of "firmament" and "the waters which were above the firmament": either to seek the "firmament" in the region between the lower sphere, the lunar sphere, and the earth and the water, or to seek it beyond the spheres. But according to his knowledge of physics, which does not include the *Meteorology*, the only things to be found in the region between the earth and water and the lunar sphere are the elements of water and fire: there is no room for an additional body that could be identified with the "firmament." He is also unable to imagine the existence of waters "above the air," as according to Aristotle's doctrine of natural place the place of the water is above the earth and below the air, not above it. He may now make another attempt to identify the "firmament" and the "waters which were above the firmament." By making use of his power of imagination, he may imagine the existence of such bodies above and beyond the spheres—but such a solution is even more absurd within the framework of Aristotelian physics than the former one for, according to Aristotle's doctrine, there is nothing beyond the highest sphere. The reader is thus forced to the

35 According to S. Munk (*Guide*, II, p. 242, n. 6), Maimonides intends to say that this commentator identifies "firmament" with "heaven," and therefore thinks that only the "waters which were above the firmament" are located above the spheres, but not the firmament itself. My interpretation differs from that of Munk.

conclusion that the "firmament" and "the waters which were above the firmament" whose creation is described in the story of the second day of Creation do not exist at all. This being the case, from his point of view there is no basis for saying of their creation "it was good":

> But there is something hidden, as you will see, with regard to the *firmament* and the thing above it, which is called *water*. For if the matter is considered according to its external meaning and with a recourse only to superficial speculation, it does not exist at all. For between us and the lowest heaven, there exists no body except the elements, and there is no water above the air. This judgment applies all the more if someone imagines that this *firmament* and what is above it are above the heaven. In that case the thing would be even more impossible and remote from apprehension. (p. 353)

If, however, the text is interpreted according to its hidden meaning, Maimonides says, there is no room to say "it was good" regarding the creation of the "firmament" or "the waters which were above the firmament," for "it was good" is only stated with regard to a thing "that is of externally visible and manifest utility for the existence and permanence of that which exists" (p. 354)—that is, something whose existence is evident to the eye, whereas here one is explicitly speaking about something whose existence is hidden from the broad masses of people. None of the vulgar know what the firmament is or what the upper waters are; hence he is unable to judge them as existent things that were created in accordance with the Divine intention. It follows from this that even according to the "hidden" meaning of "firmament" and "water which were above the firmament" it is impossible to say of them that "it was good":

> If, on the other hand, the matter is considered according to its inner meaning and to what was truly intended, it is most hidden. For in that case it was necessary for it to be one of the concealed secrets so that the vulgar should not know it. How then could it be proper to say of such a matter "that it was good"? For the meaning of the words, "that it was good," is that the thing in question is of ex-

> ternally visible and manifest utility for the existence and permanence of that which exists. But in a manner whose meaning is hidden and that, understood in its external meaning, does not exist in such a way as to appear useful, what utility externally visible to the people at large could there be so that the words, "that it was good," could be said with reference to it? (pp. 353-354)

However, Maimonides felt that this latter explanation is not yet complete. For it is still possible that, according to the hidden meaning of "firmament" and "the waters which were above the firmament," one might still say "it was good" from the viewpoint of the ideal reader of the Holy Scriptures. One is speaking here of a person with considerable philosophical training in Aristotelian physics, who knows not only Aristotle's *Physics* but also his *Meteorology*, who is aware of the fact that the text at hand is equivocal and includes "hidden" meaning in addition to its apparent meaning, and who understands it in the spirit of Maimonides' earlier explanation of these two existent things. He is a member of the third group described by Maimonides in the *Introduction* to *Perek Ḥeleq*.[36] Therefore, Maimonides says on this point:

> I cannot help adding for you the following explanation: The thing in question, though it represents a very great part of the existents, does not constitute the purposed end for the permanence of that which exists; and therefore the words, "that it was good," could not be said with reference to it. This could rather occur with reference to a compelling necessity that the earth be uncovered. Understand this. (p. 354)

This further clarification is none other than the explanation according to which, even from the viewpoint of the ideal reader, it is impossible to say "it was good" regarding the "firmament" and "the water which were above the firmament." This is so, because "it was good" is only said with regard to a thing that is an end in its own right, something whose existence was intended as such. However, the "firmament" and the "up-

36 Or the "perfect man" of the type mentioned in the Introduction to the *Guide*. See note 34 above.

per waters" are not ends in their own right. They are no more than a necessary condition of the uncovering of the earth: had the water which is above the dry land not evaporated and became the moist exhalation that penetrates to the air which is above them, the dry land would not have been uncovered.[37] It is therefore impossible to say of them "it was good" even from the viewpoint of the educated reader. This explanation is likewise appropriate to the summary of the story of Creation that Maimonides gives in *Guide* III.13.

> If you consider that book which guides all those who seek guidance toward what is correct and therefore is called *Torah*, the notion that we have in view will become manifest to you from the commencement of the *Account of the Beginning* till the end. For with reference to none of them is the statement made in any way that it exists for the sake of some other thing. He only says that He brought every part of the world into existence and that its existence conformed to its purpose. This is the meaning of His saying: "And God saw that it was good [*tov*]." (p. 453)

There is no contradiction between Maimonides' words here and what he says in *Guide* II.30 on the impossibility of saying "it was good" regarding the "firmament" and "the waters which were above the firmament," even from the viewpoint of the reader with a thoroughgoing philosophi-

37 Crescas comments on the phrase, "a necessary condition of the uncovering of the land," as follows: "Perhaps the intent of this was that by means of the warmth that arrives by means of the reflection of the rays of the sun, and by the warmth coming from the stars, the land was uncovered, as has been explained: that through the warmth of the sun [some of] the water in the seas was removed, rising as exhalation in quantity corresponding what enters from the streams. For this reason the sea neither added to nor lacks. And he said that this is the reason for the uncovering of the land, because of the rising of the exhalations through the warmth of the sun and the warmth of the stars, drying it out, lifting up the waters until the land was uncovered" (*Perush le-Moreh Nevukhim*, 60b). Crescas' interpretation is evidently based upon *Meteorology* I.14; however, according to the *Meteorology* there is a fixed cyclicity in the relationship between the land and the sea: certain parts which had been sea become dry land, and parts of the land become sea. Crescas also accepts the *Meteorology's* explanation of the uncovering of the land. He rejects the "natural" explanation as to why the dry land remains uncovered by saying: "And the philosophers say that the warmth of the sun and the warmth of the stars preserve the uncovered part of the earth so that it will not be covered by the water, because of the evaporation and drying out of the water. But our opinion differs from theirs, for everything depends upon God's will and His intention."

cal education. According to *Guide* III.13, all of those things about which it says "it was good" are intended for themselves, and this statement does not contradict what he says in *Guide* II.30, that that of which it does not say "it was good" is not an end in itself.

The final interpretation of the omission of the phrase, "and God saw that it was good," from the story of the second day of Creation also enables us to understand why, at the beginning of his explanation of this stylistic deviation in the Creation story, Maimonides claims that the best interpretation among all those given by the Rabbinic Sages was that in *Genesis Rabbah* 4.8: "for the labor of [creating] the water was not completed." This interpretation is close to the last view arrived at by Maimonides himself, according to which the making of the firmament and the separation of the water above the firmament were not ends in their own right. Maimonides may have thought that, according to the Sages as well, "it was good" is only said with regard to something whose existence is a deliberate end in its own right. The existence of the water and the dry land is an intended result in its own right, and therefore it says "it was good" only once "the labor of the water was completed"—that is, when they were gathered together into one place and became seas and dry land became visible—i.e., on the third day of Creation.

On Maimonides' Interpretation of the Story of the Garden of Eden in the *Guide of the Perplexed* I.2

Maimonides' interpretation of the story of the Garden of Eden is the most complex and the most interesting interpretation of a biblical text in the whole of the *Guide of the Perplexed*. In this interpretation Maimonides makes use of a great variety of literary devices, techniques of interpretation, and methods of hiding and uncovering. Only a meticulous scrutiny of these devices, techniques and methods is likely to help the reader in fully understanding the meaning of the story. It was because of its importance and its central position in the *Guide*, that the story of the Garden of Eden received this special attention. One can realize the importance of this story by examining Maimonides' intentions in writing this work.

In the Introduction to the *Guide* and elsewhere in this work, Maimonides himself points out his aims in writing it. Maimonides claims the *Guide* to be an interpretative work, intended to explain equivocal words appearing in the books of prophecy; also, to point out certain biblical texts, which the reader is used to understand literally, as parables and interpret them, at least in part.[1]

Maimonides intends in the *Guide* "to explain what can be explained of the Account of the Beginning and the Account of the Chariot"[2] which "belong to the mysteries of the Torah."[3] Maimonides is concerned with Bible exegesis not merely in order to satisfy intellectual curiosity. He has a practical purpose in mind: to help the readers of the *Guide*. In his Introduction to the *Guide* he draws the image of "a man ... perfect in his religion and character..." who is "in a state of perplexity and confusion" because what he knows of philosophy disagrees with the literal sense of the biblical text.[4] The main benefit, which these readers will derive from this exegesis, is, that it will free them of their perplexity.

1 Introduction, pp. 2-3/ pp. 5-8.
2 Introduction to pt. III, p. 297/p. 415.
3 *Ibid.*
4 p. 2/p. 5. See also p. 6/p.10, "Instruction with respect to this treatise," pp. 9-10/pp.16-17.

But the man of the "multitude" is not free from perplexity either. His is a pre-philosophical perplexity caused by the disagreement between what he has been taught by "traditional authority," and the literal sense of the biblical text. This perplexity centers on questions concerning the nature of God.[5] These two kinds of perplexity Maimonides has in mind when writing the *Guide*. It is them he wishes to overcome by his biblical exegesis.[6]

But it appears that Maimonides' central aim and his ultimate goal in writing the *Guide* is not merely to relieve people of their perplexity, but to *guide* his reader, mainly his disciple "and the like of him," for whom the *Guide* is intended according to the "Epistle Dedicatory,"[7] towards to rank of the ideal human being. This aim is even more conspicuous in the Hebrew epistle to the disciple,[8] in the chapters of the *Guide*, which discuss the divine attributes,[9] as well as in *Guide* III.51. Moreover, Maimonides stresses this aim by the very structure of the *Guide*. The work starts and ends with a description of the ideal human being. The presentation of this image is the "framework theme" of the book. Within it, as an "interior theme," all the rest of the problems of interpretation as well as the philosophico-theological ones are presented.

It appears that by giving the book such a structure, Maimonides implies that all its contents and the rest of its aims are to be seen as a means of achieving its ultimate goal of directing the reader towards the rank of the ideal human being.

This being the work's ultimate goal, the interpretation of the story of the Garden of Eden, which is to be seen as part and parcel of the story of the creation of man,[10] plays a central role in the book. As interpreted by Maimonides the theme of the story of the Garden of Eden is the doctrine of man. It presents the ideal man; man who has fallen from the ideal rank; the reasons for this fall and its corollaries. Thus the interpretation of this story is in itself the presentation of the central theme of the doctrine of man. It indicates that this doctrine is the biblical doctrine of man.

5 *Guide*, I.35, pp. 54-55/p. 81.

6 For these two types of perplexity see also (in this volume) "Maimonides Exoteric and Esoteric Biblical Interpretations in the *Guide of the Perplexed*," pp. 198-199.

7 p. 1/ p. 4.

8 See D.Z.H. Baneth, *Iggerot ha-Rambam* (Jerusalem, 1946), pp. 12-16.

9 I.50-60.

10 See II.30, p. 249/p. 355.

The story, as interpreted by Maimonides, may lead man towards achieving the rank of an ideal human being and towards guarding against arriving at the level of one who has fallen from this rank. For knowing the doctrine of man enables man to choose the right behavior.

Seen from another angle, knowing the contents of this biblical story enables man to perfect himself, for the doctrine of man is a part of physics, as well as in some way, a part of metaphysics. As such this doctrine is knowledge constituting human perfection.

As seen from yet other angles there is in the interpretation of the story of the Garden of Eden a realization of all the rest of the partial aims of the *Guide*. In virtue of its theme the story belongs to the Account of the Beginning (*Maʿaseh Bereshit*). Indeed, it is on the borderline between the Account of the Beginning and Account of the Chariot (*Maʿaseh Merkavah*). Therefore, its "secrets" too are "secrets" of "the divine knowledge."[11]

By the interpretation of the story Maimonides fulfills his promise "to explain what can be explained of the Account of the Beginning and the Account of the Chariot."

The literary form of the story is that of a classical text which may be read as history and taken literally. Maimonides points out that it is a parable and interprets it as such. In his explanations he also fulfills his promise to explain equivocal terms occurring in the books of prophecy. Finally, his interpretation of the story is likely to relieve of their perplexity both him who has studied the wisdom of the philosophers and the man of the multitude.

In this paper I would like to put forward some suggestions as to whom the interpretation of the story of the Garden of Eden in *Guide* I.2 is addressed, and as to its structure, as well as to indicate its place and importance within the framework of the complete interpretation of the story of the Garden of Eden in the *Guide*.[12]

The general structure *Guide* I.2 appears at first sight to be analogous to the general structure of the *Guide of the Perplexed* as a whole. It is also the only chapter in the *Guide* in which there is a "framework story" whose theme is the "addressee" of the chapter. Just as the ideal "ad-

11 p. 4/p. 7.

12 These remarks, presented in my lecture in the conference "Maimonides in Egypt" in 1982 have been excerpted from an extensive piece of research on Maimonides' interpretation of the story of the Garden of Eden that was then in preparation. They were integrated into my book: *Adam Stories*.

dressee" of the *Guide* as a whole is the figure of Maimonides' disciple and "the like of him," so Maimonides presents as the figure of the ideal reader of the interpretation of the story of the Garden of Eden "the man busy with sciences" (*rajul ʿulūmī*).[13]

It is possible that by giving the chapter this special structure, Maimonides stresses the central role the interpretation of the story of the Garden of Eden plays in the *Guide*, and hence the central role the theme of the doctrine of man plays in the book.

But whereas the disciple and "the like of him" are figures of "readers" only, though undoubtedly "active" readers,[14] the "man busy with sciences" is also a figure of one who *interprets* the biblical text. He is the first interpreter of the story of the Garden of Eden in the *Guide*.

"The man busy with sciences" is the antithesis of the perplexed "man perfect in his religion" whom Maimonides describes in three places in his Introduction to the *Guide*,[15] and whom he claims to address throughout the book. The perplexed man is described as "a religious man in whose soul the validity of our Law has become established, and in whose belief this has become actual."[16] This is a believing Jew who accepts the Bible as a holy and authoritative book, which guides men towards perfection of body and soul. The "man busy with sciences," on the other hand, is one who does not acknowledge the holiness of the biblical text, and that the Torah is "guidance for all men in the past and in the future."[17] It seems likely that he is a non-religious type, a "free thinker."[18] The perplexed

---

13 S. Pines translates "a learned man."

14 For the "active" readers of the *Guide* see (in this volume) "Maimonides Exoteric and Esoteric Biblical Interpretations in the *Guide of the Perplexed*," pp. 199-200.

15 See above note 4. The perplexed "man perfect in his religion" could be the disciple himself after having acquired further knowledge in philosophy. In the Hebrew letter to the disciple (see above, note 8) Maimonides tells him, "if you set aright your heart and its thoughts toward the ways of the wise and holy men of this time, imitate their deeds, and *eat from their savory dishes*, you will find whatever you desire if you follow me" (p. 16). Maimonides here, as well as in the interpretation of the story of the Garden of Eden, employs "eat" in the sense of learning the sciences. He uses "food," in this case "savory dishes," to mean sciences and philosophy. In order to understand the *Guide* the disciple has to study philosophy and other sciences. On the other hand it is possible, as L. Strauss does, to see in the perplexed "man perfect in his religion" another kind of reader (see L. Strauss, "How to Begin to Study the Guide of the Perplexed." In: *The Guide of the Perplexed*, tr. S. Pines (Chicago, 1963), pp. xi-lvi, at p. xix). For my part, I prefer the first interpretation.

16 p. 2/p. 5. I have slightly changed Pines' rendition of this sentence.

17 p.16/ p. 24. S. Pines translates: "the guide of the first and the last men." –According to *Guide* III.13, the word *Torah* itself indicates its function: "If you consider that book which guides all those who seek guidance toward what is correct, and therefore is called *Torah* ..." (p. 327/p. 453).

18 This interpretation has already been given by Abravanel in his Commentary on the *Guide*, *ad loc.*,

man is described as "perfect in his ...character,"[19] while the objector is described as wanton and addicted to the pleasures of the flesh.[20]

The perplexed man is described as "having studied the sciences of the philosophers and come to know what they signify," as "one who has philosophized and has knowledge of the true sciences."[21] One wonders whether "the man busy with sciences" differs from the perplexed "man perfect in religion" in this as well, or whether just this trait is common to both of them. Since the perplexed one is described as having acquainted himself with the sciences, it appears that he and "the man busy with sciences" have the same kind of philosophic education, and that they differ mainly in their attitude toward the biblical text. Such a figure of a reader of a text, this time a midrashic text, is presented by Maimonides in the *Guide* I.70. He presents there "a man who has knowledge (*al-rajul al-ʿālim*) but is not equitable." And when he studies midrashim, "he laughs at them at the beginning of his study, because he sees that their external meanings [i.e,. literal meaning] diverge so widely from the true realities of existence."[22] This reader of midrashim on the one hand does not *a priori* accept the Sages' interpretations as authoritative texts conveying an eternal truth; on the other hand he understands them in their literal sense. Since this literal sense conflicts with physics which represents "the true realities of existence" he sneers at these texts.[23] It is noteworthy that the reader of midrash in *Guide* I.70 is called *al-rajul al-ʿālim*,[24] while the objector in I.2 is called *rajul ʿulūmī*. *Rajul ʿulūmī* is a somewhat unusual expression meaning "a man dealing with sciences." It has a pejorative tint.[25]

It appears that by calling the objector *rajul ʿulūmī*, Maimonides indicates that although the objector is interested in sciences, he is not "one

---

and in his Commentary on the Pentateuch. See also I. Heinemann, "Abravanel's Lehre vom Niedergang der Menschheit," *MGWJ* 82 (1938), pp. 381-400.

19 p. 2/p. 5.

20 p. 16/p. 24

21 p. 6/p. 10 (see Pines' notes 24 and 25 *ad loc.*).

22 p. 120/p. 174.

23 The figure of the reader of midrashim in the *Guide* I.70 resembles "the perfect man of virtue" whom Maimonides presents in the Introduction to the *Guide*:" If, however, a perfect man of virtue should engage in speculation on them, he cannot escape one of two courses: either he can take the speeches in question in their external [scil., literal] sense and, in so doing, think ill of their author and regard him as an ignoramus, etc." (p. 6/p. 10).

24 As we have seen, Pines. p. 174, translates "a man who has knowledge."

25 So I was told by S. Somekh during the colloquium "Maimonides in Egypt." He suggested the translation "bothered with sciences."

who knows" (*al-rajul al-ʿālim*); he is not "one who has philosophized and has knowledge of the true sciences." He has fragmentary, superficial, loose knowledge of the sciences (including apparently philosophy), but has to be seen as having only "the first notion" of them, and has not gone into them any deeper nor acquired knowledge of them. In formulating his question the objector makes use, as it seems, of philosophical notions. But not being a true philosopher, and his knowledge of philosophy being fragmentary, he does not take into account all existing possibilities of reading the biblical text along the philosophico-semantic axis. His question is in a sense semi-philosophical. Thus the objector is one who does not accept that the Bible conveys eternal truths and thereby guides its reader towards perfection of his soul. But on the other hand he is not, either, a perfect philosopher like the perplexed "man perfect in his religion," whose perplexity arises from a *real contradiction* between the biblical text and the sciences and philosophy. Thus the objector may be seen as the opposite of the ideal reader of the *Guide*.

The objector's attitude towards the biblical text is not an attitude of perplexity at any level. It is rather a critical attitude. The "man busy with sciences" is in his character rather close to the second class of readers of the words of the Sages which Maimonides presents in his *Introduction* to *Pereq Ḥeleq*, the tenth chapter of Mishnah Sanhedrin.[26] The readers of the second class are those who understand the aggadic text literally, but are not prepared to accept its authority. They consider their own intellect and knowledge to be a criterion for truth. They are not prepared to assume *a priori* that the text necessarily indicates the truth. Therefore, finding a contradiction between *what appears to them as the truth* and the literal meaning of the text, they do not fall into perplexity like the

26 *Maimonides' Commentary on the Mishnah*, Arabic and Hebrew translation, ed. Y. Qāfiḥ, *Nezīqīn* (Jerusalem, 1963), pp. 201-202: "The second class (of readers of the midrashim of the Sages) is also a numerous one. They are those who have seen or heard the words of the Sages, and understand them literally. They claim that the Sages did not intend by this anything but what is indicated by the literal meaning of (their) words. Hence they embark upon calling (the words of the Sages) silly and evil, and upon describing as repugnant what is not repugnant. Eventually they deride the words of the Sages, and claim that they themselves are more intelligent and have brighter minds than the Sages; and that the Sages were dupes, lacking insight, ignorant of existence as a whole, so that they did not comprehend anything. Into holding such a belief tumble in the main those who claim to know medicine and the ravings concerning the decree of the stars. For they claim to be clever, wise men, and philosophers ... How far are they from humanness when seen by true philosophers." (Translated from the Arabic by Michael Schwarz; for earlier English renderings, all based on the Hebrew version, see *Maimonides' Commentary on the Mishnah, Tractate Sanhedrin*, tr. into English by F. Rosner (New York, 1981), p. 141 and p. 169-170, notes 111-125) – For these readers see also *Creation*, pp. 48-50.

perplexed "man perfect in his religion," described in the Introduction to the *Guide*, but embark immediately upon criticizing the text they have before them.[27] This attitude as such is not productive of interpretation since it implies judging the text rather than asking questions about it. But Maimonides sets this interpretation into a dialogic situation, and thus makes it a starting-point of a debate about interpretations and of a discussion of the story of the Garden of Eden. Just as the perplexed man's perplexity may serve as a starting-point or stimulus to an interpretation of the biblical text, so the objector's position as well may serve this purpose in a situation of debate. Presenting the matter as a debate is psychologically more effective. There is also much more tension in presenting the problem as a dispute between two opposing positions, than in presenting it as a reflection upon the biblical text. Also, the *ad hominem* attack on the objector, which includes a short description of him from several aspects, makes more of an impression on the reader, stirs him up, and thus draws his attention to the problem at issue, which is, as we have pointed out, one of the central problems of the *Guide of the Perplexed*. As I have already mentioned, the presentation of the problem in this manner makes it possible to introduce the figure opposite to the ideal reader of the *Guide*.

By way of this figure, which is the antithesis of the figure of the perplexed man, Maimonides introduces an interpretation of the story of the Garden of Eden which is the opposite, or antithesis, of the correct interpretation of the story. Thus the starting-point for the interpretation of the story is its most incorrect interpretation. Apart from the

---

27 The typical readers of the second class of midrashim are "those who claim to know medicine and the ravings concerning the decrees of the stars. For they claim to be clever, wise men and philosophers" while in fact "how far are they from humanness when seen by true philosophers" (see the previous note). Thus the members of this class are not philosophers, but dabble with philosophy and do not understand it properly. A similar judgment Maimonides passes on Galen, the Greek doctor, in treatise XXV of *Pirqei Moshe*: "Galen imagined that to understand logic and the rest of the theoretical subjects was like understanding medicine, and that he was as well-versed in them as in medicine. Therefore he got into all these difficulties" (ed. S. Muntner, *Medical Aphorisms of Moses* [Jerusalem, 1959], p. 371 (Hebrew); ed. Y. Qāfiḥ in: Iggrot, She'elot u-Teshuvot, Arabic and Hebrew translation with notes by Y. Qāfiḥ [Jerusalem, 1972], p. 154). It is very likely that the objector was a physician who read philosophy superficially and did not achieve a real and thorough knowledge of it. This hypothesis may be reinforced by comparing the story about "the man busy with sciences" and his question with another question raised by "some distinguished individuals of our religious community, who were physicians" as Maimonides tells his reader in Guide III.19 (p. 346/p. 478). Maimonides formulates their question in a similar way to that which he formulates the question raised by the objector. See *Adam Stories*, pp. 56-58. On Maimonides attitude towards the physicians see *ibid*., pp. 58-59.

psychological effect which this manner of presenting things has, it allows Maimonides to pass gradually from the literal interpretation of the story of the Garden of Eden along an erroneous semantic axis,[28] to comprehending it, along a correct philosophic-semantic axis, as a philosophical allegory. Thus he leads his reader to achieve, at the end of the interpretative path, in *Guide* II. 30, a level analogous to that of a reader of the third class of the readers of the midrashim of the Sages according to the classification in the *Introduction of Pereq Ḥeleq*.[29]

But the chapter is more complex than it appears to be at first sight. The figure of the objector is only the figure of *one* of the readers of the interpretation of the story of the Garden of Eden which Maimonides here presents. Actually the chapter has a twofold address: 1) the "disciple" to whom Maimonides tells about the objection put forward by "the man

---

28 Understanding the text literally and along a natural semantic axis, this is the manner of understanding of the simple "man of the multitude." This befits his power of apprehension. In accordance with the parable of "apples of gold in settings of silver" (p. 6/ p. 11), it is useful on the political level as well. The interpretation of the story of the Garden of Eden does not start from the manner the man of the multitude understands the story, but from a possible mistake made by one who has a fragmentary philosophical education and is likely to be in unwarranted perplexity or to criticize the text unjustly, as the objector did. The interpretation of the story of the Garden of Eden not only amends the manner of reading of the reader of the text who understood it literally. It amends his philosophical perceptions as well.

29 *Maimonides' Commentary on the Mishnah, Neziqin*, Arabic and Hebrew, ed. Y. Qāfiḥ (Jerusalem, 1963), pp. 202-203: "The third class – by the life of God! its members are very few; so much so that they cannot be called a class, unless in the sense as the sun is called a species. [The sun was considered a species comprising one single particular.] They are the people who have been convinced of the greatness of the Sages and of the good quality of their thoughts on account of expressions indicating very true notions, to be found throughout the Sages' discourse, although these expressions are few and scattered in various places in their writings. But these expressions indicate the perfection of the Sages and their apprehension of truth. The people of this class also know the impossibility of what is impossible and the necessity of what is necessary. Hence they know that the Sages did not say absurd things. Therefore they know for sure that the words of the Sages have an external (literal) meaning and an inner (esoteric) one. They know that whenever the Sages say impossible things, they speak by way of riddles and parables. And why, o people, should one deem it strange for them to have written wisdom in the way of parables and comparisons to base commonplace things? For you see that the wisest of men has done this under the spirit of holiness, namely Solomon in Proverbs, the Song of Song and parts of Ecclesiastes. Why should one disapprove of interpreting the Sages' sayings and giving them a non-literal explanation which would conform with Reason and agree with truth and the Revealed Books seeing that they themselves interpreted the text of [holy] Books, took them not in their literal sense and saw them in parables, this being the truth? So as we find them saying (B. Berakhot 18b) that what the Bible says "And he smote the two ariels of Moab" (2 Samuel 23:20) is altogether a parable, and likewise His words "he slew a lion in a pit" (*ibid.*) is a parable; and likewise His words "O that someone would give me water" (*ibid.*, verse 17) and all the rest of that story is a parable (B. Baba Qama 60b). Similarly some of the Sages said that the whole of Job was a parable (B. Baba Batra, 15a), and in the same manner some said the dead of Ezekiel (ch. 37) was a parable. There is much of this kind." (Translated from the Arabic by M. Schwarz. Trans. F. Rosner, pp. 141-142, Cf. above n. 26,).

busy with sciences" and about the answer he gave to this objection, 2) "the man busy with sciences" himself, to whom this answer was addressed initially. Thus the interpretation of the story of the Garden of Eden has at least two central meanings, one given by the objector to what Maimonides says, and another likely to be given to it by the ideal reader of the *Guide of the Perplexed*. When distinguishing between these two meanings one has to take into account that the objector has not had a complete philosophic education, and that, apart from this, the other chapters of the *Guide* are unknown to him. Thus he cannot "connect its chapters one with another"[30] in order to understand the interpretation of the story Maimonides offers here. Thus his way of understanding Maimonides' answer is likely to differ from the way the ideal reader of the *Guide* will understand it.[31]

Yet it appears to me that this duality is restricted to the first part of our chapter. If we have a closer look at the structure of the chapter, we shall see that a whole interpretative circle in it is addressed to the *Guide*'s reader only, and not to the objector. Namely, the interpretation of Genesis 3:5.

Before Maimonides presents the objector's objection to the reader of the *Guide*, he puts in a kind of aside, an interpretation of the equivocal term *Elohim* in Genesis 3:5.[32] This aside is clearly addressed to the *Guide*'s reader only. It is not included in the dialogue between the objector and Maimonides. Thus its contents are altogether unknown to the objector.

The aside is presented in the classical form of those chapters of the *Guide* which deal with the interpretation of equivocal terms, but with utter concision: "Every Hebrew knew that the term *Elohim* is equivocal, designating the deity, the angels, and the rulers governing the cities."[33] Since we have to do with a lingual fact known to whomsoever has been brought up in the Hebrew language, Maimonides does not take the trou-

---

30 p. 9/p. 15.

31 In a similar way there is also a kind of duality in the way the objector's objection is presented. Maimonides explicitly tells his reader, "This was the intent and the meaning of the objection, though it was not textually as we have put it" (p. 16/p. 24). So there is a duality in the relation between the original objection and the way in which Maimonides presents it to his reader, perhaps in a way calculated to serve his interpretative aims in the *Guide*.

32 On the interpretation of the equivocal term *Elohim*, see Klein-Braslavy, *Creation*, pp. 70-78 and Klein-Braslavy, *Adam Stories*, pp. 43-44

33 p. 15/p. 23. Ibn Tibbon has "judges" instead of "rulers." Both are correct translations of *al-ḥukkām*. But Maimonides' reference to Onqelos' *ravrevāyā* indicates that he meant "rulers," as indeed Pines translated.

ble to quote Bible verses in which the term occurs as examples of its use in its various meanings. Moreover, from the way he discusses the term, it appears that he is not interested at all in an overall discussion of the equivocal term *Elohim*. Rather does he list the various meanings of the terms as an introduction to the interpretation of one particular verse in the understanding of which he is interested, namely Genesis 3:5.[34] Nevertheless the mention here of the meanings of this term enables the ideal reader of the *Guide*[35] to use them, in the manner he uses Maimonides' other interpretations of equivocal terms, and to apply them in understanding the Bible verses in which the term *Elohim* occurs and in understanding Maimonides' allusions in quoting such Bible verses.

Elohim in "Ye shall be as *Elohim*, knowing good and evil" is to be understood, in accordance with the third meaning in the list of the meanings of this term, as designating "the rulers governing the cities." For the *Guide*'s reader this interpretation complements Maimonides' interpretation of *ṣelem* and *demut* in *Guide* I.1. According to the story of the creation of man in Genesis 1: 26-27, man was created "in *Elohim's* image (*be-ṣelem Elohim*), and in His likeness (*bidmuto*)."[36] The literal meaning[37] of Genesis 3:5 seems to contradict this description. According to this verse man will be like *Elohim* only after he eats from the tree of knowledge. Thus, before he ate from it he was not like *Elohim*. Reading this verse is likely to perplex the ideal reader of the *Guide*. To this reader Maimonides explains this as a contradiction of "the fourth cause," a type of contradiction to be found, according to the Introduction to the *Guide* "in the prophetic books." A contradiction of

34 In *Guide* II.6, Maimonides enlarges upon the equivocal term *Elohim*. There he also quotes Bible verses as examples for its use in its various meanings.

35 The ideal reader of the *Guide* is the disciple with the intellectual qualifications described in the Letter to the Disciple with which the work begins, provided he has followed Maimonides' instructions how to read the *Guide*, and has studies the sciences including philosophy, —and, of course, those who are like him.

36 The expression *be-ṣelem Elohim u-bidmuto* ("in the image of God and in His likeness") (p. 16; p. 23), which occurs *in Hebrew* in the Arabic text is a formula created by Maimonides himself on the basis of Genesis 1:26-27. It occurs three times in the *Guide*: *Guide* I.1, I.2 and III.8.

37 By "literal meaning" I mean here a spontaneous reading by a simple reader. This is to be distinguished from a "literal meaning" (*peshāt*) as opposed to an "inner meaning," that is reading a text in accordance with its "external meaning" (*ẓāhir*) as opposed to reading it in accordance with its "internal meaning" (*bāṭin*). In our case Maimonides does not argue that the text has two meanings, one external and one internal, but that the text has *one* meaning which one understands when one applies that meaning of the equivocal term *Elohim* which is here the *right one*. To apply here the meaning "God" would not create an external level of meaning. It would be simply an *error*.

"the fourth cause" arises when "there is a proviso which, because of a certain necessity, has not been explicitly stated in its proper place; *or the two subjects may differ, but one of them has not been explained in its proper place*, so that a contradiction appears to have been said, whereas there is no contradiction."[38] In Genesis 1:26-27 *Elohim* is God, or, according to another possible interpretation, the Active Intellect. But in Genesis 3:5 *Elohim* are "the rulers governing the cities." The apparent contradiction has arisen because of the use of an equivocal term. This use has created the impression that in both passages the same referent is spoken of. Whereas in fact "the two subjects ... differ" so that there is no contradiction between the two passages.

Seen from a different angle, the *Guide*'s reader's perplexity when reading Genesis 3:5 "literally," corresponds to the objector's interpretation of the story of the Garden of Eden. According to Genesis 3:5 it is only after he eats from the tree of knowledge that man comes to be like God. Thus he rises in the ontological hierarchy after his sin and is not punished for it. The interpretation of the term *Elohim* removes this perplexity as well. According to Maimonides' interpretation of *Elohim* in this verse, the verse does not speak of becoming like God altogether. Hence we cannot deduce from it that man has risen to a higher rank after his sin, and that he has not been punished for it. From this angle the interpretation of the term *Elohim* prepares the reader of the Guide to hear the objector's objection and Maimonides' answer to it. The problem of interpretation which arises from this verse, and its solution, are "the first edition" of the objection of the objector and Maimonides' response to it.

After Maimonides sets forth the various meanings of the term *Elohim*, and which of them is to be applied in Genesis 3:5, he goes on to state the objector's objection, which is the first, and the wrong, interpretation of the story of the Garden of Eden. According to this interpretation man was created on the ontological level of the other animals. On account of his sin he was endowed, as a reward, with intellect, and thus rose in the ontological hierarchy.

After setting forth the objection, Maimonides again addresses his reader, "hear now the intent of our reply," and presents him with his own interpretation of the story.

---

38 p. 11 and p. 12; p. 17 and p. 19.

Maimonides' answer to the objector consists of four parts: 1) an *ad hominem* attack on the objector which enables the reader to get a picture of the man's character; 2) a refutation, based on Bible verses, of the objector's interpretative argument; 3) a clarification of philosophic terms indispensable to understanding the biblical story of the Garden of Eden; 4) Maimonides' interpretation of the story of the Garden of Eden presented as an alternative to the objector's interpretation. Maimonides' interpretation is in its turn again divisible into four parts: a) a description of man's condition before the sin in accordance with his relation to two areas of cognition, cognition of what is cognized by the intellect (*al-maʿqūlāt, ha-muskalot, intelligibilia*) and cognition of generally accepted opinions (*al-mashhūrāt, ha-mefursamot*, endoxa).[39] Man knew "what is cognized by the intellect," but he did not know, and could not know "the generally accepted opinions." b-c) description of the sin and the inversion that occurred in man's relation to these two areas of cognition; b) description of the first phase of the sin: inclining towards the lusts of imagination and the sensual pleasures, and loss of the perception of what is cognized by the intellect; c) the second phase of the sin: eating from the tree of knowledge, apprehension of "the generally accepted opinions" and becoming "absorbed in judging things to be fine or bad." d) end of Maimonides' answer: man's condition after the sin.

At the end of this explanation with its symmetric well-planned structure, Maimonides adds a remark: "Hence it is said, 'And ye shall be like *Elohim* knowing good and evil' and not 'knowing the false and the true' or 'apprehending the false and the true'. With regard to what is necessity, there is no good or evil at all, but only the false and the true."[40] Here Maimonides comes back to the interpretation of Genesis 3:5. But now what interests him is the end of the verse "knowing good and evil." He bases his interpretation on the clarification of the concepts "good" and "evil" which he has accomplished in his answer to the objector. "Knowing good and evil" is nothing but knowing "fine and bad," knowing what is generally accepted, i.e. laws agreed upon by men in a given society. Such laws change from time to time, from place to place, from one human society to another. This kind of knowledge, or

39 cf. Pines, p. 24, n. 7.
40 p. 16/p. 25

cognition, is promised to man after the fall.

For the reader of the *Guide* this remark serves as a winding up of an interpretative circle which encompasses the objector's objection and Maimonides' answer to it as a kind of "framework interpretation." Man has been promised to be "like *Elohim*" in the sense of "rulers governing the cities," to become like them in that he will know "good and evil," i.e. the laws conventional in a certain human society. From the answer to the objector, the reader knows that knowing good and evil is inferior to apprehending the *intelligibilia*. Therefore its achievement is evidence of degradation and not of ascent to a higher rank or level. We may ask ourselves whether Maimonides' interpretation of "knowing good and evil" here is addressed to both the objector and ideal reader of the *Guide*, or to the *Guide*'s reader only, like the interpretation of the term *Elohim* and of "ye shall be like *Elohim*," and is not a part of Maimonides' answer to the objector. It seems to me that we have to decide in favour of the second alternative.

At the beginning of Maimonides' exposition the objector is described as one who takes the biblical text literally. He no doubt takes the term *Elohim* to mean God. Probably he is not included among all the "Hebrews," who know that in Hebrew this term has other meanings as well, for in the course of his answer to the objector, Maimonides tells him, "Similarly one expresses *in our language* the notions of truth and falsehood by means of the terms *emet* and *sheqer*, and those of fine and bad by means of the terms *tov* and *ra'*"[41] "In our language" refers to the Hebrew language, and the insistence that it is our language shows that it is not the objector's language.[42] Thus the objector will understand the verse to mean: men will become like God in knowing fine and bad, in cognizing relative judgments. For him Maimonides' interpretation of the verse will be much more absurd than his own interpretation of the story. According to the objector's interpretation God had a knowledge of absolute values of good and evil. After sinning man apprehended those values by

41 *Ibid.*

42 Maimonides believes that even the reader of the *Guide* has at least to be reminded of the fact that in Hebrew the term *Elohim* has three meanings, for not every Jew is sufficiently acquainted with the Hebrew language to know of the equivocality of this word. In his article "Maimonides on the Fall of Man," *AJS Review* 5 (1980, p.5 n.7 L.V. Berman says that Maimonides "is quite conscious of the fact that the traditional knowledge of Hebrew has been interrupted. Therefore, he implies that one of the difficulties in understanding the biblical text is simply semantic. i.e., the range of meanings easily accessible to the ancient Hebrew is not easily accessible to us."

means of his intellect, and thereby became like God.[43] According to the way he has to interpret the verse following Maimonides' remark, it is in an inferior kind of knowledge that man becomes like God, i.e., in the knowledge of what is neither necessary nor eternal. Moreover according to this interpretation the Bible claims for God the knowledge of relative and variable judgments, and this is sheer absurdity. Thus Maimonides' interpretation of "knowing good and evil" which he adduces at the end of his own interpretation of the story of the Garden of Eden is nonsensical for the objector, and makes sense to the *Guide*'s reader only, who knows from the remark at the top of the chapter that *Elohim* in Genesis 3:5 signifies "the rulers governing the cities" and not God.

On the basis of this argument we may say that the interpretation to Genesis 3:5, which is presented as a "framework interpretation," encompassing the objector's objection and Maimonides' response to it, serves also as a structural device to delimit the story about the objection and the response and separate it from the remarks and explanations Maimonides adds in the rest of this chapter, as these are meant for the ideal reader of the *Guide*, and not for the objector.

This interpretation may be reinforced by a number of additional arguments:

a) In the first remark following upon the interpretation of "And ye shall be like *Elohim* knowing good and evil" in the course of the interpretation of Genesis 3:7, Maimonides reiterates his characteristic formulas "Reflect on His dictum," "Know moreover," by means of which he calls the reader's attention to the most important clues he gives him. The appearance of these formulas in this place might also indicate to the reader that now Maimonides addresses him alone. It is also worthwhile mentioning that the interpretation of the story of the Garden of Eden in *Guide* II.30 abounds in these formulas. Each interpretative remark in that chapter starts with such a formula. There Maimonides explains in so many words that these remarks are meant for the "disciple" and "those like him." He says, "However, it will suffice *for someone like you* (*li-mithlika*) if I mention them (i.e., the Sages' midrashim interpreting the story of the Garden of Eden) in a certain order and by means of slight

---

43 Thus the objector accepts the Mu'tazili opinion of the position of "good and evil" and of the way they are cognized.

indications."[44] It is possible that the fact that at this stage of *Guide* I.2, he uses these formulas (which are so common in *Guide* II.30) indicates that here he already starts the interpretation intended for the disciple and the like of him.

b) Maimonides' interpretation of the story of the Garden of Eden in the framework of the answer to the objector gives the biblical text the right philosophic axis. In it he amends the objector's reading, which was based apparently on a partial and therefore faulty philosophic knowledge.[45] But in the framework of this interpretation Maimonides does not explain equivocal words, which understood in one way make possible one interpretation, and understood in another way make possible another interpretation. On the other hand, in his opening remark to the interpretation of the story of the Garden of Eden, and in his remark following upon the interpretation of Genesis 3:5, after presenting the objector's objection and the answer to it, Maimonides interprets equivocal terms, namely "*Elohim*" and "*paqaḥ*" (opened). In the remark following upon the interpretation of Genesis 3:5, Maimonides thus comes back to the technique of interpretation characteristic of the first part of the *Guide*, i.e., the interpretation of equivocal terms, the application of the correct meaning of which in a given context makes it possible to free the perplexed one from his perplexity. This coming back to the interpretation of equivocal terms may also indicate that Maimonides now turns again to his reader and fulfills his promise at the opening of the work to explain to him equivocal terms.

c) In the remarks following upon the first interpretation of the story of the Garden of Eden, Maimonides interprets two biblical verses which

---

44 P. 250/p. 355. According to the epistle to the disciple at the head of the work "those like you" (p. 1/p. 4) are those who are similar to the disciple described in the epistle. They constitute the ideal "addressee" of the *Guide of the Perplexed*. Apart from *Guide* II.30, Maimonides uses this expression in the final sentences of the whole work, at the end of *Guide* III. (p. 471/ p. 638): "This is the extent of what I thought fit that we should set down in this treatise, and what I consider very useful *to those like you*." A similar formula appears also in the Hebrew epistle to the disciple (see above, note 8): "I have set a table for you and because of you; *and for those like you, even though they are few*" (p. 16).

45 Maimonides' remark stating that he does not give the verbatim text of the objector's question leaves open the possibility of arguing that originally the question was not based on philosophic concepts and has then been adapted by Maimonides to serve his aims in the *Guide*. Such a course of interpretation was taken by I. Heinemann (see above, note 18), who holds that the objector's objection echoes a pagan question put in the course of an inter-religious debate. Still, the description of the objector as one who engages in sciences turns the scales in favor of the interpretation saying that the objector indeed used in his objection concepts borrowed from philosophy and posed his objection from what Maimonides considers a pseudo-philosophic standpoint.

are not at all included in the story of the Garden of Eden: Job 14:20 and Psalms 49:13. In both cases Maimonides relies implicitly on the fact that these verses have already been interpreted in midrashim as referring to Adam in the story of the Garden of Eden.[46] Only by relying on the connection brought about by the Sages between these verses and the biblical story of the Garden of Eden can Maimonides quote them, within the framework of his interpretation of the story, as support to his interpretation of Genesis 2. If the assumption that the objector was a free thinker is correct, it is difficult to suppose that he was acquainted with these midrashim and that an interpretation of the story of the Garden of Eden by means of verses, not to be found in that story, would convince him. The reader of the *Guide*, on the other hand, accepts Maimonides' basic assumptions in interpreting the biblical text. He accepts the assumption that the Sages are a link in a chain of transmitters of the mysteries of the Torah in Judaism, and that in their midrashim they interpret the biblical texts or hint to their interpretation. In his view one may rely on the midrashic connection which the Sages made between the story of the Garden of Eden and Job 14:20 and Psalms 49:13 and to chain to it another link in the interpretation of the biblical story. Moreover, the method of relying on midrashim in the interpretation is the main method Maimonides applies in his interpretation of the story of the Garden of Eden in the *Guide* II.30, which—as we have seen—is explicitly addressed to the disciple and the like of him.[47]

According to this analysis we get an interesting picture of the structure of the interpretation of the story of the Garden of Eden in the *Guide of the Perplexed.* It is an allegorical interpretation toward which Maimonides leads his reader in stages. He starts by setting forth through the objector the antipode of the correct interpretation. In a terminology parallel to that of the parable of the ruler's palace in III.51, one would say

---

46 *Genesis Rabbah* 11.5 and 12.6 (and the parallel passages in other midrashim) refer to both verses. *Genesis Rabbah* 16.1 and 21.14 refer to Job 14:20. B. Sanhedrin 38b (and parallel passages) refers to Psalms 49:13.

47 However, there is a difference between Maimonides' attitude towards the interpretation of the Sages here and in II.30. Here Maimonides relies only on the *linkage* established by the Sages between Job 14:20 and the story of the Garden of Eden but he does not accept *the interpretation* given by them to the verse. In II.30, on the other hand, he bases his argument on the Sages' interpretations of the story of the Garden of Eden in their midrashim For the use of the midrashim in the interpretation of story of the Garden of Eden in *Guide* II.30 see Klein-Braslavy, *Adam Stories,* pp. 187-192 and (in this volume) "Interpretative Riddles in Maimonides' *Guide of the Perplexed.*"

that he starts by presenting the interpretation of one who "has turned his back upon the ruler's habitation," i.e. one who takes the words of the biblical text literally, and understands it by means of a partial philosophic knowledge, and thus errs in comprehending its meaning. Then Maimonides begins to present the interpretation of those who, according to the parable of the ruler's home are said to "turn toward the ruler's habitation." These interpretations are graded in an upward gradation of approaching the real meaning of the story of the Garden of Eden, an upward gradation of the profundity of the allegoric interpretation of the story.

In the first interpretation of the story of the Garden of Eden, Maimonides engages mainly in correcting the semantico-philosophic axis along which the story has to be understood in his opinion. He only hints that "the tree of knowledge" is not a real tree but a figure of speech, the meaning of which the reader of his interpretation has to gather from his hints here and in what follows. Thus Maimonides provides an initial opening toward understanding the story of the Garden of Eden as a story made up of figures of speech taken from the physical world, the meaning of which is to be looked for on the psychological level. Maimonides encompasses the objector's interpretation and his own initial interpretation of the story with the interpretation of Genesis 3:5. In the latter the two interpretations actually recur in the guise of a search for the meaning of the verse and then a statement of its correct meaning. This meaning removes the perplexity that a literal interpretation of the verse might have brought about. After this "framework interpretation" appear a number of remarks which lead the reader towards understanding the story as a parable. The most important remark is that which interprets Job 14:20.[48] For our purpose it is important that when he interprets this verse Maimonides indicates clearly "the Garden of Eden" is not a geographical place, but a rank of perfection, the stage of apprehending the *intelligibilia*. Through interpreting Job, Maimonides comes to interpret the punishment in Genesis 3:18-19, and sets forth a second interpretation of the story of the Garden of Eden. Here Maimonides at first describes man's condition before sinning, then he explains the two stages of the sin together, and immediately afterwards—their outcome, that is he presents parts (b) and (c) of the first interpretation together.

48 For a full interpretation of the verse see Klein-Braslavy, *Adam Stories*, pp. 101-106.

He winds up his interpretation by describing man's condition after the sin by means of Psalm 49:13, "Man, unable to dwell in dignity, is like the beasts that speak not."[49] Instead of couching his words in scientific language as he does in his first interpretation of the story when answering the objector, he here falls back upon Arabic phrases altogether parallel to the biblical ones. In the main he makes use of the Arabic verb *akala*, to eat, which parallels the Hebrew verb *akhol*. But the intelligent and sensitive reader, who is already acquainted with the first interpretation of the story of the Garden of Eden, realizes the structural parallelism of this interpretation and the second interpretation of the story. He understands the second interpretation in the light of the first. Since it has been hinted to this reader that "the tree of knowledge" and "the Garden of Eden" are not to be taken in their literal sense, he thereby got the clue that he should not understand the verb "to eat" in the story in its primary meaning, but in some kind of metaphorical meaning which this equivocal term has.

The first two interpretations of the story of the Garden of Eden already indicate that this story is a parable, but they do not explicitly deny the assumption that the story of the Garden of Eden is an historical story, the hero of which is the first specimen, temporally, of the genus "man." The reader can go on understanding that everything described in the story happened to Adam, but on the psychological rather than on the physical level. In *Guide* II.30, Maimonides completes the allegoric interpretation of the story of the Garden of Eden. Here he indicates that the dramatic personae of the story are also only figures of speech representing the faculties of the soul, mental representations, and the elements of the substance "man" according to Aristotelian philosophy and not historical figures. The parable as a whole is a philosophic allegory dealing with the doctrine of man, not a historical narrative. A reader, who has got to the point of understanding it in this way, becomes the ideal reader of the biblical text, and is an antipode to the objector with whose reading Maimonides opens the series of his interpretations. Such a reader is analogous to a reader of the third class of readers of midrashim in the *Introduction* to *Pereq Ḥeleq*.[50]

These three stages of interpretation are to be found by reading the

---

49 For a full interpretation of the verse see Klein-Braslavy, *Adam Stories*, pp.122-129.
50 See n. 29 above.

Guide in a linear way. But for a reader who desires to grasp the full meaning of the story of the Garden of Eden this kind of reading is insufficient. Such a reader must combine this kind of reading with a reflective reading of the interpretations, based on the method of "connecting its chapters one with another."[51] Each phase in Maimonides' interpretation must be read again on the basis of what has been understood from the phase following it. The reader has to "lift" it (in the Hegelian sense of "aufheben") to the new level of interpretation, with which he has been presented in the more advanced phase, and combine it with it. A full and exhaustive reading of the interpretation of the story of the Garden of Eden and a full-scale comprehension of it are possible only after one has finished reading the interpretation given in II.30, and understood the two preceding phases in its light. Such a reading I presented in my Hebrew book *Maimonides' Interpretation of the Adam Stories in Genesis - A Study in Maimonides' Anthropology.*[52]

51 p. 9/p. 15.
52 pp. 254-261.

The Creation of the World and Maimonides' Interpretation of Genesis 1-5

The problem of Maimonides' position on the creation of the world is one of the most controversial aspects of his thought. Scholars are generally divided into those who claim that Maimonides maintained the doctrine of creation *ex-nihilo*[1] and those who claim that he accepted the doctrine of the eternity of the world.[2] It has also been suggested that Maimonides held Plato's view.[3]

Most of the discussions concerning Maimonides' position on the creation of the world are based upon his philosophical and theological arguments in *The Guide of the Perplexed.* In this paper I would like to examine this problem from a new perspective—that of his biblical exegesis. I shall examine two central themes: (1) Maimonides' interpretation of the verb *bara'* in Genesis 1:1; (2) the question as to whether or not Maimonides interpreted the stories about *Adam* historically. I will attempt to demonstrate that the analysis of these two themes may lead us to another solution of the creation problem, namely that Maimonides behaved in this issue as a skeptic who maintained *epochē*, that is, he abstained from judging a matter which he was unable to decide logically or philosophically.

I

As I have already shown in my book, *Maimonides' Interpretation of the Story of the Creation of the World*, Maimonides interprets the "six days

---

1 See I. Ravitzky, "The Question of a Created or Primordial World in the Philosophy of Maimonides," *Tarbiṣ* 35 (1965-66), pp. 333-48, (Hebrew); A.L. Ivry, "Maimonides on Possibility," *Mystics, Philosophers and Politicians*, ed. J. Reinharz and D. Swetshinski (Duke U. P., 1982), pp. 67-84; H. Davidson, "Maimonides' Secret Position on Creation," *Studies in Medieval Jewish History and Literature*, ed. I. Twersky (Harvard U. P., 1979), pp. 16-40 (as one of two possibilities).

2 See S. Pines, "Translator's Introduction," *Guide* p. cxxvii ff.; J. Glücker, "Modality in Maimonides' *Guide to the Perplexed*," *Iyyun* 10 (1959), pp. 177-91 (Hebrew); L.V. Berman, *Ibn Bajja and Maimonides—A Chapter in the History of Political Philosophy*, Ph.D. Dissertation (Jerusalem, 1959), pp. 156-63 (Hebrew); A. Nuriel, "The Question of a Created or Primordial World in the Philosophy of Maimonides," *Tarbiṣ* 33 (1964), pp. 372-87 (Hebrew).

3 H. Davidson, see note 1 above (as one of two possibilities).

of the Creation" as the order of priority referring to the "cause" and the "nature" of simultaneous existents, and not as a sequence of six different units of time. Hence, the biblical account of "the six days of creation" is not a *cosmogony*—i.e., it does not tell us about the *way* in which the world came into being in time—but rather a *cosmology*, i.e., it tells us about the *structure* of the created world. Therefore, the problem of the creation of the world is dependent on the interpretation of Genesis 1:1, in which the verb *bara*ʾ is the keyword.

Having interpreted the story of the Creation in Genesis 1:1-2:4, the story of the Garden of Eden in Genesis 2-3 and the stories of Adam's sons in Genesis 4, Maimonides proceeds, in *Guide* II.30, to interpret a group of four different words used in the Bible to describe the relationship between God and heaven. The first word in the group is the verb *bara*ʾ in Genesis 1:1: "God (*Elohim*) created (*bara*ʾ) the heaven and the earth." Maimonides explains here that *baro*ʾ is: "bringing into existence out of nonexistence (or privation) (*min ʿadam*)" (p. 252/ p. 358). This interpretation is repeated in an abridged manner in III.10, where he says that *baro*ʾ is "out of nonbeing (or privation) (*min ʿadam*)" (p. 316/p. 438).

The Arabic word *ʿadam* (nonexistence), by which Maimonides explains the Hebrew verb *baro*ʾ, is an equivocal term, which can mean either "nothing" or "matter."[4] Hence, Maimonides' explanation of the verb *baro*ʾ is itself an equivocal explanation: it can either mean "bringing into existence out of nothing," or "bringing into existence out of matter." This equivocal interpretation of the verb *baro*ʾ enables us to understand the biblical story of the Creation according to each one of the three opinions described by Maimonides in II.13. If *ʿadam* in the expression "bringing into existence out of *nonexistence*" means "nothing," *baro*ʾ implies *creatio ex-nihilo*. But if *ʿadam* means "matter," so that *baro*ʾ is "bringing into existence out of matter," two different opinions about the creation of the world are possible: (1) We may claim that *bara*ʾ in Genesis 1:1 means that heaven and earth were created *all at once* from an antemundane matter. In this case, Maimonides maintains the second opinion presented in II.13, namely, the Platonic position on the cre-

4 See H.A. Wolfson, "The Kalam Problem of Nonexistence and Saʿadiah's Second Theory of Creation," *Studies in the History of Philosophy and Religion*, ed. I. Twersky and G.H. Williams (Harvard U. P., 1977), 2, pp. 345-46.

ation of the world. (2) Alternatively, we can claim that *bara'* in Gen. 1:1 does not indicate a single action of "information" of matter, but rather a process of *eternal* "information" of matter. In this case, Maimonides adopts the Aristotelian position on the creation of the world. In this view, Genesis 1:1 indicates that heaven and earth were eternally created by an eternal "information" of matter.

The difficulty in Maimonides' explanation of the verb *baro'* thus consists not only in the fact that the explanation is an equivocal one, but in the fact that *Maimonides gives an equivocal explanation to the keyword of the story of creation itself.*

In the *Guide*, Maimonides uses two univocal expressions for the idea of *creatio ex-nihilo*: the expression "after pure and absolute nonexistence" *(ba'd al-'adam al-maḥḍ muṭlaq)* and the expression used by Sa'adiah before him: "not from something" (*la min shai*).[5] The fact that these two expressions are used whenever he wishes to express the idea of *creatio ex-nihilo* proves that he was clearly aware of the possibility that an alternative expression might be equivocal and might be understood as expressing the idea of creation *out of something*. Using these two univocal expressions, Maimonides shows us that he intends to be extremely precise about the expression of the idea of *creatio ex-nihilo*.

The expression which interests us in this paper is "after pure and absolute nonexistence." This univocal expression replaces the equivocal one, "bringing into existence out of nonexistence." There are two differences between these expressions: first of all, in his univocal expression of the idea of *creatio ex-nihilo*, Maimonides does not speak of "bringing into existence *from* (or out of) nonexistence," but of "bringing into existence *after* nonexistence." It would appear that he was afraid that the expression "out of nonexistence" (or "from nonexistence") might be taken to mean that the world was created from "nonexistence," that is, "*something*," i.e., from "matter." Similarly, he does not simply write "after nonexistence," but adds "after *pure and absolute* nonexistence." This precision in his use of language indicates that Maimonides was clearly aware of the equivocal nature of the word "nonexistence." Thus, when he wished to express the idea of *creatio ex-nihilo*, he added the words "pure and absolute." which made it mean, univocally, "nothing."

Therefore, had Maimonides wished to explain *bara'* in Genesis 1:1

5 *Ibid.*, pp. 355-57.

univocally as *creatio ex-nihilo*, and had he really thought, as he wrote in II.25, that we must "take the texts [of the Torah] according to their external sense [in this case]," (p. 329) he would have used the more exact expression, "after pure and absolute nonexistence." The fact that this expression was not used in either of the chapters (II.30, III.10) where he explains the word *bara*ʾ in Genesis 1:1, proves that this explanation was intentionally formulated equivocally. If this is so, we must ask *why* Maimonides chose an equivocal explanation of the verb *bara*ʾ, which is the keyword for the understanding of the biblical position on the Creation. The answer to this question will give us an answer to the question of Maimonides' genuine view of the Creation as well.

Two basic presuppositions may be distinguished here.

1. According to the former, Maimonides behaves as an *esotericist*, who holds a secret doctrine concerning the Creation. Scholars maintaining this interpretation of Maimonides' position would claim that, in explaining *bara*ʾ equivocally, Maimonides imitates the Torah, which uses equivocal terms in order to transmit "the mysteries of the Torah" in such a manner "that the multitude might comprehend them in accord with the capacity of their understanding and the weakness of their representation, whereas the perfect man, who is already informed, will comprehend them otherwise" (I, Introduction, p. 9). If Maimonides uses an equivocal explanation in order to *hide* his genuine opinion from the multitude, then it must be that the opinion he tries to conceal is that which is most remote from the position of the multitude and closest to that of the philosophers. The multitude thinks that *bara*ʾ is *creatio ex-nihilo*; hence, Maimonides' genuine opinion must be that Creation takes place out of nonexistence that is "something," i.e., "matter."

As we have already seen, two possible positions on the Creation may be maintained on the assumption that *bara*ʾ refers to creation from matter: the Aristotelian position of the eternity of the world, and the Platonic position of the creation of the world from an antemundane matter at some defined point in the past. The Aristotelian position is the most distant from the multitude's understanding of the biblical verse. Hence, it is more plausible that, according to the esotericists, this is Maimonides' hidden position on the Creation. Nevertheless, the esotericist approach does not completely rule out Plato's position.

2. The second presupposition is that Maimonides relates to this

problem as a *skeptic* who maintains *epochē*, i.e., who abstains from judging a matter which he is unable to prove. This is based on Maimonides' discussion of the limits of human knowledge in I.31-32 and his recommendation

> That man should not press forward to engage in speculative study of corrupt imaginings. When points appearing as dubious occur to him or the thing he seeks does not seem to him to be demonstrated, he should not deny and reject it, hastening to pronounce it false, but rather should persevere and thereby *have regard for the honor of his Creator.* He should refrain and hold back. (I.32/ p. 70)

In I.71 (p. 180), Maimonides claims that the problem of the Creation is such a case: "With regard to this question—namely the eternity of the world of its temporal creation—no cogent demonstration can be reached and that it is a point before which the intellect stops." According to this presupposition, Maimonides gave an equivocal explanation of the verb *bara*ʾ, not because he wanted *to conceal* his genuine position from the unprepared reader, but because, as he could not arrive at a philosophical conclusion, he did not wish to decide the issue on any other grounds (such as theological considerations or traditional conventions). His indecision is a consequence of his attitude as a rigorous philosopher who would not accept either the opinions of the multitude concerning theological problems or those of the philosophers, unless they are perfectly demonstrated.

We must ask ourselves which of the two presuppositions is the more plausible one and, hence, what Maimonides' position on the Creation was.

I think that we should lean towards the latter position. The *Guide* is an exegetical book, which uses philosophical discussions to clarify, support and prove its exegetical conclusions. Hence, Maimonides' interpretation of *bara*ʾ should be treated as the culmination of his discussions of the problem of the Creation. In this paper, I shall only deal with the philosophical discussions, although the same conclusion may be drawn from the analysis of his theological argument for *creatio ex-nihilo*, from his statements on the interpretation of biblical passages concerning the relationships between God and the world, and from the actual interpretations in the *Guide*.[6]

When we consider the philosophical debates which preceded Maimonides' interpretation of the story of the Creation, we notice that, though it appears that Maimonides tries to persuade us that *creatio ex-nihilo* is the more plausible opinion on the Creation, his discussions do not really lead us to this conclusion. An analysis of his philosophical arguments shows that in fact they do not favor one particular opinion on the Creation. Maimonides tries to solve the problem of the Creation by two sets of philosophical arguments. (1) In the first one, he asks whether it is possible to *demonstrate* either *creatio ex-nihilo* or the eternity of the world, and in both cases answers in the negative.[7] Both positions are "possible"; moreover, the position of *creatio ex-nihilo* is perfectly compatible with Aristotelian physics, as the latter prevails in the world only *after* it was created. (2) Having shown that it is impossible to *demonstrate* either of the positions on the Creation, Maimonides proceeds to a lower type of scientific verification. Following Alexander in his treatise *On the Principles of the All*, he claims that we should choose the position "to which fewer doubts attach" (II.22, p. 320). Apparently he demonstrates that the hypothesis of *creatio ex-nihilo* is more reasonable than that of the eternity of the world, but a closer examination of his arguments reveals that such is not the case.

In II.19 and 22 Maimonides uses the Kalām's method of *particularization*, which is then applied to select aspects of the celestial realm. He explains, "by means of arguments that come close to being a demonstration" (II.19, p. 303), that the lack of order in astronomical phenomena may only be explained on the basis of the hypothesis that there is a purposeful particularizing agent for the celestial realm. As "the notions of purpose and of particularization only apply to a non-existent thing for which it is possible to exist just as it was purposed and particularized and for which it also is possible not to exist in this fashion" (II.20, p. 314). The fact that on the one hand, we cannot explain the astronomical phenomena by the principles of Aristotelian physics, and on the other hand, we do explain them on the basis of the

6 I have dealt with these two themes in my article: "Maimonides' Interpretation of the Verb *bara'* and the Problem of the Creation of the World," *Da'at* 16 (1986), pp. 39-55 (Hebrew).

7 See I.71-74 for *creatio ex-nihilo*; II.14, 17, 18 for the eternity of the world.

hypothesis that there is a purposeful and particularizing agent for the celestial realm, leads us to the conclusion that the world was created *ex-nihilo*.

But in II.24 Maimonides himself claims that the philosophers and the astronomers of his time have only limited knowledge of the celestial realm. As a matter of fact, Maimonides maintains that "The deity alone fully knows the true reality, the nature, the substance, the form, the motions and the causes of the heavens" (p. 327), and that the purpose of the astronomer "is not to tell us *in which way the spheres truly are*, but to posit an astronomical system in which it would be possible for the motions to be circular and uniform and to correspond to what is apprehended through sight, *regardless of whether or not things are thus in fact*" (p. 326, italics added). Thus, he does not reject the hypothesis that there is a concatenation of causes and effects that constitutes an order in the celestial realm. He merely claims that human knowledge is limited and cannot provide a rational causal explanation of the celestial phenomena. Moreover, it would seem that God knows the order of the celestial spheres and their motions. Hence, according to Maimonides' own claim, a better knowledge of the celestial realm would enable us to explain its phenomena without the presupposition of a particularizing agent.

The esotericist may claim that Maimonides' arguments in II.19-24 only serve a theological and hence political purpose.[8] They are not addressed to the ideal reader of the *Guide*, but to one who, while not belonging to the multitude, has yet to reach the stage of the ideal reader, that of the "perfect man...devoted to the Law...and...perplexed." Maimonides' genuine opinion, according to the esotericists, is that there is a rational order in the celestial realm.

Yet the traditionalists, who claim that Maimonides adopted *creatio ex-nihilo*, may argue that it is inconceivable that Maimonides made so many efforts to establish his arguments in II.19-24 merely in order to mislead the non-ideal reader of the *Guide* into thinking that he believed in *creatio ex-nihilo* while he genuinely believed in the eternity of the world. They may also claim, as did H. Davidson, that "we can hardly conceive, though, of a philosopher's taking pains to fashion and publish *brand new arguments that undermine his position*" (p. 36).

---

8 See Pines, Introduction, pp. cxxix-cxxx.

Those who claim that Maimonides maintained a skeptical attitude concerning the problem of the way in which the world was created, may argue that Maimonides claimed no knowledge of the celestial realm. Therefore, he did not know whether there is a rational causal order in this realm beyond human understanding, or whether there is only a purposive order, determined by God's wisdom and will, which therefore requires a purposive and particularizing agent. Hence, he was unable to decide to which position on the creation of the world "fewer doubts attach."

It seems to me that we should consider Maimonides' arguments in II.19-24 as a genuine philosophical endeavor to show that one can argue for the position of *creatio ex-nihilo* within the framework of Aristotle's physics and with its tools. Nevertheless, I do not believe that this enables us to decide that Maimonides really believed in *creatio ex-nihilo*. If that were the case, Maimonides would not have refrained from explaining the verb *bara*ʾ in Genesis 1:1 univocally as "bringing into existence *after pure and absolute* nonexistence," after having formulated all the arguments of II.19-24.

The rejection of the proofs for the eternity of the world (II.7, 18); the claim that the position holding the eternity of the world is "possible" (II. premise 26); the establishment of the "possibility" of the position of *creatio ex-nihilo* (II.17); the claim that there is no criterion which enables us to determine what is "possible" (III.15); the claim that the position of *creatio ex-nihilo* is more plausible (II.19-24); and finally the equivocal explanation to the keyword *bara*ʾ in the creation story—all these tend towards the view that Maimonides maintained a skeptical approach to the problem of the Creation, although this is insufficient for a complete rejection of the esotericist interpretation.

It seems to me that Maimonides tried to exhaust all possible rational arguments in his discussion of the problem of the Creation but, being aware of the limits of human knowledge, was unable to decide between the various positions on this issue and so decided not to decide. He therefore maintained *epochē*, expressed in his equivocal interpretation of the keyword *bara*ʾ in the biblical story of the Creation.

II

In the second part of this paper, I wish to examine Maimonides' interpretation of the stories about Adam in Genesis 1-5, and will attempt to determine whether his interpretation there confirms or denies the conclusion of the first part.

In *Guide* I.14 Maimonides explains the equivocal term "Adam," stating that "Adam" has three different meanings. It may designate: (1) the proper name of the first human being (*Adam ha-Rishon*); (2) the species (man); (3) the multitude. This list enables Maimonides to interpret the stories about "Adam" in two different ways. He may claim that "Adam" designates "the first man"; hence, the biblical stories about "Adam," even in their hidden sense, are historical stories, their "hero" being the first created specimen of the human genus. But he can equally claim that the term "Adam" in Genesis 1-5 designates the species "man." Hence, according to their inner sense, the stories about "Adam" are a-historical or, to be more accurate, they represent a philosophical anthropology. The "hero" of these stories is every individual to whom the definition "rational animal" may be applied.

If Maimonides believed in *creatio ex-nihilo*, as the traditionalists claim, or in Plato's position—i.e., in creation out of an antemundane matter—as some of the esotericists claim, it is more plausible that he maintained the historical interpretation of the stories about "Adam." Indeed, there is no reason why he should not do so. According to this interpretation, the biblical narrative of the Creation is a cosmogony; it tells us *how* God created the world in time. Then it tells us about the first things that were created, including the first man, and what happened to him at the beginning of human history.

But if, as most esotericists claim, Maimonides believed in the eternity of the world, or if he maintained a skeptical attitude towards the problem of the Creation, as I have tried to establish, then he would not interpret the stories about "Adam" as historical stories. According to the esotericist view, there *cannot* be any historical interpretation of the stories about "Adam" in Genesis 1-5, because if the world is eternal, there was no "first man" created in time. A similar conclusion may also be drawn from the skeptical position: if Maimonides could not decide whether the world was created in time (from nothing or from antemundane matter) or whether it is eternal, then he also could not have considered the stories about "Adam" as historical stories. This interpretation only fits with *creatio ex-nihilo* and with Plato's opinion, while the a-historical interpretation fits all three views of the Creation. According to this interpretation, the story of the creation of the world is a *cosmology* and not a *cosmogony*; it tells us about the *structure* of the created world, and not about its generation. Similarly, the stories about "Adam" are not an *anthropogony* but a *philosophical anthropology*; they tell us about the structure of man, about his ultimate goal, how he should behave in order to reach it, and what will happen to him if he does not do so. This interpretation of the story of the Creation and the stories about "Adam" is indifferent to the question of how the world and man were created. The answer to this question is found exclusively in the interpretation of the verb *bara*ʾ at the beginning of Genesis 1; the balance of the first five chapters of Genesis tells us about the *created world* and about the species "man."

In the interpretation of the stories about "Adam" we are confronted with a similar problem to that of the interpretation of the story of the Creation: the keyword of these stories is again an equivocal term ("Adam") as was the verb *bara*ʾ, and Maimonides does not state here explicitly in which sense we should understand it.[9] In this section of my paper, I wish to show that, although there is no conclusive evidence that Maimonides understood the biblical stories about "Adam" in an a-historical manner, this is the most plausible understanding of his thought.

In Genesis 1-5, there are three stories about "Adam": (1) the story of the creation of man (Gen. 1:26-27); (2) the story of the Garden of Eden (Gen. 2-3); (3) the story of Adam's sons (Gen. 4-5). I shall examine Maimonides' interpretations of each one of these stories in order to determine whether there are any hints as to the meaning that Maimonides attached to the equivocal term "Adam" in them.

(1) *The Creation of Man*. In *Guide* I.1 Maimonides interprets Genesis 1:26-27. In this chapter he uses the Arabic term *al-insān* which means Man. This use indicates that he chose the second meaning of "Adam" according to the list of meanings of this term in *Guide* I.14—i.e., the species "man."

(2) *The Story of the Garden of Eden*. Maimonides interprets the story of the Garden of Eden in two different passages of the *Guide*: in chapters I.2 and II.30. In I.2 he twice uses the term "Adam," which is an equivocal term. Hence, this chapter *by itself* can be interpreted in either a

9 Maimonides could also hold an ambiguous interpretation of the term "Adam," and thus not need to decide also between the two possible interpretations of this term but, as I shall show, he did not do so.

historical or an a-historical manner. But his interpretation of the story of the Garden of Eden in I.2 is not sufficient unto itself, but must be read in conjunction with II.30 which completes it.[10] In II.30 Maimonides explains that the equivocal term "Adam" not only has the meaning of *Adam ha-Rishon*, the species of man and the multitude, as he said in I.14, but also the meaning of "form," one of the constituents of the substance "Adam." Nevertheless, it is unclear whether this substance "Adam" is the first man or the human species. I think that it is more plausible that Maimonides uses "Adam" here in the sense of the human species, as the opposite hypothesis entails far more difficulties in the understanding of his interpretation of the story of the Garden of Eden. I would like to bring two arguments to support my claim.

First, in II.30 (p. 355) Maimonides follows "all the Sages" who "are unanimous in thinking that all this story [of the Garden of Eden] occurred on Friday and that nothing was changed in any respect after the *six days of the Beginning*." As I have already indicated, according to Maimonides "the six days of the Beginning" do not refer to units of time, but to the order of priority according to "cause and nature" of the existents to each other. If that is so, then the "events" of the "sixth day" of the creation of the world cannot be temporal events. Hence, the story of the Garden of Eden should be construed as philosophical anthropology rather than a story which tells us what happened to the first man in the beginning of human history.

Secondly, at the beginning of chapter I.2, before Maimonides presents a possible objection, he offers, in a kind of aside, an interpretation of the equivocal term *Elohim* in Genesis 3:5: "Ye shall be as *Elohim*, knowing good and evil." He explains that *Elohim* in Genesis 3:5 is not the deity, but "the rulers governing the cities." At the end of his own explanation of the story of the Garden of Eden, Maimonides returns to this biblical verse, this time interpreting its end, "knowing good and evil." On the basis of his earlier clarification of the concepts of "good" and "evil" he identifies "good and evil" with "fine and bad." As I have

10 In I.2 Maimonides does not mention the woman and the snake, although the biblical verses on which he comments (Gen. 3:5, 6) do deal with them. Moreover, he relates Genesis 3:6 to Adam and explains that 3:7 speaks of Adam as well (he uses the singular here). The reader must read *Guide* II.30 in order to understand that "Adam" of I.2 is a substance constituted from "Adam and Eve"—i.e., form and matter.

indicated elsewhere,[11] the literal sense of Genesis 3:5 corresponds to the objector's interpretation of the story of the Garden of Eden, while Maimonides' interpretation corresponds to his answer to the objector. This interpretation also plays an important role in the structure of *Guide* I.2, and corresponds to Maimonides' view on the rulers of the cities.[12] Therefore, it is not plausible that Maimonides' interpretation of this verse is intended ironically, but must be taken seriously. Nevertheless, it is sheer absurdity to say that *Naḥash* (the snake) persuaded the first man to become like the "rulers governing the cities." In the beginning of human history there were no "rulers governing the cities" whom Adam and his wife could wish to resemble. Maimonides' interpretation of Genesis 3:5 is thus only comprehensible on the assumption that he considered "Adam" as a term designating the human species, and not as the first specimen of the human species.

(3) *The Story about Adam's Sons*. In two different chapters of the *Guide*, Maimonides interprets two different stories about Adam's sons.[13] In I.7 he interprets Genesis 5:3, "And Adam lived a hundred and thirty years and begot [a son] in his own likeness after his image," in conjunction with an aggadic passage from B. ʿErubin 18b, which explains this verse in its turn and completes the biblical story. According to this *aggadah*, Genesis 5 does not refer only to Seth but also to Adam's two other sons, Cain and Abel. In II.30 Maimonides interprets Genesis 4, which deals explicitly with all three of Adam's sons.

The main idea of Maimonides' first interpretation of the story about Adam's sons in Genesis 5 (as completed by B. ʿErubin 18b) is that Adam taught his sons "opinions": he taught Cain and Abel false opinions, and Seth correct opinions. This interpretation presupposes that Genesis 4 speaks of the birth of Adam's *biological sons*.

In *Guide* II.30 Maimonides refutes the conclusion which one would necessarily draw from his interpretation of Genesis 5 in *Guide* I.7. He explains that the story about Adam's sons in Genesis 4 is a parable and is part of the story of the Garden of Eden. "The sons of Adam" are—according to this interpretation—the thoughts engendered by Adam, and not his biological sons. The "Adam" who engendered these thoughts as

---

11 In the paper presented at the conference "Maimonides in Egypt." See (in this volume) "On Maimonides' Interpretation of the Story of the Garden of Eden in the *Guide of the Perplexed* I.2."

12 See W.Z. Harvey, "Political Philosophy and *Halakhah* in Maimonides," *Bina* 3 (1994), pp. 49-50.

13 See Klein-Braslavy, *Adam Stories*, pp. 263-89.

"Adam," the hero of the story of the Garden of Eden, might be either "the first man" or any individual belonging to the human species. If he is "the first man," then the story about the sons of Adam is a parable of the first man; if he is any individual belonging to the human species, then it is part of a philosophical anthropology. The second interpretation seems to me the more plausible.

In III.50 (p. 613) there is a quasi-historical proof for the creation of the world in time. Maimonides tells us that "it is a pillar of the Law that the world was produced in time, that at first a single individual of the human species, namely *Adam* was created, and that approximately two thousand five hundred years elapsed between *Adam* and *Moses our Master*," "The pillar of the Law" is not only the statement that the world was created in time, but also that at the beginning a single individual of the human species was created and that the time that elapsed between Adam and Moses was approximately two thousand five hundred years. According to this remark, the history of the generations from Adam to Moses (i.e., the beginning of the history of the people of Israel) is inseparable from the statement that the world was created in time; the two entail one another. The assertion that a finite time elapsed between Moses and the first man supports the assertion that *there was* a first man, and this in turn supports the creation of the world in time. The refutation of an historical interpretation of the stories about Adam and the generations who followed him would exclude the possibility of deducing from this biblical story that there was a first man, from whom were descended all the generations up to Moses. Hence, according to this interpretation, the biblical story does not prove the creation of the world in time.

If Maimonides thought that "Adam" was the first man and hence that the world was created in time, he would have been interested in maintaining this "historical proof." It is not plausible to assert that, though he thought that "Adam" designates "the first man," he explained the story about his sons as a parable.[14]

14 As I have stated in some of my articles and in my book (*ibid.*), we must consider Maimonides' interpretation of the story of Adam's sons in Genesis 5 as addressed to those who no longer belong to the "multitude," but have not yet reached the stage of the "perfect man." This description includes Maimonides' disciple before he has read *Guide* II.30, which completes the interpretation of the story of the Garden of Eden and "lifts" it (in the Hegelian sense of *Aufhebung*) to a new level of interpretation. In this "new level," there is no longer room for the first interpretation of the story about Adam's sons, in *Guide* I.7, and it should be dropped. Nevertheless, the existence of two different interpretations of the

Moreover, a close examination of his interpretation of Genesis 1-5 shows that he is consistent in his a-historical interpretation. The first exegetical remark on the story of the Garden of Eden in *Guide* II.30 is an Arabic paraphrase of a well known aggadic text, apparently in the version of *Genesis Rabbah* 8.1. This midrash tells us that the first man was created as an hermaphrodite. The "creation" of Eve consisted in the division of this hermaphrodite into two parts: male and female. Maimonides does not cite this midrash, but calls the attention to its most important elements which he takes as clues. One of them interests us here.

The midrash cites the view of two talmudic Sages, R. Jeremiah b. Leazar and R. Samuel ben Naḥman. R. Jeremiah b. Leazar says: "When the Holy One Blessed be He created *Adam ha-Rishon*, He created him hermaphroditic, as is said: 'male and female created He them and called their name Adam' (Gen. 5:2)"; R. Samuel b. Naḥman said: "When the Lord created *Adam ha-Rishon* he created him double-face." Maimonides substitutes his own words for theirs and says: "*Adam* and *Eve* were created together, having their backs joined" (p. 355). This rewording is very significant as he substitutes for *Adam ha-Rishon* (the first man), "Adam and Eve." He thereby indicates that "male and female" in Genesis 1:27 and 5:2 corresponds to "Adam and Eve" of the biblical text in Genesis 2-3. In other words, Maimonides *explains that male and female = Adam and Eve = form and matter.* Hence, he does not think that Genesis 1:27 refers to the two first individuals of the human species, one of them a male and the other a female, but to the two parts which constitute "man."

"Adam" might be the first individual of the human species who was created in time, or the term that designates the species "man." But, if the first created human being was Adam alone (without Eve), how can we understand the biblical stories about the birth of his sons as being historical? According to this interpretation, the biblical text does not mention the creation of the female of the human species who gave birth to these sons.

---

stories about Adam's sons explains why Maimonides used the equivocal term "Adam" in I.2. This term, when understood to mean *Adam ha-Rishon*, facilitates the historical interpretation of the story of the Garden of Eden, which is completed by the interpretation of the story of the sons of Adam in I.7, but it also permits the *Aufhebung* of the interpretation of the story of the Garden of Eden in I.2 to the level of the interpretation of II.30, where Adam is understood to mean the human species.

This point has already been noted by Gersonides. In his *Commentary on the Torah* he states that the story about "Eve" does not contain any "impossibilities," that is, elements which contradict reason or the "nature of being," such as the story about the snake which can talk. Hence, the biblical text does not necessitate any interpretation that will reveal its "inner sense," but may be perfectly well understood according to its "external sense." Maimonides' interpretation of "Eve" is only comprehensible if we presuppose that he intended to exclude a historical interpretation of the story of the creation of man and of the Garden of Eden.[15] According to Gersonides, the denial of a historical interpretation of these two stories would entail a denial of a historical interpretation of the story about Adam's sons.[16] That is exactly what Maimonides has done in *Guide* II.30, in giving an allegorical interpretation to the story about Adam's sons in Genesis 4. Thus, the interpretation of the story about Adam's sons completes that of "Eve" and that of "male and female."

To summarize, my analysis of the stories about Adam in Genesis 1-5 indicates that it is more plausible that Maimonides interpreted these stories as philosophical anthropology, rather than as historical stories whose protagonist is "the first man." These stories are thus compatible with either the esotericist position concerning the creation of the world (viz., the theory of eternity) or the skeptical position on the Creation.[17] As I have tried to establish in the first part of my paper, the second hypothesis is the more plausible. According to Maimonides it would seem that the greater part of Genesis 1-5 consists of texts concerned with the Account of the Beginning, i.e., of physics, and therefore includes anthropology as a part of physics. Physics in the sense of the description of the structure of the world is indifferent to the question as to *how* God created the physical world, and is thus compatible with all the

---

15 See pp. 114-115. See also Abravanel's remark in his *Commentary on the Torah, Bereshit* (Jerusalem, 1964), p. 123. Page reference to Gersonides' Commentary on Genesis is to: B. Braner and E. Freiman, ed., *Rabbinic Pentateuch with Commentary on the Torah by R. Levi ben Gerson (Gersonides,* 1288–1344*): Genesis,* 2nd ed. (Jerusalem, 1993).

16 That is why, according to Gersonides, the story about Adam's sons is not a parable, and Eve is the female of the human species.

17 If that is so, we cannot accept Davidson's conclusion (see note 1 above), according to which Maimonides believed either in the creation of the world out of matter or in *creatio ex-nihilo*. In both cases, the world was created before a finite time and Maimonides should have interpreted the stories about Adam historically.

possible positions on the creation of the world. The biblical text speaks of the Creation only in Genesis 1:1: "In the beginning God created (*bara*ʾ) the heaven and the earth." Yet, as it is beyond human capacity to know how God created the world, we are unable to understand the meaning of *bara*ʾ in this biblical verse.

Part Two

Maimonides' Methods of Biblical Interpretation

Maimonides' Interpretation of Jacob's Dream of the Ladder*

One of the most interesting phenomena in Maimonides' biblical exegesis is his manner of interpreting a given biblical text by means of a midrash regarding it. The present paper will be devoted to three different kinds of biblical exegesis involving midrashim, which I shall exemplify by means of three different interpretations given by Maimonides to Jacob's Dream of the Ladder in Genesis 28.

Maimonides interprets the Dream of the Ladder in three different places in his writings:[1] in *Hilkhot Yesodei ha-Torah (Fundaments of the Torah)* 7.3; in *Guide of the Perplexed* I.15; and in *Guide* II.10. In each of these interpretations, Jacob's dream is seen as having a different meaning: according to *Hilkhot Yesodei ha-Torah*, it is a prophecy of future events, whereas according to the *Guide of the Perplexed* it is concerned with "mysteries of the Torah" (i.e., esoteric teachings). Moreover, whereas according to the interpretation offered in *Guide* I.15 the dream revolves

---

* In this version I have corrected the Hebrew original of this article that appeared in the *Annual of Bar-Ilan University, Studies in Judaica and Humanities, Moshe Schwarcz Memorial Volume*, 22-23 (1987), 329-349.

1 The "fourth" interpretation of the Dream of the Ladder appears in Maimonides' response to R. Ḥasdai ha-Levi (published in *Qoveṣ Teshuvot ha-Rambam ve-Iggerotav* [Leipzig, 1859], 23a-24b, republished in a critical edition by I. Shailat in *Letters and Essays of Moses Maimonides* [Maaleh Adumim, 1988] vol. 2, pp. 677-684). This interpretation is problematic for several reasons: a) The authenticity of the letter remains to be proven; b) Even if the letter is authentic, according to its introduction it was written by a disciple of Maimonides who recorded his master's words in his own language, making it difficult to know to what extent the words of this letter in fact reflect Maimonides' original words; c) Even if this interpretation is in fact Maimonides' authentic response to R Ḥasdai, it seems quite likely that Maimonides created a compromise interpretation that would satisfy him, particularly because he did not see him as the ideal reader for whom he had written the *Guide of the Perplexed*; d) The interpretation itself is uncharacteristic of Maimonides' biblical interpretations, which are generally marked by a certain elegance and exegetical-homiletic logic that are absent in this case; e) The very fact that he compromises between two different interpretations does not derive directly from the basic exegetical intuition displayed by Maimonides in his interpretation of the Dream of the Ladder—i.e., his interpretation of the Dream on the basis of midrashim, and his giving three different meanings to it on the basis of three different midrashim which were expounded on it. For all of the above reasons, it does not seem to me that the interpretation found in the epistle to R. Ḥasdai ha-Levi reflects Maimonides' authentic view, for which reason I have not discussed it here. See also I. Shailat (ibid, pp. 673-675), who considers the letter to be a literary fiction; see the arguments he adduces there.

around the physics of the sublunary world and the world of spheres, human consciousness and the figure of the prophet as the ideal leader, in *Guide* II.10 the Dream of the Ladder is a simpler parable, concerned with the physics of the sublunary world alone. The physics that includes his anthropology is none other than the "Account of the Beginning," one of the two central esoteric sciences to whose interpretation the *Guide of the Perplexed* is devoted. Whereas the doctrine of prophecy is not part of the "Account of the Beginning," it is, according to *Guide* I.35, in fact part of "the mysteries of the Torah."

The existence of these three different interpretations of the Dream of the Ladder may be justified, on the one hand, by Maimonides' doctrine of prophecy and, on the other, by his theory of the nature of the biblical parable. According to Maimonides' interpretation, Jacob's dream is a prophetic dream.[2] This being so, it works as a "parable" which, according to Maimonides' doctrine of prophecy, may have two different levels of meaning: the revelation of future events, and "mysteries of the Torah." The existence, in the case of the Parable of the Ladder, of two different interpretations of the contents of the "mysteries of the Torah," may be partially justified by the theory of the biblical parable, which Maimonides presents at the Introduction to the *Guide*. He speaks there of different kinds of parables in the prophetic books, which he classifies according to the relationship between the symbols used in the parable and the object of the parable, and the place of the object of the parable within the parable. Maimonides notes a type of parable that has two different interpretations or meanings: "Sometimes the whole is a parable referring to two cognate subjects within the particular species of science in question" (p. 4/p. 8).

According to his interpretations, the Dream of the Ladder is a parable of this type, even though it does not serve as a perfect example thereof: one of the meanings of the Dream of the Ladder, according to the interpretation given in *Guide* I.15, and that given in *Guide* II.10, belong to the same science, that of the "Account of the Beginning."[3] How-

2 See *Guide* II.45 (p. 284/p. 399); *Hilkhot Yesodei ha-Torah* 7.3; and also A. Altmann, "The Ladder of Ascension," in his *Studies in Philosophy and Religious Mysticism* (London, 1969), p. 59.

3 In a similar manner, Joseph Ibn Kaspi justifies the existence of two different interpretations of the dream of the ladder. See *Maskiyot Kesef*, in *Sheloshah Qadmonei Mefrashei ha-Moreh* (Jerusalem, 1961: facsimile edition of Salomo Werbluner, ed., Frankfurt am Main, 1848), pp. 32, 92. On Maimonides' theory of biblical parables, see Klein-Braslavy, *Creation*, pp. 39–46.

ever, even though it is possible to justify the giving of three different interpretations to the Dream of the Ladder, in accordance with both Maimonides' doctrine of prophecy and his theory of the biblical parable, this fact may also be explained, as I demonstrate here, by the fact that the midrashim give differing interpretations of Jacob's dream,[4] and that in each of his interpretations of the Dream Maimonides made use of a different midrash.

1. *The Interpretation of the Dream of the Ladder in Hilkhot Yesodei ha-Torah*

The briefest interpretation of the Dream of the Ladder appears in the "Laws of the Fundaments of the Torah" (*Hilkhot Yesodei ha-Torah*) 7.3, where Maimonides interprets the biblical text by adopting the literal meaning of the midrashic interpretation rather than seeing it as a parable. Thus, the interpretation of the biblical text is expressed here by the very choice of midrash—one out of many—selected to interpret the text. This type of interpretation is similarly characteristic, for example, of the cosmological part of the story of the Creation in *Guide* II.30.[5] In *Hilkhot Yesodei ha-Torah* 7.3, Maimonides integrates this type of interpretation with an exegetical technique specifically characteristic of the second type of biblical interpretation, by means of a midrash which I shall discuss—namely, the interpretation of the Bible by means of a midrash which is itself a parable. Maimonides does not present here the entire midrash, and does not quote so much as an entire sentence in its original language, nor even present it in paraphrase; rather, he alludes to this midrash by means of selecting certain key phrases that indicate its meaning.

The Dream of the Ladder is presented here as one of six examples of a prophetic parable in which the prophet saw the parable "in a prophetic

---

4 In his edition of *Genesis Rabbah*, Theodor comments that the existence of a multiplicity of different midrashim about Jacob's dream may be explained by the fact that the Sages evidently wished to exclude the interpretation widely held among the early Christian authors: namely, that the Dream of the Ladder alluded to the crucifixion of Jesus. See ibid, p. 798.

5 See Klein-Braslavy, *Creation*, pp. 134–136, 162–163, 178. It may be possible to divide this type into two subcategories: a) acceptance of a midrashic interpretation that sees the biblical text as a parable and that interprets its hidden level. The Dream of the Ladder will belong to this type; b) acceptance of a midrashic interpretation that expounds the Bible according to its "literal meaning." To this type belong the interpretations of the cosmological section in the story of the Creation.

vision,"[6] and immediately thereafter its meaning (*pesher*) was written in his heart. But whereas Maimonides mentions the other five examples[7] without interpreting them, he adds an exegetical gloss to the Dream of the Ladder: "like the ladder seen by the patriarch Jacob with the angels ascending and descending thereon; and this was a metaphor for the kingdoms and their oppression of Israel." Maimonides does not explicitly state that he is adopting a midrashic interpretation of the dream; however, to anyone familiar with midrashic literature, two key words, "kingdoms" (*malkhuyot*) and "their oppression" (*shi'abudan*), suggest that he is here adopting in interpretation of this biblical text a midrash that sees the Ladder Dream as a parable concerned with revealing the future. This midrash appears in *Pesiqta de-Rav Kahana, Leviticus Rabbah* 29.12, and in *Tanḥuma, Parashat Vayeṣe*;[8] I will bring it here in the version of the *Pesiqta:*

> "And behold, angels of God ascending and descending thereon" (Gen. 28:12)—these are the princes of the nations of the world. This teaches us that the Holy One blessed be He showed Jacob the prince of Babylonia, ascending and descending, that of Media ascending and descending, and that of Edom ascending and descending. The Holy One blessed be He said to Jacob: Why do you not ascend? That very moment Jacob was frightened and said: Just as these also descend, shall not I too descend? He said to him: If you ascend, you shall not descend. He did not believe and he did not ascend.
>
> R. Shimon ben Yosina expounded it as follows: "In spite of all this they still sinned, despite his wonders they did not believe" (Ps. 78:32). The Holy One blessed be He said to him: Had you ascended and believed, you would never

6 According to *Hilkhot Yesodei ha-Torah* 7.2, the expression "prophetic vision" indicates the images seen by the prophet, whether in a dream or in a vision.

7 The creatures seen by Ezekiel; the boiling pot and the almond staff seen by Jeremiah; the scroll seen by Ezekiel, and the ephah seen by Zechariah.

8 A different text appears in *Genesis Rabbah* 68.13. However, from the opening words quoted by Maimonides, it clearly follows that this was not the version which he had before him. Ibn Ezra alludes to the interpretation of *Genesis Rabbah* 68.13 in his *Torah Commentary* when he says: "And it is the nature of the ladder to be a symbol or regarding the number of 'Sinai' which it expounds."

> have descended. But since you did not believe, your children will be subjugated to these four kingdoms in this world. Jacob said to Him: Can it be thus forever? He said to him: "Fear not, my servant Jacob, and be not afraid, O Israel, for behold, I shall redeem you from afar, and your seed from the land of their captivity" (Jer. 46:27). (Mandelbaum edition, pp. 334-335)

The first key word cited here by Maimonides is *malkhuyot*—"monarchies" or "kingdoms." This word suggests to the reader that he accepts the midrashic interpretation of Genesis 28:12—"And behold, angels of God ascending and descending thereon"—in which the "ladder" symbolizes the axis of time, and the "angels of God" who "ascend and descend" thereon symbolize the four monarchies: Babylonia, Media, Greece and Rome, which shall both ascend to greatness and descend from it during the course of human history. This interpretation is very suitable to the doctrine, put forward in *Guide of the Perplexed*, of equivocal terms, such as *mal'akh* ("angel") and *yarad ve-ʿalah* ("ascended and descended"). According to *Guide* II.6, the primary meaning of the word *mal'akh* is that of "messenger"—i.e., one who executes orders—which is used in the borrowed sense to signify whatever can possibly be perceived as such. The four monarchies of which the midrash speaks are "messengers," because in practice they fulfill the "command of God" who rules over human history. "To ascend and descend" has, according to *Guide* I.10, a borrowed meaning of ascending and descending in rank or level, and it is in this sense that it is also used by the midrash in question.

Mention of the key word "and their subjugation," suggests to the reader that Maimonides also accepted the aggadic expansion found in the midrashim, according to which, as Jacob himself refused to ascend the ladder, the people of Israel will indeed be subjugated to these four kingdoms, albeit they will eventually be delivered from this subjugation. According to this aggadic expansion, the center of gravity of the dream is turned to the people of Israel—that is, Jacob's dream is one concerning the future history of the Jewish people. Although the people of Israel will in fact be subjected to these four kingdoms, it will not be thus forever, and in the end they will be delivered. As we shall see below, accepting an aggadic expansion in the midrashic interpretation of the biblical text is extremely characteristic of this type of biblical interpretation by means of midrash, which is itself a "parable."

It is interesting that in another of his works, the *Epistle to Yemen*, Maimonides returns to the interpretation of Jacob's dream, giving the very same meaning to another verse. In dealing with the ascent and descent of those religions that challenge the Jewish religion, he interprets Genesis 28:14, "and your descendants shall be like the dust of the earth"—a verse from that part of the chapter in which Jacob receives in his dream explicit speech from God, rather than from the first part, which is defined as a "prophetic vision"—as follows:

> Indeed, God assured our father Jacob that although his children would be humbled and overcome by the nations, they and not the nations would survive and would endure. He declares, "Your descendants shall be as the dust of the earth" [Gen. 28:14], that is to say, although they will abased like the dust that is trodden under foot, they will ultimately emerge triumphant and victorious. And, as the simile implies, just as the dust settles finally upon him who tramples upon it and remains after him, so will Israel outlive its oppressors. (p. 102)[9]

Dust has two qualities: on the one hand, it is trodden down by all; on the other hand, it goes onto the foot of the one trampling it and covers it. According to Maimonides' interpretation, the image "as the dust of the earth" exploits these two different meanings of dust in order to express the idea that the people of Israel will indeed be subjugated, "trampled down" by the nations, but will ultimately overcome them. According to this interpretation, God's explicit words here parallel the "prophetic vision" seen earlier by Jacob; thus, we have here a case of an interpretation of a prophetic vision within the dream itself. This interpretation is particularly fitting to the interpretation of the third level of prophecy as given in *Guide* II.45: "a prophet's seeing a parable in a dream according to all the conditions set forth before with regard to the true reality of prophecy. And it is in the dream of prophecy itself that the meaning of the parable—what was intended thereby—is made manifest

9 Page references are to *Epistle to Yemen*, translated in Abraham Halkin and David Hartman, *Epistles of Maimonides: Crisis and Leadership* (Philadelphia–Jerusalem, 1985), pp. 91-131.

to the prophet, as for instance in most of the parables of Zechariah" (p. 285/p. 400).

It seems to me that in the interpretation of this verse, as in that of the vision of the ladder, Maimonides adopts the core exegetical idea of the midrash which expounds this verse. *Genesis Rabbah* 69.5 interprets this verse, saying: "Just as the dust of the earth wears out metal utensils and endures forever, so shall your sons outlive all the nations of the world and endure forever. Just as the dust of the world is stepped upon, so shall your children be stepped upon by the kingdoms" (p. 794).[10]

While Maimonides infers his exegetical idea from the selfsame image—the dust of the earth being trodden down, but also covering the feet of the one trodding—the midrash infers the same idea from two different qualities of dust: that dust wears away metal, and that dust is trodden underfoot. The midrash connects the quality of the dust as wearing away metals with the dream of Nebuchadnezzar concerning the statue, in which the four kingdoms are alluded to by four kinds of metal. According to *Genesis Rabbah* 68.13, this dream also relates to the Dream of the Ladder: that is, of the vision seen by Jacob.[11]

2. *The Interpretation of the Dream of the Ladder in Guide II.10*[12]

The interpretation of Jacob's Dream of the Ladder in *Guide* II.10 is more extensive than its predecessor. This interpretation sees the biblical text itself as a "parable," whose significance is found on the hidden, esoteric level. The interpretation takes the form of an "interpretative riddle,"[13] which is itself written partly in the form of a "parable." Maimonides makes use therein of aggadic expansions found in the midrashim; that is, of those same elements that the midrash adds to the biblical text, seeing therein the "comments" that allude to the topic of the riddle.[14]

---

10 Compare also *Genesis Rabbah* 40 (41).9, where this is interpreted as referring to God's words to Abraham, "and I shall make your descendants as the dust of the earth" (Gen. 13:16). Page references are to *Midrash Bereshit Rabbah*, ed. J. Theodor & H. Albeck, (Jerusalem, 1996).

11 As we have seen, Maimonides also interprets the vision of the ladder on the basis of the midrashic parallel, in which ladder=symbol=the image of Nebuchadnezzar.

12 This section has been reworked in light of my study written twenty-one years after the original publication of this paper: (in this volume) "Interpretative Riddles in Maimonides' *Guide of the Perplexed*." It is also innovative in relation to what I wrote about this subject in the entry: s.v. "Bible Commentary." In Kenneth Seeskin, ed. *The Cambridge Companion to Maimonides* (Cambridge, 2005), pp. 259-261, which was based upon the earlier version of this section.

13 On the nature and structure of the "interpretative riddle," see *ibid.*, pp. 145-147.

14 The interpretations of the creation of man and that of the figure of the serpent in the Garden of

The unique feature of the interpretation of the ladder dream in *Guide* II.10, as opposed to the other interpretations of this type, lies in the distinction drawn by Maimonides between his presentation of the level of meaning of the parable and the hints regarding the interpretation of its hidden level. At the beginning of the chapter Maimonides presents in scientific language a broader realm of meaning than that of the visual part of the Dream of the Ladder (Gen. 28:12-13), which he interprets at the end of the chapter as an "interpretative riddle." This level of meaning is, in effect, the same as that of Ezekiel's vision of the Chariot; the present chapter thus serves, not only as an introduction to the interpretation of Jacob's Dream of the Ladder and Zechariah's Vision of the Chariot, which he presents at the end of this chapter, but also as an introduction to the allusions to the interpretation of the Account of the Chariot, which he only presents in *Guide* III.1-7. Jacob's Dream, and Zechariah's Vision of the Chariot, present by way of parable—that is, by means of figurative language—a part of its realm of meaning.

The central idea in the theoretical part of *Guide* II.10 is that, in the view of the philosophers, the number four bears special significance for the description of the governance of the lower world: the spheres are divided into four groups or "spheres" (the sphere of the moon, the sphere of the sun, the sphere of the other wandering stars [i.e., the planets], and that of the fixed stars). Each sphere moves as the result of four causes: the form of the sphere, its soul, its intellect, and the separate intellect "which is its beloved" (p. 189/p. 271). Each one of them is responsible for one of the four elements: the sphere of the moon moves the water; the sphere of the sun—fire; the third sphere—air; while the fourth sphere moves the element of the earth. From these four spheres there also proceed four forces toward the lower world: the force causing the generation of the minerals, the force of the vegetative soul, the force of the animal soul, and the force of the rational soul.

Having presented this level of meaning, Maimonides turns to the interpretation of Jacob's Dream of the Ladder, which he views as a parable that, according to his interpretation, presents on its hidden level a part of the realm of meaning mentioned at the beginning of the chapter: namely, a certain phenomenon in the sublunary world involving

---

Eden story in *Guide* II.30 belong to a similar kind of "interpretative riddle." For an analysis of both these interpretations, see Klein-Braslavy, "Interpretative Riddles."

the number four. However, Maimonides does not find the number four in the biblical text of Jacob's dream, but only in the aggadic expansion found in the midrashim that interpret it. He therefore turns to the midrashim, interpreting the Dream of the Ladder by their means:

> They said in *Midrash Rabbi Tanḥuma*: *"How many steps were in the ladder? Four"*—which refers to the dictum, *"And behold a ladder set up on the earth"* [Gen. 28:12]. And in all the *Midrashim* it is mentioned and repeated that *there are four camps of angels*. However, in some manuscripts I have seen the text: *"How many steps were in the ladder? Seven."* But all the manuscripts and all the Midrashim agree that *the angels of God*, whom [Jacob] saw *ascending and descending*, were only four and not any other number—*two ascending and two descending*—and that the four gathered together upon one step of the *ladder*, all four being in one row—namely, the two who *ascend* and the two who *descend*. They even learned from this that the breadth of the *ladder* seen *in the vision of prophecy* was equal to the dimension of the world plus one-third. For the breadth of one *angel in the vision of prophecy* is equal to the dimension of one-third of the world, according to the dictum: *"and his body was like tarshish"* [Dan. 10:6]. Accordingly the breadth of the four is equal to that of the world plus one-third. (pp. 189-90/p. 272)

In effect, by bringing these midrashim Maimonides presents his interpretation of the Dream of the Ladder as an interpretative riddle that attempts to answer the question: Who are the angels that ascend and descend the ladder seen by Jacob in his dream, and what is the ladder upon which they ascended? The words of the Sages in these midrashim are the comment alluding to the solution of this interpretative riddle.

The central hint involved in the solution of this riddle is the number four, whose importance Maimonides notes in the first part of the chapter and which appears as an aggadic expansion in a number of midrashim interpreting Jacob's Dream. As in his two other interpretative riddles—namely, his interpretation of the story of the creation of man, and that of the serpent in the Garden of Eden story—here too Maimonides explicitly states that the hints to the solution of the interpretative riddle he presents are found in the midrashim. Here he even cites the name of one of the midrashim upon which he relies—*Midrash Tanḥuma*; quotes the original Hebrew text of another midrash, or perhaps a Hebrew paraphrase in his own language of another midrash—namely, *Pirqei de-Rabbi Eliezer* 4.12 and its parallels (*Gen. Rab.* 68.12; B. Ḥullin 91b); and an Arabic paraphrase of the midrash and its above-mentioned parallels.

The allusions given by Maimonides in his interpretation of the riddle of the Dream of the Ladder are thus rooted in the selection of midrashim used to interpret the dream, pointing towards those elements that he sees as comments on the interpretative riddle, while removing those elements that do not support these comments and therefore are of no importance for understanding the hidden level. Hence, there is no need to attempt to interpret them or to take them into consideration in attempting to answer it.

Maimonides made use here of three aggadic expansions found in the midrashim, which he saw as comments:

1. *Midrash Tanḥuma* (in a textual version that is not extant today)[15] interprets the verse "and behold a ladder set up on the earth" by answering the question, "How many steps were in the ladder? Four." While Maimonides admits that some versions of this midrash mention *seven* steps on the ladder, it is important for him to note that there is a text which counts *four* steps on the ladder.

2. The most important aggadic expansion for resolving the interpretative riddle that he presents here is the answer given by the midrashim to the question: How many angels ascended and descended on the ladder? Here, Maimonides notes that there is agreement among all the midrashim as to the number four. The formulation, "There are four camps of angels" is closest to the statement found in *Pirqei de-Rabbi Eliezer* 4.12: "There are four classes of ministering angels who exalt before the Holy One, blessed be He. The first camp... the second camp... the third camp... the fourth camp..." By saying "all the midrashim," Maimonides is doubtless referring as well to the parallels to *Pirqei de-Rabbi Eliezer*: *Numbers Rabbah* 2.1; *Pesiqta Rabbati* Ch. 47; as well as *Genesis Rabbah*

---

15 See S. Munk, *Le Guide des Égarés* , vol. II, p. 90, n. 1; and cf. M. Schwarz, *Moreh Nevukhim le-Rabbenu Moshe ben Maimon*, translated, with notes, addenda and indexes, by Michael Schwarz (Tel Aviv, 2002), I, p. 288, n. 27.

and its parallels, to whose aggadic expansions he shall refer presently.

3. The third aggadic expansion is that found in *Genesis Rabbah* 68.12 and its parallel in B. Ḥullin 91b:

> Rabbi Berechiah said: He showed him the world and one-third of the world. Ascend (*'olim*) - those who ascend do not ascend with less than two, and those who descend—do not descend in less than two. The angel is one-third of the world. From whence do we know that the angel is one-third of the world? As is said: "And his body was like tarshish, and his face was like the appearance of lightning…" (Daniel 10:6). (p. 787)

Maimonides does not mention the midrashim here by name, but cites one phrase in Hebrew—"two ascend and two descend"—which is closest to the formula in B. Ḥullin: "there ascend two and descend two," and gives an Arabic paraphrase of the midrash in *Genesis Rabbah*. This aggadic expansion serves him primarily as confirmation of the central comment that he derives from the midrash, according to which the number of angels who ascended and descended the ladder was "four and no more." The midrash in *Genesis Rabbah* explains how it arrived at the conclusion that there were at least four angels: namely, from the plural form of the verbs "ascend" and "descend" in the biblical verse (*'olim veyordim*), it infers that "'ascend' cannot be less than two, and 'descend' cannot be less than two." But what is important for Maimonides is the idea that the number of angels can be no greater than four, specifically—an idea inferred from the continuation of the midrash in *Genesis Rabbah* 68.12, according to which Jacob saw "in a prophetic vision" a world and a-third of the world. This midrashic calculation is based upon the statement that "an angel is one-third of the world," combined with the assumption that Jacob saw specifically four angels. Had he seen more than four angels, he could not have seen "a world and a-third thereof"—that is, one-third times four.

Maimonides also emphasizes another idea which he inferred from this aggadic expansion, which he also saw as a comment towards the solution of the interpretative riddle of the ladder dream—namely, that the four angels who ascended and descended the ladder gathered together on one step of the ladder. This comment is implied in the remark of the

Sages that Jacob saw, in his "prophetic vision," "a world and a-third of the world." Jacob was able to see a world and a-third when all of the angels, each one of whom was one-third the width of the world, stood together upon one step. This idea is formulated more clearly in B. Ḥullin 91b, which speaks of the breadth of the ladder in units of parsangs: "They taught: How great was the width of the ladder? Eight thousand parsangs; as is written, 'and behold the angels of God were ascending and descending upon it.' Two ascended and two descended, and when they met one another they were four. And it is written concerning the angels, 'and his body was like tarshish,' and we have learned that tarshish was two thousand parsangs." It seems reasonable to assume that in *Guide* II.10, Maimonides had in mind both versions—that of *Genesis Rabbah* and that of Ḥullin—and that his interpretation was constructed on the basis of both.

In addition to emphasizing those points that serve as a key to understanding the hidden level of this midrash, Maimonides takes care to ignore those elements in the midrash which, according to his interpretation, are not relevant to understanding its hidden level. He emphasizes that the dimensions of each angel—one-third of the world—and that of all four angels together—the world and one-third of the world—appear as such according to the Sages only in the "prophetic vision." They belong to the external, visual level of the parable, to the metaphorical garment given by the dream to its theoretical message. What is significant on the hidden level is only the idea implicit within the presentation of these dimensions—namely, that the four angels gathered on one step of the ladder, and it was that which served as a comment to the interpretative riddle which he presents here.

But this riddle cannot be resolved on the basis of the comments contained in the midrashim alone. In order to solve it, the reader of the *Guide of the Perplexed* needs to draw the connection for himself between the theoretical part presented at the beginning of the chapter and the midrashic comments regarding the Dream of the Ladder. In order to understand the comments he must also have certain prior knowledge: he must know something of Aristotelian philosophy and must know other chapters of *The Guide of the Perplexed*. His knowledge of those chapters will enable him to make use of the method of "connecting its chapters one with another," to apply what he learned from them in understanding the comments found in other midrashim, and thereby to resolve the interpretative riddle inherent in the Dream of the Ladder; he must know *Guide* II.6, in which Maimonides interprets the equivocal term "angel," and *Guide* I.10, in which he discusses the equivocal terms "descend" and "ascend." He must also know *Guide* I.72, in which Maimonides presents in narrative form the structure of reality as proven by philosophic demonstration, and to implement in his interpretation what he learned from it.

According to the theoretical portion of that chapter, there are four phenomena in the physical world that may correspond to the exegetical hint implied by the number of angels seen by Jacob in his dream: the four spheres; the four causes of their motion; the four elements; and the four forces that proceed from the spheres. According to *Guide* II.6 and II.7, only two of them may be called "angels": the spheres[16] and the four elements.[17] However, only the meaning of the four elements is suitable to the description of the angels as beings that are in movement of ascent or descent. In Aristotelian physics, the elements of earth and water have a natural tendency to move "downwards," while those of air and fire tend to move "upwards." The midrashic description cited here by Maimonides, "two ascend and two descend," therefore corresponds to this principle of Aristotelian physics and to the description of the motion of the elements in *Guide* I.72: "The motions in a straight line, which are found to belong to these four elements when they move in order to return to their places, are two: a motion toward the encompassing sphere, which motion belongs to fire and to air, and a motion toward the center of the world, which belongs to water and to earth" (p. 128/p. 185). It follows from this that the "angels" are the four elements, while the verbs "ascend" and "descend" appear here in their original significance; that is, as ascent and descent in physical space. [18]

The third aggadic expansion used by Maimonides in his interpretation is brought primarily, as we said, in order to confirm the statement that Jacob saw in his dream four angels and no more. However, according to his interpretation, the Dream of the Ladder also alludes to an additional matter—namely, that the four angels gathered together in a single row, standing together on one rung of the ladder. This aggadic

16 See *Guide* II.7 (p. 185/p. 266).
17 *Guide* II.6 (p. 182/p. 262); II.7 (p. 185/p. 266).
18 See *Guide* I.10 (p. 24/pp. 35-36).

expansion, according to Maimonides' interpretation, evidently alludes to another natural law related to the four elements, described by Maimonides in *Guide* I.72: "Inasmuch as the fifth body as a whole is engaged perpetually in a circular motion, it thus engenders forced motion in the elements because of which they leave their places. I have in view fire and air, which are pushing toward the water. All of them penetrate toward the body of the earth, in the valleys. In consequence a mixture of the elements comes about" (p. 128/p. 186). These four elements mix with one another in a forced motion that originates in the world of spheres, and this mixture creates the various temperaments from which all things that exist in this lower world are composed. It is therefore possible that, according to Maimonides, this comment in the words of the Sages indicates that the angels who ascend and descend not only allude to the four elements as distinct, separate elements, but also to the four elements as they mix with one another to create the mixtures of those things existing in the sublunary world.

On the basis of this interpretation of the second and third aggadic expansions, the reader may also attempt to interpret the comment found, according to Maimonides' interpretation, in the first aggadic expansion, according to which the ladder had four rungs, and thereby answer the question of the meaning of the ladder seen in Jacob's dream. The "ladder" is a kind of "place." It is therefore reasonable to interpret that, if the four angels that ascended and descended the ladder are the four elements, than the ladder itself refers to the four natural places of these four elements. These natural places are described in *Guide* I.72: "Every one of these four elements has a natural place proper to it and is not found elsewhere if left to its nature" (p. 128/p. 185).

According to this interpretation of the Dream of the Ladder, its significance belongs to the realm of "mysteries of the Torah." Jacob saw in his dream a part of the "Account of the Beginning"—the basic principles of physics from which those things existing in the sublunary world are composed, and their mixture with one another. His perception therefore corresponds to the lowest level of apperception of the chariot in Ezekiel, the vision of the wheels.[19]

---

19 For an interpretation of the wheels in Ezekiel's Chariot Vision as the four elements, see *Guide* III.2. In Jacob's dream there is added to this the perception of the "ladder," and hence the natural places of the elements.

3. The Interpretation of the Dream of the Ladder in the Introduction to the Guide and in Guide I.15

The most interesting, complex and fullest interpretation of the Dream of the Ladder appears in *Guide of the Perplexed* I.15. In this interpretation, Maimonides does not openly rely upon any particular midrash. Rather, he seemingly approaches the interpretation of the biblical text directly, on the basis of the semantic–philosophical axis and of the biblical–philosophical lexicon constructed in the *Guide* of *the Perplexed*. Nevertheless, this interpretation, like the two discussed previously, seems to be rooted in a midrash that expounds the Dream of the Ladder, the main portion of which represents a third type of biblical interpretation via midrashic means used by Maimonides. In this case Maimonides does not accept the literal meaning of the midrashic interpretation, nor does he see the midrashic interpretation as a "parable" which is to be interpreted and understood according to its hidden layer. The midrash serves here only as a factor which "awakens" or inspires him to understand the significance of the biblical parable. A similar type of biblical interpretation via midrash is found, for example, in Maimonides' interpretation of the story of the Garden of Eden in *Guide* I.2[20] albeit there in a less developed form.

The midrash which "awakens" Maimonides to this interpretation is found, like the central midrash on whose basis he interprets the Ladder Dream in *Guide* II.10, in *Genesis Rabbah* 68.12:[21]

> The Rabbis interpreted it as referring to Sinai: "And he dreamed that there was a ladder" (Gen. 28:12)—this refers to Sinai. The letters of this are like the letters of that. "Set up on the earth"—"And they stood at the foot of the mountain" (Exod. 19:20). "And the top of it reached to heaven"—"while the mountain burned with fire to

20 As I have shown in Klein-Braslavy, *Adam Stories*, pp. 95–96, 101–104, 122–123, in *Guide* I.2 Maimonides interprets Job 14:20 and Psalm 49:13 as referring to "Adam" as the hero of the story of the Garden of Eden. This may be explained on the basis of the fact that, already in the midrashim, these two verses are interpreted as referring to Adam. Job 14:20 is explained thusly in *Genesis Rabbah* 11.12; 12.6; *Tanḥuma* (Buber ed.), 7a; *Genesis Rabbah*. 16.1 and 21.14, while Psalm 49:13 is interpreted in *Genesis Rabbah* 11.2; 12.6; B. Sanhedrin 35b; and *Pesiqta Rabbati* to Gen. 3:22. See also (in this volume) "On Maimonides' Interpretation of the Story of the Garden of Eden," pp. 65-66.

21 This midrash is paralleled in *Tanḥuma* (Buber ed.), *Vayeṣe* §3 and in *Midrash Leqaḥ Tov*, *Vayeṣe*.

> the heart of heaven" (Deut. 4:11). "And behold, the angels of God"... Another thing, "And behold, the angels of God"—this refers to Moses and Aaron, of whom it is written, "Then Haggai, the messenger of the Lord, spoke to the people with the Lords' message" (Haggai 1:13). "Ascending"—"and Moses ascended" (Exod. 19:3). "And descending"—"and Moses descended from the mountain" (ibid., 14). "And behold, the Lord stood above it"—"and the Lord descended on Mt. Sinai" (ibid., 20). (p. 786)

Characteristic of this midrash is that it does not contain any aggadic expansion that elaborates or adds to what is already stated in the biblical text itself. The midrash divides the biblical text into seven units of meaning, interpreting each one on its own. Thus, on the basis of the interpretation that "Sinai equals *sulam* (ladder),"[22] the midrash implies that the Dream of the Ladder alludes to the level of meaning of Moses' ascent to Mt. Sinai and his descent therefrom; the rest of the biblical text is expounded on the basis of this biblical spirit.

In the Introduction to *Guide of the Perplexed*, where Maimonides deals with the theory of the parable, he cites the Parable of the Ladder as an example of one of two central types of parables found in the Bible:[23] the Parable of the Ladder is presented as an example of one constructed out of a mosaic of equivocal terms; thus, every word or group of words therein bears a distinct significance on the esoteric level of the parable. In order to understand a parable of this type, one first needs to analyze its basic units of meaning, to interpret each one on the basis of its general semantic axis, and finally to undertake a synthesis, combining all those meanings derived during the course of this exegetical process and to construct from them the "meaning of the parable." The interpretation of each of the units of meaning of the parable on the basis of its semantic axis and their combination with one another is necessary for a full understanding of the concealed or esoteric level of the parable, as

---

22 On the basis of the *gematria* (numerological equation): *Sinai* in Hebrew is written *sameḥ, yod, nun yod*; in *gematria, sameḥ*=60 *yod*= 10 and *nun*=50, hence *Sinai*=130; in the defective spelling of *slm* as it appears in the biblical textual tradition *slm* = 130 as *sameḥ*= 60 *lamed*=30 and *mem*=40.

23 See note 3 above. For the second type of parables see (in this volume) "Maimonides' Strategy for Interpreting 'Woman' in the *Guide of the Perplexed*," pp. 134-135.

each word contributes to our understanding of its overall meaning. In order to exemplify this type of biblical parable, Maimonides undertakes an analysis of Jacob's Dream of the Ladder. He divides it into seven basic units of meaning, identical to the seven units of meaning into which it is divided by the midrash in *Genesis Rabbah* 68.12:

> An example of the first kind of prophetic parable is the following text: "And behold a ladder set up on the earth," and so on. In this text, the word "ladder" indicates one subject; the words "set up on the earth" indicate a second subject; the words "and the top of it reached to heaven" indicate a third subject; the words "and behold the angels of God" indicate a fourth subject; the word "ascending" indicates a fifth subject; the words "and descending" indicate a sixth subject; and the words "And behold the Lord stood above it" indicate a seventh subject. Thus every word occurring in this parable refers to an additional subject in the complex of subjects represented by the parable as a whole. (p. 8/pp. 12-13)

Maimonides does not interpret here the units of meaning of the parable, nor does he provide any hint as to their general field of meaning.[24] Nevertheless, the very assertion that "And behold the Lord stood above it" is the seventh unit of meaning of the Parable of the Ladder already implies a certain interpretation. If we examine the biblical text, we discover that Jacob's dream is divided into two parts: a visual part—i.e., the vision seen by Jacob; and a verbal part—God's words to Jacob in his dream. "And behold the Lord stood above it" introduces the second part of the dream: God's explicit speech to Jacob. Jacob sees God standing above the ladder—that is, standing at its top, speaking to him, and revealing to him the future. This image is extremely characteristic of dreams of incubation experienced in holy places and temples in the ancient world; the individual sleeping in the holy place would dream that the god of the place was standing by him and speaking with him, revealing to him the future or telling him how he would be healed from his

24 The early commentators on the *Guide* engaged in "creative interpretation" when they read the formal analysis in the Introduction as a metaphysical interpretation to the Dream of the Ladder.

illness.[25] Indeed, in wake of the midrash in *Genesis Rabbah* 68.12, Maimonides sees "And behold the Lord stood above it" as a unit of meaning belonging to the visual part of the dream. According to the theory of the type of parable, which he exemplifies by means of the Parable of the Ladder, this unit must add to "the totality of the thing alluded to" of this visual part. By means of this statement, we already infer that "stand" means to stand upon or above the ladder, and not to stand over Jacob, who is lying down and dreaming.[26]

The formal discussion of the Parable of the Ladder requires completion, which takes note of the significance of this parable. Maimonides brings such a completion in *Guide* I.15, and in this chapter alone. According to the interpretation of the parable of the dream in *Guide* II.10, the "ladder" is the lower world whose upper end reaches to the heaven—that is to say, the spheres. Those found upon it are the spheres and not God. It follows from this that the phrase "And behold, the Lord stood above it" cannot serve as a seventh unit of significance adding to the overall significance of the parable of this dream. Indeed, the midrashim upon which Maimonides relies here do not mention or interpret the units of meaning "and the top of it reached to heaven" nor the unit "and behold the Lord stood above it." This being so, it may be that by the very division of the parable of the ladder into seven units of meaning Maimonides is suggesting that the Parable of the Ladder, which he will interpret in *Guide* I.15, ought to be understood on the basis of the midrash in *Genesis Rabbah* 68.12.

In *Guide* I.15, Maimonides interprets the dream of the ladder within the framework of the chapter dealing with the interpretation of the equivocal terms, *naṣov / yaṣov*.[27] *Naṣov* and *yaṣov* are two different roots with the same significance in all of their various uses. Their primary meaning is the "rising and being erect" of a physical body, while their derivative sense is "to be stable and permanent." They may also be used in this latter sense with regard to non-corporeal entities or of intellectual apprehension. According to the dominant model given in those chapters

---

25 Cf. J. G. Frazer, *Folklore in the Old Testament* (London, 1923), pp. 225–228.

26 Already the midrashim disagreed among themselves as to the meaning of the word *ʿalav* (here translated "above"). There were those who saw it as meaning "above the ladder," and those who read it as "above Jacob."

27 On the lexicographical chapters in Book I of the *Guide* and the manner of interpreting the words therein, see: Klein-Braslavy, *Creation*, pp. 35-39; (in this volume) "Maimonides' Strategy for Interpreting 'Woman' in the *Guide of the Perplexed*," p. 126.

dealing with the interpretation of equivocal terms in the First Part of the *Guide*, Maimonides argues here, after presenting the two meanings of these verbs and exemplifying each meaning by means of a suitable biblical verse, that when *naṣov* or *yaṣov* refer to God or His activities, they always have the sense of "to be stable and permanent"—that is, the secondary or borrowed meaning of these verbs. As an example of the biblical use of *naṣov* in relation to God, Maimonides cites the beginning of Genesis 28:13, "And behold the Lord stands above it." According to his interpretation, God did not appear to Jacob as having a physical form, but rather as one "that was stably and constantly upon it [i.e., the ladder]." This example for the use of *naṣov* in its borrowed meaning leads Maimonides to deviate from the explicit subject of the chapter—i.e., the interpretation of equivocal terms—to the interpretation of the visual part of Jacob's dream as a whole.[28]

If we examine closely the visual part of the Dream of the Ladder, we will find that it is possible to distinguish two elements therein: static and dynamic. The static element is composed of units of meaning (1), (2), (3), and (7): "ladder," "standing upon the earth," "its head reaches the heaven," "and behold the Lord stands above it." The dynamic component, by contrast, is composed of units (4), (5), and (6): "angels of God," "ascending," and "descending." Maimonides, who has great sensitivity to text and extraordinary exegetical-homiletical ability, interprets each of the elements in *Guide* I.15 separately, while remaining loyal to the logic of the biblical text. As we shall see later, he thereby also remains loyal to his fundamental intuition regarding the meaning of the Ladder Dream, which he interprets within the broader framework of his overall thought and his biblical exegesis.

The static element is interpreted by Maimonides from two different perspectives: cosmological or ontological, and cognitive. The cosmological perspective is rooted in the starting point of the interpretation: "And behold the Lord stands above it" serves, on the one hand, as an example for the interpretation of *niṣav* in the sense of "to be stable and permanent," thereby concluding the discussion of the equivocal terms *yaṣov* and *naṣov;* on the other hand, this part of the verse serves as an introduction to the interpretation of Jacob's Dream of the Ladder. The

28 This structure of a lexicographical chapter is also found in *Guide* I.7; cf. Klein-Braslavy, *Adam Stories*, pp. 267-270.

beginning of the interpretation of the dream with the seventh unit of meaning involves a change in the original order of units of meaning of this parable. This change serves Maimonides as a starting point for interpreting the static portion of the dream of the ladder from the viewpoint of God, who stands "above" the ladder, rather than from that of Jacob, who lies upon the ground and sees the ladder standing upon the ground. This point of view also requires Maimonides to change the original order of units of meaning (2) and (3) in the Ladder Dream, and to place (3), "and the top of it reached to heaven," prior to (2), "set up on the earth." He does not make this change in an arbitrary manner, but bases it upon his interpretation of the word, "and the top of it" in the third unit of meaning. Maimonides understands *rosho*, "its head," as meaning "first"; from this, he arrives at the interpretation of "the top of it reached to heaven" as "*the first end* of which is in heaven" (*ṭarafuhu al-awwal fī l-samāʾ*; p. 27/p. 41). He concludes from this that "*its last end is upon the earth* (*wa- ṭarafuhu al-ākhar fī l-arḍ*)." (*ibid.*)[29] To the interpretation of this aspect of the static element in the dream, Maimonides adds an interpretation that confirms that which was already given by the reader to "And behold the Lord stood erect above it," when he read the Introduction to the *Guide*: "'*And behold the Lord stood erect above it*,' that is, was stably and constantly upon it—I mean upon the ladder" (*ibid., ibid.).* Maimonides does not respond to the expectations of the reader, who is familiar with the formal discussion of the Parable of the Ladder in the Introduction to the *Guide*, such that he will interpret here each of the units of meaning of the parable in a clear manner in its own right. He does not interpret the unit of meaning of "ladder," nor that of "heaven" and "earth" in units (2) and (3). The reader must complete the interpretation given here for himself, using the method of "connecting its chapters one with another," and applying the meaning of "heaven" and "earth," to which Maimonides relates in other chapters of *Guide of the Perplexed,* here. On the basis of this interpretation, he may also conclude the meaning of "ladder."

Maimonides interprets the term "heaven" (*shamayim*) in *Guide* I.70. His interpretation there is another example of the first type of biblical interpretation by means of midrash which I presented here earlier. This is an interpretation that adopts the literal meaning of a homiletic inter-

29 I have here corrected the translation of Pines on the basis of Ibn Tibbon and Schwarz.

pretation, and it is quite similar in its nature to the interpretations of the cosmological part of the story of the creation of the world in *Guide* II.30.[30] Just as in *Guide* II.10 Maimonides relies upon a general agreement among the Sages in the midrashim who claimed that the number of angels which went up and down on the ladder was four, so here as well he relies upon "the textual words of the Sages... which are repeated (*al-mutakarrir*) in every relevant passage" (p. 118/p. 171) which relate to the world of the spheres, according to which: 1. the number of heavens is seven; 2. "'*Aravot* is the highest [heaven] encompassing the universe" (*ibid., ibid*)."[31] Since Maimonides assumes that the Sages thought in terms of concepts of Aristotelian philosophy, he understood that "firmament" in the language of the Sages refers to a "sphere," from which he concluded that *ʿAravot* is the highest sphere: that is, the starless or most encompassing sphere. He sees this interpretation of the words of the Sage as the literal interpretation of their words; there is, in his opinion, no other interpretation of *raqiʿa* or *ʿAravot* in their words.[32] On the basis of the assumption that this is the only correct interpretation of the concepts of *raqiʿa* and *ʿAravot*, Maimonides accepts as is, without any addition or interpretation, the interpretation given by the Sages to the word *shamayim*. Here, he relies explicitly on B. Ḥagigah, bringing its interpretation there in its language:

> *ʿAravot* ("the heavens"), He who is high and uplifted dwells upon it, as is said, "Lift up a song to Him who rides upon the clouds [*ʿAravot*]" (Ps. 68:5). And from whence do we know that it is called *shamayim* ("heavens")? It is written here, "He who rides upon the *ʿAravot*" and it is written there, "who rides upon the heavens" (Deut. 33:26). (B. Ḥagigah 12b)

On the basis of the view that *ʿAravot* is equivalent to the highest sphere that encompasses all, and the homiletical interpretation of the

30 See note 5.

31 See B. Ḥagigah 12b; *Pirqei de-Rabbi Eliezer* Ch. 18; *Pesiqta Rabbati* 20.3; *Deuteronomy Rabbah*. 5.3, and more.

32 The words of the "Sages" concerning "heaven" and "earth" in Gen. 1:1, upon which Maimonides relies in his interpretation of the Creation story in *Guide* II.30, are likewise understood as referring to the highest sphere or the spheres, and to the element of the earth or the four elements, seeing this as the straightforward understanding of the biblical text.

Sages in B. Ḥagigah 12b, according to which ʿ*Aravot* equals *shamayim*, Maimonides arrives at the equation that *shamayim*, the heavens, is identical to the highest, all-encompassing sphere. The reader then needs to apply this meaning to the interpretation of the Dream of the Ladder in *Guide* I.15, in which the first end of the ladder is none other than the highest sphere.

The noun ʾ*ereṣ* ("earth") is interpreted by Maimonides within the context of his interpretation of the story of the Creation in *Guide* II.30. According to his interpretation there, ʾ*ereṣ* is an equivocal term "used in a general and in a particular sense. In a general sense it is applied to all that is beneath the sphere of the moon, I mean the four elements. In a particular sense it is applied to one element, the last among them, namely, earth" (p. 246/p. 350). It follows from this that ʾ*ereṣ*, "earth," in the second unit of meaning in the ladder dream, means either the element earth, which according to Aristotle's doctrine of the natural place is at the center of the sublunary world, or all four elements from which things in the lower world are composed.

The determining of the meaning of the two ends of the ladder—the highest sphere and the element of the earth or the four elements—enables the reader to understand the first unit of meaning of Jacob's dream, the ladder itself. The "ladder" is none other than the material reality—that is, all the existing things that are composed of form and matter, and are arranged in a hierarchy according to their ontological level.

Maimonides does not explain the expression "set upon the earth," in the second unit of meaning, in any particular way. However, it is reasonable to assume that he expects the reader to apply here the secondary meaning of *niṣav* and to explain that the "ladder" "is stable and permanent"—that is, that the material, hierarchical reality persists and is eternal.

According to this interpretation of the four units of meaning that establish the static component within the dream of the ladder, one can understand that in its hidden level this aspect of the static component presents a picture of the physical world from the viewpoint of God, as the "beginning" of the physical world. The physical world begins from the highest sphere and concludes with the four elements. Precisely such a description, in conceptual language, is brought by Maimonides in *Guide* II.4: "Just as bodies begin similarly with the highest sphere and come to an end with the elements and what is composed of them" (p. 180-179/p. 258). To use the terminology of Maimonides' biblical exegesis, the subject of this aspect in the Parable of the Ladder is "the Account of the Beginning" which is "among the mysteries of the Torah."

Having interpreted the static element in the Parable of the Ladder from its ontological or cosmological aspect, Maimonides goes on to interpret the selfsame element from an additional point of view: from that of Jacob lying on the ground and seeing the ladder set upon the ground, its top reaching into the heaven and God standing above it. It must be emphasized that this vision is distinct from that of the angels ascending and descending the ladder; rather, it is that perception by which Jacob perceives the static element of the ladder alone. From this point of view, the Dream of the Ladder alludes to the graduated cognition of physical reality that serves as a means of metaphysical cognition—that is, the knowledge of the reality of the existence of God as He who is "stably and constantly" at the top of the ladder. From the cognitive (or epistemological) viewpoint, the "ladder" "begins" from "the earth"—i.e., the element of earth or the four elements—and "concludes" in the highest sphere. "Behold the Lord stands above it" is parallel to "He who rides upon the heavens" or "He who rides upon the ʿAravot" which, according to *Guide* I.70, means: "He who makes the encompassing heaven revolve and who moves it in virtue of His power and His will" (p. 120/p. 175).[33] *Guide* I.70 serves not only as a key to understanding the noun *shamayim* (heaven) in the Dream of the Ladder, but also as its parallel in terms of contents. Moses' words in his blessing in Deuteronomy 33:26-27 and Psalm 68:5, interpreted by Maimonides in this chapter of the *Guide* primarily by means of B. Ḥagigah 12b,[34] as well as Jacob's dream, present, according to his interpretation, the selfsame picture of the world—God is He who is "the mover of the first sphere" (*Guide* II.1; p. 171/p. 246). This conclusion, based upon biblical exegesis, is paralleled in the realm of pure philosophical discussion by the first proof of the existence of God given by Maimonides in *Guide* II.1—namely, the proof of the existence of God by means of the movement of the sphere, i.e., that God is He who moves the sphere. According to *Guide* I.70, "It is the greatest

---

33 This parallel has already been noted by the commentators: Efodi, Crescas, Shem Tov, and Abravanel, in their commentaries to *Guide* I.15, pp. 32a-b.

34 He also interprets Psalm 68:5 on the basis of *Pirqei de-Rabbi Eliezer*, Ch 18.

proof through which one can know the existence of the Deity" (p. 121/p. 175).[35]

According to this interpretation of the static element in the Parable of the Ladder, the subject of the dream is the highest possible level of cognition that man may attain and the manner in which he may attain it. One who learns the science of physics in an organized and systematic way can arrive, in the final analysis, at an apprehension of the existence of God as He who moves the highest sphere, and one must understand—by means of the first proof of the existence of God presented in *Guide* II.1. Maimonides' words, "*wa-fihi yatasallaqu wa-yaṭṭaliʿu kull man yaṭṭaliʿu ḥattā yudrika man ʿalayhi ḍarūra*" ("upon which climbs and ascends everyone who ascends,[36] so that he necessarily apprehends him

---

35 There is a certain contradiction in the *Guide* pertaining to the relation of God to the highest sphere. On the exegetical level, the dream of Jacob, Deuteronomy 33:26–27, and Psalm 68:5—all according to the interpretation which Maimonides gives them on the basis of B. Ḥagigah 12b, and *Pirqei de-Rabbi Eliezer* Ch. 18—stand in opposition to Ezekiel's Vision of the Chariot, again according to Maimonides' interpretation. As has already been noted by Shalom Rosenberg in a lecture given at the Ninth World Congress of Jewish Studies (August 1985), in *Guide* III.7 Maimonides states that "'the likeness of a man that was on the throne' and that was divided, is not a parable referring to Him, who is exalted above all composition, but to a created thing" (p. 309/p. 430). It follows from this that, according to Maimonides' interpretation of Ezekiel's vision of the chariot, it is the created (*makhlūq*) "first intellect" that is the first cause that moves the highest sphere, and not God Himself. In his lecture, Rosenberg presents this contradiction as one between *Pirqei de-Rabbi Eliezer* and Ezekiel's chariot vision. But this statement does not seem correct to me. As I have shown here, the contradiction on the exegetical level is among the biblical texts themselves. Some of the biblical texts—Deut. 33:26–27 and Ps. 68:5—are interpreted by means of a midrashic interpretation—i.e., B. Ḥagigah 12b and *Pirqei de-Rabbi Eliezer,* Ch. 18. Moreover, this contradiction also exists between Jacob's dream, which is "a prophetic dream," and Ezekiel's vision of the chariot. It follows that the contradiction is between two prophetic visions, and not between *Pirqei de-Rabbi Eliezer* and a prophetic vision. It must also be stressed that this contradiction does not only exist on the exegetical level, and does not derive from exegetical exigencies alone, from an honest attempt to understand the meaning of different texts in the Bible and in rabbinic thought, but also on the level of pure philosophical discussion. In the first proof of the existence of God in *Guide* II.1—i.e., the argument from the motion of the sphere—Maimonides proves the existence of God as the direct cause of the motion of the highest sphere. As against that, in *Guide* II.4, he explicitly claims that "the deity, may He be exalted, has... brought into existence the first intellect, who is the mover of the first sphere in the way that we have explained" (p. 179/p. 258). It seems to me that the fourth proof of the existence of God in *Guide* II.1, in which Maimonides is influenced by Avicenna, proving the existence of God as being necessary of existence in respect of its own essence, as opposed to the separate intellects, that are "possible of existence in respect to their own essence," presents the selfsame picture as in *Guide* II.4. Regarding the contradiction between the dream of Jacob and *Guide* I.70, and *Guide* II.4, it has already been noted by Isaac Abravanel in *Sefer Shamayim Ḥadashim*, B. Heidenheim, ed., (Rodelheim, 1828; repr.: Jerusalem, 1966), Fifth Sermon, pp. 47b–48a. Abravanel thinks that Maimonides' authentic view is that which follows from the first proof of the existence of God in *Guide* II.1

36 Already here, Maimonides interprets by implication the meaning of "ascent." He uses the Arabic word, *wa-yaṭṭaliʿu* which is parallel to the Hebrew *ʿalah*, and from his words here it is clear that "ascent" of the ladder means an ascent in apprehension

who is upon it; p. 28/p. 41),"[37] leave room to think that the apprehension of God spoken of here is not unique to the prophet. This is the ultimate level of discursive intellectual apprehension, and it is that which is attained by the philosopher. The prophet attains this level by virtue of him being the perfect philosopher.[38]

Having clarified these two aspects of the static element in the parable of the ladder, Maimonides turns to an interpretation of the dynamic element therein, in units (4), (5), and (6): "angels of God," "ascend" and "descend." It seems to me that, in the interpretation of this element in the Dream of the Ladder, Maimonides' attention was turned by a "pointer" *(tanbīh)* found, according to his understanding, in the midrash, in *Genesis Rabbah* 68.12. The "pointer" he derived from this midrash also influenced the interpretation he gave to the two aspects of the static element in the parable. Nevertheless, one ought not to ignore the fact that, in the interpretation of the dream of the ladder, there are also "weak echoes" of the motifs of the "ladder of wisdom" and the "ladder of ascent," as has been argued by Alexander Altmann.[39]

The dynamic element in the parable of the ladder is composed of three equivocal terms of the logical type, which Maimonides explains elsewhere in the *Guide of the Perplexed* in a systematic manner—of the noun *mal'akh* ("angel"), interpreted primarily in *Guide* II.6; and of the verbs "descend" and "ascend" (*yarad* and *ʿalah*), interpreted in *Guide* I.10.

His interpretation of the noun *mal'akh* ("angel") is of particular interest. In *Guide* II.6, Maimonides develops a linguistic theory to explain the various meanings of this equivocal noun. He explains, "Now you already know that the meaning of angel is messenger [*rasūl*]. Accordingly every-

37 As one is speaking here of cognition, of the philosopher's gradual progress towards knowledge of God, it is reasonable to interpret the phrase "so that he necessarily apprehends him who is upon it," as meaning that the necessity relates to the apprehension and not to the reality of God. Pines writes "so that he necessarily apprehends Him who is upon it," but the correct translation should be "him." Maimonides does not refer here explicitly to the deity, though "him who is upon it" is certainly God. Pine notes (p. 41 n. 7) that "the Arabic phrase might also be translated: so that he apprehends Him who is upon it necessarily. However, for syntactic and other reasons, the translation in the text is probably the correct one." In fact, Ibn Tibbon chose the second alternative (he does not translate 'Him who is upon it' but '*he* who is upon it," which is preferable to Pines' translation here. Similarly, Munk translated here: "et où s'élancent et montent tous ceux qui montent, afin de percevoir celui qui est nécessairement en haut" (*Le Guide des Égarés*, vol. I, p. 65). Schwarz translates as does Pines.

38 This is likewise the view of Shem Tov, who writes: "It follows of necessity that the enlightened ones and the knowledgeable Sages who ascend this ladder will comprehend that there is a Cause of Causes over all" (p. 32b).

39 See note 2, above.

one who carries out an order is an angel" (p. 182/p. 262). This being the case, this noun is applied to every thing which can be seen as a "messenger" that is "carrying out orders." On the basis of the analogy between God's activities in the world and those of man, he demonstrates that the noun "angel" may be applied to everyone or everything that mediates between God and the lower world or between specific things therein. Every intermediary of this type is understood as a "messenger" in the sense of carrying out God's commands. The first significance of "angel" in the sense of "messenger" of which Maimonides takes note here is "prophet." A "prophet" is an angel because he is God's messenger to man. The biblical use of the word "angel" in the sense of "prophet" is exemplified here by Maimonides by means of two biblical verses: "Now the angel of the Lord went up from Gilgal to Bochim" (Judg. 2:1) and "And He sent an angel and brought us forth out of Egypt" (Num. 20:16).

Maimonides likewise interprets the noun "angel" in the interpretation of the Dream of the Ladder in *Guide* I.15, albeit there he is interested in its meaning in the context of the ladder dream alone, and not in the various meanings of this equivocal term. He cites here the same verses which he subsequently quotes in II.6 to exemplify the use of the word "angel" in the sense of "prophet," albeit not as an exemplification of the biblical use of this equivocal noun, but rather as prooftext for his interpretation of "angels of God" in the Dream of the Ladder as "prophets." His interpretation here is not at all based on that of "angels" in his general theory of this noun. What is unique to Numbers 20:16 and Judges 2:1 is that the meaning of the word *mal'akh* is clear therein from the context. One may therefore rely upon these verses to argue that the word *mal'akh* ("angel") has the sense of "prophet" in the biblical lexicon. It would seem as if Maimonides here infers the meaning of the word *mal'akh* from the biblical text itself. Nevertheless, it seems to me that in this case as well we encounter one of the manifestations of biblical interpretation that relies in a covert way upon the midrash—in this case, the interpretation of equivocal words in the Bible on the basis of an interpretation already given them in the midrash. Maimonides evidently had in mind *Leviticus Rabbah* 1.1 (or one of its parallels),[40] which infers from these selfsame verses that the noun "angel" in the biblical lexicon also has the meaning of "prophet." Maimonides evidently relies here,

---

40 *Numbers Rabbah*. 16.1; *Tanḥuma* (Buber ed.,) *Shelaḥ* §1.

by implication, on the fact that the Sages already learned the equation, "angel=prophet," from these verses:

> The prophets are called angels. It is written there, "And He sent an angel and brought us forth out of Egypt" (Num. 20:16). And was he an angel? Are we not speaking of Moses; why then did he call him an angel? Rather, we learn from this that the prophets are called angels. Similarly, "Now the angel of the Lord went up from Gilgal to Bochim" (Judg. 2:1). And was this an angel? Was it not Phinehas? Why then was he called an angel? Rather, R. Simon says: At the time that the Holy Spirit rested upon Phinehas, his face burnt like a torch. R. Yohanan said: From their classical case (*Beit Av*), we infer that the prophets are called angels. It is written, "Then Haggai, the messenger [*mal'akh*] of the Lord, spoke to the people with the Lord's message" (Haggai 1:13). Of necessity, you infer from this classical case (*Beit Av*) that the prophets are called angels. (*Leviticus Rabbah* 1.1)

This midrash is itself mentioned by Maimonides in *Guide* II.42 in the name of the "Sages," and he even quotes a passage from it:

> With regard to the dictum: *And the angel of the Lord came up from Gilgal... And it came to pass, when the angel of the Lord spoke these words unto all the children of Israel* [Judg. 2:1-4]; the Sages have already literally stated that the *angel of the Lord* mentioned here was Phinehas. They said: *This was Phinehas who, when the Indwelling descends upon him, resembles an angel of the Lord.*[41] We have already explained that the term *angel* is equivocal and that a prophet may likewise be called an *angel*, as is said in the text: *And sent an angel, and brought us forth out of Egypt* [Num. 20:16]. It also says: *Then spoke Haggai the Lord's angel in the Lord's message* [Hag. 1:1]. And it says: *But they mocked the angels of God* (2 Chron. 36:16). (p. 276/

41 In the extant text: "his face was burning like torches."

pp. 389-390)[42]

From his words here it is clear that he relies upon the midrash in determining that angel means prophet. It would appear that in *Guide* II.6 he integrates his linguistic theory of the equivocal term "angel" with the prooftext which the midrash finds in the Bible for the interpretation, angel=prophet.[43]

Maimonides does not at all interpret the meaning of the verbs *yarad* and *ʿalah* in *Guide* I.15. He assumes that the reader is already familiar with *Guide* I.10, in which he systematically explains this pair of opposing verbs and their significances, and that he is capable of choosing here that meaning most suitable to the interpretation of the Dream of the Ladder. According to *Guide* I.10, "descend" and "ascend" are equivocal terms of the logical type that relate to one another in a relationship of opposition. Thus, in each one of their meanings, the meaning of the one will be the opposite of the other. In fact, "descend" and "ascend" are the dynamic aspects of "place," whose equivocal nature has already been discussed by Maimonides in *Guide* I.8, and whose meanings are parallel to those of *maqom* ("place"). As the primary meaning of the word "place" is physical, "a particular and general place," so too "descend" and "ascend" have a primary meaning in the sense of "moving from a certain place to a lower place" and "moving from a certain place to a higher place than the place in which it was." Parallel to this, in the borrowed sense, "place" refers to "an individual's rank and situation; I mean to say with reference to his perfection in some manner" (p. 22/p. 33). In similar fashion, "descend" and "ascend" refer in the borrowed sense to "sublimity and greatness." Thus, "when an individual's rank was lowered, he was said to have descended (*yarad)*; when, on the other hand, his rank became higher in respect of sublimity, he was said to have ascended (*ʿalah).*" (p. 24/p. 36). From this borrowed meaning of "descend" and "ascend," an additional pair of meanings is derived. Just as place may refer to "a rank in theoretical speculation and the contemplation of the intellect" (p. 23/p. 34), so, too, "descend" and "ascend" may refer to the dynamic

42 The verse from Chronicles only appears in the printed edition of *Tanḥuma, Shelaḥ*, §1.

43 A similar phenomenon also appears in Maimonides' interpretation of the word *ben* ("son") in *Guide* I.7. Maimonides interprets the word here in the sense of "disciple," inferring this meaning from the expression "the sons of the prophets." Here too he relies by implication upon the midrash, at *Sifrei, Va'etḥanan*, §34; and see on this *in extenso* in Klein-Braslavy, *Adam Stories*, pp. 267–270.

aspect of speculation. From the human viewpoint, the apprehension of the intelligibles and of God would be an "ascent," whereas directing their gaze in the opposite direction—towards the realm of action as opposed to the realm of theory—would be a "descent." Or, to use Maimonides' language: "When a man directs his thought towards a very mean object, he is said to have descended; and similarly when he directs his thought toward an exalted and sublime object, he is said to have ascended" (p. 24/p. 36).

The reader who has already seen the allusion to this in Maimonides' words in Arabic: "Everyone who ascends does so climbing up this ladder, so that he necessarily apprehends him who is upon it" will understand that the "ascent" upon the ladder is an ascent in theoretical apprehension, and that he needs to apply the latter pair of borrowed meanings in his interpretation of the verbs "ascend" and "descend" in the Dream of the Ladder.

Maimonides' only exegetical comment in *Guide* I.15 regarding the meaning of the terms *yarad* and *ʿalah* ("descend" and "ascend") in the Dream of the Ladder refers to the order in which these verbs appear therein. According to his interpretation, the order of these verbs is the key to understanding the dynamic element in the Dream. In his view, this order is deliberate: "How well put (*mā aḥkam*) is the phrase *ascending and descending* (*ʿolim ve-yordim*), in which *ascent* comes before *descent*" (p. 28/p. 41). By means of the order of the verbs, the biblical parable conveys one of the central ideas of the biblical doctrine of prophecy and that of politics: that the prophet is an angel in the sense of being a messenger. His mission is expressed specifically in his descent, in his turning his thoughts towards the practical realm, towards human leadership. However, ideal political leadership is only possible after the "ascent," after intellectual apprehension. Therefore, for the prophet as ideal political leader, the ascent must precede the descent: "For after the *ascent* and the attaining of certain rungs of the ladder that may be known comes the descent with whatever decree[44] the prophet received[45]—with a view to governing and teaching the people of the earth"[46] (p. 28/p.

---

44 Pines, p. 41 n. 13, comments: "The Arabic word *amr* may also be translated 'matter' or 'thing.'" Ibn Tibbon translates likewise.

45 Here I have accepted the translation of Schwarz. Pines translated here, "the prophet has been informed of."

46 It may be that "and teaching the people of the earth" refers to instruction relating to the

41).[47]

As we have seen, the "ladder," according to Maimonides' interpretation of Jacob's dream here, is the physical world: the sublunar world and the world of the spheres. It is depicted in Jacob's dream from three different perspectives: in itself, or from the ontological perspective; from the viewpoint of the human being, who knows the physical world in a hierarchical manner (and, in man's cognition, the ladder is transformed into "the ladder of wisdoms"); and finally, as it is known by the prophet, the ideal leader who sees in it a model for emulation in the process of political leadership. Maimonides relates to this last level of cognition in his explanation of the dynamic aspect of the Dream of the Ladder, which requires here some further explanation.

The interpretation of the dynamic element in the Dream of the Ladder parallels Maimonides' interpretation of Moses' request prior to the revelation in the Cleft of the Rock and his interpretation of that revelation per se; thus, it may be explained by its means. In *Guide* I.54, Maimonides explains God's words to Moses prior to the revelation in the Cleft of the Rock: "I will make all My goodness pass before you" (Exod. 33:19) as God's promise to Moses: "This dictum—*All My goodness*—alludes to the display to him of all the existing things, of which it is said: *And God saw everything that He had made, and, behold, it was very good* [Gen. 1:31]. By their display, I mean that he will apprehend their nature and the way they are mutually connected so that he will know how He governs them in general and in detail" (p. 84/p. 124).

This apprehension is none other than apprehension of the "ways" of God, which are His attributes of action. In the revelation in the Cleft of the Rock, Moses is thus promised knowledge of the entire physical world and its internal connections, not as themselves, but as an attribute of God's action. By means of this cognition, physics is elevated to the level of metaphysics, and knowledge of physics becomes the positive knowledge of God that is possible for man.

This interpretation well suits Maimonides' interpretation of Jacob's

---

commandments. However, it seems more likely that this phrase refers to instruction relating to theoretical, philosophical contents. The political leader conveys to the inhabitants of the state the philosophical principles, knowledge of which leads to the attainment of that "happiness" which is the goal of the ideal state.

47 The aspect of "descent" in the Dream of the Ladder is emphasized by L.V. Berman, "Maimonides on Political Leadership." In *Kinship and Consent* (Ramat Gan, 1981), p. 117 and n. 18 (Hebrew).

Dream of the Ladder. The "ladder," as we have seen, is none other than the physical world. Its knowledge by the prophets is their cognition thereof as God's attribute of action. This cognition is different from that of "he who ascends on the ladder"—that is, from advanced philosophical knowledge in a graduated manner of physics, or study of the science of physics in order to arrive in the final analysis at knowledge of the existence of God as the cause of motion of the highest sphere.

Moses expresses his apprehension of the revelation in the Cleft of the Rock in the words: "The Lord, the Lord, a God merciful and gracious, slow to anger and abounding in steadfast love and faithfulness," etc. (Exod. 34:6-7). According to Maimonides' interpretation, Moses here translated into the language of the "Thirteen Qualities (13 *middot*)," which is that of ethical qualities, his apprehension of those aspects of the physical world concerned with giving existence to man and providence over him. He drew an analogy between the human being, who performs various activities, and God, who performs similar actions within nature, expressing the apprehension of these Divine actions by means of the names of those same qualities which are the source of analogous activities in man. In interpreting the Thirteen Qualities, Maimonides explains: "Scripture has restricted itself to mentioning only these thirteen qualities, although [Moses] apprehended all His goodness—I mean to say, all His actions—because these are the actions proceeding from Him, may He be exalted, in respect of giving existence to the Adamites [i.e., human beings] and governing them" (pp. 84-85/pp. 124-125). These Thirteen Qualities are none other than part of God's attributes of action; that same portion that served Moses as the model according to which he led the people. This interpretation of the Thirteen Qualities is most suitable to the description of the prophets who "ascend" the "ladder" according to Maimonides' interpretation: "For after the *ascent* and the attaining of certain rungs of the ladder that may be known..." (p. 28/p.41)

"Certain rungs of the ladder," based upon the parallel between the Dream of the Ladder and the revelation in the Cleft of the Rock, refers to the Thirteen Qualities.[48] The prophets who "ascend" the ladder

48 On the basis of this analogy, it seems to me that one should not accept the proposed interpretation of A. Altmann, according to which "certain levels of the ladder" are certain different levels of prophecy. See his article cited above (n. 2), p. 58.

only "descend" after they attain apprehension of those attributes of Divine action whose concern is the giving of existence of human beings and their guidance, for only these attributes of action serve them in guiding the people in accordance with the principle of *Imitatio Dei*.[49] In the Dream of the Ladder, the idea of imitation of God is presented by means of the order of the verbs, "ascend" and "descend"; it is for that reason that Maimonides so strongly emphasizes this order. The verbs "ascend" and "descend" in themselves indicate the manner and value of these actions from the viewpoint of speculation. In the revelation in the Cleft of the Rock, according to the interpretation given to it by Maimonides, the idea is clearer. In Exodus 33:13, Moses asks God: "Show me now Your ways, that I may know You and find favor in Your sight. Consider too that this nation is Your people." This verse, according to Maimonides' interpretation, is divided into four units of meaning: 1) Moses' request from God for apprehension of the attributes of action; 2) the claim that by apprehending the attributes of action man arrives at knowledge of God or, to be more precise: that knowledge of God which it is possible for a human being to attain in a positive manner, is none other than knowledge of the attributes of action; 3) the personal goal of apprehending God's attributes of action or of knowledge of God is drawing close to God, another aspect of which is individual providence; 4) the ultimate purpose of Moses' apprehension of the Divine attributes of action is not only intellectual perfection, drawing close to God, and attaining individual providence, but a political goal—namely, leadership of the people by imitating God's actions in the world: "This was [Moses'] ultimate object in his demand, the conclusion of what he says being: *That I may know Thee, to the end that I may find grace in Thy sight and consider that this nation is Thy people*—that is, a people for the government of which I need to perform actions that I must seek to make similar to

49 On the question of *Imitatio Dei*, see especially L.V. Berman, "The Political Interpretation of the Maxim: The Purpose of Philosophy is the Imitation of God," *Studia Islamica* 15 (1961), pp. 53-61; *idem*, "Maimonides on Political Leadership" (op cit.) p. 122, n. 7; A. Altmann, "Maimonides' 'Four Perfections,'" *Israel Oriental Studies* 2 (1972), pp. 15–24; S. Pines, *Between Jewish Thought and Thought of the Nations* (Jerusalem, 1977), pp. 162-163 (Hebrew); E. Goldman, "The Special Labor in Attaining Truths," *Shenaton Bar-Ilan* 6 (1968), pp. 309-312 (repr in E. Goldman *Expositions and Inquiries – Jewish Thought in Past and Present*, A. Sagi and D. Stattman, ed. (Jerusalem 1996) (Hebrew); Z. W. Harvey, "Political Philosophy and Halakhah in Maimonides – Appendix: The Perfection of Man and the Political Imitation of God," *Bina* 3 (1994), pp. 58-59.

Thy actions in governing them (pp. 84-85/p. 125).[50]

Towards the end of his interpretation of the revelation in the Cleft of the Rock, it becomes clear that Maimonides understands this revelation as a model for proper conduct of the prophet-leader in general, and not only as an interpretation of the historical story of Moses' ascent to Mt. Sinai—and hence as pertaining to the issue of the uniqueness of Moses' prophecy. He writes: "It behooves the governor of a city, if he is a prophet, to acquire similarity to these attributes, so that these actions may proceed from him" (p. 86/p. 126).

In terms of this aspect, the dynamic part of the parable of the ladder, concerned with the model of behavior of the ideal prophet–leader, is parallel to the revelation in the Cleft of the Rock. The "angels" are parallel to Moses, in that they served him as a model of emulation for the behavior of the prophet-leader.[51]

It seems to me that the parallel between the interpretation of the dynamic element in the Dream of the Ladder and the revelation in the Cleft of the Rock may be explained by means of the assumption that what led Maimonides to interpret this aspect of the dream was the midrash in *Genesis Rabbah* 68.12, which I presented at the beginning of my discussion of the interpretation of the Dream of the Ladder in *Guide* I.15. According to this midrash, the "angels" are Moses and Aaron, who are referred to as "angels" (*mal'akhim*) in the plural, but the one who "ascends" and "descends" the ladder is in fact Moses alone. Nevertheless, as may easily be demonstrated, Maimonides does not use the midrash here to interpret the biblical text. Rather, he borrows from the midrash only its interpretation of the realm of meaning of the Dream of the Ladder—namely, that it relates to Moses' ascent of Mt. Sinai. The significant ascent of Mt. Sinai is not Moses' first ascent, described by the Bible in Exodus 19, to which the midrashim relate in their interpretations of "ascending" and "descending" and "behold the Lord stands above it," but rather the second ascent—namely, the revelation in the Cleft of the Rock related in Exodus 33–34. As we have seen, the revelation in the Cleft of the Rock plays a central role in *Guide of the Perplexed,* where it

---

50 See Shem Tov's interpretation, in which he compares the parable of the ladder to Maimonides' interpretation of the revelation in the Cleft of the Rock (pp. 32b-33a). Both Efodi and Crescas interpret the "ladder" as parallel to Moses' apprehension in the revelation of the Cleft of the Rock.

51 To both of these interpretations there is an additional exegetical parallel: namely, the interpretation of Jer. 9:23 in *Guide* III.54.

is used to explain the apprehension of the ideal man, the significance of the knowledge of God, the means of drawing close to God and attaining providence, and the image of the prophet as the ideal political leader. Maimonides thus interprets the midrashic idea, according to which the subject of the Dream of the Ladder is Moses' ascent of Mt. Sinai, in terms of the revelation in the Cleft of the Rock. Through the interpretation given this in the *Guide*, he sees the hidden level of Jacob's prophetic dream as parallel in meaning to that of a historical event—namely, the revelation in the Cleft of the Rock.

In light of this statement, one may reexamine Maimonides' interpretation of the static element in the Dream of the Ladder. It seems that there, too, a parallel exists between the Dream of the Ladder and the revelation in the Cleft of the Rock. In the latter revelation, God says to Moses, "Behold there is a place by Me, where you shall stand upon the rock." Maimonides interprets this verse in Book I of the *Guide,* in Chapters 8, 15 and 16, as well as alluding to it in Chapter 54, where he interprets the revelation in the Cleft of the Rock in detail. "Behold there is a place by Me" signifies "a rank in theoretical speculation and the contemplation of the intellect—not that of the eye" (p. 23/p. 34), whereas "you shall stand upon the rock" means "Rely upon, and be firm in considering, God, may He be exalted, as the first principle. This is the entryway through which you shall come to Him, as we have made clear when speaking of His saying [to Moses]: *Behold, there is a place by Me* (*Guide* I.16; p. 28/p. 42). The ascent to Sinai of Moses, "the Master of the Sages," is parallel to the first "ascent" of which Maimonides speaks in his interpretation of the Dream of the Ladder, that of: "everyone who ascends does so, climbing up this ladder, so that he necessarily apprehends him who is upon it" (p. 28/p.41). This is by way of discursive apprehension of the perfect philosopher, who comes to know gradually the physical world, and at the end of this path apprehends God as "standing upon it (the ladder)" or as the "rock" who is the "principle (*al-mabda'*) and the efficient cause of all things other than Himself" (p. 28/ p. 42). The apprehension of God as "the principle and efficient cause" precedes the revelation in the Cleft of the Rock, in which Moses sees, according to Exodus 33:23, the "back" of God. "And you shall see My back" is interpreted by Maimonides as "thou shalt apprehend what follows Me, has come to be like Me, and follows necessarily from My will—that is, all the things created by Me" (*Guide* I.38; p. 59/p. 87). It is this apprehension that is expressed in Exodus 34:6-7 by the Thirteen Qualities. The apprehension of the attributes of action of God in the sense of the "back" of God or the "Thirteen Qualities" is paralleled, in Maimonides' interpretation of the Parable of the Ladder, to a further "ascent": the ascent of the prophets on the ladder. The ascent of the prophets is thus not parallel to Moses' ascent on Mt. Sinai, as interpreted by the midrash, but rather to the second revelation to Moses after he ascended Mt. Sinai. In this respect, Maimonides deviates from the midrashic interpretation, although remaining loyal to its spirit. He reworks here the interpretation of the midrash and incorporates it within the frame of his own biblical interpretation in the *Guide of the Perplexed*—the interpretation of the revelation in the Cleft of the Rock—and to the philosophical–theological ideas that lie at its basis.

To summarize: it seems to me that the fact that Maimonides, in his writings, offers three different interpretations of Jacob's Dream of the Ladder is well explained by the fact that his interpretations are rooted in the midrashim which were expounded on this dream. In each one of his interpretations, Maimonides made use of a different midrash in order to understand the hidden level of the parable of the ladder. The three interpretations we have seen here may serve as a basic model for different types of biblical interpretation by means of midrash as found in Maimonides' writings.

Strategy for Interpreting "Woman" n the *Guide of the Perplexed*

In the *Guide of the Perplexed,* Maimonides is especially preoccupied by the motif of "woman." He interprets three types of biblical literary units that are concerned with woman: a word, a metaphor, and an allegory. In this paper I will focus on his strategy for interpreting these literary units. I will argue that the main strategy he employs is that of a "structure of relation"— the types of relations that "woman" has with other objects, mostly "man." These relations are the key for understanding the meaning of "woman" in the biblical texts.

I will analyze his explanations by increasing scale of the literary unit, proceeding from the single word, the equivocal term "woman" [*ʾishah*] (*Guide* I.6), to the metaphor of the "married harlot" (*ʾeshet ʾish zonah*), derived from Proverbs 6:26 (*Guide* III.8), and finally two allegories— the "married harlot" [*ʾeshet ʾish zonah*] in Proverbs 7 (Introduction to the *Guide*) and "a woman of virtue" [*ʾeshet ḥayyil*] in Proverbs 31:10–31 (*Guide* III.8).[1]

Maimonides believes that the Bible contains esoteric doctrines that should be concealed from the masses and conveyed only to the intellectual elite. These are truths that are liable to harm the masses' religious belief.[2] The most important such doctrines are the "Account of the Beginning" and the "Account of the Chariot," which deal, according to Maimonides, with Aristotelian physics and metaphysics, respectively. Esoteric doctrines should be transmitted by esoteric methods. In the *Guide,* Maimonides elaborates special methods of transmission that enable him to teach these truths to qualified readers and conceal them from the uneducated masses. An analysis of his biblical interpretations shows, however, that in the *Guide* he provides exoteric philosophical interpretations, too, of biblical texts. Evidently he saw no reason to

---

1 Although Maimonides regards Proverbs 31:10–31 as an allegory, he interprets (as we shall see) only the metaphor "a woman of virtue" on which it is based.

2 On Maimonides' concept of esotericism, see Klein-Braslavy, *Esotericism*.

conceal philosophical truths that are not liable to harm the belief of the masses of his time, although they would not always be able to understand them.[3]

Because Maimonides does not think that explanations of the figurative meaning of the equivocal term *'ishah*, the metaphor "a married harlot," and the allegories of "a married harlot" and of "a woman of virtue" can harm the masses' belief, he provides clear exoteric interpretations for all of them.

1. *The Interpretation of the word "woman" ['Ishah]*

As it is well known, most of the first part of *Guide* I (42 chapters) consists of what can be called a biblical-philosophical lexicon of equivocal terms. Maimonides presents it as the basis for interpreting those biblical verses and passages in which a faulty comprehension of equivocal terms is liable to cause the entire verse or passage to be misunderstood. Most of these terms refer to God: some are words used to depict God and his actions; others, to convey the human apprehension of God and attitude toward Him. The primary purpose of this lexicon is to eliminate any corporealization of God in the Bible, although it does have other goals in supporting Maimonides' interpretation of the "Account of the Beginning," the "Account of the Chariot," and prophecy— esoteric verses and passages and "secrets of the Torah." Some chapters in the lexicon explain equivocal terms that are not related to God in the Bible. *Guide* I.6, which explains the words "man" [*'ish*] and "woman" [*'ishah*], is one of them.[4]

Most of the equivocal terms explained in the lexicon of the first part of the *Guide* are derived terms, with an original sense and a "borrowed" meaning or meanings. The original signification generally refers to physical objects and their properties or to their sensory or imaginative apprehension. The derivative meaning or meanings are more abstract. They are constructed on the basis of properties common to the original object and the object that borrows its name. An object borrows the name of another object when it has the same property or properties that characterize the original object.

3 For the issue of exoteric and esoteric biblical interpretations in the *Guide*, see (in this volume) "Maimonides' Exoteric and Esoteric Biblical Interpretations in the *Guide of the Perplexed*."

4 Similar chapters include *Guide* I.7, which explains "to bear children" [*yalod*], and *Guide* I.14, which explain the word *adam*.

The nouns "man" and "woman" are of this type. Their primary and best-known meaning is human male and human female. They also have two derivative meanings. The first is "male or female among the other species of living beings" (p. 31) and not just the human species. Maimonides explains the second derivative meaning only for "woman." It is this meaning that interests us for an understanding of his biblical exegesis.

Maimonides regards the noun "woman" in its second derivative meaning as a term that has an intension or a meaning but not an extension or a reference.[5] This type of term specifies the feature a thing must possess in order to be recognized as referred to by it. In other words, it designates a class of objects that share a common feature. The specific referents of the class can be identified by the context in which the member of the class appears and by its supposed semantic axis.[6]

The common feature shared by the members of the class "woman" is not a property but a type of relation that every member of the class has with another object. "Woman" is "any object apt for, and fashioned with a view to being in conjunction with some other object" (p. 31). Every object that has this type of relation is a member of the class "woman" and can be called, figuratively, "woman."

Because the second derivative meaning of the word "woman" is "a structure of meaning," "woman" can turn texts in which it appears into metaphors or allegories. On the literary level, "woman" may have either its original meaning or its first derivative meaning. On the inner level, readers must identify its referent on their own, taking into account the intension of the word—i.e., its "structure of meaning"— the context in which it appears, and its semantic axis. Because Maimonides believes that the semantic axis of the inner meaning of biblical texts is Aristotelian philosophy, understanding "woman" in this way permits a philosophical non-literal interpretation of biblical texts alongside a

5 The intension of an expression is the way in which the reference is presented (see *The Encyclopedia of Language and Linguistics*, edited by R. E. Ashen et al. (New York, 1994), vol. 3, p. 1198). I use the expression as Richard Montague defined it: the intension of an expression is a rule that allows one to determine its extension in each context (*ibid.*, vol. 4, p. 1700). The extension is what the expression refers to (*ibid.*, p. 1699).

6 Such terms include the words *'aḥot* (sister) and *'aḥ* (brother), which Maimonides mentions in this chapter, *reshit* (beginning) in Genesis 1:1 (*Guide* II.30), *ṣur* (rock) (I.16), *mal'akh* (angel) (II.6), and apparently *sulam* (ladder) (I.15), Maimonides only alludes to its interpretation. For an analysis of *reshit*, see (in this volume) "Exoteric and Esoteric Biblical Interpretations." pp. 215-219.

literal interpretation of the same texts.

Maimonides does not provide any direct examples of objects that are "apt for, and fashioned with a view to being in conjunction with some other object." In each chapter of the lexicon of biblical language Maimonides first presents the equivocal term or terms he will explain, followed by the various meanings. For each meaning he cites biblical verse(s) whose context allows one to understand the term there, thereby corroborating the meaning he attributes to it. The biblical verse Maimonides cites as his proof text for the contention that "woman" has a second derivative meaning—"Five curtains shall be coupled together, a woman to her sister" (Exod. 26:3)—confirms only the statement that the term has an intension, i.e., that it denotes a class of objects that have a common feature. It says nothing about the referent of the noun. The referents of the class "woman" (as well as of class "sister" [*'aḥot*]),[7] are mentioned in the first part of the verse: the five curtains. Citing the verse, Maimonides indirectly provides an example of a member of the class "woman" (and also the class "sister")—a curtain. Curtains can be called "woman" and "sister." However, the member of the class is referred to explicitly in the verse and is not denoted by the words "woman" and "sister."

Because Maimonides does not explain a second derivative meaning of "man" [*'ish*], we do not know whether he considers it to be a derivative term parallel to "woman," i.e., a noun that has an intension that is a "structural meaning." It is quite plausible that Maimonides does consider it to have an intension only, even though he nowhere defines the common features shared by the members of the class "man."

Maimonides does not explain how the figurative meanings of "woman" and "man" were derived. The derivation of the first figurative sense, "male or female among the other species of living beings," is clear. It is derived from the meanings male and female of the human species. Because human beings are members of the class "animal," the gender difference between the male and female of the human species was borrowed to designate the male and female of all members of the class "animal."

The second derivative meaning is not derived from the mere fact that a "woman" is a female, of the human or the animal species, but from what Maimonides considers to be the nature of the female. In his view,

7 According to this chapter, the noun "sister" (*'aḥot*) has the same derivative meaning as "woman."

the female is always apt to join the male and has a disposition to conjunction with the male. The derivative meaning of the noun "woman" builds on the female's relation with the male. But instead of applying it to an object that has the same type of relationship to another object— the normal way in which derivative or "borrowed" terms are constructed—here the borrowed relationship becomes the very meaning of the word "woman."

I do not know whether Maimonides is relying here on simple observation of nature, on a biblical verse, or on a philosophical doctrine. He may have in mind Gen. 3:16, "your desire shall be for your husband," and consider it to be a description of the female's nature. He may have been thinking of an Aristotelian text, such as *Physics* I, 9 $192^{a}22$–23[8] or Alfarabi's summary of Aristotle's *Sophistical Refutations*.[9] According to these, it is the nature of the female to yearn for the male. However, Maimonides does not say that "woman" designates any object that yearns for another object, as the verse in Genesis, Aristotle, and Alfarabi all assert. I tend to think that even if he relied on the biblical text he had the philosophical texts in mind as well. As we shall see later, there is a striking similarity between his interpretation of the metaphor "a married harlot" in *Guide* III.8 and Aristotle's contention, in the *Physics*, that matter is analogous to the female and form to the male. This similarity suggests that Maimonides may have had Aristotle's *Physics* and/or Alfarabi's summary in mind, though he formulated the relationship between the object designated by the figurative term "woman" and another object differently. But even if Maimonides did have these texts in mind, he could not have written *in the lexicon* that the noun "woman" denotes matter, because the lexicon relies on biblical language. From his biblical proof text for the second derivative meaning of "woman" he could infer only that "woman" is something with a predisposition to join another thing. There is no verse whose context can support the idea that, in biblical language, "woman" denotes matter.

8 The text was translated into Arabic by Isḥāq b. Ḥunayn. See J. T. Robinson, "Some Remarks on the Source of Maimonides' Plato in *Guide of the Perplexed* I, 17," *Zutot: Philosophy and Science* 3 (2003), pp. 54–55. Robinson refers to these texts for another purpose, namely, as possible sources for Maimonides' contention that "Plato and his predecessors designated Matter as the female and Form as the Male" (*Guide* I.17).

9 Cf. Robinson, "Some Remarks."

2. *The Interpretation of the Metaphor "a married harlot" ['eshet 'ish zonah]*

As we have seen, the name "woman" in its second figurative meaning has only an intension and not an extension or a referent. It has "a structure of meaning" consisting of the type of relationship that members of the class "woman" have with other objects. The "structure of meaning" makes it possible to determine the extension (referent) of the name in each given biblical text.[10]

Maimonides also provides an explanation based on the same strategy of interpretation—an explanation by a "structure of meaning"—for larger literary units involving "woman": a compound metaphor and allegories. In these interpretations he discerns a more complicated structure of relations. As with the explanation of the noun "woman," he regards the structure of relation of these units as the key for determining their referents and hence for understanding them.

Maimonides accepts the traditional view that King Solomon wrote the book of Proverbs. He considers him to be one of those who "speak through the Holy Spirit" (*Guide* II.45). In his view, Solomon is a philosopher who composed metaphors and allegories in order to convey philosophical truths and practical lessons.[11] In the Introduction to the *Guide* (p. 13), Maimonides asserts that the entire book of Proverbs is based on the compound metaphor "a married harlot," though he does not offer a demonstration thereof. He explains only the metaphor "a married harlot" (Prov. 6:26) and the allegories of "a married harlot" (chapter 7) and of "a woman of virtue" (31:10–31).

Maimonides does not cite any chapter or verse as the source of the metaphor. In fact, the expression "a married harlot" does not exist in the Bible and is Maimonides' own coinage, based on Proverbs. He probably derived it from the parallelism in Proverbs 6:26: "For a harlot's [*'ishah zonah*] fee is only a loaf of bread but a married woman [*'eshet 'ish*] preys on a precious soul."[12] The parallelism enables Maimonides to identify the harlot mentioned in the first half of the verse with the married woman in its second half and create the metaphor "a married

10 Note that the structure of relation constitutes the meaning of the noun "woman" independently of any context. Only the referent of the noun is context-dependent.

11 For Maimonides' view of Solomon, see Klein-Braslavy, *Esotericism*, pp. 109–188.

12 In *Guide* I.1 and III. 8 Maimonides himself creates an expression based on a biblical verse: the "image of God and His likeness" from Gen. 1:26, "Let us make man in our image, after our likeness."

harlot" (*'eshet 'ish zonah*).

Maimonides does not interpret the expression "a married harlot"; rather, he explains how Solomon created it. The philosophical interpretation of the text and the method of its composition are two sides of the same coin. The interpretation moves from the text to its philosophical meaning, while the explanation of its composition moves from the philosophical ideas to the biblical text and explains why the author chose to present it in the way he did.

In Maimonides' view, the philosophical idea that Solomon wanted to convey by the metaphor is the concept of sublunar matter. In *Guide* I.6 he does not explain how the figurative term "woman" was derived; here, by contrast, he does explain why Solomon chose the metaphor "a married harlot" to represent sublunar matter. The explanation is based on the properties of matter according to Aristotle. Because matter has no form it cannot be defined in itself, but only in its relation to form. In a brilliant exegetical insight, Maimonides has Solomon understand this property and choose an appropriate metaphor to represent it.

According to Maimonides, Solomon created the metaphor on the basis of an analogy between sublunar matter and a married harlot.[13] He says: "How extraordinary is what *Solomon* said in his wisdom when **likening** [*tashbīhihi*] matter to *a married harlot*" (p. 431, [emphasis mine]).[14]

The vehicle of Solomon's metaphor—a married harlot—has a structure of relations that is analogous to that of sublunar matter with forms. Her relations with men are like those between matter and forms. Their common dominator is not their properties but the type of relation they maintain with another object. The relationship defines the character of each of them.[15] On the one hand, in the sublunar world, matter is always

---

13 Maimonides' interpretation is easier to understand if we remember that the literal translation of *'eshet 'ish zonah* is "woman of a man*–harlot" (*i.e., married woman).

14 Maimonides does not distinguish between similes and metaphors. His explanation of the origin of the metaphor "a married harlot," however, suggests that he regards it as derived from a simile. The first step was, sublunar matter is *like* a married harlot. Then the word "like" drops out and the expression turns into a metaphor, "a married harlot."

15 Maimonides evidently believes that Solomon based the metaphor of a "married harlot" on the *image* of a married harlot and not on the linguistic consideration of the figurative meaning of the term "woman." It is possible, though, that he thinks that Solomon did take into account that the figurative term "woman" means "any object apt for, and fashioned with a view to being in conjunction with some other object" (p. 31). As we have seen, the figurative term "woman" has only an intension and not an extension. Its referent is to be identified by the context in which it appears and its semantic axis.

tied to a form. On the other hand, it does not have a permanent relation to one specific form. When substances composed of matter and form are generated and corrupted they put on a form and then discard it for another.

The metaphor "a married harlot," too, consists of both a binding and a non-binding relation. On the one hand, she is a wife, a "married woman" [*ʾeshet ʾish*] bound to the man who is her husband. On the other hand, she is a harlot [*zonah*] who is unfaithful to her husband and has transient relationships with other men. From the perspective that matter is always tied to a form, Solomon likened it to a married woman. In that it continually puts on one form and discards another, he likened it to a harlot:[16]

> The nature and the true reality of matter are such that it never ceases to be joined to privation; hence no form remains constantly in it, for it perpetually puts off one form and puts on another. How extraordinary is what *Solomon* said in his wisdom when likening matter to *a married harlot* (*ʾeshet ʾish zonah*) for matter is in no way found without form and is consequently always like *a married woman* (*ʾeshet ʾish*) who is never separated from a *man* (*ʾish*) and is never *free* (*penuyyah*). However, notwithstanding her being *a married woman* (*ʾeshet ʾish*), she never ceases to seek for another man to substitute for her husband, and she deceives and draws him on in every way until he obtains from her what her husband used to obtain. This is the state of matter. For whatever form is found in it, does but prepare it to receive another form. And it does not cease to move with a view to putting off that form that actually is in it and to obtaining another form. (p. 431)

The metaphor "a married harlot" has a far richer meaning than does the figurative noun "woman"; in fact, it extends the meaning of that word. As we have seen, the common feature shared by the members of the class "woman" is a type of relation that each has with another thing. The metaphor "a married harlot" specifies the relation between

---

Solomon identifies the referent of the term "woman" in the metaphor "a married harlot" with sublunar matter on the basis of the context in which the term appears, i.e., on the basis of the specific relations this "woman" is said to have with men; she is both a wife and a harlot.

16 In fact, the analogy is not perfect: the married harlot is a wife and a harlot at the same time, but matter is always tied to one form. It merely changes the form to which it is tied. Maimonides seems to have overlooked the dimension of time in the relations of matter and forms and set up the metaphor only on the basis of the types of relations that matter has with forms and a married harlot has with men.

the member of the class "woman" referred to in Proverbs 6:26 and other objects. The class of objects defined by this relation is not that of objects that are merely "apt for, and fashioned with a view to being in conjunction with some other object," but the class of objects that are always joined to another object, but not necessarily always the same object.

The related objects of the members of the class "woman" are not specified. They are provided by the context in which the term appears. The metaphor "a married harlot" also indicates the object that "woman" is related to. She is *ʾeshet ʾish*, the woman of a man. The related object is "man."

In *Guide* I.6, Maimonides does not explain the second derivative meaning of the word "man" [*ʾish*]. The explanation of the origin of the metaphor "a married harlot" enables him to identify the referent of "man" in this context, on the basis of the analogy with the relations between matter and forms. "Woman" is the sublunar matter and "man" is the form—both the "husband" — the form of matter of each sublunar substance, and "other men," the forms that matter receives when it discards the form it currently has and puts on another one.

The explanation of the origin of the metaphor "a married harlot" and hence of how Proverbs 6:26 should be interpreted is exoteric. Maimonides explains the "structure of meaning" of the metaphor and identifies its referent. He does not think that explaining that Solomon conveyed the philosophical concepts "matter" and "form" by means of metaphors can harm the masses. However, he does not explain why Solomon conveyed this philosophical truth metaphorically rather than in scientific language.

As we have seen, it is plausible that the interpretation of the second derivative meaning of "woman" was influenced by Aristotle's *Physics* (I.9 192ᵃ22–23) or by Alfarabi's summary of Aristotle's *Sophistical Refutations*. The explanation of the way Solomon created the metaphor of "a married harlot" may also have been inspired by one of these texts, though here too Maimonides does not depict the female as "yearning" for the male but only as "seeking" for man [*ṭālibat rajul*]. It is worth noting, though, that the metaphor of "a married harlot" is subtler than that of the female in these texts; not only does it refer to matter, it also indicates its characteristic.

3. *The Interpretation of the Allegory of "a married harlot" ['eshet 'ish zonah]*

The largest literary unit concerned with "woman" that Maimonides interprets in the *Guide* is the allegory or the parable[17] (*mashal, mathal*), a text that has two meanings: an external literal meaning (*ẓāhir*) and an inner meaning (*bāṭin*).

In the Introduction to the *Guide* (p. 6), Maimonides promises to point out allegorical passages texts that are not explicitly identified as such in the Bible and to interpret some of them. Later in the Introduction, when he expounds a theory of the types of prophetic allegories, he identifies Proverbs 7 as one such. He presents it as an example of the second type of biblical allegory distinguished by this theory. Allegories of the second type are those that intend to convey a main idea. Not every detail on the external level has meaning on the inner level. Rather, most of them serve a literary purpose—to construct a well-written piece of literature in accordance with literary principles and conventions—and/or an esthetic purpose—to ornament and embellish the literal meaning. They may also serve an esoteric purpose—to create deliberate obscurity by burdening the text with details that have no meaning on the inner level. In this type of allegory, "*the parable as a whole* indicates *the whole* of the intended meaning" (p. 12; emphasis mine). This type of allegory is well-suited to philosophical interpretations of biblical texts. It can convey a philosophical idea, on the one hand, and overcome the problem of an "excess of information" on the literal level of the text, on the other.[18] An allegory works when it contains enough elements that can be interpreted allegorically. But it misses its goal if it contains too many elements, because these obscure the main idea the allegory intends to convey or do not fit in with its inner sense. Moreover, too many elements oblige readers to employ complicated methods of interpretation in order to make them tally with the main idea conveyed by the allegory. Maimonides seems to be aware of this danger and avoids it through this second type of allegory. Readers of such an allegory do not have to find a correlative on the inner level for every word or literary unit of the external level. They need only explain the main image and some of the

---

17 S. Pines usually translates *mashal, mathal* "parable."

18 For this problem, see J. Whitman, *Allegory: The Dynamics of an Ancient and Medieval Technique* (Cambridge, 1987), pp. 3–4.

important adjectives and verbs used. By asserting that most biblical allegories are of this type, Maimonides has the best of all possible worlds: he can interpret biblical texts as philosophical allegories without having to interpret every detail and without engaging in philological or pseudo-philological explanations of their meanings.

As we have seen, Maimonides does not explain why Solomon used the metaphor of a "married harlot" to convey the idea of the sublunar matter. Two explanations, both in accordance with Maimonides' doctrines, can be suggested. First, Maimonides held that Solomon considered the idea of sublunar matter to be an esoteric doctrine and concealed it from the masses using an expression that can be understood both literally and metaphorically. Second, Maimonides believed that Solomon was behaving like the ruler of the perfect state, as depicted by Alfarabi. According to Alfarabi, the religion of the perfect state presents philosophical ideas in figurative language in order to convey them to the masses in a way they can understand. In order to adapt his teaching to the comprehension of the masses, then, Solomon used an image that can be understood both literally and metaphorically. The metaphor of a "married harlot" should be considered to be an "educational myth" as understood by Alfarabi.

Interpreting Solomon's "married harlot" allegory, Maimonides says explicitly that it is esoteric. If so, perhaps the "married harlot" metaphor is also esoteric. But Maimonides does not think that, in his time, the meanings of the metaphor and allegory are liable to undermine the faith of the masses. Therefore, reducing the scope of biblical esotericism, he explains their esoteric content in an exoteric way.

According to Maimonides' interpretation, Proverbs 7 is an allegory built around the "married harlot." The key for understanding it is therefore the interpretation of this image. The details of the description of the married harlot and her behavior have no meaning in the hidden level; they are merely a literary device, a rhetorical description of the temptation exercised on a young man by a married woman who is also a harlot. Here Maimonides cites, one after another, parts of vv. 6–21 to show that they have no meaning on the internal level.

The allegory is a warning against pursuing a "married harlot." The warning itself is stated in vv. 24–25, verses that Maimonides does not cite: "And now, my children, listen to me and be attentive to the words of my mouth. Do not let your heart turn aside to her ways; do not stray into her paths." The description of the married harlot and her behavior (vv. 6–21) constitutes the object of the warning and hence its content. Because Maimonides presents Proverbs 7 as an example of an allegory of the second type, he is interested in the parts of the allegory that contain details that have no meaning on the inner level as well as in the metaphorical image that conveys the essential idea on which it is based. It is clear, though, that vv. 24–25 are also a part of the allegory.

As noted above, the collocation "married harlot" is not found in Proverbs 7. Maimonides coins it on the basis of the biblical text. Here he does not derive it from a single verse (Prov. 6:26) as in *Guide* III.8, but from the whole passage that describe the behavior of a married harlot (vv. 6–21).

Maimonides regards the allegory of a married harlot as a compound or creative allegory rather than an interpretative allegory.[19] He presents it as an allegory composed by Solomon in a way similar to how he presents the creation of the metaphor "a married harlot" in *Guide* III.8: "He [Solomon] likens matter which is the cause of all these bodily pleasures to a *harlot* who is also a *married woman*" (p. 13). Because compound and interpretative allegories imply each other, the explanation of how the allegory is produced is the key to interpreting it.

The "married harlot" is an "ethical allegory." Both its external and inner meanings deal with a practical rather than a theoretical issue: warning men against the pursuit of desire. Maimonides evidently believes that Solomon chose the literary form of allegory because it is a way to convey instruction to two types of audience: the masses and the intellectual elite. He adjusted the lesson to the intellectual capacities of each of them: the external level for the uneducated masses and the inner level for readers with philosophical knowledge. The external literal meaning teaches good behavior in a particular case, warning young men against pursuing a harlot who is married. Its aim is to educate young men. The inner meaning is philosophical. Because philosophy does not deal with particular cases, but only with general statements, it is a general instruction for conduct formulated in general terms: "a warning against the pursuit of bodily pleasures and desire" (p. 13). The young

19 For the two types of allegory, see Angus Fletcher, "Allegory," *Dictionary of the History of Ideas*, ed. Philip Wiener (New York, 1973), vol. 1, p. 41; Whitman, *Allegory*, pp. 3–4; *The New Princeton Encyclopedia of Poetry and Poetics*, ed. A. Preminger and T. V. F. Brogan (Princeton, 1993), p. 31.

man represents the human species and the warning is addressed to all its members. Though the allegory concerns a practical issue, it is based on principles of theoretical philosophy—more precisely, on philosophical anthropology—as represented by the metaphor of the married harlot. Hence the idea conveyed by "the whole allegory" is a warning based on a philosophical theory.

Though Maimonides does not say so explicitly, it is obvious that he considers the external meaning of the allegory to be important, just as it is in the case of Solomon's "well-constructed allegory" of "apples of gold in settings (*maskiyyoth*) of silver" (Prov. 25:11).[20] But as with the "well-constructed allegory" the external meaning of the allegory seems to be less important than the inner meaning.[21]

Because the image of the "married harlot" is derived from the verses that provide the content of the warning and (as we shall see) its reason as well, it is context-dependent and must be understood within the context of the chapter as a whole. Hence, even though here Maimonides explicitly relies on his explanation of the metaphor of the "married harlot" in *Guide* III.8, writing, "we shall explain in various chapters of this Treatise his [Solomon's] wisdom in likening matter to a *married harlot*" (p. 13), he interprets the expression in a different way than he does in *Guide* III.8. The context in which the metaphor appears is a warning against the pursuit of desire. So Maimonides does not identify the married harlot with the sublunar matter in general, as he did in *Guide* III.8, but with a specific kind of sublunar matter, namely, human matter, the matter of which human beings are composed.

Maimonides does not explain how Solomon derived the image of the married harlot. Since, however, he announces that in other chapters of the *Guide* he will explain Solomon's wisdom in likening matter to a married harlot, it is obvious that he attributes to Solomon the same strategy of composition that he ascribed to him with regard to the coinage of the "married harlot" metaphor in Proverbs 6:26: Solomon derived that image from an analogy between the relations that Aris-

20 Introduction, pp. 11–12.

21 It is important to note that the "married harlot" allegory is similar to the "well-constructed allegory" but is not an example of that type. In Maimonides' interpretation, both levels of the "well-constructed allegory" convey knowledge. The inner meaning conveys theoretical truths, whereas the external level conveys knowledge that is "useful in many respects, among which is the welfare of human societies" (p. 12). The allegory of the married harlot is practical and not theoretical. It conveys instruction for ethical behavior at both levels.

totelian philosophical concepts, or the objects they designate,[22] have with one another and the relations that the components of a figurative image have with one another. The relations are the key provided by Solomon for understanding the philosophical ideas conveyed by the allegory, just as they are the key for understanding the "married harlot" metaphor in *Guide* III.8.

Maimonides states that the relations between human matter and form are analogous to the relations between wife and husband and between the married harlot and other men. The meaning Maimonides attributes to the relations between the married harlot and her husband and with other men can be inferred from the end of the passage, where Maimonides promises to explain the character of another kind of woman described in the book of Proverbs, the "woman of virtue" (Prov. 31:10). He does not mention the actual expression (*'eshet ḥayyil*) but alludes to it by referring to its literal meaning:

> We shall explain how he concluded this book of his with a eulogy of the *woman* (*'ishah*) who is not a *harlot* (*zonah*) but confines herself to attending to the welfare of her household and husband. (Introduction, p. 13)

Maimonides mixes the literal and the inner meanings of the expressions when he contrasts a "woman of virtue" with a "married harlot."[23] The contrast reveals his conception of the role of the married woman and her ideal relations with her husband. The role of the wife is to serve her husband and to attend to the welfare of the household. This is a fair description of the wife's role in Maimonides' contemporary society.[24] The "woman of virtue" is the woman who fulfills this vocation. Because the "married harlot" is her antithesis, we may infer that she is a woman who does not do so: she serves men other than her husband and does not attend to the welfare of her household. The literal meaning of a "woman of virtue" supplies the basis for understanding the metaphor

---

22 In Aristotelian philosophy there is a correspondence between objects and concepts. Cf. Aristotle's *De Interpretatione*, I, 16^{a}3–8. Maimonides endorses this idea, probably under the influence of Alfarabi's *Commentary on De Interpretatione* (see *Al-Farabi's Commentary and Short Treatise on Aristotle's De Interpretatione*, trans. F. W. Zimmermann [London, 1981], p. 17), in *Guide* I.50.

23 As we shall see, in *Guide* III.8 he returns to the expression *'eshet ḥayyil* and explains it as a metaphor.

24 For a description of the wife's role, see Maimonides' *Mishneh Torah, Laws Concerning Marriage*, chapter 21.

of the "married harlot." Maimonides does not draw the conclusions from the contrast between the two kinds of women on the literal level of the text and skips immediately to explaining the "married harlot" as a metaphor without explaining its literal meaning.

Maimonides does not directly explain the word "man" (*'ish*) in the expression *'eshet 'ish zonah* (a married harlot). As in *Guide* III.8, however, the meaning he assigns to it is clear from his interpretation of the image of "a married harlot"; "man" (*'ish*) means man's form, the intellect.

The metaphorical "married harlot" refers to the role played by human matter in the substance "man"; human matter is the cause of the pursuit of bodily desires, a pursuit that prevents the intellect (*'ish*) from attaining its perfection.

The interpretation of the "married harlot" allegory is based on philosophical anthropology, a different philosophical theory than that used for the "married harlot" metaphor. The theory is presented in *Guide* III.8, in clear scientific language, immediately after Maimonides explains the origin of the "married harlot" metaphor. In this chapter Maimonides explains some principles in philosophical anthropology and does not refer to the "married harlot" allegory. However, this explanation completes the interpretation of the allegory of the married harlot in the Introduction to the *Guide* by providing its philosophical basis. In *Guide* III.8, Maimonides expands on the role played by human matter in the substance "man." He describes it as the cause of the body's "passing-away and corruption or deficiency" (*ibid.*), of the

> deformity of his [man's] form, the fact that his limbs do not conform to their nature, and also the weakness, the cessation, or the troubling of all his functions. ... Similarly every living being dies and becomes ill solely because of its matter. ... All man's acts of disobedience and sins are consequent upon his matter and not upon his form. (p. 431)

It is matter in this sense that is described here as the cause of bodily desires, namely, "his eating and drinking and copulation and his passionate desire for these things, as well as his anger and all bad habits found in him" (*ibid.*). In the Introduction to the *Guide,* Maimonides considers the married harlot to be a metaphor that represents only one of these functions: human matter is the cause of the pursuit of bodily pleasures and desires.

Because all sublunar matter is always tied to a form,[25] human matter is always tied to the human form, the intellect. Hence Solomon likened it to a married woman, a woman who is bound to a man (*'ish*). But matter is the cause of the bodily desires that prevent man from attaining his goal, intellectual perfection. Hence, Solomon likened it to a harlot who, instead of serving her husband, pursues other men and does not maintain the household.[26] The household is analogous to man's goal.

As we have seen, the allegory is centered on the metaphor of a "married harlot." The details of the description of the woman and her allures do not convey its meaning. The meaning of the allegory is conveyed by the allegory as a whole and not just by the image of the married harlot. The allegory is not just a statement about the role played by human matter, but a lesson of conduct based on the role of human matter. Because matter is the cause of bodily desire, which keeps man from attaining his goal, the warning against a married harlot is a warning against the pursuit of these desires and the pleasures of their realization.

Maimonides does not explain what human matter is. Matter is the substrate of form, that to which the form is joined. So human matter may refer either to the body, which is composed of the four elements and the two lower faculties of the soul (which, in Aristotelian psychology, are bodily forces), the vegetative and the animal souls; or solely to the animal soul, the soul that man shares with animals and which is the substrate of his form, the intellect. Because here he refers to *Guide* III.8 where he provides the philosophical doctrine on which the "married harlot" allegory is based, it is plausible that he regards matter as the temperament of the body. According to *Guide* III.12 (p. 445),[27] the temperament of the body is the cause of bodily desires.[28]

---

25 Maimonides states this explicitly in *Guide* III.8: "It is impossible for matter to exist without form" (p. 431).

26 If Maimonides considered that the analogy between a married harlot and the behavior of man's matter to be perfect, we must infer that the noun "man" does not always refers to "form" but only to the object woman it relates to. Man's matter is the cause of the pursuit of bodily desires, just as the harlot pursues other men. Here "men" are the objects of bodily desire. It follows from this analogy that the figurative term "man" is of the same type as the figurative term "woman"; it has an intension and not an extension. It denotes the object that the woman is "apt for, and fashioned with a view to being in conjunction with". This object should be identified by the context in which the word "man" figures.

27 Cf. also *Guide* II, premise twenty-six, p. 240.

28 It should be noted, however, that the sense of touch and the imagination are corporeal forces.

4. The Interpretation of the Allegory of "a woman of virtue" ['eshet Ḥayyil]

As we have seen, in the Introduction to the *Guide* Maimonides explains the plain meaning of the expression "a woman of virtue" (*'eshet ḥayyil*) in Proverbs 31:10. In *Guide* III.8 he returns to the expression. This time he interprets it as a metaphor and regards Proverbs 31:10–31 as an allegory. The chapter completes the interpretation of the images of the "two women" presented in the Introduction to the *Guide* and the allegories based on them.

Maimonides does not specify which type of parable the "woman of virtue" allegory is. Yet, it is obvious that, like the parable of "a married harlot," he considers it to belong to the second type described in the Introduction to the *Guide*. It too hinges on a metaphorical image, this time that of the "woman of virtue." Most of the words and the descriptions therein have aesthetic and literal functions and are meaningful only on the external. Consequently, in his explanation of the "woman of virtue" allegory, in *Guide* III.8, Maimonides does not even refer to the verses that describe her (Prov. 31:11–31), but only interprets the image "a woman of virtue" that conveys the meaning of the allegory.

The allegory of "a married harlot" is an ethical lesson that includes a statement about a philosophical doctrine—the role that matter plays in the substance "man." The allegory of "a woman of virtue" is not an ethical lesson but a description of the ideal woman. It conveys a theoretical truth—the role played by the matter of the ideal man. Maimonides does not explain the origins of the metaphor and the allegory and merely identifies the referent of the expression "a woman of virtue":

> As for [Solomon's] dictum *a woman of virtue who can find?* and this whole parable, it is clear. For if it so happens that the matter of a man is excellent, and suitable, neither dominating him nor corrupting his constitution, that matter is a divine gift. (p. 433)

It is obvious from the descriptions of the two kinds of woman and the identification of their referents that, in Maimonides' view, Solomon

(For the imagination as a corporeal force, see *Guide* II.36.) Hence elsewhere in the *Guide* Maimonides speaks of the sense of touch (*Guide* III.8) or of imagination (*Guide* III.12) as the cause of bodily desires.

created the expression "a woman of virtue" and the allegory constructed on it in a way similar to that he used to create the "married harlot" metaphor and allegory; that is, by an analogy between the relations represented by the image of "a woman of virtue" and by its referent. A married harlot and a woman of virtue are antithetical kinds of women and have antithetical types of relations. The married harlot is a woman who is not faithful to her husband, does not serve him, and serves other men. The woman of virtue serves her husband and her household and does not serve other men.

The metaphors are created on the basis of the analogy between the relations of man and woman in each case and the relations of the principles of philosophical anthropology. Hence their referents should be identified by these relations. In the expression "woman of virtue," "woman" is human matter (as in the metaphor "a married harlot"), but another kind of matter, a kind of that serves man and helps him to attain his goal—the perfection of the intellect. It is matter that does not provoke the pursuit of bodily desires.

According to *Guide* III.8, human matter is the temperament of the body. A "woman of virtue," like a "married harlot," represents the role of human matter in the pursuit of bodily desires. A "woman of virtue" is a special temperament of body, a harmonious temperament that does not cause the pursuit of bodily desires as human matter usually does. Maimonides describes it as "a divine gift" and rare phenomenon. We can infer from this statement that human matter usually triggers the pursuit of desires; i.e., it is more often a "married harlot" than a "woman of virtue."

Conclusion

We have seen that Maimonides employs the same strategy in all his interpretations of "woman"—an explanation by "a structure of relation" and by analogy. The referent of the term "woman," the metaphor "a married woman," and the images of a "married woman" and a "woman of virtue" at the center of the women allegories in the book of Proverbs are identified by the relations women maintain with another object or with men.

The noun "woman" has an intension but no extension. It designates the structure of relation itself. "Woman" is "any object apt for, and fashioned with a view to being in conjunction with some other object."

The referent of the noun must be identified by the context in which it appears.

The metaphor "a married harlot" and the metaphorical images "a married harlot" and "a woman of virtue" refer to two types of relation: the relation between a woman and her husband and between the woman and other men. Maimonides assumes that Solomon was a philosopher and expounded philosophical principles, doctrines, and lessons in figurative language. In his view, Solomon created the metaphors on the basis of an analogy between the relations that matter has with form or forms and the relations that "woman" in each of the metaphors has with men. The relations constitute "the structure of relation" on which the analogy is grounded.

The metaphor of the "married harlot" represents matter as a concept in Aristotelian physics—sublunar matter. Matter is always tied to a form, but not always the same form: it puts off and puts on forms. Hence it is analogous to the married harlot, who has a husband but also has relations with other men. The metaphors of a "married harlot" and a "woman of virtue" convey an idea in philosophical anthropology—the role that human matter plays in the attainment of man's vocation. "A married harlot" represents human matter as causing the pursuit of bodily desires and hence as an impediment to attaining perfection of the intellect. She is a wife, bound to one man; but she pursues other man instead of serving him and his household. She is analogous to human matter, which is joined to its form, the intellect, but also causes man to pursue bodily desires and thus prevents him from attaining his goal. The metaphor of a "woman of virtue" is created on the basis of only one type of relation—the relation of a woman to her husband. It represents a rare and special kind of human matter—matter that helps man attain his goal. The woman of virtue is a wife; she is bound to one man, serving him and his household, just as the man's good matter is tied to his form, the intellect, does not cause him to pursue bodily desires, and thereby helps him attain his perfection and the vocation of humankind.

Interpretative Riddles in Maimonides' *Guide of the Perplexed*

This paper offers an analysis of one of Maimonides' methods of esoteric biblical interpretation in the *Guide*—the method I call "the interpretative riddle." I maintain that this method has much in common with the riddle, especially the literary riddle, and that the theory of the literary riddle can help us understand its application in the *Guide*.

1. *The Theory of the Interpretative Riddle and its Presuppositions*[1]

Maimonides is a riddler. Rather than explain the meaning of biblical texts openly, he poses riddles (to which he knows the solution) and manipulates readers into finding the answer to them. The reader of the *Guide* is the "riddlee" and must come up with the correct answer in order to understand the hidden meanings of biblical allegories

The riddling situation is not public, as it often is in folk riddles, but private, as it is in literary riddles. Although the interpretative riddle is written in a book that is public, every reader has a private dialogue with Maimonides. Moreover, in his introduction to the *Guide* Maimonides asks readers to read the book for themselves "and not to explain to another anything in it" (Instructions with respect to this treatise, p. 15).

Whereas in the traditional riddling situation the poser approves or rejects the answer orally (in the case of the folk riddle) or in writing (the literary riddle),[2] Maimonides generally does not provide answers to his interpretative riddles in the *Guide*.[3] Readers cannot check their solutions and know whether they figured out the right answer.

The interpretation of biblical texts is a challenge for readers, as

---

1 In this part of my paper I relied mainly on: Robert A. Georges and Alan Dundes, "Toward a Structural Definition of the Riddle," *Journal of American Folklore* 76 (1963), pp. 111–118; Dan Pagis, "Toward a Theory of the Literary Riddle." In G. Hasan-Rokem and D. Shulman, ed., *Untying the Knot: On Riddles and Other Enigmatic Modes* (Oxford, 1996), pp. 81–108; Annikki Kaivola-Bregenhoj, *Riddles: Perspectives on the Use Function and Change in a Folklore Genre* (Helsinki, Finnish Literature Society, 2001).

2 It can be found at the end of the book or upside down at the bottom of the page. Cf. Pagis, "Theory of the Literary Riddle,"p. 84.

3 But see below on the Satan riddle.

riddles always are, but it serves a different function. Whereas the traditional riddle game is a competition between riddler and riddlee, the interpretative riddle of the *Guide* is a mode of communication, a way of teaching or conveying information to its readers. Maimonides' *Guide* is written according to the tradition, widespread in Greek and Islamic thought, that knowledge should be divulged only to those worthy of receiving it and able to understand it and withhold from others.[4] The riddle suits the esoteric purpose of the book because it conceals and conveys information at the same time.

Riddles have two parts: the image or the question and the answer. According to Georges and Dundes, the image or question generally contains a descriptive element, which is the minimal structural unit of the riddle. The descriptive element consists of a "topic" and a "comment." "The topic is the apparent referent; that is, it is the object or item allegedly described. The comment is an assertion about the topic, usually concerning the form, function, or action of the topic";[5] it describes the characteristics of the referent. In most (but not all) cases, the image stands in metaphorical relationship with the answer.[6] The topic and the referent form a pair that have some characteristics in common. These characteristics are the object of the comments. They direct the riddlee to the identification of the referent. Riddles may contain several descriptive elements and hence several comments that enable the riddlee to solve them.

Maimonides' interpretations of biblical and midrashic allegories concentrate on the nouns in the text, though he also explains verbs, thereby offering an interpretation of the entire story told by the allegory, and not just of separate words (as in the Stoic allegorical interpretations of Homer and Hesiod). Accordingly, the interpretative riddles turn on the objects of the story, animate or inanimate substances, and ask "who is?" or "what is?"

Some of the riddles are short and simple, with only one descriptive element. Most of them are complex and sophisticated, with several de-

4 Cf. Klein-Braslavy, *Esotericism*, pp. 15–27; Dimitri Gutas, *Avicenna and the Aristotelian Tradition: Introduction to Reading Avicenna's Philosophical works* (Leiden and New York, 1988), pp. 225–234.

5 Georges and Dundes, "Structural Definition of the Riddle," p. 13.

6 The metaphorical character of the riddle was already stated by Aristotle in *The Rhetoric* III.2. For a modern analysis of metaphor in riddles, see, for example, Elli Kongais-Maranda, "Theory and Praxis of Riddle Analysis," *Journal of American Folklore 84* (1971), p. 54.

scriptive elements and comments of diverse types. The complexity of these riddles is increased by another method of Maimonides' esoteric interpretation—the method of scattering hints throughout the *Guide*.

There are two kinds of riddles: riddles for which the only precondition is that readers possess wit and intelligence, and riddles that require prior possession of some specific knowledge. Maimonides' interpretative riddles are of the second kind, addressed to the ideal reader of the *Guide* who knows Aristotelian philosophy. As we shall see, readers are also supposed to know Hebrew, to be familiar with the other chapters of the *Guide*, and to be able to apply them to solve the interpretative riddles. Only readers with this knowledge can cope with the challenge posed by Maimonides' interpretative riddles and answer them.

In the following pages I will present two related interpretative riddles from the *Guide*, one dealing with the creation of Adam and Eve and the other with the character of the serpent in the Garden of Eden pericope. I want to show that Maimonides uses the method of the interpretative riddle as an esoteric device to convey his interpretations. I will analyze the structure of the riddles, explain the type of comments he employs, and point out the kinds of knowledge readers must have in order to solve each of them.[7]

I will also show that because the comments of the interpretative riddles are comments on biblical and midrashic allegories they shed light on the ways in which, according to Maimonides, the allegories were created.

Because my approach is experimental and I examine only two examples from the *Guide*, I do not pretend to exhaust the subject here, but only to point out some characteristics of this genre of biblical exegesis as manifested in the *Guide*. I believe that my approach is conducive to a better understanding of Maimonides' biblical exegesis in the *Guide*.[8]

2. *The Interpretative Riddle of the Story of the Creation of Man*

In *Guide* II.30 Maimonides interprets the stories of the creation of Adam and Eve and of the Garden of Eden. He views them as allegories

---

7 This paper analyzes the technique of the interpretative riddle. A full interpretation of the stories can be found in Klein-Braslavy, *Adam Stories*. Nevertheless, here I offer some revisions of my earlier interpretations.

8 For another type of "interpretative riddle" – the interpretation of the word *reshit* in *Guide* II. 30 see now (in this volume) "Maimonides' Exoteric and Esoteric Biblical Interpretation in the *Guide of the Perplexed*," pp. 215-219.

composed of personification of the human faculties of the soul, mental representations, and the elements of the substance "man" according to Aristotelian philosophy. The interpretation of the allegories consists mainly of identifying the philosophical concepts that correspond to these personifications.

In both cases he answers the interpretative question with Midrashim that he considers to be interpretative riddles. Because the function of the comments in the descriptive elements of the riddle is to provide information on the topic, Maimonides can use the aggadic expansions in the Midrashim (which add elements not found in the biblical text) as comments. Readers must take them into account in order to understand the text. This method is perfectly legitimate in the literary genre of the riddle.

The exegetical question addressed by the first interpretative riddle is: who are Adam and Eve? Maimonides cites a midrash from *Genesis Rabbah* (8.1), on Genesis 1:26, as the interpretative riddle that answers the exegetical question.

The midrashic riddle is a story that recounts an event in figurative language and contains a verbal image. According to it, Eve was not created after Adam but together with him. At first Adam and Eve were joined by their backs and formed one entity, a *diphrosophon*. The diphrosophon was the "first man." Only later was it split into two—Adam and Eve—and Eve was juxtaposed to Adam.

Maimonides does not quote the midrash verbatim but paraphrases it in Arabic. "*Adam and Eve* were created together, ... their backs joined, and ... this being was divided and one half of it, namely *Eve*, [was] taken and brought ... to [Adam]" (pp. 355–56). He does not add his own comment to the midrash but extracts the riddle it contains, phrasing it in scientific language. He eliminates the temporal meaning of the story and turns it into a timeless statement. The image of the diphrosophon and its division into two separate entities indicate the relationships between Adam and Eve. Translating the figurative language of the midrash into scientific language, Maimonides shows that the midrashic interpretative riddle is based on an antithesis:[9] "They were two in a certain respect and ... they were also one" (*ibid.*). The riddle of Adam and Eve is

9 Maimonides does not treat the two opposites equally. He emphasizes the unity of Adam and Eve and supports it by two biblical verses, Gen. 2:23–24.

similar to "oppositional riddles," the form of many traditional riddles.[10] Oppositional riddles contain only a seeming contradiction, which riddlees must resolve in their answer. Maimonides presents the opposition as noncontradictory; Adam and Eve were two "in a certain respect" and one in another respect. In his formulation, the midrash presents an opposition but provides the clue for understanding it as a seeming contradiction only.

The midrashic interpretative riddle is: Who are Adam and Eve, who were two in a certain respect but also one?

Riddles are based on common characteristics of the topic and the referent. The comment in the midrash, according to Maimonides' interpretation, is a "formal" one. It refers, not to common properties of Adam and Eve and their referents, but to relationships shared by them with their referents. These relations define their nature.

The interpretative riddle of Adam and Eve is addressed only to the ideal reader of the *Guide*. To solve it, readers must posses some prior knowledge—Aristotelian philosophy, especially Aristotelian anthropology—and have an acquaintance with other chapters of the *Guide*. They are then supposed to identify, in Aristotelian philosophy, the concepts or principals of the topic that the Bible and Midrash present in figurative language.

Readers can proceed in the following way. The biblical story speaks of Adam and Eve. They are male and female, man and woman. But because they are man and woman that are one entity, not two separate entities, they cannot be two historical persons. The biblical story is an allegory whose inner meaning is philosophical. Hence, readers must look for elements or principles of Aristotelian physics that have the same relationships as Eve and Adam in the external meaning of the allegory: both two and one. In the sublunar world, two principles satisfy this condition: matter and form. Matter and form are the two components of every physical substance. They are two; but because they never exist separately they are one substance.

The reader can also refer to other parts of the *Guide*: *Guide* I.17, where Maimonides writes that "Plato and his predecessors designated Matter as the female and Form as the male" (p. 43); *Guide* III.8, where he offers an explicit interpretation of "woman" and "man" in Proverbs

10 Cf. Georges and Dundes, "Structural Definition of the Riddle."

6:26 and identifies them with matter and form in the sublunar world (p. 431); and the introduction to the *Guide*, where he explains clearly that "woman" in Proverbs 7:6–22 is man's matter (pp. 13–14).

Because the biblical story speaks of the creation of man and woman and the Midrash speaks explicitly of "the first man," matter and form in the allegory of the creation of man and woman must be the matter and form of the substance "man" and not the general physical principles "matter" and "form." Readers can solve the interpretative riddle and identify Eve=female=woman with the matter of human beings and Adam=male=man with their form. Together they compose the substance "man."

3. *The Serpent in the Garden of Eden*

This riddle is more complex than the previous one and contains several descriptive elements. Finding its answer requires more preliminary knowledge as well.

This interpretative riddle answers the exegetical question, who is the serpent that seduced Eve in the story of the Garden of Eden? The riddle comprises two sets of descriptive elements—one found in the Midrash, as in the first riddle we looked at, the other offered by Maimonides himself.

Maimonides first cites midrash from *Pirqei de-Rabbi Eliezer* (ch. 13), which, he says, is an allegory written in figurative language that functions as an interpretative riddle.

As with the Adam and Eve riddle, Maimonides does not quote the midrash verbatim. This time he does not even paraphrase it, but only extracts the descriptive elements he believes it contains. Nor does he reformulate them in scientific language, as he did in the Adam and Eve riddle. He retains the figurative language of the midrash and translates it into Arabic. The midrashic interpretative riddle is composed of the narrative of an event, and a verbal description of an image, and an interpretative comment. For Maimonides, they are all descriptive elements of the riddle. The image, more precisely a moving picture, is of a serpent that looks like a camel and a supernatural being named Sammael that climbs up and rides it. The midrashic comment explains that it was Sammael and not the serpent that seduced Eve.

Maimonides identifies four descriptive units here. The first two refer directly to the serpent, which is the topic of the riddle: (1) "The serpent was ridden";[11] (2) "it was the size of a camel." The other two refer to the rider and to its role: (3) "It was the rider who led Eve astray" and (4) "the rider was Sammael." The identification of the rider and the explanation of its role are the comments. Their implicit topic is the Serpent. (3) means that it was the rider *and not the serpent* that led Eve astray. (4) means that the rider *of the serpent* was Sammael.

The additional information provided by the comments is the introduction to the story of another character—Sammael—and the statement that it was he who seduced Eve and not the serpent, as one would understand from the biblical text.

Using the midrash, Maimonides composes a riddle similar to that of Adam and Eve. The introduction of Sammael enables him to hint at the interpretation of the serpent by pointing to the *relationships* between the two protagonists. As in the Adam and Eve riddle, the relationships provide the clue to the solution. But the serpent riddle has more descriptive units and hence more comments than that of Adam and Eve.

In order to understand this clue readers must identify Sammael. Maimonides presents Sammael's identity in the form of a new interpretative riddle, thus constructing a riddle within a riddle.

The type of comment he uses here can be called an "equation hint." He tells his readers that the Sages identified Sammael with Satan.[12] Thus he prompts him to inquire about Satan in order to understand who Sammael is. Readers are supposed to be familiar with the entire *Guide* and should know that in *Guide* III.22 Satan is the subject of another interpretative riddle—this one about Satan in the scenes in heaven of the first two chapters of Job.

When posing the Sammael riddle Maimonides uses another exegetical device—linking two interpretative riddles: here, those of the serpent and of Satan. The link between the two enables readers to use the solution to one riddle to help answer the other riddle. Only readers who have correctly solved the Satan riddle can be helped by the "equation hint" Maimonides offers in *Guide* II, 30. Hence not only do riddlees have to possess philosophical knowledge and knowledge of other

11 Munk translates: "Le serpent, disent-ils, était monté par un cavalier" (II, p. 243); Pines translates: "That the Serpent had a rider "(p. 336). Schwarz translates: "it was a riding animal" (p. 368). I accept Ibn Tibbon's and Munk's translations.

12 He cites as a proof text Gen. 57:4 and adds an allusion to its parallel in B. Sanhedrin 89b. See Klein-Braslavy, *Adam Stories*, pp. 211–212.

chapters of the *Guide,* they must also come up with the right answer to the Satan riddle.

The Satan riddle in the book of Job is very complicated. Evidently Maimonides believed that there are two Satans in the story—one Satan who appears in the first scene in heaven and another Satan who appears at the second scene.[13] The identification of the second Satan is the clue for understanding Sammael.

As in the previous riddles, Maimonides finds the hint to the referent of Satan in the Talmud, this time in B. Baba Batra 16a. The hint is of the same type as Maimonides' own hint—an "equation hint."

Rabbi Simeon ben Laqish identifies Satan with both the *yeṣer ha-raʿ* (the Evil Inclination) and the *mal'akh ha-mawet* (the Angel of Death): "Satan, the evil inclination, and the angel of death are one and the same." For Maimonides, this statement is a riddle. The topic is "Satan"; the comment is "identical with the Evil Inclination and with the Angel of Death." Readers can try to solve it by themselves on the basis of their previous philosophical knowledge. They can also realize that Maimonides provides the solution elsewhere in *Guide* (II.12). Thus they can either learn the solution of the riddle from that chapter or use it to verify their own answer.

Here Maimonides behaves like the author of literary riddles who provides the solution to his riddles in the same book he poses them in. But the riddling situation in the *Guide* is different; Maimonides does not pose his riddle to entertain his readers or to examine their intellectual capacities, but rather as a device to teach them esoteric knowledge. Hence he uses one of the methods for conveying esoteric knowledge—scattering hints in different chapters of the *Guide* and offers the answer in an unexpected place in the book.

In *Guide* II.12 he explicitly identifies the referent of "the Evil Inclination," which is one of the members of the equation in ben Laqish's saying, as "imagination" (*khayāl*).[14] Readers who are acquainted with the

13 See S. Rosenberg, "On the Interpretation of the Bible in the *Guide,*" *Jerusalem Studies in Jewish Thought* 1/1 (1981), p. 134 (Hebrew); A. Nuriel, "Le-berur musag ha-Satan be-Moreh Nevukhim*: ṣiūnim shonim shel ha-Satan,*" *Jerusalem Studies in Jewish Thought* V (1986), pp. 83-91 (Hebrew).

14 Maimonides is not consistent in the use of *khayāl* in the *Guide* and gives it two meanings. In some chapters he understands *khayāl* as the images created by the imaginative faculty or stored in it (cf. Introduction to part 2, premise twenty-six, p. 240; II.1, p. 245; II.4, p. 255; II.37, p. 374; II.38, p. 377). On the other hand, in *Guide* II.29 he writes, "the correct thing to do is to refrain, if one lacks knowledge of the sciences, from considering these texts merely with the imagination

Introduction to the *Guide* understand the methodological statement there—"even [the chapter headings] are not set down in order or arranged in coherent fashion in the Treatise, but rather are scattered and entangled with other subjects that are to be clarified" (p. 6)—as a direction for reading the book. Thus they can apply it to understand ben Laqish's "equation hint." They can also note Maimonides' explicit instruction in the Introduction to the *Guide,* "you must connect its chapters one with another" (p. 15) and combine the two "equation hints"—that of the Sages: Sammael = Satan, and that of ben Laqish: Satan = the Evil Inclination = the Angel of Death—and add "imagination" to the equation. This creates a new equation: Sammael = Satan = the Evil Inclination = the Angel of Death = imagination and solve the Sammael riddle by identifying Sammael with imagination.

To solve the Serpent riddle, readers must draw on all four midrashic comments as well as the solution of the Sammael-Satan riddle. One comment makes it possible to understand the other or confirms its meaning.

As we have said, both the midrashic descriptive elements and Maimonides' report of them are written in figurative language. Three of them emphasize aspects of the image of the rider and his mount. Riddlees can regard them as metaphors and interpret them on their own: A mount—a "ridden" beast—is an animal that is controlled by its rider and does not move at its own initiative; the rider is a controller. These are relative terms, defined by their relations to each other. The controlled object is controlled when something controls it and the controlling subject is dominant when it has an object or objects to control.

Readers can also regard the comments as linguistic hints and arrive

(*khayāl*)" (p. 347). Here he opposes the imagination to the intellect (*'aqel*): "On the other hand it is obligatory to consider them with what is truly the intellect after one has acquired perfection in the demonstrative sciences" (*ibid.*). Here he seems to understand *khayāl* as the imaginative faculty. It is plausible that this is also the meaning of *khayāl* in *Guide* II.12, where Maimonides speaks twice of the *act* of the imagination and hence of the act of a faculty of the soul: "For just as the imagination cannot represent to itself an existent other than a body or a force in a body, the imagination cannot represent to itself an action taking place otherwise than through the immediate contact of an agent or at a certain distance" (pp. 279–80); "every deficiency of reason or character is due to the action of the imagination or consequent upon its action" (p. 280). In *Guide* II.6 Maimonides writes, "Individual natural and psychic forces are called *angels* [*mal'akhim*]" (p. 264). According to ben Laqish, Satan is an angel, namely, the Angel of Death. In his own interpretation of the book of Job, Maimonides states that Satan is an angel (III.22, p. 490). Sammael seems to be the imaginative faculty and not the images presented by it.

at the same results. Though Maimonides formulates what he considers to be the midrashic descriptive elements of the interpretative riddle in Arabic, readers are supposed to understand that the words *markūb* and *rākib* are translations of Hebrew words derived from the root *r.k.b* to ride. Thus they realize that the key words of three of the comments are all derived from this root: "The Serpent was *ridden*"; "It was the *rider* who led Eve astray"; and "the *rider* was Sammael." From their reading of the rest of the *Guide* they remember one of its lexicographic chapters, I.70, where Maimonides explains the equivocal root *r.k.b.* According to that chapter, *r.k.b* is a derivative term. Its first meaning is physical; its derivative meaning is "domination over a thing" (p. 171). From the derived meaning of *r.k.b* readers can infer the meanings of other words derived from this root: a "rider" is a dominant thing and "to be ridden" is to be dominated.

Hence, in order to understand the comments on the basis of linguistic considerations readers must possess knowledge not only of other chapters of the *Guide* but also of the Hebrew language. Only Hebrew-speaking readers can understand Maimonides' explanation of *r.k.b* and apply it to the names derived from it.

According to the linguistic interpretation, the Midrash uses equivocal Hebrew terms as a device to create a text with a double meaning: a text that has an external figurative meaning and an internal philosophical meaning. The words derived from the root *r.k.b* are the clues to understanding the internal meaning of the midrashic hint.

In both cases—both the metaphoric and linguistic interpretation of the comments—readers have a double task. First they must understand the hidden meaning of the comments and translate their figurative language into scientific language; then they can use them to discover the answer to the interpretative riddle. Both ways lead to the realization that, according to the midrash, the Serpent is a controlled object and Sammael is a controlling subject and Sammael controls the Serpent. Because the comments of a riddle correspond to its solution, readers must now identify those concepts or things in Aristotelian psychology concepts that have the same relationship as those of that figure in the comments.

The fourth descriptive element is, "the rider was Sammael": Sammael is the controlling subject. Because riddlees have already solved the Sammael riddle and know that the referent of Sammael is imagination, they also know the identify of the controlling factor in the riddle of the Serpent. The riddle becomes simpler: namely, what faculty of the soul is dominated by imagination? As in the Adam and Eve riddle, the characteristic shared by the image and its referent is the relationship that exists between the protagonists of the allegory on its external level and the concepts or things to which they refer. Because readers already know the referent of one of the related things, Sammael, the relationship between Sammael and the Serpent provide a hint for the identification of the Serpent. The Serpent must be a faculty of the soul that is dominated by imagination.

The third hint is based on the comment the midrash provides for the image it presents: "It was the rider who led Eve astray." That is, imagination was responsible for the seduction of Eve. This hint explains the sin of Eve, but I am not sure that it contributes much to the solution of the Serpent riddle.

The second hint to the nature of the Serpent, that the Serpent "was the size of a camel," may help riddlees identify the referent of the Serpent if they decipher it correctly. On the other hand, the interpretation of the other comments may help decipher the second hint. Note that in traditional riddles, riddlees are supposed to interpret all the comments and not only to give an answer to the riddle. This is also the case with the midrashic comments that constitute the Serpent riddle. Readers of the *Guide* are supposed to interpret each of them and not merely figure out the identity of the Serpent in the Garden of Eden. Maimonides does not offer readers any hint as to the method to be used to understand the second comment. Readers must discover it on their own and then apply it in order to interpret the comment.

In the next section Maimonides adds two descriptive elements of his own to the midrashic riddle. The comments are methodological hints that direct readers to a linguistic interpretation of the midrash and of the biblical text. The first is a riddle on a riddle —a riddle on the midrashic riddle, as in the case of the Satan riddle; the second is a riddle on the biblical text itself. They are both of the same type; they turn readers' attention to a device used by the allegorical or metaphorical comments of the midrash as well as by the biblical allegory—the use of names with a significant etymology to indicate the things or concepts referred to by the characters they name: "This name [Sammael] is used with a view to a certain signification, just as the name Serpent (*Naḥash*) is used with a view to a certain signification" (p. 336). Thus Maimonides directs readers to use the etymological method in order to understand Sammael and *Naḥash*.

The Bible gives some of its characters names that have a meaning. These include: Eve (*Ḥawwah*), "because she was the mother of all life (*ḥay*)" (Gen. 3:20)—the Bible emphasizes her role. *'Ishah*, "she shall be called woman (*'ishah*) because she was taken out of man (*'ish*)" (*ibid.* 2:23)—the Bible emphasizes woman's dependence on man; Jacob, who is renamed Israel after he struggles with the Angel—"Your name shall no longer be called Jacob, but Israel, for you have striven *(sarita)* with God and with men and have prevailed "(*ibid.* 32:28). The same is true of the etymological interpretations of names in the Midrash. Solomon was called Qohelet, "Because his words were uttered in public assembly *(haqhel)*" (*Ecclesiastes Rabbah* 1.2) But these names are meant to be understood primarily on the literal level of the text. They are the names of the historical characters; the Midrash merely explains why they got them. Maimonides is not carrying on this tradition here,[15] but rather another well-known tradition of allegorical interpretation that originated in the second half of the fifth century BCE and was applied especially by the Stoics in their interpretation of the works of Homer and Hesiod. The philosophers maintained that the works of the early poets were allegories intended to convey scientific knowledge. This assumption justified their allegorical interpretation of the poems. One method of this allegorization was the etymological interpretation of names. The assumption was that the protagonists of the poems are personifications of philosophical concepts, personifications that can be extracted by means of etymology.[16] The names resemble the things they name and indicate them. Maimonides does not rely openly on this Greek tradition, which lasted until the Neoplatonists, but asserts that he found the method in the Bible, in the language of the prophets. He demonstrates that in their visions the latter saw objects whose names were etymologically related to their referents[17] or used names that indicate their

15 I no longer believe that Maimonides is applying here an exegetical method already used in the Bible and Midrash, as I claimed in *Adam Stories* (p. 184) and in the chapter on "Bible Commentary." In Kenneth Seeskin (ed.), *The Cambridge Companion to Maimonides* (Cambridge, 2005), pp. 250-252.

16 See Felix Buffière, *Les mythes d'Homère et la pensée grecque* (Paris, 1956), p. 60; J. Tate, "Cornutus and the Poets," *Classical Quarterly* 23 (1929), pp. 41–45; Y. Amir, "Ha-allegoriyah shel Philon be-yaḥasah la-allegoriyah ha-homerit," *Eshkolot* 6 (1971), p. 39 (Hebrew).

17 *Guide* II.43.

referents via the etymology of the latter.[18] He also finds the method in the aggadic corpus of the talmudic Sages—implicitly claiming that it was used by wise men acting on their own and not only by prophets who spoke through revelation.[19]

Maimonides applies this method in his interpretation of the Serpent in the Bible and Sammael in the Midrash. His interpretation of these characters is based on the supposition that we can identify the philosophical concepts personified by *Naḥash* and Sammael through the etymology of their names.

As in the case of the previous linguistic hint—the meaning of *r.k.b* and its derivatives—here too an etymological grasp of the word is only a hint. Readers must still identify the referents that have the characteristics indicated by the names. This is a very difficult task. Because Maimonides does not provide the solutions of the interpretative riddles in the *Guide*, readers cannot know whether their solution is the one intended by Maimonides. In fact, the early commentators understood the etymologies of these names in different ways and proposed different identifications of their referents.[20]

Understanding the etymologies of the names of *Naḥash* and Sammael is not of great help in answering the Serpent and Sammael riddles. They can be solved only on the basis of the comments offered by the midrash. Nevertheless, understanding the etymologies and identifying their referents may confirm readers' solution of the midrashic riddle. Because the comments are part of the Serpent riddle, readers must interpret them as in the case of the traditional riddle.

I believe that the descriptive elements Maimonides added to the midrashic riddle also play another function in his biblical exegesis beyond helping riddlees solve the *Naḥash* riddle or confirming their solution.

---

18 *Guide* II.29. For a fuller discussion of this issue see Klein-Braslavy *Adam Stories*, pp. 183–187; iadem, "Bible Commentary," pp. 250-252.

19 It is interesting to note that both the earlier Greek philosophers and the Neoplatonists offered two explanations for poetic allegories. One was that poets were wise men who expressed the truth about reality via myths and symbols. This was the basis of the Stoic allegorism. The other explanation was that poets were inspired and possessed by some supernatural power. Hence their works were in a sense not their own, but a divine revelation, and as such expressed in some measure the divine truth. See J. Tate, "On the History of Allegorism," *Classical Quarterly* 28 (1934), pp. 105–114. These two explanations of allegory in early Greek poetry correspond to some extent to Maimonides' two explanation of allegory in Jewish literature: the prophets who had divine revelation; and the prophets and Sages who invented the allegories themselves.

20 For the early commentators' interpretations, see Klein-Braslavy, *Adam Stories*, pp. 215–217.

These elements explain the technique used by the Bible and the Midrash to create the allegories and answer the question why the Bible and Midrash used these supernatural creatures to convey the corresponding philosophical concepts. According to Maimonides, they did so because their names indicate their meaning and hence their referents. Both used a linguistic device to create their allegories and to convey their hidden meanings.

As noted above, Maimonides does not tell readers what method to use in order to understand the second comment: "It [the Serpent] was the size of a camel." According to the unwritten laws of the literary genre of the allegory, philosophical concepts are personified either in the guise of a character that has traits corresponding to the philosophical concept, or linguistically, as a character whose referent is indicated by the etymology of its name. Because Maimonides does not tell readers which method to use here, either one might be applied. In fact, the early commentators of the *Guide* applied both of them.[21]

I believe that the best interpretation assumes that the allegorical interpretative comment in the midrash is based on the etymological method, which Maimonides finds in both the Bible and the Midrash.[22]

As with the linguistic hint of *r.k.b,* understanding this hint requires knowledge of the original midrash and of the Hebrew language. Readers must know that the Hebrew word for camel is *gamal.* This can be interpreted as derived from the name of the third letter of the Hebrew alphabet—*gimel*—which has the numerological value of three. In other words, readers must identify characteristics of the Serpent that are three in number.

The second comment follows the comment that the Serpent was "ridden"—i.e., that it did not act at its own initiative but was controlled by another. On the basis of knowledge of Aristotelian psychology, read-

21 Narboni (the first interpretation of camel) and Profiat Duran (Efodi) apply the first method. Narboni, who understands the camel as humane desire, explains: "It was in the size of a camel with regard to the body" (first interpretation of the camel, Commentary on the *Guide*, 40b). Efodi, who identifies the camel with the imaginative faculty, says that what the two have in common is "that camel is a large and inferior animal" and the imagination is also "a large and inferior faculty that composes and fabricates forms that have no existence" (commentary on the *Guide* II.30, 61b). Narboni also proposes another, etymological interpretation of *gamal* (camel)—that *gamal* is derived from *higgamel*, to be weaned: "Because its effervescence [*retiḥato*] [that of human desire] is at the time when man is weaned (*be-ʿet higgamel ha ʾadam*") (Commentary on the *Guide*, 40b).

22 My interpretation is not the same as Narboni's, however.

ers can then identify the Serpent with the faculty of desire or the appetitive faculty.[23] This faculty moves human beings toward the objects offered by the senses[24] (or by changes in the body's temperament[25]), by the faculty of imagination, or by the intellect.[26] Hence these three faculties of the soul control human desire. Because readers already know that the Serpent in the Garden of Eden was dominated by imagination, it is plausible to interpret that the number three alludes to all three types of human desire.[27]

The answer to the midrashic riddle may shed light on the interpretation of the etymology of *Naḥash* and Sammael. Because Maimonides claims that *Naḥash* should be understood etymologically and because the most plausible interpretation of the second comment is that it refers to human desire, we may conclude that the noun *Naḥash* is derived from the verb *Ḥas*,"agile in carrying out a task." Humane desire is what moves human beings towards the desired object. Because this etymology of the noun *Naḥash* corresponds to the identification of *Naḥash* with human desire, the interpretation of the name *Naḥash* according to its etymology confirms the answer to the riddle of *Naḥash* derived from the midrashic comments.

Given that readers have already identified Sammael with imagination, the etymology of the name Sammael should be easier to discover. The name seems to be derived from the verb *samme*ʾ, blind.[28] Imagination blinds human beings; it offers them wrong aims, inducing them to pursue physical desires and preventing them from seeing their true purpose, which is to achieve human perfection by contemplation of the intelligibles.[29] Narboni adds another suggestion for an etymological interpretation of Sammael: Sammael is derived from *smo*ʾ*l* (left).[30]

---

23 Narboni, whose interpretation, though different than mine, is also based on the supposition that the clue to the interpretation of the second comment is the etymological method, arrived at the same conclusion.

24 Cf. al-Farabi, *The Perfect State*, 10.6. This also seems to be Maimonides' view in *Guide* II.1 (p. 245).

25 Cf. Introduction to part II, premise twenty-six (p. 240).

26 Cf. al-Farabi, *The Perfect State*, 10.6.

27 Those who hold that Sammael is the images or representations produced by the imaginative faculty, and not the imagination itself, may identify the Serpent in the same way.

28 This is also one of the interpretations offered by Narboni, Efodi, and Shem Tov.

29 Readers can confirm this interpretation on the basis of Maimonides' explanation of the etymology of "Satan" in *Guide* III.22 (p. 489): Satan "turns people away from the ways of truth and makes them perish in the ways of error." Because Satan, according to the Sages, is Sammael, this statement applies to Sammael as well.

30 This interpretation is based on Ecclesiastes 10:2, "a fool's heart is at his left," and is compatible

Because Maimonides does not provide the solution of the Serpent riddle and the descriptive elements that compose it in the *Guide*, readers are left to decide which is the "correct" answer to the riddle and what are the "correct" meanings of the comments offered in its descriptive elements.

To sum up: We have seen that Maimonides uses interpretative riddles as a device to convey his esoteric understanding of biblical texts. He uses midrashic allegories and statements by the Sages as the "comments" of these riddles, along with his own comments, thereby creating riddles that combine the biblical text, the midrashic text, and his own hints. The Midrash employs several types of comments: structural comments, in which the clue to solving the riddle is the relationships between the protagonists of the story;[31] equation comments; and linguistic comments, which use equivocal terms to hint at the solution. Maimonides offers both equation hints and methodological hints that direct riddlees to use another linguistic method in order to answer the interpretative riddle: the etymological method.

The technique of the interpretative riddle sheds light on the way Maimonides understands the creation of biblical and midrashic interpretative allegories. The comments correspond to the techniques by which the allegories were composed; namely, linguistic devices—the use of equivocal terms and of terms that indicate the referent by their etymology—and structural devices, or creating allegories that indicate the hidden meaning through the corresponding relationships between two protagonists of the story and their referents.

---

with Maimonides' interpretation of B. Shabbat 119b in *Guide* III.22 (p. 490).

31 Maimonides himself employs a "structure of relation" as a clue for understanding the meaning of "woman" in his interpretations of the biblical texts. See (in this volume) "Maimonides Strategy for Interpreting 'Woman' in the *Guide of the Perplexed*."

Part Three

Maimonides and Esotericism

King Solomon and Metaphysical Esotericism According to Maimonides

One of the central characteristics of Maimonides' intellectual enterprise is his great attachment to the basic written texts of Jewish tradition—the Bible, the Talmud, and the Midrash—and his attempt to demonstrate that he is essentially continuing this tradition. The talmudic Sages had the same sense that they were preserving the continuity of the Jewish textual tradition; they demonstrated that they were, in essence, continuing an existing tradition, and not making innovations, by citing biblical verses in support of their opinions. Borrowing his approach from the Sages, Maimonides builds his system of philosophical-theological thought as a further link in Judaism's written tradition.

Even though Maimonides adopts the principles of Aristotelian philosophy as taught by Alfarabi and Avicenna, he makes enormous efforts to demonstrate that the Aristotelian world-view is not foreign to Judaism, but is an integral element of its faith and principles, expressed in central texts of its literature. He accomplishes this by an interpretive process that invests traditional Jewish texts with philosophical meaning. From this point of view, Maimonides' enterprise may be seen as exegetical in the broad sense of the word: working within the framework of Aristotelianism, he reinterprets and gives philosophical meaning to fundamental theological terms, to biblical, talmudic, and midrashic texts, and to Jewish historical figures and the events that befell them. From the standpoint of exegesis, Maimonides is very close to the hermeneutical tradition of the Sages. He frequently uses rabbinic midrashim to interpret biblical verses, and he takes ideas from the Sages regarding the exegetical connections between their views and the biblical texts they cite in support of them.

One of the most interesting reinterpretations in the writings of Maimonides is his exegesis of the esoteric doctrine of the Sages, the *locus classicus* of which is *Ein Dorshin*, the second chapter of the tractate Ḥagigah. Both in his halakhic writings and in the *Guide of the Perplexed*, Maimonides makes use of the esoteric tradition of the Sages in his teaching, giving a philosophical meaning to their mystical basic concepts. He thus identifies the Account of the Beginning (*Maʿaseh Bereshit*) with Aristotelian physics, and the Account of the Chariot (*Maʿaseh Merkavah*) with Aristotelian metaphysics; he likewise interprets the "secrets" (*sodot*) or "mysteries of the Torah" (*siṭrei Torah*) of ancient mysticism as being identical with philosophical ideas. It is from his reinterpretation of the basic concepts of ancient mysticism that Maimonides derives one of the legitimations for his reading of the biblical texts dealing with *Maʿaseh Bereshit* and *Maʿaseh Merkavah* as belonging to the same sphere of meaning as Aristotelian physics and metaphysics.

But Maimonides is not satisfied merely to identify the contents of the Sages' esoteric doctrine with the central elements of Aristotelian philosophy; he applies to his own teachings all of the formal rules which the Sages lay down concerning the study of esoteric teachings and their transmission to others. Through his reinterpretation of the esoteric teachings, these rules took on a new meaning that made it possible to apply them to the study and teaching of physics and metaphysics, and to the interpretation of biblical passages and rabbinic sayings whose subject matter, according to Maimonides, is physics and metaphysics. By adopting the formal rules of the Sages, Maimonides was able to rely upon the Jewish tradition to justify the literary form of the biblical and midrashic texts whose significance, according to his interpretation, lies in the realm of Aristotelian physics and metaphysics; he was also able to argue that they convey philosophical content through symbolic language, in "parable and riddle." This literary form makes it possible to conceal "secrets" from those who do not deserve to receive them, and at the same time provides hints for those who are able to comprehend such lore. His acceptance of the formal guidelines of the Sages regarding the transmission of the Account of the Chariot to others also enables Maimonides to use Jewish tradition to justify his own way of writing about *Maʿaseh Bereshit* and *Maʿaseh Merkavah*, and to argue that, in writing in a concealing and allusive manner, he is continuing an existing tradition on how to convey "secrets of the Torah."[1]

There is an additional aspect to the adoption of the esoteric doctrine

1 Alexander Altmann, "Das Verhältnis Maimunis zu der jüdischen Mystik," *MGWJ* 80 (1936), pp. 305-30. See also Klein-Braslavy, *Creation*, pp. 27-34; Klein-Braslavy, *Esotericism*, pp. 195-202.

of the Sages in Maimonides' teaching. In *Ein Dorshin*, and apparently also in B. Taʿanit 7a, according to Maimonides' interpretation, the Sages held that the warnings and words of wisdom of King Solomon referred to the conduct of a mystic, and not to that of an ordinary person or to practical, everyday conduct. They justify their own conduct or explain the conduct of other mystics by citing verses from the books traditionally attributed to Solomon. These verses can only be used in support of the mystic's conduct if it is implicitly assumed that they are not to be understood literally, but as what Maimonides calls a "parable" or an "allegory" (*mashal*), i.e., as texts written in symbolic language which require interpretation in order for their true significance to be apparent. Thus, by the very act of citing Solomon's words as pertaining to the conduct of mystics, the Sages identify Solomon with ancient mysticism, implicitly claiming that he was "wise" in the mystical sense, helped others to attain mystical knowledge, and spoke about the obligation to conceal its "secrets."

Both in his halakhic works and in the *Guide*, Maimonides accepted this exegetical idea. But since he identified the mystic with the Aristotelian philosopher who strives to attain the maximal understanding of God possible for a human being, this idea took on a new meaning. For Maimonides, Solomon's words pertain to metaphysics, and not to mysticism, as in the Sages' view.

Thus Maimonides inherited from the talmudic Sages an elaborate structure for discussing esoteric doctrine. This structure included the idea of an exegetical connection between the conduct of the mystic and Solomon's words of warning and wisdom. In this respect, Maimonides is merely repeating what was said by the sages who preceded him. But he reinterprets the structure and gives it a totally new direction. On the one hand, he adheres closely to the Jewish textual tradition that preceded him; on the other, he revitalizes it by giving it new meaning.

In the course of doing so, Maimonides is not satisfied merely to borrow what the Sages said about *Maʿaseh Merkavah* and the Solomonic sources they cited about the conduct of the mystic. Instead, he develops their fundamental exegetical idea further by identifying Solomon with the metaphysician. He does this in two ways. First, for any given idea, he cites sources over and above those brought by the Sages. Second, he substantiates the instruction on metaphysical matters given to the wise man with proof from Solomon's statements, deriving morals from the biblical stories or interpreting and developing the Sages' esoteric doctrine.

The aim of the present paper is to trace the ways in which Maimonides adopts, interprets, and develops the exegetical tradition connecting Solomon's warnings and wise sayings with the Account of the Chariot. In consequence, it will also discuss the identification of the Account of the Chariot with metaphysics, and with the instruction given the philosopher on the proper method of attaining metaphysical knowledge.

1. Solomon's Warning Against the Public Teaching of Esoteric Doctrine

The Babylonian Talmud, in its discussion of the prohibition of publicly expounding *Maʿase Merkavah* (B. Ḥagigah 13a), gives an account of an actual incident, evidently an exemplary story intended to teach conduct worthy of imitation. Rabbi Joseph, we are told, studied the Account of the Chariot, while the elders of Pumbedita studied the Account of the Beginning. Rabbi Joseph asked the elders of Pumbedita to teach him *Maʿaseh Bereshit*, which they did. They then asked Rabbi Joseph to teach them *Maʿaseh Merkavah*. He refused, basing himself on Song of Songs 4:11, "Honey and milk are under thy tongue," which he interpreted as follows: "Those things which are as sweet as honey and milk should be kept under one's tongue"; in other words, esoteric matters like the Account of the Chariot, which are compared to honey and milk, are to be kept (figuratively) under one's tongue and neither discussed nor taught publicly.

According to this story, Solomon originated the proscription against publicly revealing the meaning of the Account of the Chariot. Rabbi Joseph justified his conduct by saying that he was following Solomon's warning; in other words, he based himself upon the authority of an earlier sage. Further on in the same story, Rabbi Abahu is said to have agreed with Rabbi Joseph that the proscription was of Solomonic origin, but to have derived it from another verse in Solomon's writings, "the lambs will be for thy clothing" (Prov. 27:26). Abahu read *kevasim* ("lambs") as *kevashim*, which is etymologically related to *kivshon*, "secret" or "hidden thing." On the basis of this reading, he interpreted the verse to mean, "Things that are secrets of the world (*kivshono shel ʿolam*) shall be beneath your clothing," i.e., things that are "secrets," the esoteric teachings of the Account of the Chariot, are to be kept to oneself and not freely transmitted to others.

In his halakhic writings, though not in the *Guide*, Maimonides repeats the Sages' exegetical claim that Solomon had condemned the public dissemination of *Ma'aseh Merkavah* in Song of Songs 4:11 and Proverbs 27:26. Since, however, Maimonides holds that the Account of the Chariot is about metaphysics, Solomon's words are reinterpreted in his reading: they are understood as support for the argument that metaphysics should not be taught in public, and not, as they were for the Sages, as a prohibition against teaching mysticism in public.

The fullest presentation of Maimonides' reinterpretation of the mishnaic-talmudic doctrine on the teaching of esoteric matters appears in *Hilkhot Yesodei ha-Torah* 2.12. After summarizing what the Sages say in the Mishnah (Ḥagigah 2.1) and the Talmud (B. Ḥagigah 12a and 13a), he makes the following brief comment:

> Our former Sages commanded that one is not to expound these things [i.e., the Account of the Chariot] save to one person alone, and that [on condition that] he be wise and understand things by himself [from Mishnah Ḥagigah 2.1]. Thereafter, one conveys to him chapter headings [from R. Ḥiyya's remarks in B. Ḥagigah 12a] and informs him of a bit of the thing, and he understands by himself, and comprehends the end of the thing and its profundity.

Maimonides adds to this summary the lesson to be derived from the account of the four people who entered into *Pardes* (B. Ḥagigah 14b): "and these things are very profound matters, and not every intellect is capable of comprehending them." The term *Pardes*, like the other terms used for the Sages' esoteric teachings, such as *Ma'aseh Merkavah* and *Ma'aseh Bereshit*, is reinterpreted and given a philosophical meaning over and above its original mystical meaning in the sayings of the Sages. In *Hilkhot Yesodei ha-Torah* 4.13, Maimonides explains that *Pardes* includes both *Ma'aseh Bereshit* and *Ma'aseh Merkavah*, namely, physics and metaphysics. Accordingly, the four who "entered *Pardes*" engaged in philosophical speculation. In the above-mentioned source, Maimonides explains in a general way why R. Akiva's three companions failed: "for even though they were great ones of Israel and great sages, not all of them had the strength to know and to comprehend all of these things fully." The "strength" of which Maimonides speaks here is intellectual power, meaning that some of them had not developed their intellects sufficiently to comprehend the contents of *Pardes*. He evidently alludes to this interpretation in his comments here, where he derives the more general conclusion that not every person has the appropriate intellectual ability or preparation to comprehend metaphysical notions.

After concluding his reconstruction and brief commentary on the words of the Sages in Ḥagigah concerning the public teaching of the Account of the Chariot, Maimonides goes back to cite the verses from Solomon with which the Sages justified their conduct. But Solomon's remarks are connected here with others concerning the nature of *Ma'ase Merkavah*: "and these things are very profound matters, and not every intellect is capable of comprehending them"; and Maimonides adds: "and concerning them [i.e., the same profound things] Solomon said..." By placing his remarks in this context, Maimonides indirectly explains why Solomon warned that matters concerning the Account of the Chariot should be concealed: since these things are profound and not everyone is able to comprehend them, they should not be expounded in public.[2]

Maimonides prefaces two explanatory remarks to his citation of the verses from Solomon. First, he notes that Solomon said these words "in his wisdom," i.e., as a philosopher, and therefore they are to be read as the instructions of a "sage" who preceded the Sages of the Mishnah and the Talmud. The comment may also mean: and not as a prophet.[3] Second, Maimonides here claims that Solomon's words were as in a "parable." It may be that the stress upon Solomon's saying these things "in his wisdom," and writing them in the form of a "parable," is an echo of Maimonides' claim, in the *Introduction to Pereq Ḥeleq*, that "the great sages" wrote their words "in parable and riddle." Maimonides explicitly states there that Solomon, who was wiser than any other man, wrote words of wisdom "in parable and riddle." While in this passage Maimonides is discussing the contents of this wisdom and not its transmission, one may assume that he sees his statement as a general rule applying to all the

2 As we shall see in *Guide* I.34, the argument that matters of the Account of the Chariot are deep is attributed to Solomon himself.

3 Following the midrashic tradition (in *Canticles Rabbah* and *Ecclesiastes Rabbah)*, Maimonides sees Solomon as a prophet. See "Solomon as a Prophet." In Klein-Braslavy, *Esotericism*, pp. 164-188.

words of the Sages in reference to wisdom, and therefore to Solomon's words of instruction concerning the teaching of "wisdom" to others. On the other hand, the claim that Solomon wrote Song of Songs 4:11 as a parable is based upon the same exegetical assumption that underlies the interpretation of this verse by the talmudic Sages, upon which their homiletic interpretation of the verse is based.

Maimonides presents the verses quoted in *Ein Dorshin* in an order different from theirs. First he cites Proverbs 27:26, "the lambs will be for thy clothing (*li-levushekha*)." Next, he could have cited the version of R. Abahu found in our editions of the Talmud, "the secrets of the world (*kivshono shel ʿolam*) shall be under (*taḥat*) your clothing," a wording that brings this verse in line with the phrasing of Song of Songs 4:11, "*under* your tongue" (*taḥat leshonekh*). Instead, however, Maimonides cites Rabbi Abahu's words in line with the original text of the biblical verse, "*to* your clothing," which is interpreted to mean, "they shall be *to you alone*, and do not expound them in public." He immediately observes that the source for this interpretation is a parallel Solomonic verse, Proverbs 5:17, which contains the very same idea: "Let them be *only thine own*, and not strangers' with thee."

Proverbs 5:17 is not cited in *Ein Dorshin* in support of the proscription against expounding *Maʿase Merkavah* in public, but in B. Taʿanit 7a it is interpreted as being concerned with the teaching of the Torah to others. R. Ḥanina bar Ḥama poses a question arising from an apparent contradiction between two consecutive verses in the Book of Proverbs. In 5:16 we read, "Let thy springs be dispersed abroad," while in verse 17 we read, "let them be only thine own." Like other Sages cited in Taʿanit 7a, R. Ḥanina states that "water" is used in Scripture as an image for Torah.[4] Thus, he explains, both verses from Proverbs deal with the teaching of Torah; they seem to contradict one another only because verse 16 requires the sage to teach the Torah to others, while verse 17 tells him to keep it to himself. R. Ḥanina resolves the contradiction by adding an appropriate "condition" to each verse: "If he is a worthy student, 'let

4 R. Ḥanina bar Pappa explicates two verses about water in a manner similar to R. Ḥanina bar Ḥama's exposition of Prov. 5:16-17: "Unto him that is thirsty bring ye water!" (Isa. 21:14) and "Ho, every one that thirsteth, come ye for water" (Isa. 55:1). R. Ḥanina bar Pappa says, "If he is a worthy student, they say of him, 'Unto him that is thirsty bring ye water!', and if not, 'Ho, every one that thirsteth, come ye for water'." It is possible that Maimonides had this very homily in mind when he says in *Guide* I.30: "Similarly they often designate knowledge as water. Thus: 'Ho, every one that thirsteth, come ye for water'" (p. 43/ p. 64; see below, n. 11).

thy springs be dispersed outward'; and if [not], 'let them be only thine own'."[5] According to R. Ḥanina b. Ḥama's interpretation, Proverbs 5:16-17 revolves around the question of the conditions for teaching Torah to others: if the student is worthy, one is to teach him the words of Torah; if not, one should not teach him, in which case one should keep things to oneself. In Maimonides' view, R. Ḥanina is not speaking here about the teaching of halakhic matters, but about the teaching of "secrets of Torah," so that his remarks apply to *Maʿaseh Merkavah*.[6] Accordingly, R. Ḥanina's statements in B. Taʿanit 7a parallel what the Sages say in the second chapter of Ḥagigah, and thus Maimonides can add Proverbs 5:17 to the list of Solomonic verses cited by the Sages there in support of the argument that *Maʿase Merkavah* may not be expounded in public.[7]

After effectively interpreting Proverbs 27:26 in light of the parallel to Proverbs 5:17, Maimonides returns to the verse originally adduced by the Talmud against the public dissemination of *Maʿaseh Merkavah*, Song of Songs 4:11, as interpreted by Rabbi Joseph. He does not add any exegetical observations of his own.[8]

Maimonides does not interpret Song of Songs 4:11 in his Introduction to the Mishnah, where he again deals with the prohibition of public expositions of the Account of the Chariot:[9]

> And they [i.e., the Sages], of blessed memory, interpreted it, saying that the subject matter of this verse is that it is fitting that those sweet things which are pleas-

---

5 This is, in effect, a "contradiction" of the fourth cause mentioned by Maimonides in the Introduction to the *Guide*, where he argues that this is common in the books of the prophets. This argument relies on the Sages' interpretation of verses which they saw as contradictory, such as those found in B. Taʿanit 7a.

6 Rashi explains it in the same way here: "and if he is worthy tell him the secrets of the Torah."

7 Maimonides gives this verse a different interpretation in *Guide* III.54, where he says that it refers to the "true human perfection...belonging to him alone [i.e., the individual] " (p. 469; p. 635).

8 In his *Commentary on the Mishnah*, Ḥagigah 2.1, he explains this verse in the same manner as Prov. 27:26: "They already warned in the Talmud against teaching them in public [i.e., those matters which are fundaments of the bodies of Torah, i.e., *Maʿase Merkavah*], and they were very strict about this. And they commanded that a person ought to teach them to himself by himself, and that he not pass them on to others. And they based this upon the saying of Solomon in this matter, by way of parable: 'Honey and milk are under thy tongue'" (Qāfiḥ, p. 378; see below, n. 10). Maimonides stresses here an additional idea—that *Maʿaseh Merkavah* is a subject which a person studies by himself and does not learn from others. One concludes from this that the "chapter headings" which the teacher conveys to his disciple are only intended to assist him in learning *Maʿase Merkavah* by himself.

9 Here too, as in the *Commentary on the Mishnah*, Ḥagigah 2.1, Maimonides does not mention any other Solomonic verses concerning this matter.

> ing to the soul, as the palate finds pleasures from honey and milk, not be spoken of or come upon one's tongue in any circumstances, and this is what is said, "under your tongue"—for these notions are not among [the things] which should be taught or in which instruction should be given in the [public] schools of learning. (ed. Qāfiḥ, pp. 35-36)[10]

In the Introduction to the Mishnah, Maimonides not only mentions that *Maʿase Merkavah* is not to be expounded in public, but refers to the story of Rabbi Joseph and the sages of Pumbedita, although he does not mention its principals by name. By drawing inferences from this incident concerning the actual conduct of a specific talmudic Sage, Maimonides hoped to derive conclusions regarding the conduct expected of sages in general, namely: "that some of the Sages, of blessed memory, withheld the secrets of wisdom from one another" (ed. Qāfiḥ, p. 35). He interprets Song of Songs 4:11 here as implying a prohibition against teaching *Maʿase Merkavah* to other Sages, it being understood that this refers to cases in which the Sages in question do not satisfy the requirements making it permissible to teach them these subjects. In order to make explicit the general argument that *Maʿase Merkavah* may not be expounded in public under any circumstances, Maimonides adds that not only is it prohibited to teach the secrets of *Maʿase Merkavah* to Sages lacking the proper qualifications, but it is also prohibited to teach them to "foolish people." This supplementary argument is likewise derived from the words of Solomon, and in this case Maimonides himself cites the support for it rather than simply rely upon a verse already explained by the Sages:

> Because if they set it before the fool, if they do not deride it in his presence it will certainly not be pleasing in his eyes; therefore, the wise man [i.e. Solomon] said, "Speak not in the ears of a fool, for he will despise the wisdom of thy words" (Prov. 23:9). (ed. Qāfiḥ, p. 36)

---

10 The Introduction to the Mishnah is quoted from the *Commentary on the Mishnah*, Arabic text and Hebrew translation, edited by Y. Qāfiḥ (Jerusalem, 1963-68). On occasion, I have preferred the translation of al-Ḥarīzī or corrected the translation myself.

Maimonides here continues an exegetical line started by the Sages, explaining Proverbs 23:9 on the basis of the assumption that Solomon warned against any public exposition of *Ma'ase Merkavah*.

Maimonides does not repeat this proof in the *Guide of the Perplexed*, relying instead on the words of the Sages themselves in *Ein Dorshin*. Nevertheless, it seems to me that the *Guide* echoes the exegetical tradition associating Solomon with the prohibition of publicly disseminating the "secrets of the Torah." In II.30, Maimonides tells his disciple how to interpret the story of the Garden of Eden. He states that he will explain this biblical text by means of the homiletical interpretation of the Sages found in the Talmud and midrashim, and then adds:

> Know that these things that I shall mention to you from the dicta of the sages are sayings that are of utmost perfection; their allegorical interpretation was clear to those to whom they were addressed, and they are unambiguous. Hence I will not go too far in interpreting them, and I will not set forth their meaning at length. For I will not be "one who divulges a secret." (p. 249-50/p. 355)

The words "one who divulges a secret" (*megalleh sod*), quoted in Hebrew in the Arabic text, are doubtlessly an allusion to Proverbs 11:13, "He that goeth about as a talebearer revealeth a secret, but he that is of a faithful spirit concealeth a matter." Maimonides understands the word "secret" in this verse as referring to the "secrets of the Torah"; he therefore explains that Solomon is denouncing one who reveals those secrets. Like Rabbi Joseph in B. Ḥagigah 13a, Maimonides justifies his own conduct by citing a Solomonic statement. He argues by implication that in conveying to others his interpretation of what the Sages said about the story of the Garden of Eden, he has avoided following the examples of negative conduct pointed to by Solomon in Proverbs 11:13. Maimonides therefore maintains here that by refusing to expound more extensively the words of the Sages on *Ma'aseh Bereshit*, he is following a long-standing tradition that requires the concealing of these "secrets."

2. Solomon's Instruction on the Apprehension of God

In his halakhic writings Maimonides presents Solomon as a "wise man" who warns against the public exposure of *Maʿase Merkavah*, i.e., as a sage engaged in conveying these "secrets" to others. In *The Guide of the Perplexed*, however, he depicts Solomon as cautioning his readers against attempting to go beyond the limits of human capability in the effort to apprehend God, and as guiding and instructing them toward a proper understanding of God within their mortal limitations.

Since Maimonides identifies *Maʿaseh Merkavah*, the secret doctrine of the Sages, with metaphysics, it follows that instruction for the apprehension of God is synonymous with instruction toward apprehending the "secrets" of *Maʿase Merkavah*. This being so, Maimonides relies upon *Ein Dorshin* even in those chapters which deal with instruction concerning the attainment of metaphysical knowledge (*Guide* I.31-34), implying that here too he is only continuing, explaining, and explicating an existing tradition in Judaism, and not innovating anything.[11]

The Chapters of Instruction in the first part of the *Guide* deal with two central concerns: (1) the limitations of human knowledge (chaps. 31-32), and (2) why the subject matter of *Maʿase Merkavah* is concealed, the conditions under which it may be transmitted to others, and the method of transmission (chaps. 33-34). The former concern is developed by way of a commentary on the story of the four sages who entered *Pardes*, while the latter is developed through a commentary on what the Mishnah and Talmud say about *Maʿaseh Merkavah* in chapter 2 of Ḥagigah.

In the *Guide* as in the halakhic writings of Maimonides, we find the same basic model of discussion, namely one that connects the study of metaphysics, the commentary on the passages in *Ein Dorshin* dealing with *Maʿase Merkavah*, and support for these arguments from the words of Solomon. However, in the *Guide*, not only does Maimonides adopt an existing exegetical structure of the Sages by connecting Solomon and his writings with instruction concerning matters of *Maʿase Merkavah*, but he continues that exegetical tradition and develops it along independent lines.

In *Guide* I.32, Maimonides continues the discussion of the limitations

---

11 As we shall see below, one should also add to these chapters *Guide* I.5, in which Maimonides' words of instruction are not connected with any esoteric doctrine of the Sages.

of human knowledge that began in chapter 31. He opens the chapter with a general argument, noting that in sense perceptions, the attempt to overreach human capabilities has the effect of weakening the sense, preventing it from achieving even what would earlier have been within its ability. Similarly, when man attempts to achieve or understand something that is beyond the capability of the human intellect, not only is he unsuccessful, but he loses his former ability for intellectual apprehension, and thereby also for human perfection, which is intellectual perfection. In light of this, Maimonides instructs his disciple:

> For if you stay your progress because of a dubious point; if you do not deceive yourself into believing that there is a demonstration with regard to matters that have not been demonstrated; if you do not hasten to reject and categorically to pronounce false any assertions whose contradictories have not been demonstrated; if, finally, you do not aspire to apprehend that which you are unable to apprehend—you will have achieved human perfection...(p. 46/p. 68)

These words of instruction are buttressed with historical examples. Maimonides presents the contrasting patterns of conduct of two sages who attempted to apprehend God, R. Akiva and Elisha ben Abuyah, as related in the story of the four who entered *Pardes* (B. Ḥagigah 14b ff.). The reinterpretation of the term *Pardes* suggested in *Hilkhot Yesodei ha-Torah* is assumed here. On this basis it follows that the four who entered Pardes engaged in philosophic speculation. According to Maimonides, R. Akiva and Elisha were at the highest level of philosophical speculation—metaphysics. R. Akiva serves as an example of a properly conducted attempt to attain metaphysical knowledge, for he acted in accordance with Maimonides' instructions to his disciple in this passage: i.e., he did not attempt to apprehend that which is beyond the capability of the human intellect. Thus R. Akiva serves as an example of a properly conducted attempt to attain metaphysical knowledge, for he acted in accordance with Maimonides' instructions to his disciple in this passage: i.e., he did not attempt to apprehend that which is beyond the capability of the human intellect. Thus R. Akiva "'entered in peace and went out in peace' when engaged in the theoretical study of these metaphysical matters" (p. 46/p. 68), thereby achieving human perfection. Elisha, on the other hand, did not follow the right path; he attempted to attain that which is beyond human ability. Therefore, as Maimonides warned his own students, not only did he fail to apprehend God properly, but he lost the faculty of intellectual apprehension, and thereby his intellectual perfection, which is human perfection.[12] Elisha exchanged the intellectual apprehension he had previously possessed for its opposite, imaginative apprehension. As a result, his attempt to go beyond human limitations had consequences in the realm of practical conduct. His behavior was guided by the imagination and not by the intellect, and he tended toward matter and things defective, evil, and wicked.

As in his halakhic writings, here too Maimonides accepts the exegetical tradition connecting Solomon's words of instruction with ancient esoteric doctrine (Ḥagigah, chap. 2). He comments that the verse "Hast thou found honey? eat so much as is sufficient for thee, lest thou be filled therewith, and vomit it" (Prov. 25:16) refers to conduct like Elisha's, maintaining that the Sages read it as a "parable" concerning Elisha. In the extant text of the Talmud, the Sages apply this verse to Ben-Zoma, but Maimonides may have had another version in which it was applied to Elisha.[13] In any event, Maimonides understands that in the view of the Sages, it was Elisha and not Ben-Zoma who sinned by overreaching in his philosophical speculations. This comment well serves his purposes in the chapter under discussion.

Maimonides' contribution to the exegetical tradition that uses Solomon's statement about honey to explain Elisha's fate consists in his explanation of Proverbs 25:16. Maimonides fits Solomon's words to his own admonition to his disciple at the beginning of the chapter, where he referred to the consequences that might follow from a failure to obey the warning to keep metaphysical speculation with the natural limits of human knowledge:

12 Maimonides covertly relies here upon B. Ḥagigah 15a: "'Since that person [i.e., Elisha ben Abuyah speaking of himself] has been expelled from the next world, let him go and enjoy this world.' Thus Aḥer [Elisha ben Abuyah] became an apostate." One must remember that Maimonides identifies the next world with the survival of the soul, which is dependent upon the perfection of the intellect; he therefore understands the passage to mean: since he lost the perfection of the intellect and therefore the world-to-come, he turned toward the appetites of the senses.

13 Another, less likely, possibility is that Maimonides simply erred in arguing that the Sages attributed this verse to Elisha.

> How marvelous is this parable, inasmuch as it likens knowledge to eating, a meaning about which we have spoken [in *Guide* I.30]. It also mentions the most delicious of foods, namely, honey. Now, according to its nature, honey, if eaten to excess, upsets the stomach and causes vomiting. Accordingly, Scripture says, as it were, that in spite of its sublimity, greatness, and what it has of perfection, the nature of the apprehension in question—if not made to stop at its proper limit and not conducted with circumspection—may be perverted into a defect, just as the eating of honey may. For whereas the individual eating in moderation is nourished and takes pleasure in it, it all goes if there is too much of it. Accordingly Scripture does not say, "Lest thou be filled therewith and loathe it," but rather says, "and vomit it." (p. 46/p. 69)

In his commentary Maimonides specifically stresses the second half of the honey metaphor, and not the first part, which embodies the actual warning given by Solomon in this verse. He speaks of the wise man's loss of the wisdom he had before he attempted to grasp that which was beyond his comprehension, or to decide on matters for which there is no rational proof, and of the consequent decline of his intellect as wisdom deteriorates to though about imaginary things, which is the opposite and absence of rational thought.

Maimonides had laid the groundwork for this parable in *Guide* I.30, a lexicographical chapter devoted to the various meanings of the verb *ʾakhal* ("ate"), the noun *maʾakhal* ("food"), and of specific "foods," in particular:

> The term *eating* is applied figuratively to knowledge, learning, and, in general, the intellectual apprehensions through which the permanence of the human form endures in the most perfect of states, just as the body endures through food in the finest of its states. (p. 43/p. 63)

As examples of the scriptural use of the verb "to eat" in this sense, Maimonides cites, among other verses, Proverbs 25:27, which warns against overindulging in honey ("It is not good to eat much honey"), and Proverbs 24:13-14, which recommends eating honey ("My son, eat thou honey, for it is good, and the honeycomb is sweet to thy taste; so know thou wisdom to be unto thy soul"). The meaning of "eating honey" in the latter verse is inferred from the textual context: "honeycomb," which is parallel to "honey," is equivalent to wisdom. It follows that the eating of honey referred to in verse 13 is intellectual apprehension. Maimonides almost certainly relies here implicitly upon the exegetical tradition of the Sages in chapter 2 of Ḥagigah, where "honey" is a metaphor for *Maʿaseh Merkavah* (in R. Joseph's interpretation of Song of Songs 4:11, "honey and milk are under thy tongue"), and the "eating of honey" denotes the apprehension of matters relating to it (this, in the context of the claim that Proverbs 25:16, "Hast thou found honey? eat so much as is sufficient for thee, lest thou be filled therewith, and vomit it out," refers to Elisha). Maimonides applies the same exegetical principle to other Solomonic verses about "eating honey."

In citing the two verses from Proverbs, Maimonides alludes to a central idea developed in *Guide* I.32 and 34: that a person must guard against the temptation to apprehend that which is beyond his ability; the positive goal toward which one should strive is the rational apprehension of God in accordance with human capability.

As in *Hilkhot Yesodei ha-Torah* 2.12, so also in *Guide* I.32, Maimonides adds other verses from Solomon's writings to the Solomonic quotations cited by the Sages in *Ein Dorshin*. All of the passages teach the same central idea, but in this case, Maimonides no longer relies upon the rabbinic interpretations, as he did in *Hilkhot Yesodei ha-Torah*. Instead, he supplies the parallel verse in Solomon's words. By doing so, he strengthens and confirms the exegetical tradition received from the Sages. The first verse Maimonides cites is Proverbs 25:27, "It is not good to eat much honey," used in *Guide* I.30 as an example of the biblical use of "eat" in the sense of apprehension of the intelligibles. In I.32, however, he discusses the whole verse and does not simply infer the meaning of an equivocal term, as he does in chapter 30. Proverbs 25:27 is parallel in meaning only to the first half of Proverbs 25:16, the exhortation of Solomon.[14]

---

14 In *Hilkhot Deʿot* 3.2, Maimonides interprets this verse as defining a norm for conduct in everyday life. But even there it is seen as a kind of parable, in which "honey" in Solomon's words is taken to refer to tasty foods generally.

Maimonides here adds to the two "parables of honey" (Prov. 25:16 and 25:27) two other verses from Solomon's writings that allude to the same prohibition, Ecclesiastes 7:16, "neither make thyself overwise; why shouldest thou destroy thyself?" and Ecclesiastes 4:17, "Guard thy foot when thou goest to the house of God." The first verse warns against overreaching in the attempt to acquire wisdom. Maimonides evidently understood "why shouldest thou destroy thyself?" as parallel to "and vomit it out" in Proverbs 25:16: why should you destroy yourself, i.e., make yourself devoid of intellectual apprehension and human perfection?[15] The second verse, Ecclesiastes 4:17, indicates that one must follow the right path in order to apprehend "divine matters." In *Guide* I.18 Maimonides explained the verb *qarov* as meaning to advance or move forward in the realm of intellectual apprehension; now he indicates that "goest to" refers to approaching the realm of metaphysical knowledge, symbolized by "the house of God," through intellectual apprehension. The caution that Solomon counsels in this verse, Maimonides says, refers to refraining from judgment in cases where the human intellect is unable to decide on the basis of definite proof, and to refraining from efforts to attain that which is beyond the capacity of the human intellect.

In the *Guide of the Perplexed*, Maimonides ascribes further activity to Solomon in the area of providing instruction to the wise man regarding questions of metaphysical knowledge, citing him as one who cautions against haste in the path toward apprehension of God, and who teaches the proper way of acquiring it. His discussion here differs from what we have seen so far. Instead of taking a ready-made model of discussion from the Sages, he presents his own words of instruction, in some cases derived from biblical interpretation, and in others presented by way of interpretation of the words of the Sages in chapter 2 of Ḥagigah.

The warning against haste in attempts to apprehend God is first presented in *Guide* I.5. This chapter does not belong to the Chapters of Instruction, and its main purpose is not to guide the reader toward the proper apprehension of God, but to complete the discussion of the ambiguous verbs *ra'oh*, *habbit*, and *ḥazoh* ("to see," "to look at," and "to

15 Baḥya Ibn Paquda makes similar use of this verse in *Duties of the Heart*, Eighth Treatise, chap. 3. Baḥya also sees this verse as a restriction upon intellectual investigation, but he limits such investigation to those sciences which lead to obedience to God and understanding of His wisdom and His power, recommending that one not engage in sciences which do not serve this end.

vision") that began in chapter 4. It does so by means of an exegesis of biblical stories in which these verbs are used as key words for understanding the description of the apprehension of God. As is well known, the avowed purpose of the lexicographical chapters in book I of the *Guide* is to explain away the anthropomorphic descriptions of God occurring in the Bible. Maimonides points out that since the terms referring to God in the Bible have multiple meanings, the implication that God is corporeal can be eliminated by reading biblical passages in which God is the subject or object in accordance with the meaning that does not convey this notion. There are two main ways in which the Bible's anthropomorphic descriptions of God occur: anthropomorphic descriptions of God Himself, and anthropomorphic descriptions of man's apprehension of God. The interpretation of biblical passages devoted to man's apprehension of God, which appear in lexicographical chapters of the *Guide*, have then as their primary purpose to remove anthropomorphic attributes from God. From another perspective, however, they can be viewed as passages dealing with prophetic apprehension. In the latter respect they form part of Maimonides' account of prophecy. Thus, in completing the discussion in chapter 4, chapter 5 serves, at one and the same time, two functions: to remove anthropomorphic attributes from God and to explain prophecy.

One of the characteristic features of Maimonides' writings in general, and of the lexicographical chapters in book I of the *Guide* in particular, is that each chapter has several different goals, and may be read from several different perspectives and in the context of several different chapters or groups of chapters simultaneously. Another striking aspect of the discussion in chapter 5 is the instruction toward proper apprehension of God. In this respect, chapter 5 must be read alongside the Chapters of Instruction in *Guide* I.31-34. Maimonides evidently anticipates in chapter 5 a number of the ideas to be presented in chapter 34 and, as in chapter 34, he brings Solomonic sources to support his words of instruction.

Chapter 5 is similar in structure to chapter 32, which we have already analyzed. It consists of instructions to a disciple, contrasting models from the conduct of historical figures, and biblical verses which can be interpreted, on the one hand, as parallel to Maimonides' words of instruction, and on the other, as the conclusions to be derived from the historical incidents.[16]

At the beginning of chapter 5, Maimonides presents, in concentrated form, his own view concerning the proper mode of investigation to be adopted by someone who wishes to attain proper knowledge of God in accordance with his ability to follow this path:

> ...man should not hasten too much to accede to this great and sublime matter at the first try, without having made his soul undergo training in the sciences and the different kinds of knowledge, having truly improved his character, and having extinguished the desires and cravings engendered in him by his imagination. When, however, he has achieved and acquired knowledge of true and certain premises and has achieved knowledge of the rules of logic and inference and of the various ways of preserving himself from errors of the mind, he then should engage in the investigation of this subject. When doing this he should not make categoric affirmations in favor of the first opinion that occurs to him and should not, from the outset, strain and impel his thoughts toward the apprehension of the deity; he rather should feel awe and refrain and hold back until he gradually elevates himself. (p. 19/p. 29)

According to this passage, a certain degree of ethical preparation is required if one is to apprehend God in accordance with one's ability. It is necessary to restrain the desires of one's soul, to gradually learn the sciences, and know the rules of logic, which is an "instrument" for scientific investigation.

The examples of correct conduct deserving of imitation, and of improper behavior to be avoided, are derived from the Bible, and not from the Talmud, as in chapter 32. Here, however, Maimonides interprets Scripture on the basis of the rabbinic exegesis found in the Talmud and the midrashim to these texts. The heroes of the biblical accounts are

16 On the interpretation of this chapter, see S. Regev, "The Vision of the Nobles of the Children of Israel (Exod. 24:9-11) in Medieval Jewish Philosophy," *Meḥqerei Yerushalayim be-Maḥshevet Yisrael* 4, nos. 3/4 (1985), pp. 281-86 (Hebrew).

not "Sages" but "prophets" i.e., individuals who were worthy of divine revelation. Maimonides equates their understanding, as well as that of the mystics in the second chapter of Ḥagigah, with the intellectual apprehension of the philosopher. This being so, he sees them as both positive and negative examples for the "wise man" who wishes to apprehend God.

The example of conduct worthy of imitation is Moses. Maimonides bases himself upon the Sages, who connect God's revelation to Moses in the burning bush, of which the Bible says, "And Moses hid his face; for he was afraid to look upon God" (Exod. 3:6), with the description of Moses' vision in Numbers 12:8, "and the similitude of the Lord doth he behold." The Talmud comments: "As a reward for '[he was afraid] to look' (Exod. 3:6), he merited 'and the similitude of the Lord doth he behold' (Num. 12:8)" (B. Berakhot 7a).[17] In other words, the conception of the Godhead enjoyed by Moses was a reward because he had earlier refrained from looking upon God. The Sages evidently understood Numbers 12:3, which speaks of Moses' modesty or meekness ("Now the man Moses was very meek, above all the men that were upon the face of the earth"), as alluding to his conduct at the revelation of the burning bush. But Maimonides interprets Moses' modesty in a different manner. He does not see it as a personality trait or an ethical quality, but as the conduct of a sage engaged in intellectual inquiry.[18] "And Moses hid his face" refers to the fact that Moses refused an immediate apprehension of God because he was unprepared for it and had not learned all the preparatory disciplines that would make it possible. As a reward for this correct conduct, "the similitude of the Lord doth he behold"; according to Maimonides in *Guide* 1.3, this means, "he grasps the truth of God" (p. 18/p. 27).

The "nobles of the children of Israel," identified by Maimonides with the seventy elders, are cited as an example of those who did not follow the correct path, but "were overhasty, strained their thoughts, and achieved apprehension, but only an imperfect one" (p. 20/p. 30). They attempted to apprehend God but were inadequately prepared. This improper way of pursuing the apprehension of God had consequences

17 See also *Tanḥuma*, Genesis 1; Exodus 19; *Exodus Rabbah* 3.1; *Leviticus Rabbah* 20.10; *Numbers Rabbah* 2.25.

18 One must take into account that according to Maimonides' doctrine of prophecy, Moses did not prophesy by means of the power of the imagination; therefore, his apprehension was purely intellectual.

similar to those that followed Elisha ben Abuyah's attempt to apprehend that which was beyond human comprehension: the nobles of the children of Israel apprehended God in a confused way, in an imaginary rather than an intellectual manner, and as a result, "they inclined toward things of the body." That is the meaning of "and they visioned God, and did eat and drink" (Exod. 24:11); i.e., when they failed to attain an intellectual apprehension and had not achieved intellectual perfection, they were guided by the power of the imagination, which drew them toward the physical appetites, represented by eating and drinking. "Eating and drinking" were therefore the result of this imaginative apprehension.

As in *Guide* I.32, here too Maimonides argues that the lesson to be learned from the story, in this case a biblical account, was already formulated by Solomon in the form of a general exhortation:

> Accordingly Solomon has bidden the man who wishes to reach this rank to be most circumspect. He said warningly in parabolic language: "Guard thy foot when thou goest to the house of God." (p. 20/p. 30)

We have already seen that in *Guide* I.32 Maimonides also cites Ecclesiastes 4:17 in support of his words of warning, interpreting it as a "parable" without reference to any exegetical tradition of the Sages, associating this verse with instruction for the apprehension of God. Here, too, Maimonides assumes that Ecclesiastes 4:17 is a "parable," but he sees it as an exhortation concerning the path toward apprehension of God, not, as in chapter 32, as a warning against attempts to attain that which is beyond the limits of human comprehension. According to Maimonides here, Solomon's exhortation included all of the words of personal instruction which Maimonides himself presents at the beginning of the chapter. Maimonides says that his own words of instruction are no more than an interpretation of the words of instruction of a wise man who preceded him, Solomon.

In the Chapters of Instruction, *Guide* I.34, Maimonides returns to the subject of the care to be exercised regarding the path toward the apprehension of God. This chapter completes the discussion begun in chapter 33, and therefore must be understood in the light of that discussion. In chapter 33, Maimonides presents two arguments which serve as an interpretation of the terms used by the Sages in chapter 2 of Ḥagigah and their remarks concerning *Ma'aseh Merkavah*. First, instruction should not begin with metaphysics, because the study of metaphysical subjects will weaken the faith of those who lack the necessary preparation. Thus metaphysics should not be taught to the masses and, in fact, should be concealed from them. At the same time, one may, allusively, reveal a few small metaphysical points to those who have the preparation to understand them. The terms "secret" and "mysteries of the Torah" (*sod* and *siṭrei Torah*), which appear in the Bible and in the rabbinic literature, and are used by Maimonides to denote metaphysics, suggest the idea of concealing metaphysical topics from those who are not fit to receive them, and of communicating them allusively to those who are fit.

Second, metaphysical matters can only be taught to one who is "wise and able to understand by himself." Maimonides interprets this condition, set forth in Mishnah Ḥagigah 2.1, as follows:

> ...the one who is to be taught is *wise*, I mean that he has achieved knowledge of the sciences from which the premises of speculation derive; and the other, that he be full of understanding, intelligent, sagacious by nature, that he divine a notion even if it is only very slightly suggested to him in a flash. This is the meaning of the dictum of the sages: "able to understand by himself." (p. 48/p. 72)

As most people do not satisfy these conditions, it is impossible to teach them metaphysics. The teaching of metaphysics to the masses would constitute a situation in which metaphysical matters were taught directly, without any advance preparation.

Maimonides develops the latter subject in *Guide* I.34, where he lists five "causes that prevent the commencement of instruction with divine science, the indication of things that ought to be indicated, and the presentation of this to the multitude" (p. 49/p. 72). In effect, Maimonides explains here why only unique individuals, constituting an intellectual elite, and not the masses, are able to attain knowledge of God by means of man's ability to know Him. He sets forth the difficulties that stand in the way of one who wishes to apprehend God, the conditions that must be fulfilled, and what one must do in order to succeed in this project. The latter point is identical with the words of instruction to the sage who wishes to apprehend God, and parallels Maimonides' words of instruction in *Guide* I.5. Here, as in I.5, Maimonides bases his argument on what Solomon says in Ecclesiastes and Proverbs. But while in *Guide* I.5 he is satisfied with a general warning from Solomon, here he shows that Solomon also provided a more concrete and detailed warning about the apprehension of God. This warning is presented in the framework of three out of the five items in Maimonides' list of causes preventing the beginning of study with metaphysics. Sometimes in this discussion Maimonides cites a verse from Solomon without offering any interpretation, so that his understanding of the verse must be inferred from the fact that it is used in support of specific words of warning. At times he also provides an interpretation of the verse in order to justify its citation in support of his words of instruction. By finding appropriate verses in support of his own words of instruction, Maimonides here develops, independently of the Sages, the exegetical principle that Solomon's words are to be associated with the question of occupying oneself with metaphysics.

The first cause or reason why instruction should not begin with metaphysics, or "divine science," is "the difficulty, subtlety, and obscurity of the matter itself" (p. 48/pp. 72-73). In other words, there is a certain objective difficulty, in that the subject is in itself a complex one. Maimonides supports this idea by citing, among other sources, Ecclesiastes 7:24: "That which was is far off and exceeding deep; who can find it out?" The use of this verse to support the argument that divine science is profound and difficult to comprehend indicates that Maimonides read it as referring to divine science. This interpretation makes sense when the verse is read within the overall context of Ecclesiastes 7. Since the preceding verse deals with wisdom ("All this have I tried by wisdom; I said, 'I will get wisdom'; but it was far off from me"), Maimonides understood verse 24 as likewise dealing with "wisdom," concerning which it says, "That which was is far off and exceeding deep," etc. According to *Guide* III.54, "the term wisdom (*ḥokhmah*), used in an unrestricted sense and regarded as an end, means in every place the apprehension of Him" (p. 469/p. 636). In applying this meaning of "wisdom" to verse 23, Maimonides is able to interpret Solomon's words in verse 24 as applying to the apprehension of God, the goal of all wisdom.

Maimonides had already cited Ecclesiastes 7:24 in the Introduction to the *Guide*, in support of the claim that a certain branch of the esoteric teachings of the Sages is so profound that it cannot be adequately understood. However, in this instance Maimonides is speaking about *Maʿaseh Bereshit* (physics) and not about *Maʿaseh Merkavah* (metaphysics or divine science):

> And because of the greatness and importance of the subject and because our capacity falls short of apprehending the greatest of subjects as it really is, we are told about these profound matters—which divine wisdom has deemed it necessary to convey to us—in parables and riddles and in very obscure words. As [the sages], *may their memory be blessed*, have said: *It is impossible to tell mortals of the power of the Account of the Beginning. For this reason Scripture tells you obscurely: 'In the beginning God created,' and so on.* They have thus drawn your attention to the fact that the above-mentioned subjects are obscure. You likewise know Solomon's saying: *that which was is far off, and exceeding deep; who can find it out?* (p 5/p 9)

The Maimonidean commentator Efodi (Profiat Duran) found it difficult to understand how Maimonides could cite this verse in one place as referring to the Account of the Beginning (physics) and in another to the Account of the Chariot (metaphysics). He attempted to resolve the difficulty by arguing that the first half of the verse, "that which was is far off," refers, in Maimonides' interpretation, to the Account of the Beginning, and the latter half, "and exceeding deep; who can find it out," to the Account of the Chariot. But since Maimonides uses the same Arabic word for "deep" in both citations of this verse (*al-umūr al-ghāmiḍa* ["the profound matters"] at the beginning of the *Guide*, and *ghumūḍuhu* ["its profundity"; Pines translates "obscurity"] in I.34) this indicates that the Arabic phrase relates to the second half of Solomon's statement: "and exceeding deep; who can find it out." Thus this part of the verse refers to the difficulty in apprehending the contents referred to in both places.

It seems to me that Maimonides' comments on the Account of the Beginning and the Account of the Chariot in the Introduction to the *Guide* explain why he cites the same verse in one place to teach that the Account of the Beginning is "a profound matter," and in another to teach that the apprehension of God is a "deep" thing. Following the Sages, Maimonides distinguishes sharply between these two esoteric sciences, in terms of both their contents and their degree of esotericism, but he also has a certain tendency to somewhat obscure the distinction. Speaking of the Account of the Beginning in the Introduction to the *Guide*, he says of the principles of physics that "they too are secrets of that divine science" (p. 3/p. 7). That is, there is a certain realm which is common to physics and metaphysics, the area in which these two sciences border upon one another. Maimonides is alluding here, among other things, to the causal relationship between the metaphysical world and the physical world, and thus also to the question of the creation of the world. Understanding the creation of the world is, on the one hand, a question of physics, since the explanation of the structure of the created world and the connections among its various parts is physics in the strict sense, but the creation of the physical world and its relation to the metaphysical world is also a metaphysical question. When Maimonides speaks about the "greatness and importance of the subject," "the greatest of subjects," and "these profound matters" in the Introduction to the *Guide*, he is not saying that the Account of the Beginning is physics in the sense of a description of the physical world, but that an aspect of the natural sciences may properly be seen as "secrets of that divine science" (p. 3/p. 7), namely, the creation of the physical world. Ecclesiastes 7:24 refers to this aspect of the Account of the Beginning. Moreover, the very use of this verse, which Maimonides afterwards understands as referring to the Account of the Beginning, indicates that an analogous interpretation is to be given to his comments here. It follows that in both cases in which he uses Ecclesiastes 7:24 to support his own statements, Maimonides understands it as referring to the difficulty in apprehending metaphysical matters: in the Introduction to the *Guide* it is applied to the connection between God and the physical world in the ontological realm, whereas in *Guide* I.34 it is applied to the connection between the physical world and the metaphysical world in the realm of human knowledge, to man's apprehension of God through knowledge of physics. In both instances, there is a certain point of contact between physics and metaphysics, where the "profound thing" relates to the transition to metaphysics.

Another Solomonic verse which evidently refers to the same idea is cited by Maimonides in *Guide* III.54. At the beginning of this chapter, Maimonides discusses the various meanings of the noun *ḥokhmah* ("wisdom"). The first of these is "the apprehension of true realities, which have for their end the apprehension of Him, may He be exalted" (p. 466/p. 632). This definition encapsulates the fundamental idea stated in the explanation of the third reason militating against the commencement of study with metaphysics; namely, that the apprehension of God is the ultimate aim of the process of graduated study of the sciences. Understanding "wisdom" as the comprehension of God made possible by the study of the preparatory sciences, Maimonides says further on in the chapter that "the term *wisdom* [*ḥokhmah*], used in an unrestricted sense and regarded as the end, means in every place the apprehension of Him, may He be exalted" (p. 469/p. 636).

Maimonides illustrates the biblical use of the word "wisdom" in this sense by means of two verses from the Hagiographa: Job 28:12 ("But wisdom, where shall it be found?"),[19] cited in *Guide* I.34 in support of the first reason against commencing study with metaphysical matters, and Proverbs 2:4a ("If you seek her as silver..."). The word "wisdom" does not appear in the half-verse from Proverbs, which must be read, similarly to Ecclesiastes 7:24, in its overall context: "So that thou make thine ear attend unto wisdom, and thy heart incline to discernment; yea, if thou call for understanding, and lift up thy voice for discernment. If thou seek her as silver, and search for her as for hid treasures; then shalt thou understand the fear of the Lord, and find the knowledge of God" (Prov. 2:2-5). From verses 2-3, it is possible to derive the equation: wisdom = understanding (*binah*) = discernment (*tevunah*). From this it may be inferred that verse 4 speaks of wisdom. Thus verse 4 is simply the first half of a conditional sentence continued in verse 5: "If thou seek her as silver...then shalt thou understand." Verses 4-5 state that one who seeks wisdom will achieve knowledge of God. By citing Proverbs 2:4a, Maimonides is saying that the biblical text itself teaches us that "wisdom" has the significance which he indicates here: "the apprehension of true realities, which have for their end the apprehension of Him, may He be exalted" (p. 466/p. 632).

---

19 Chapter 28 of Job deals with the limitations of human as distinguished from divine wisdom. "Wisdom" appears in this chapter in the sense of knowledge of the principles of physical phenomena and their manifestations, by which human life is guided. Maimonides chose here a verse in which the word "wisdom" appears in a way indicative of its sense in the chapter as a whole.

But in citing Proverbs 2:4 in support of the claim that *ḥokhmah* in the Bible has the first meaning discussed here, Maimonides had an additional aim. This verse, like Job 28:12 ("But wisdom, where shall it be found?"), speaks of the difficulty of attaining wisdom. In *Guide* I.34, Maimonides brings Job 28:12 in support of the first reason why instruction should not begin with divine science, namely, "the difficulty, subtlety, and obscurity of the matter itself" (p. 49/pp. 72-73), together with Solomon's words in Ecclesiastes 7:24, "That which was is far off, and exceeding deep; who can find it out?" The citation of the same verse together with a verse stating that the acquisition of wisdom, like the unearthing of silver and hidden treasures, requires much effort, indicates that here too Maimonides wished to allude to the idea of the profundity of wisdom and the difficulty of attaining it. The use of Job 28:12 indicates to the reader that he must reread *Guide* I.34 in order to connect the significance of the noun "wisdom" with the idea of the difficulty of attaining metaphysical truths, and perhaps also with all of the words of instruction found in that chapter.

The third cause against beginning study with metaphysics is "the length of the preliminaries," i.e., the need to master many different sciences, a process which takes a great deal of time. There are two reasons why preliminaries are needed. (1) God can only be comprehended through knowledge of His activities in the world, i.e., by means of physics. Since knowledge of physics is in turn dependent, both directly and indirectly, upon knowledge of mathematics and logic, it is impossible to arrive at knowledge of God without first learning all of these disciplines in a systematic and gradual fashion.[20] Maimonides attributes to Solomon the argument that one must study all these preparatory sciences in order to arrive at the apprehension of God: "Solomon has made it clear that the need for preliminary studies is a necessity and that it is impossible to attain true wisdom except after having been trained" (p. 51/p. 75). According to Maimonides, Solomon said this twice, in Ecclesiastes 10:10 and in Proverbs 19:20, and he quotes both passages without commentary. But the very claim that in these verses Solomon explained the need for scientific studies as preparation for the apprehension of God

20 Compare *Guide* I.5, "man should not hasten too much to accede to this great and sublime matter at the first try, without having made his soul undergo training in the sciences and the different kinds of knowledge" (p. 19/p. 29).

indicates the interpretation which Maimonides gave them. He evidently understood Ecclesiastes 10:10 ("If the iron be blunt, and one do not whet the edge, then must he put to more strength; but even more preparation is needed for wisdom") as meaning that wisdom is made possible by the "preparation" (i.e., the preliminary studies), just as the axe is prepared for use by whetting it. Similarly, he interpreted Proverbs 19:20 ("Hear counsel and receive instruction, that thou mayest be wise in thy latter end") to mean that man must begin by preparing himself through the study of sciences and then "at his end," will arrive at apprehension of God and acquire "wisdom" in the first sense of the word used in *Guide* III.54.[21] (2) Rapid investigation arouses doubts regarding the subject of investigation. It is only possible to have a firm basis for one's doctrine, not susceptible to doubt, if the investigative process leading up to it is gradual and systematic, with the premises of its syllogisms all deduced from the science previously learned.

As in other instances where he deals with the correct method of apprehension, here too Maimonides appends some remarks about its opposite, the incorrect method of apprehension, and the results following it. He does this by means of the "parable of walking," which is similar to the parable of Solomon in Ecclesiastes 4:17:

> One engaged in speculation without preliminary study is therefore comparable to someone who walked on his two feet in order to reach a certain place and, while on his way, fell into a deep well without having any device to get out of there before he perishes. It would have been better for him if he had foregone walking and had quietly remained in his own place. (p. 51/p. 76)

As elsewhere in his discussion of the correct and incorrect methods of apprehension, Maimonides again observes that he is not the first to state that anyone who hopes to apprehend God must first learn all the sciences that prepare for this apprehension, for otherwise he will lose the ability to apprehend God in the proper manner. Maimonides claims that this observation was anticipated by Solomon. He begins with a

21 Similarly, Abravanel interprets here: "which is the wisdom that comes after the preliminaries, and this is 'at your end'."

general exegetical rule pertaining to the Book of Proverbs: namely, that all of Solomon's proverbs concerning the "slothful" or "slothfulness" are to be read as parables whose real subject is "the incapacity to seek knowledge of the sciences" (p. 51/p. 76), i.e., laziness as regards the study of the sciences that prepare man for the apprehension of God. The parables of the slothful describe the conduct of the slothful and what happens to them. Maimonides indicates through these remarks that the reader must himself interpret the parables of the slothful in Proverbs, using the exegetical key provided here.[22] Together with this general directive concerning the parables of the slothful, Maimonides quotes some sayings about wisdom in Proverbs 21:25-26. The first part of this passage is a parable about the slothful, and he gives it a broad interpretation: "The desire of the slothful killeth him; for his hands refuse to labor. He coveteth greedily all day long; but the righteous giveth and spareth not."

In *Guide* I.5 and 32, Maimonides supports his admonitions with stories about the conduct of biblical and talmudic heroes, arranged in pairs of antinomies. Here, however, he brings Solomonic sayings about wisdom that present two contradictory human types, described in terms of the paths they follow: the "lazy" and the "righteous." According to Maimonides, Solomon is speaking here of the means of apprehending God.

Maimonides understands the word *ta'avah* ("appetite") in Proverbs 21:25 as meaning "longing." Thus, the appetite of the "lazy person" is "desirous to achieve his ends" (p. 51/p. 76). His laziness is expressed in his "making no effort to achieve knowledge of the preliminary studies leading up to those ends" (p. 51/p. 76). The combination of desire and laziness kills the lazy person: "the reason why the desire of the slothful kills him is to be found in the fact that he makes no effort and does not work with a view to that which would allay that desire; he has only an abundance of longing and nothing else, while he aspires to things for which he has not the necessary instrument" (p. 51/p. 76). Maimonides

22 It seems reasonable to assume that Maimonides understands the parables of the slothful as belonging to that type in which understanding of the parable depends upon understanding of a central image or its key words, and not upon every single word therein. He in fact makes such a point in the comment to his disciple concerning the meaning of these parables. On this type of parable see (in this volume) "Maimonides' strategy of Interpreting 'Woman'," pp. 134-135. On the two kinds of parables appearing in the Bible, see Klein-Braslavy, *Creation*, pp. 42-44.

does not elaborate upon the meaning of the "death" undergone by the lazy-longing person, but on the basis of the parallel with the parable of the person who falls into a pit, and of the explanation of the words "life" and "death" in *Guide* I.42, we may understand that the lazy person arrives at "false opinions" (p. 63/p. 93) instead of "correct opinions." As a result, he does not acquire that human perfection in which survival of the soul is rooted, and therefore "dies" in the absolute sense of the word "death," for he does not acquire eternity of the intellect.

Maimonides complements Solomon's statement here with a comment of his own: "It would be healthier for him if he renounced this desire" (p. 51/p. 76). By adding this comment, Maimonides establishes a complete parallel between the proverb of the walker who falls into a pit and Solomon's words in Proverbs 21:25. The important idea here, which he sees perhaps as only an expansion of Solomon's words, is presented in a similar context in *Guide* I.32: that one should not draw hasty conclusions and thus avoid falling into error. Maimonides spoke in I.32 about absolutely refraining from drawing conclusions, and about refraining from drawing conclusions concerning matters which are not susceptible to man's understanding; here he recommends the same policy, albeit as a temporary expedient: one should not draw conclusions until the necessary studies have been completed, for otherwise one's conclusions will be hasty and incorrect. This temporary abstention from drawing conclusions opens the door for future progress in one's philosophical inquiries, and serves as preparation for the correct apprehension of God in accordance with one's ability after the necessary scientific studies have been completed. In practice, the approach advocated here is similar to that practiced by Moses at the revelation of God in the burning bush: "And Moses hid his face, for he feared to gaze upon God" (Exod. 3:6). According to Maimonides' interpretation in *Guide* I.5, based upon the interpretation already given by the Sages, this act of restraint enabled Moses ultimately to achieve the apprehension of God—"and the image of God he shall see" (Num. 12:8).[23]

At the opposite pole from the "slothful" is the "righteous." Solomon's statement about the righteous is explained by Maimonides at length,

---

23 Compare also *Guide* I.5: "He should not make categoric affirmations in favor of the first opinion that occurs to him and should not, from the outset, strain and impel his thoughts toward the apprehension of the deity; he rather should feel awe and refrain and hold back until he gradually elevates himself". (p. 19/p. 29).

because in his opinion what Solomon says about the righteous illuminates his view-point on the image of the lazy person who is opposed to the righteous. "But the righteous giveth and spareth not" is interpreted by Maimonides to mean: "the just one [i.e., righteous] among men is he who gives everything its due; he means thereby that he gives all his time to seeking knowledge and spares no portion of his time for anything else" (p. 51; p. 76). The interpretation of this portion of the verse is summarized in a Hebrew interjection within the Arabic text as follows: "He says, as it were: *But the righteous gives his days to wisdom and is not sparing of them...*" (p. 51/p. 76).

As in *Hilkhot Yesodei ha-Torah* 2.12 and in *Guide* I.32, here too Maimonides observes that Solomon presented the same ideas differently at different points in his writings. The idea contained in "the righteous giveth and spareth not" is formulated negatively, as a warning, in Proverbs 31:3: "Give not thy strength unto women." According to Maimonides, "to give" in Proverbs 21:26 means, "to give of your time." The symbolism of "woman" in the Book of Proverbs is explained in the Introduction to the *Guide*, and further elaborated in *Guide* III.8. Maimonides maintains that in the Book of Proverbs, "woman" is synonymous with man's material component, specifically his animal soul, which desires physical things.[24] Thus Solomon's warning in Proverbs 31:3 is a warning against becoming obsessed with one's physical appetites.[25] The person who is attentive to this warning is the righteous "who spareth not" and devotes all of his time to wisdom.

This interpretation of "righteous" sheds further light upon the meaning of "slothful" in the previous verse. The slothful person is not only too lazy to study the preparatory disciplines in order to arrive at a proper knowledge of God, but also devotes most of his time to satisfying his sensual appetites, and therefore is not free to study the sciences that would enable him to acquire proper knowledge of God. Thus the slothful one "gives to women his strength." In this interpretation, Maimonides connects the argument that proper apprehension of God requires systematic study of all the preparatory disciplines in the proper sequence with the claim that proper apprehension of God

24 For the interpretation of the term *'ishah* ("woman"), see Klein-Braslavy, *Adam Stories*, pp. 198-205; (in this volume) "Maimonides' Strategy for Interpreting 'Woman' in the *Guide of the Perplexed.*"

25 Maimonides gives another interpretation of this verse in *Hilkhot De'ot* 4.19, reading it as an instruction concerning man's sexual conduct.

requires ethical preparation. Restraining the appetites is a necessary precondition for proper apprehension of God because only someone who restrains his appetites can devote all of his time to reflection and study.

The antithetical parallel between Proverbs 21:26 and Proverbs 31:3 suggests that the motif of the married harlot in Proverbs, interpreted by Maimonides in the Introduction to the *Guide* and in III.8, is to be associated with the chapters instructing the wise man in the proper apprehension of God. The warning against being led astray by a married harlot is seen as a warning not to be drawn after the corporeal appetites, which prevent man from attaining the final perfection, identified by Maimonides in many places with the stage of apprehending God in accordance with human capability.

The interpretation of Proverbs 21:25-26 is a logical transitional link between the third and the fourth of the causes that prevent the commencement of instruction with metaphysics, according to *Guide* I.34. In practice, the latter part of this interpretation deals with the subject of its cause. The fourth cause against the commencement of study with metaphysics is "the natural aptitudes" (p. 52/p. 76), i.e., the acquisition of those qualities which are "preparation for the rational virtues" (p. 52/pp. 76-77). Here Maimonides cites an additional Solomonic verse in support of his position, Proverbs 3:32:

> It is accordingly indubitable that preparatory moral training should be carried out before beginning with this science, so that man should be in a state of extreme uprightness and perfection; *For the perverse is an abomination to the Lord, but His secret is with the righteous.* (p. 52/p. 77)

Maimonides does not interpret this verse, but anyone familiar with his reading of the Bible will understand how he read it and why he used it to support the argument that the acquisition of moral virtue is a condition for attaining knowledge of God. The two key words upon which Maimonides' interpretation of this verse is based are "the upright" and "His secret." In *Hilkhot De'ot*, Maimonides uses "the upright path" (*ha-derekh ha-yesharah*) to signify the middle path, which is the ideal ethical path.[26] The upright person follows the middle path[27] and possesses the virtues acquired by following it. As we have already seen, Maimonides understands the word "secret" (*sod*) as referring to the secrets of divine science. It follows that "but His secret is with the righteous" means that in order to obtain the "secret," i.e., metaphysical knowledge of God, a person must be upright, i.e., possess moral qualities, namely the intermediate qualities.

Thus, Maimonides reiterates in *Guide* I.34 what he also says in I.5: that the person who wishes to achieve proper knowledge of God must possess proper ethical qualities and learn the sciences in their proper order; and that these words of guidance and instruction to the seeker of wisdom were already uttered by Solomon, "the wisest of all men."

26 *Hilkhot De'ot* 1.4; cf. 1.6, "and we are commanded to walk in these intermediary ways which are the good and upright ways."

27 It is thus that we are to understand Eccles. 7:29, cited by Maimonides in *Guide* III.12: "Behold, this only have I found, that God made man upright." Cf. Klein-Braslavy, *Adam Stories*, p. 157, n. 24.

Maimonides' Exoteric and Esoteric Biblical Interpretations in the *Guide of the Perplexed*

Maimonides' *Guide of the Perplexed* is often considered as belonging to the genre of esoteric literature. In this paper I do not want to undermine this claim, which I have myself maintained in previous studies, but to moderate it. I will argue that in the *Guide* Maimonides also engages in exoteric biblical exegesis and offer some examples of it. Then I will focus on his treatment of the cosmological part of the Creation story and show that this interpretation, which deals with one of the esoteric subjects Maimonides promises to explain in the Guide, is not entirely esoteric.

Maimonides' biblical exegesis should be understood in the light of the aims of his book and its underlying postulates. One of the purposes of the *Guide* is to teach everyone that God is not a corporeal being. Maimonides explains the fact that the Bible speaks of God in corporeal terms by what he considers to be an exegetical rule formulated by the Sages:[1] "The Torah speaks in the language of human beings."[2] He understands this rabbinic dictum to mean that the Torah teaches about God's existence and perfection in a way suitable to the mental capacity of the masses. In the age when the Torah was given, the Israelites could only comprehend the existence of corporeal beings and accept only qualities resembling their own. Consequently the Torah had to speak of God in anthropomorphic and anthropopathic language. Though Maimonides does not say so explicitly, it is most plausible that he understands the

---

1 B. Baba Meṣi'a 31b, B. Berakhot 31a, B. Qiddushin 17b, et *passim*.

2 See *Guide* I. 26, 29, 33, 47, and in Maimonides' halakhic writings: *Introduction to Pereq Ḥeleq, Third Principle*; *Mishneh Torah, Yesodei ha-Torah* 1.9; *Epistle of Resurrection*. In *Moshe be Maimon, Iggerot*, ed. M. D. Rabinovich (Jerusalem, 1970), p. 355. For the interpretation of the dictum, see: A. Nuriel, "'The Torah Speaks in the Language of Human Beings' in the *Guide of the Perplexed*." In M. Hallamish and A. Kasher, ed. *Religion and Language* (Tel Aviv, 1982), pp. 97–103 [repr. in A. Nuriel, *Concealed and Revealed in Medieval Jewish Philosophy* (Jerusalem, 2000), pp. 93-99] (Hebrew); Klein-Braslavy, *Creation*, pp. 24-26, 27, 42, 92, 105, and 106; iadem, "The Flourishing Era of Jewish Exegesis in Spain: The philosophical Exegesis." In M. Saebø, ed., *Hebrew Bible / Old Testament - The History of Its Interpretation*, vol. I (Göttingen, 2000), pp. 314–315.

dictum in a way very similar to the educational myth in Alfarabi's perfect state. The Torah adapted the religious discourse about God to the mental capacity of the multitude at the time and the place it was given, just as the religion of the perfect state, according to Alfarabi, translates philosophical truths into figurative language that suits the multitude's understanding in a certain time and place.[3] Because the religious discourse in the perfect state is time and place dependent, it varies from place to place and from one period to another. According to this implicit interpretation of the rabbinic dictum, the Sages' rule is dynamic: the Torah spoke "the language of human beings" living at the time it was given to Israel. But with the passage of time and the advance of the people who read the Torah, the educational myth can and should be amended. In the case of the corporealization of God, the educational myth should be totally eliminated. The masses, too, are not to think of God as an incorporeal being. The demand that everyone adhere to the doctrine of an incorporeal deity, made in a normative chapter of the *Guide* (I.35), indicates that in Maimonides' mind *all* the people of his era are capable of understanding an incorporeal conception of God and hence can believe in His existence and perfection without having recourse to corporeal language.[4] Speaking "the language of human beings" in his age means proclaiming explicitly that God is not a corporeal being.

In his "Lecture on Maimonides' *Guide of the Perplexed,*"[5] Shlomo Pines argued that Maimonides' attitude towards the denial of God's corporealization was influenced by the dogmatic requirement by the Muwaḥḥidūn of his era that all people, including the masses, acknowledge the incorporeality of God. I think that Pines' explanation of Maimonides' attitude supports my understanding of his interpretation of the rabbinic dictum. Because this dictum states that the Torah is an educational myth, the dogmatic demand by a prominent contemporary theological movement persuaded him that the people of that age could believe in the existence of God and His perfection without having to use corporeal language.

3 I do not believe that the Sages' principle, understood this way, is identical with Alfarabi's educational myth. The educational myth conveys philosophical truths in figurative language, whereas the talmudic dictum refers to the teaching of a religious truth that is not necessarily philosophical. See, however, n. 7 below.

4 See also H. Kreisel, *Maimonides' Political Thought* (Albany, 1999), pp. 193-209.

5 *Iyyun* 47 (1998), pp. 115–128. The lecture was published from Pines' manuscript by S. Stroumsa and W. Z. Harvey.

In *Guide* I.33, Maimonides attributes an esoteric character to this rabbinic dictum. He claims that the masses should not commence their studies with the science of metaphysics, seeing that they cannot understand it adequately. Metaphysical truths must be transmitted to them according to their mental capacity. According to this chapter, the metaphysical topics that should be withheld from the multitude are God's knowledge, God's will, His providence, and His attributes. All of these are "truly *the mysteries of the Torah*." Given that in chapter 33 he states that hiding the truth from the masses, "is the cause of the fact that the *Torah speaks in the language of human beings*, as we have made clear,"[6] he evidently believes that when the Torah was given to Israel the masses might have been harmed by references to God as an incorporeal entity. Because they could apprehend only the existence of a corporeal God, any negation of His corporeality might lead them to doubt His very existence. Maimonides explains the multitude's way of thinking in a similar way in *Guide* I.1. Here he is not speaking of the style in which the Torah is written but of the masses' interpretation of the biblical verse "Let us make man in our image, after our likeness" (Gen. 1:26). Nevertheless, the explanation teaches us about the danger the doctrine of incorporeal God poses for the masses:

> The pure doctrine of the corporeality of God was a necessary consequence to be accepted by them. They accordingly believed in it and deemed that if they abandoned this belief, they would give the lie to the biblical text, that they would even make the deity to be nothing at all unless they thought that God was a body provided with a face and a hand like them in shape and configuration. (p. 14/p. 21)[7]

If my understanding of Maimonides' stance is right, we can conclude that in the *Guide* he restricts the scope of the esoteric teachings of the Bible and extracts the doctrine of God's incorporeality from

6 *Guide* I.26 (p. 48/p. 56); 29 (p. 71/p, 62).

7 I believe that in chapter 33 Maimonides applies the dictum "The Torah speaks in the language of human beings" to a broader range of esoteric matters, such as God's knowledge, His will, His providence, and His attributes. There is a closer analogy between the talmudic dictum, as I understand it, and Alfarabi's educational myth in this chapter than there is in chapter 26.

them. According to *Guide* I.35

> The negation of the corporeality of God and the denial of His having a likeness to created things and of His being subject to affections are matters that ought to be made clear and explained to everyone according to his capacity and ought to be inculcated in virtue of traditional authority upon children, women, stupid ones, and those of a defective natural disposition. (p. 54/p. 81)

When those people become perplexed by the contradiction between the doctrine of the incorporeal God they received from traditional authority (though not by means of demonstration) and the biblical text, the meaning of the verses should be explained to them in a way that does not imply God's corporeality. Maimonides states explicitly that "their attention should be drawn to the equivocality and figurative sense of the various terms—the exposition of which is contained in this Treatise [= the *Guide*]" (p. 55/p. 81). Hence, the biblical-philosophical lexicon provided in the first part of the *Guide* is addressed to these readers as well as to the intellectual elite. There Maimonides explains equivocal terms that may entail the corporealization of God and provides a clear exoteric explanation of these words as well as of some verses in which they appear.[8]

Another purpose of the *Guide* is to free the "perplexed" from their perplexity. Here Maimonides addresses a limited audience—people who are familiar with Aristotelian philosophy and accept it as true, but are also believing Jews, who observe the commandments and accept the authority of the Bible. These readers find inconsistencies and contradictions between the literal meaning of the biblical texts and the philosophical doctrines they accept as true. The perplexed person described by Maimonides in the Introduction to the *Guide* (p. 2/p. 5) is in fact the philosopher who lives in Alfarabi's perfect state, which Maimonides identifies with the state governed by the Law, but who is not aware of its character. He does not know that in the perfect state the philosophical truths are transmitted to the masses in form of educational myths

---

8 I do not, however, maintain that Maimonides' entire biblical-philosophical lexicon is exoteric. The lexicographical chapters also contain esoteric hints, such as the interpretation of the term "likeness" (*demut*) in chapter 1, which also alludes to the story of the chariot in Ezekiel 1:26.

adapted to their understanding, formulated in figurative language to facilitate their grasp in a non-philosophical manner. Consequently there is no real contradiction or inconsistency between philosophy and the biblical texts. The latter have an inner philosophical meaning and can be interpreted in a way that conforms to the philosophical doctrines.

The perplexity of the "perplexed" is partially due to the anthropomorphic notion of God derived from the interpretation of equivocal terms whose primary or more common meanings refer to physical objects and their properties or to their sensory or imaginative apprehension. Thus, the elimination of anthropomorphic and anthropopathic concepts of God by means of exoteric biblical interpretation is intended for two audiences: the masses, who understand them according to their capacity, and the "perplexed" philosophers. The explanation of the terms serves a dual purpose: teaching ordinary people of Maimonides' time that God is incorporeal and freeing the "perplexed" of their perplexity.

Different readers grasp Maimonides' explanations of equivocal terms that may entail an anthropomorphic image of God and of the biblical verses he explains in the lexicographic chapters in different ways. The masses (and "the beginners in speculation" whom Maimonides mentions in the Introduction to the *Guide*, p. 2/p. 5) and the perplexed intellectuals understand them according to their respective capacities.[9] Moreover, Maimonides does not regard his lexicon only as a means to convey authoritative interpretations of biblical terms and verses to his readers, but also as an exegetical tool.[10] Unsophisticated readers will be satisfied with the interpretations of the biblical verses about God that Maimonides provides in the lexicographic chapters. The sophisticated, more perceptive readers will apply the explanations of the terms found in these chapters to other biblical verses and interpret them for themselves. Because the verses may contain more than one equivocal term, perceptive readers have the ability to employ different lexicographical chapters to arrive at a full understanding of verses that Maimonides did not explain in the *Guide*.[11] Though such interpretations depend on

---

9 In *Guide* I.35, Maimonides says that "the negation of the doctrine of the corporeality of God and the denial of His having a likeness to created things and of His being subject to affections are matters that ought to be made clear and explained to everyone according to his capacity" (p. 54/p. 81).

10 See *Guide* I.8 (p. 22/pp. 33–34).

11 Readers may interpret Michaiah's vision of God in 1 Kings 22:19—"I saw the Lord on his throne, and all the host of heaven standing beside him"—in accordance with Maimonides' explanations in the lexicographic chapters of the terms that figure in the vision. Maimonides interprets part of the vision in

perceptive reading and presuppose readers of greater intellectual capacity than the masses, they are still exoteric.

The exoteric biblical interpretations addressed to the philosophers, however, are broader in scope than those directed to the multitude as well, and deal with more philosophical topics. Hence the *Guide* contains two levels of exoteric interpretations: exoteric interpretations addressed to most of the people and those meant for the intellectual elite.

As already noted, the exoteric interpretations addressed to the intellectual elite are based on Alfarabi's idea of educational myth:[12] in the perfect state, religion comes after philosophy. It teaches philosophical doctrines in figurative language so that the masses will be able to understand them according to their capacity. The identification of the "state of the Law" with Alfarabi's perfect state justifies a philosophical reading of biblical texts written in figurative language, even if they do not appear to contradict philosophical doctrines and do not cause perplexity. The philosophical reading proves that the true beliefs of the Law are in fact philosophical doctrines, albeit presented in figurative language.

The aim of freeing the perplexed of their perplexity should entail explicit and clear exegesis of biblical texts. But the *Guide* is based on another presupposition as well, the idea that the Bible contains esoteric teachings to be concealed from the masses and divulged only to a select group—the intellectual elite among whom the "perplexed" are numbered. The main subjects of the esoteric teaching are the "Account of the Beginning" and the "Account of the Chariot," which Maimonides identifies respectively with Aristotelian physics and metaphysics.[13]

Esotericism and educational myth may coexist. A text can be formulated in a way adapted to the understanding of the masses, and

---

Guide I.4, where he explains "to see" but readers can complete the interpretation from chapter 9, which explains "throne," and from chapter 11, which explains "sitting." Because "throne" has two derivative senses, there are two possible interpretations to this part of Michaiah's vision. For the interpretation of Michaiah's vision see S. Klein-Braslavy, "Bible Commentary." In Kenneth Seeskin (ed.,) *The Cambridge Companion to Maimonides* (Cambridge, 2005), pp. 252-253.

12 Maimonides acknowledges this explicitly in *Guide* III.27.

13 It is important to note that in *Guide* I.35 Maimonides lists what are "truly the mysteries of the Torah." In addition to distinctly metaphysical issues, such as God's attributes, God's knowledge, His will, and His names, the list also includes issues associated with the relationships between God and the world, such as "His creation of that which He created, the character of His governance of the world, the 'how' of His providence in respect to what is other then He" (p. 54/p. 80) and prophecy. Maimonides regards these issues as being just as esoteric as the Account of the Chariot. See Klein-Braslavy, *Creation*, pp. 45–48.

thus function as an educational myth, concealing the truth from that audience and hinting at it to the worthy. Esoteric doctrines must be transmitted in special esoteric ways. Because the interpretation of esoteric texts unlocks their secret doctrines, it must be done by the same esoteric methods of transmission. Hence, though Maimonides intends to free the perplexed of their perplexity by philosophical interpretations of the Bible, he cannot provide them with clear exoteric explanations only. He must have recourse to esoteric methods. Here, as in the case of biblical interpretations that presuppose that the Bible conveys philosophical doctrines in figurative language in order to adapt them to the comprehension of the multitude, the assumption that the Bible communicates esoteric doctrines entails esoteric philosophical interpretations of texts even when their literal meaning does not contradict philosophy and does not cause perplexity.

Maimonides adopts the method of transmission of the "Account of the Chariot" suggested by R. Ḥiyya (B. Ḥagigah 13a): "[only] chapter headings may be transmitted to him." Understanding "chapter headings" to mean allusions, he employs the latter as a method for interpreting esoteric biblical texts.[14] The method presupposes that readers are familiar with Aristotelian philosophy and hence able to understand the allusions in the light of Aristotelian physics (including anthropology and psychology) and metaphysics.

Maimonides employs another esoteric device, too: scattering allusion in different chapters of the *Guide*. In the Introduction he explicitly describes the method: "Even those [chapter headings] are not set down in order or arranged in coherent fashion in this treatise, but rather scattered and entangled with other subjects that are to be clarified" (p. 3/ p. 6).[15]

It needs to be emphasized, though, that not every biblical interpretation scattered in various chapters of the *Guide* is necessarily esoteric; nor is every interpretation that appears in a single chapter and contributes to the understanding of a topic in another chapter or chapters necessarily esoteric. There are two types of "scattering" in the *Guide*: intentional and unintentional. The first is a way to convey esoterica; the second is a result of the book's composition. The *Guide*, like most works of philoso-

14 For the meaning of "chapter headings" in the *Guide*, see Klein-Braslavy, *Esotericism*, p. 66.
15 Maimonides learns this method, too, from the Sages. See *Guide* II.29 (p. 244/p. 347).

phy, has a certain plan. The different issues it deals with are subordinated to this plan. Maimonides is aware, however, that connecting the book's chapters in a different order than the original one may promote a better understanding of some of the issues it addresses. Moreover, other combinations of ideas and biblical interpretations might yield discourses that could not be treated within the original structure of the book. The guidelines he offers to readers in the "instruction with respect to the treatise" direct them towards a more flexible reading of the book, enabling them to derive more benefit from it.[16]

The most outstanding example of a non-esoteric interpretation that is dispersed over several chapters of the *Guide* is that dealing with God's promise to reveal Himself to Moses in the Cleft of the Rock (Exod. 33: 21–23): "Behold, there is a place by me where you shall stand upon the rock. And it shall come to pass while My glory pass by, and I will cover you with My hand until I have passed. And I will take away My hand and you shall see My back, but My face shall not be seen." The fact that Maimonides does not interpret this promise in a continuous manner, but explains eight of the terms that appear in it (place, stand, rock, pass, glory, see, back, and face) in eight widely separated chapters,[17] does not prove that he considers the description of the promised revelation to be esoteric and hence employs the esoteric method of "scattering." An incorrect understanding of the terms in which God's promise to reveal Himself in the Cleft of the Rock is written is liable to entail the corporealization of God. Consequently Maimonides explains to all readers that these are equivocal terms and also have incorporeal meanings. He instructs them to apply these meanings in verses related to God. Maimonides does not resort to allusion here. Rather, each term is clearly explained and each of its meanings is illustrated by biblical verses. Understanding his explanations and the various verses, however, depends on the readers' capacity. Some will not be able to comprehend them all, even though Maimonides does not explain them allusively. The scattering of the explanation of these terms is simply the result of

16 It is interesting to note that most of Maimonides' esoteric interpretations that are conveyed by "chapter headings" are continuous interpretations of the biblical texts, although they do not always interpret the whole passage or the entire biblical chapter. The "chapter headings" that are scattered in the *Guide* help readers understand the allusions offered in the main interpretative passage or chapter.

17 "Place," chap. 8; "to stand," chap. 15; "rock," chap. 16; "to pass," chap. 21; "glory," chap. 64; "to see," chap. 4; "back," chap. 38; "face," chap. 37.

structural constraints. Because Maimonides decided to begin the book with a series of lexicographic chapters, a continuous exposition of the promised revelation in the *Guide* was not possible. All the same, he regards this as one of the most important secondary exegetical subjects of the lexicographic chapters. This is evident from the fact that, in addition to elucidating eight terms that figure in the promise of the revelation in the Cleft of the Rock in the lexicographic chapters of the *Guide*, thereby enabling intelligent readers to arrive at the full understanding of the revelation on their own, he draws on it for the examples he provides for the use of these terms in their spiritual meaning. That is, Maimonides openly and clearly interprets parts of the revelation in the lexicographic chapters themselves.[18] The choice of precisely these very verses to illustrate the biblical use of the terms applied to God shows that Maimonides intended to provide an interpretation of the promised revelation in the Cleft of the Rock within the constraints set by the structure of the first part of the *Guide*. Still, the interpretation is meant for readers with a higher intellectual capacity than the masses. Maimonides assumes that some can read the chapters actively and arrive at a full interpretation of God's revelation in the Cleft of the Rock by themselves. Not all readers of the *Guide* have these intellectual capacities. It is plausible that many of them will not be able to accomplish it. But that does not mean that the interpretation itself is esoteric and that Maimonides intends to withhold it from the unworthy.

I think that the criterion we must use for distinguishing biblical texts Maimonides considers to be esoteric and those he sees as non-esoteric for his age is the use of interpretation by "chapter heading." Only an interpretation conveyed through hints is an interpretation of an esoteric text. An overt and clear interpretation shows that Maimonides does not consider the verse or the passage in question to be esoteric, even though simple readers may not be able to understand it. Applying this criterion, we find that the *Guide* contains several interpretations that are not esoteric, even though they are addressed only to readers who

---

18 "There is a place by me." chaps. 8 and 16; "Where you shall stand upon the rock," chaps. 15 and 16; "And it shall come to pass while My glory pass by," chap. 21; "And I will cover you with My hand until I have passed," chap. 21; "And you shall see My back," chaps. 21 and 38; "But My face shall not be seen," chaps. 21 and 37. The lexicographic chapters also contain interpretations of other verses in the revelation: "My face shall go and I will give you rest" (Exod. 33:14), chap. 37; "I beseech you, let me see Your glory" (v. 18), chaps. 4 and 64; "But my face shall not be seen" (v. 20), chap. 37; "and the Lord passed by before his face" (*ibid.* 34:6), chap. 21 (two interpretations).

have a philosophical education and high intellectual capacities. There is nothing in them that can damage the faith of the masses, in Maimonides' age. Hence they should not be withheld, even if the masses cannot understand them, in part or whole. In addition the interpretation of God's promise to reveal himself to Moses in the Cleft of the Rock, Maimonides' interpretations of Moses' requests, God's answers, and the actual revelation (Exod. 33:13–20 and 34:6–7) in *Guide* I.54 are all exoteric.

Guide I.54 is not a lexicographic chapter, but one of those that discuss God's attributes. In this chapter Maimonides asserts and completes the theoretical discussion of God's attributes found in *Guide* I.51–53. He looks at this issue from a new perspective and uses a different method—the exegesis of a biblical text. Here he does not explain equivocal terms but biblical verses that raise difficulties and represent God in terms of moral qualities.

Maimonides begins with a lucid and systematic explanation of Moses' requests and God's answers, followed by a description of God's revelation in terms of moral qualities. He openly explains that the prophet as a political leader governs society by imitating God's attributes of action. He solves the contradiction between the notion of God as a spiritual, non-corporeal entity and His description in terms of moral qualities through a clear explanation of the mechanism that translates the apprehension of physical phenomena that he considers to be God's attributes of action into terms of affections of the soul or moral qualities.[19]

First he explains the process of the "translation": "Whenever one of His actions is apprehended, the attribute from which this actions proceeds is predicated of Him, may He be exalted, and the name deriving from that action is applied to Him" (p. 85/p. 125). Then he illustrates the process of translation by an analysis of two properties by which Moses describes God's revelation in the Cleft of the Rock: "merciful" and "gracious." At the end of the discussion, after interpreting "negative" characteristics applied to God in the Bible — "a jealous avenging God; the Lord is vengeful and fierce in wrath" (Nah. 1:2) — he explains at length how the prophet who is a political leader should apply the apprehension of these attributes in his governance of the city.[20]

19 It is worth noting that this interpretation is very similar to R. Judah Halevi's far-from-esoteric interpretation of God's attributes in *Kuzari* 2.2. Halevi interprets the attributes "jealous and vengeful" and "merciful and gracious" that Maimonides interprets in *Guide* I.54.

20 See p. 86/p. 126.

The open explanation of this issue proves that Maimonides does not consider the prophet-as-governor and his apprehension of God's attributes of action to be an esoteric matter, but a subject that should be explained to intelligent readers. He does not seem to believe that this interpretation of Exodus 33:13–20 and 34:6–7 can harm the masses of his era, even though they will not be able to understand it fully. Hence God's promise to reveal himself to Moses in the Cleft of the Rock, Moses' requests, God's reply, and the revelation itself are all non-esoteric and are not expounded by esoteric methods.[21]

Maimonides also provides a detailed and clear exoteric interpretation of the metaphor of the "married harlot," which he formulates himself on the basis of Proverbs 6:26 (*Guide* III.8, p. 310/p. 431), and of the parable built around it in Proverbs 7:6–21 (Introduction, pp. 8–9/ pp. 13–14).[22] In *Guide* III.8 he suggests that the metaphor of the "married harlot" concerns the physical world. It presents the principles of the sublunar world—matter, form, and privation—and their behavior:

> How extraordinary is what Solomon said in his wisdom when likening matter to *a married harlot*, for matter is in no way found without form and is consequently always like *a married woman* who is never separated from *a man* and is never *free*. However, notwithstanding her being *a married woman*, she never ceases to seek for another man to substitute for her husband, and she deceives and draws him on in every way until he obtains from her what her husband used to obtain. This is the state of matter. For whatever form is found in it, does but prepare it to receive another form. And it does not cease to move with a view to putting off that form that actually is in it and to obtaining another form; and the selfsame state obtains after that other form has been obtained in actu. (p. 310/p. 431)

---

21 However, Maimonides does not explain how Moses gave the Law to the people of Israel. He seems to have considered this issue to be esoteric and does not even offer allusions for understanding it. The way in which Moses gave the Law is left for students of the *Guide* to guess.

22 For a full analysis of the metaphor of the "married harlot" and the parable of the "married harlot" see (in this volume) "Maimonides' Strategy for Interpreting 'Woman' in the *Guide of the Perplexed*," pp. 130-133; 134-140.

Maimonides offers an explanation of the parable of the "married harlot" in the introduction to the *Guide*. He understands that the parable deals with a practical issue: while its external meaning is a concrete warning, the counsel not to follow a harlot, the inner meaning is a general warning based on the principles of Aristotelian anthropology:

> The outcome of all this is a warning against the pursuit of bodily pleasures and desires. Accordingly he [Solomon] likens matter, which is the cause of all these bodily pleasures, to *a harlot* who is also *a married woman*. ... For all the hindrances keeping man from his ultimate perfection, every deficiency affecting him and every disobedience, come to him from his matter alone, as we shall explain in this Treatise. This is the proposition that can be understood from this parable as a whole. I mean that man should not follow his bestial nature; I mean his matter. (pp. 8–9/pp. 13–14)

After elucidating the parable, Maimonides states explicitly that he offers readers an exoteric explanation of the esoteric parable: "And as I have explained this to you and *disclosed the secret* of this parable" (p. 9/p.14; [emphasis mine]). Here again he reduces the scope of biblical esotericism and explains the meaning of an esoteric biblical text to everyone.

The Account of the Beginning is one of the two esoteric subjects Maimonides promises to explain in the *Guide*: In *Guide* II.29 he declares: "The first purpose of this Treatise [the *Guide*] is to explain what can be explained of the *Account of the Beginning* and of the *Account of the Chariot*" (p. 243/p. 346).[23] According to Mishnah Ḥagigah 2.1, the Account of the Beginning is less esoteric than the Account of the Chariot. While the Account of the Beginning can be transmitted only to a single person, without however the stipulation of further qualifications, the Account of the Chariot can be conveyed to one only if he is "wise and understands by himself." In the Introduction to the *Guide,* Maimonides at first seems to follow the distinction between the two levels of eso-

23 See Introduction to *Guide* II, *Guide* II.2 (p. 176/pp. 253–254).

tericism proclaimed by the Sages. He says: "Know that with regard to natural matters as well, it is impossible to give a clear exposition when teaching some of their principles as they are. For you know the saying of [the Sages] *may their memory be blessed*: *The account of the Beginning ought not to be taught in the presence of two men...* Hence these matters too occur in parables in the books of prophecy" (p. 3/p. 7). At the end of the passage, though, he seems to blur this distinction. Pointing out that the Sages also "spoke of them [the secrets of the Account of the Beginning] in riddles and parables," he says that "there is a close connection between these matters and the divine science, and *they too are secrets of that divine science*" (*ibid.*; emphasis mine). If some of the principles of the natural matters "are secrets of that divine science," they too should be conveyed by esoteric methods and the biblical texts that transmit them should be interpreted by esoteric methods, that is, by allusions. In *Guide* II.29 Maimonides emphasizes the esoteric character of the Account of the Beginning: "Not everything mentioned *in the Torah* concerning the *Account of the Beginning* is to be taken in its external sense as the vulgar imagine" (p. 243/p. 346). But if "not everything" is to be taken in its external sense, we may infer that some things are to be so understood. In other words, some biblical texts associated with the *Account of the Beginning* should be interpreted literally.

At the end of chapter 29, Maimonides announces the subject of the following chapter: there will "give several indications as to texts concerned with the *Account of the Beginning*" (p. 243/ p. 346). These turn out to be the stories of the creation of the world, of the creation of man, of the Garden of Eden, and of Adam's sons — Cain, Abel, and Seth. The stories of the creation of man, of the Garden of Eden, and of Adam's sons are explained only by means of a "hard" esoteric method, but the cosmological portion of the story is interpreted in various ways: exoteric, "soft" esoteric, and "hard" esoteric interpretation.[24] Let us proceed to analyze these methods.

Not all of the philosophical exoteric interpretations of the cosmological part of the story of creation are meant for the masses; some of them target persons who have some knowledge of Aristotelian philosophy,

24 For an analysis of the cosmological part of the story of creation, see Klein-Braslavy, *Creation*. Here I consider Maimonides' interpretation from another point of view. The analysis that follows supplements the one I offered there.

including the intellectual elite. For them, Maimonides demonstrates that the biblical texts concerning the Account of the Beginning conform to Aristotelian physics.

Maimonides provides an exoteric interpretation of the word "earth" (*'ereṣ*). He begins by noting that it is an equivocal term and explains it as he does in the biblical-philosophical lexicon in the first part of the *Guide*:

> Among the things you ought to know is that *earth* is an equivocal term used in a general and a particular sense. In a general sense it is applied to all that is beneath the sphere of the moon. I mean the four elements. In a particular sense it is applied to one element, the last among them, namely, earth. (*Guide*, II.30, p. 246/p. 350)

Then he offers a clear explanation of the senses in which the word "earth" should be understood in the story of creation. In Genesis 1:1, "In the beginning God created the heaven and the earth," it refers to the four elements; in Genesis 1:10, "And God called the dry land earth," it means the element "earth."

Maimonides also explains that the Bible itself provides an "interpretative key" to the equivocity of the term "earth" and its meaning in verse 10. The phrase, "God called A *B*" indicates that *B* is an equivocal term and that in its second appearance in the text it has a different meaning from its first. Given that second occurrence of "earth" in Genesis 1 is preceded by "God called [the dry land earth]" (v. 10), "earth" in this verse has a different meaning than in verse 1.[25] Maimonides regards this "interpretative key" as "a great secret of the secrets" (p. 246/p. 351); nevertheless, it is a secret that he reveals to all readers. Here, as with the interpretation of anthropomorphic and anthropopathic terms in the Bible and the parable of the "married harlot," Maimonides reduces the scope of the esoteric teaching of the Bible and reveals one of its secrets. I think that he reveals the "secret" of a meta-linguistic device because he considers that it cannot damage the faith of the masses.

For readers acquainted with Aristotelian physics, Maimonides also

25 Maimonides finds this "interpretative key" also in Genesis 1:8, "and God called the firmament Heaven," and uses it to interpret the verse. See Klein-Braslavy, *Creation*, pp. 185–186 and (in this volume) "The Interpretation of the Story of the Second Day of Creation," pp. 28; 37.

offers an exoteric interpretation of Genesis 1:2: "And the earth was unformed and void, and the darkness was upon the face of the deep; and the spirit of God moves upon the face of the waters." According to this interpretation, the verse describes the four elements—fire, air, water, and earth:

> A proof of this [that *earth* in a particular sense is the element earth] is his saying: "And the earth was unformed and void, and the darkness was upon the face of the deep; and the spirit of God" and so on. Thus sometimes he called all the elements earth. Afterwards he said: "and God called the dry land earth" (Gen. 1:10). (*ibid.*, p. 246/ pp. 350–351)

Maimonides adds that the story of creation mentions the elements in their order in the Aristotelian theory of natural place:

> The elements are mentioned according to their natural position; namely, first the earth, then the water that is above it, then the air that adheres to the water, then the fire that is above the air. (*ibid.*)

Though these are philosophical interpretations, Maimonides considers them to be literal construals. These terms and verses do not have a meaning suited to the grasp of the multitude, unlike the "married harlot" metaphor. Their only import is philosophical.[26]

Maimonides does not explain the word "heaven." He must have considered its meaning to be self-evident. He does, however, explain some astronomical points that can be learned from the wording of Genesis 1:17—"And God set them [the moon, the sun and the stars] in the firmament of the heaven"—taking for granted that "heaven" means the spheres:[27]

---

26 Maimonides explains the word *maqom* (place) in the same way in *Guide* I.8. The philosophical or scientific meaning of this word is its only primary meaning. *Maqom* has no other physical meaning than "particular and general place" (p. 22/p. 33).

27 This is also the interpretation that Maimonides assumes in *Guide* I.4, 9, and 11. In *Guide* I.70 he explains that *shamayim* (heavens) in the expression "the rider of the heavens" (Deut. 33:26) is only one sphere, the sphere that encompasses the universe. See Klein-Braslavy, *Creation*, pp. 131–133 and "The Interpretation of the Story of the Second Day of Creation," p. 23.

In these words there is likewise a clear indication of what has already been demonstrated, namely, of the fact that all the stars as well as the sun and the moon are situated within the sphere—as there is no vacuum in the world—and that they are not located upon the surface of a sphere, as the vulgar imagine. This appears from his saying: in the firmament of the heaven, and not upon the firmament of the heaven. (*ibid.*, p. 247/p. 352)

The wording "*in* the firmament of the heaven" shows that the biblical description conforms to an astronomical doctrine demonstrated in Aristotelian philosophy — that the stars are located inside the spheres and not on their surface.[28] Maimonides explains that this doctrine is founded on the fact, as proven in Aristotle's physics,[29] that there is no vacuum.

The masses imagine that the stars are located on the surface of the sphere.[30] They make this mistake because they use imagination instead of intellect.[31] From this comment we may infer that although the masses are incorrect about the location of the stars, they are acquainted with the doctrine of the spheres. Hence it is most plausible that Maimonides thought that even the multitude of his time understood that "heaven" means the spheres. The term *shamayim* (heaven), like *maqom* (place) in its first sense,[32] does not have a second non-scientific or non-philosophical meaning. On this point, the multitude differs from the philosophers only in the latter's understanding that the stars are located inside the spheres. For readers conversant with Aristotle, Maimonides explains that the biblical verse conforms to the principles of the Aristotelian astronomy. His explanation is exoteric and clear. Again, he evidently believes that knowing the correct location of the stars will not weaken the faith of the masses.

Thus far we have been considering interpretations based directly

---

28 Because the music of the spheres results from the friction between the stars and the spheres, Maimonides' insistence that the stars are located inside the spheres and not upon their surface is a tacit rejection of the Pythagorean doctrine of the harmonic music of the spheres. See Aristotle, *On the Heavens* II.9. For Maimonides' discussion of the issue, see: *Guide* II.8; Klein-Braslavy, *Creation*, pp. 187–188.

29 See Aristotle, *Physics* IV. 7–9. In *Guide* II.24 (p. 227/p. 324) Maimonides states explicitly that this premise was demonstrated.

30 In *Guide* II.8 Maimonides attributes this notion to the Sages as well, but says that they changed their mind and accepted the opinion of "the sages of the nations of the world" (p. 186/p. 267).

31 According to *Guide* I.73, premise ten, it is the intellect, and not the imagination, which is the criterion of the necessary and the impossible.

32 See *Guide* I.8.

on the biblical text. In two other exoteric comments on the Account of the Beginning Maimonides relies on the Sages: *et ha-shamayim ve-et ha-'areṣ* [the heaven and the earth] (Gen. 1:1) and the growth of grass and trees on the Third Day. Although midrashic interpretations of biblical texts are frequent in the *Guide*, most of them are esoteric and use the midrashim as comments that allude to the inner meaning of the text.[33] Here Maimonides relies on explicit exoteric interpretations of the Sages and not on esoteric midrashic hints.

Expounding Genesis 1:1, Maimonides cites the Sages' understanding that the heaven and the earth were created together:

> Among the things that you ought to know is the fact that the *Sages* have *explicitly* [emphasis mine] stated in a number of passages that the word *et* figuring in his words *et h-shamayim ve-et ha-'areṣ* [the heaven and the earth] (Gen. 1:1), has in that verse the meaning: with. They mean by this that He created together with the heaven all that is in the heaven and together with the earth all that is in the earth.[34] You already know that they make it clear that the heaven and the earth were created together because He says: *I call unto them, they stand up together* (Isa. 48:13). Accordingly everything was created simultaneously.[35] (*ibid.*, p. 245/p. 350)

With regard to the growth of the grass and trees on the Third Day, he connects the biblical description in verses 11–12 with Genesis 2:6—"And there went up a mist from the earth"—and explains (on the basis of *Genesis Rabbah* 13.1) that the grass and the trees grew after

33 For example, his interpretations of the story of the creation of man and the story of the Garden of Eden in *Guide* II.30. See Klein-Braslavy, *Adam Stories*, pp. 95–96, 101–104, 122–124, 167–192, 201–212, 270–273; iadem, (in this volume) "Interpretative Riddles in Maimonides' *Guide of the Perplexed*," pp. 145-160. Another example is the interpretation of Jacob's dream of the ladder in *Guide* II.10. For a discussion of this issue, see (in this volume) "Maimonides' Interpretation of Jacob's Dream of the Ladder," pp. 95-102. See also S. Klein-Braslavy, "The Philosophical Exegesis," pp. 317–318; iadem, "Bible Commentary," pp. 256-261; J. A. Diamond, *Maimonides and the Hermeneutics of Concealment: Deciphering Scripture and Midrash in the Guide of the Perplexed* (New York, 2002). For some aspects of the method of allusion in the *Guide*, see Klein-Braslavy, "Interpretative Riddles."

34 Maimonides is referring to the statement by R. Akiva (*Genesis Rabbah* 1.14), who adopts the exegetical principle propounded by Naḥum 'Ish Gamzu .

35 Maimonides is referring to B. Ḥagigah 12b.

God caused the rain to fall:

> Among the things that you ought to know is that the *Sages* have made it clear that God only made grass and trees grow from the earth after he had caused rain to fall upon them, and that its saying: *And there went up a mist from the earth* (Gen. 2:6) is a description of the first state of matters obtaining before the command: Let the earth put forth grass. For this reason *Onqelos* translates: *And there had gone up a mist from the earth.* This is also clear from the [scriptural] text itself because of its saying: *And no shrub of the field was yet in the earth* (Gen. 2:5), *This is clear by now.* (*ibid.*, p. 248–9/p. 354; emphasis mine)

The Sages' interpretation allows Maimonides to argue that the biblical description of the created beings corresponds to the natural order of the sublunar world according to Aristotelian physics. First he uses clear scientific language to describe the order of nature according to Aristotelian physics:

> You who are engaged in speculation, know that after the forces of the sphere, the first of the causes producing generation and passing-away are light and darkness — because of the heat and the cold consequent upon them. The elements intermix in consequence of the motion of the sphere, and their combinations vary because of light and darkness. The first combination that is produced by them is constituted by two exhalations, which are the first causes of all the meteorological phenomena among which rain figures. They are also the causes of the minerals and, after them, of the composition of the plants, and after those, of that of the living beings; the final composition being that of man. Darkness is the nature of the existence of the whole lower world, light supervening in it. It should be sufficient for you to know that when there is no light, the state of matters remains permanent. (*ibid.*, p. 249/p. 354)

At the end of the description he clearly explains the correspondence between the philosophical doctrine and the biblical text: "The [scriptural] text about the Account of the Beginning *goes exactly* in this order, leaving out nothing" (*ibid.*; emphasis mine).[36] Maimonides is openly addressing the reader who "is engaged in speculation," namely the philosopher. The biblical text does not cause any perplexity. Maimonides merely wants to show readers that there the Bible and Aristotelian philosophy agree with each other.

Alongside these exoteric interpretations, Maimonides also offers two types of esoteric explanations for some of the cosmological parts of the story of creation: "soft" and "hard." Maimonides offers a "soft" esoteric interpretation of "firmament" and "the water which were above the firmament" (Gen. 1:7).[37] He openly admits that such an explication is the result of a textual constraint. There is a contradiction between the literal meaning of the text and Aristotelian physics, which may perplex readers who accept Aristotelian philosophy as the truth. If the firmament is the spheres, as readers may understand, the biblical statement that there is water above the firmament contradicts the Aristotelian doctrine that there is nothing upon the spheres.[38] The only way to free the "perplexed" from their perplexity is to interpret the biblical text in a way compatible with Aristotle. Nevertheless, Maimonides considers the philosophical meaning of the text to be esoteric and thinks that the literal meaning of the text conceals it from the multitude in order to protect their faith.

> But there is something hidden, as you will see, with regard to the firmament and the thing above it, which is called *water*. ... If on the other hand, the matter is considered according to its inner meaning and to what was truly intended, it is most hidden. For in that case it was necessary for it to be one of the concealed secrets so that the vulgar should not know it. (*ibid.*, p. 248/p. 353)

---

36 But see my comment on this statement in *Creation*, pp. 222–227.

37 It is worth noting that Maimonides does not cite this part of the verse in Hebrew, but only refers to its meaning.

38 This is how Gersonides understands Maimonides. Gersonides understands that "Maimonides interprets the term *raqiʿa* as the coldest part of the air in which the clouds and the rain are generated. He was led to this interpretation by his reluctance to believe that there is water surrounding the heavenly body" (*The Wars of the Lord* VI.2.7, (Hebrew, Leipzig, 1866), p. 425, S. Feldman's English translation: Levi ben Gershom (Gersonides), *The Wars of the Lord*, vol. 3 (Philadelphia, 1999), p. 442.)

Maimonides does not explain how the vulgar understand the literal meaning of the text. According to an opinion that Abravanel cites from Saʿadiah Gaon's lost commentary on the Pentateuch, the masses believe that the firmament is something rigid—"a spherical hard body"—with water beneath it and above it.[39]

Because the meaning of the verse is esoteric, Maimonides interprets it by an esoteric method. Instead of explaining what it is that the Bible calls "firmament" and "the water which were above the firmament," as he did in his exoteric interpretation of "earth," he merely drops hints. These hints are addressed to readers who have already studied philosophy. The first hint is that the "water which were above the firmament," the "water which were under the firmament" and the "firmament" are all created from the element "water."[40] The second is an explicit reference to Aristotle's *Meteorology*. Maimonides concludes his interpretation of the "firmament" and the "water which were above the firmament" as follows:

> Reflect, if you are one of those who reflect,[41] to what extent he [R. Akiva] had made clear and revealed the whole matter in this statement [do not say, Water, Water...], provided that you consider it well, understand all that has been demonstrated in the *Meteorologica*. (*ibid.*, p. 248/p. 353)

Here, as in the interpretation of the astronomical matters in Genesis 1:17, Maimonides relies on a scientific truth, a demonstrated doctrine. This time, it is a doctrine proven in Aristotle's *Meteorology*. Because this scientific doctrine is harmful to the multitude, he does not state it explicitly, as he did for "in the firmament of the heaven," but only

39 See Klein-Braslavy, *Creation*, p. 169-170; and (in this volume) "The Interpretation of the Story of the Second Day of Creation," p. 45 n33.

40 Maimonides explains that the verb *va-yavdel* (divided) in Gen. 1:7 does not refer merely to a division in place but to a division with regard to the form of the water that was under the firmament and the water that was above the firmament. Both are water. For the interpretation of the verb *va-yavdel* see also "The Interpretation of the Story of the Second day of Creation," p. 27. As to the claim that the firmament, too, was produced from water he relies on the exoteric interpretation of the Sages in *Genesis Rabbah* 4.2: "The middle group [of the water] congealed."

41 *Iʿtibār* means philosophical reflection and learning from it; see W. Harvey, "Averroes and Maimonides on the Obligation of Philosophic Contemplation (*iʿtibār*)," *Tarbiṣ* 58 (1989), pp. 75–83 (Hebrew).

alludes to it. Qualified readers, familiar with Aristotle's *Meteorology,* can themselves identify the substances in Aristotle's physics that are designated by the "firmament" and the "water which were above the firmament." Because Maimonides does not explain the biblical text, but only hints at its meanings, "firmament" and the "water which were above the firmament" can be understood in several ways, as is manifested by the diverse interpretations offered by the medieval commentators on Maimonides.[42]

Maimonides does not explain how the literal meaning of the text could harm the masses. I have not found a better explanation than that offered by Asher Crescas (fourteenth century): The true meaning of the biblical text is a "secret" because if the vulgar knew that rain has natural causes and does not depend on God's will they would not longer believe in divine providence.[43]

Maimonides offers a more esoteric elucidation, a "hard" esoteric interpretation, of the opening word of the creation story: *bereshit* ("in the beginning").[44] The explanation of that word (and of the verb *bara'*)[45] is a key for the understanding the Torah's doctrine of creation. It deals with one of the subjects that Maimonides considers to be "truly the mysteries of the Torah": "His creation of that which He created" (*Guide* I.35, p. 54/p. 80).[46] Because these "mysteries" should be conveyed only by "chapter headings," interpreting them entails a more esoteric method than that used for the physical substances "firmament" and "the water which were above the firmament."

Maimonides divides *bereshit* into its components, the noun *reshit* and the preposition *be-*, and treats each one separately. The explanation of *reshit* differs from those found in the lexicographic chapters of the *Guide*. In the "lexicon" he generally cites a word or words and then comments on each of its senses in Arabic. In *Guide* II.30, however, Maimonides does not explain the word *reshit* directly. He begins the chapter

42 See Klein-Braslavy, *Creation,* pp. 163–168 and (in this volume) "The Interpretation of the Story of the Second Day of Creation," pp. 34-37.

43 Crescas cites biblical verses that ascribe rain to God's action and understands them to mean that rain is caused by God's will. See his commentary on the *Guide*, p. 60a.

44 The analysis of Maimonides' interpretation of the word *reshit,* which follows, supplements the one I offered in my book *Creation*, pp. 114–131.

45 For Maimondes' interpretation of the verb *bara'* see S. Klein-Braslavy, "Maimonides' Interpretation of the verb *bara'* and the Creation of the World," *Da'at* 16 (1986), pp. 39-55 (Hebrew).

46 For the meaning of this expression, see Klein-Braslavy, *Esotericism*, p. 45.

with some remarks on two related Arabic terms, *al-awwal* and *al-mabda'*, and distinguishes among their senses. Only then does he mention their Hebrew parallels, identifying *awwal* with *teḥilla* and *mabda'* with *reshit*.[47]

It is his explanation of *mabda'* (principle) that interests us here.[48] Maimonides does not define the word, but merely offers some comments that enable readers to understand it more accurately. *Reshit* belongs to a type of words that have "a formal meaning." These are words that indicate a *class* of objects that share a common property. That is, they are defined by intension rather than by extension. The specific referents of each member of the class can be identified only by the contexts in which they figure and by its semantic axis.[49]

Maimonides' first comment on the meaning of *mabda'* is that "a principle exists in the thing whose principle it is or simultaneously with it" (p.244/p. 248).[50] This clarifies two features of a "principle": it is always a principle of something else and has a certain relation with the thing whose principle it is.[51] Maimonides speaks of two possible relations be-

---

47 It is possible that here he is disagreeing with Sa'adiah Gaon, who rendered the first verse of Genesis as *Awwal mā khalaqa Allāh al-samāwāt wa-l-arḍ* (The first thing God created was the heaven and the earth). See Y. Y. Rivlin, "Perush R. Sa'adiah Gaon la-Torah," in *Sefer ha-Yovel li-Khvod Y. N. L. Epstein* (Jerusalem, 1950), p. 134 (Hebrew). Maimonides justifies the identification of *reshit* with *al-mabda'* by the etymology of *reshit*: "For it derives from head [*rosh*], which in view of its position is the principle [*mabda'*] of the living being" (p. 245/p. 348).

48 For a discussion of the distinction between *al-awwal* and *al-mabda'*, see Klein-Braslavy, *Creation,* pp. 121–123.

49 For this type of words see (in this volume) "Maimonides' Strategy for Interpreting 'Woman' in the *Guide of the Perplexed*."

50 "Principle" (*mabda'*) is the subject of the sentence, which thus cannot be the definition of that term. Gersonides, who is influenced by Maimonides' interpretation, defines it as follows: "The term 'beginning' (*reshit*) means in Hebrew that part of a thing which is prior to all its other parts, no matter what kind of priority" (*The Wars of the Lord,* VI.2.2, p. 420 [Leipzig edition], p. 430 [Feldman's tr.]. See also Gersonides' commentary on Genesis: B. Braner and E. Freiman, eds., *Ḥamishah Ḥumshei Torah 'im Be'ur Rabbenu Levi ben Gershom: Bereshit* (Jerusalem, 1999), p. 35. Gersonides defines *reshit* as a part of the thing and speaks of the "priority" of the principle (*reshit*) and of that of which it is the principle in four of the senses of priority that Aristotle lists in *Categories* 12, 14^{a}25ff. (see also *Metaphysics* IV, 1). One of them is "priority in cause and in nature." From Maimonides' explanation of *al awwal* (first) — "sometimes, however, 'the first' is applied solely to what is prior in time even when that which is prior in time is not the cause of what is posterior to it" (p. 244/p. 348) — we can infer that the principle is a thing that is the cause of that which it is prior. But this does not tell us whether this is the only relation of the principle to that whose principle it is.

51 This explanation is similar but not identical with those offered by Rashi and Abraham Ibn Ezra. Rashi thinks that *reshit* is in the construct state *(somekh)* and always needs a dependent genitive *(nismakh)*: "There is no *reshit* in the Bible that does not cling to the word the follows it. ... Here too you have to say 'in the beginning God created etc.' " According to Rashi, the word *reshit* in Genesis 1:1 lacks its *nismakh* and the commentator must complete it. Rashi suggests two complements: *be-reshit bro'* and *be-reshit ha-kol*. Ibn Ezra mentions such an explanation: *"ve-yesh 'omerim ki be-reshit le-'olam*

tween a principle and the thing whose principle it is: the principle may exist *in* the thing or simultaneously *with it*.[52] Thus *mabda*ʾ/ *reshit* denotes a class of objects whose common characteristic is that they are principles that may have two types of relations with the thing whose principle they are: they either exist *in* it or exist alongside it. Maimonides also adds a "negative" remark: "even if it [the principle] does not precede it [the thing] in time" (*ibid.*). The turgid syntax of the sentence permits several interpretations of the possible relationships between the principle and the thing whose principle it is.[53]

After identifying *reshit* with *mabda*ʾ, Maimonides turns to the preposition *be-*. It has several meanings in Hebrew, and the commentators are divided about its meaning in *be-reshit*: is it the instrumental *bet ha*ʿ*ezer*, "by means of," or the container *bet ha-keli*, "in"? If the first, *reshit* is the means by which God created the world.[54] If the second, God created the world in *reshit*. Maimonides opts for the second, thus adding another hint for identifying the referent of *reshit* in the creation story: *reshit* is a principle (in the sense he attributed to *mabda*ʾ) in which the world was created. According to the introduction to the *Guide*, one of the literary devices used by the Bible to transmit the esoteric teaching of the Account of the Beginning is to communicate it "in very obscure words" (*umūr mubhama jiddan*)" (p.5/p. 9).[55] The creation story, which begins

---

samukh"(Some people say that *be- reshit* is always in the construct state) and cites the complement those commentators suggest: *be-reshit ha-*ʿ*erev* ʾ*o ha-laylah* ʾ*o ha- ḥoshekh* (the beginning of the evening/night/ darkness). Ibn Ezra does not agree with them. He thinks that *be-reshit* in Genesis 1:1 is a construct state, although the word can exist in the absolute state. Maimonides interpretation is different. He offers a lexical interpretation of *be-reshit* and not a syntactical one.

52 Maimonides provides two examples of specific members of the class *mabda*ʾ*=reshit*. The first is taken from biology: "the heart is the principle of the living being" (p. 244/ p. 348). The second is from Aristotelian physics: "the element [is] the principle of that of which it is the element" (*ibid.*). Because he does not explain the examples, his medieval commentators offered several. See Klein-Braslavy, *Creation*, pp. 116–120. According to *Guide* I.16, which explains the word *ṣur*, another member of the class *mabda*ʾ*=reshit* is God, who is "the principle (*al-mabda*ʾ) and the efficient cause of all things other than himself" (p. 28/p. 42).

53 The examples he provides to illustrate these relations can also be interpreted in several ways. For the possible interpretations of the two relations and the examples that illustrate them, see Klein-Braslavy, *Creation*, pp. 115–121.

54 Shem Tov, who identifies *reshit* with "wisdom and knowledge," offers such a commentary. It is also found in the introduction to the Zohar and in *Midrash ha-Ne*ʿ*elam* on Genesis. This midrash also offers another explanation of *bereshit* as a means and identifies it with the Torah.

55 The Alexandrian commentators of the fifth and sixth centuries attributed to Aristotle the use of obscurity as a method of concealing philosophical doctrines from the undeserving. The reason for its use is explained as the seventh of the ten points that students had to know before studying Aristotle's works in the prolegomena to the commentaries on the *Categories*. See I. Hadot, *Simplicius Commentaire*

with a word that indicates a class of principles but without specifying the particular member of the class referred to, may be an example of this stylistic device.

Maimonides does not fully clear up the obscurity and does not identify the principle in which the world was created and what it is the principle of. But he adds a "negative" comment that suggests an identification of the principle in which the world was created by restricting the group of possible concrete referents of *reshit* in the first verse of Genesis.[56] The principle in which the world was created does not exist in time: "The world has not been created in a temporal beginning as we have explained,[57] for time belongs to the created things" (p. 245/p. 349). Readers are supposed to find a principle of Aristotelian philosophy that matches all of Maimonides' hints.

The method of interpretation Maimonides is using here is what I call "an interpretative riddle."[58] Maimonides' hints form a riddle the readers must solve. The riddle is: what thing is it that is the principle of some other thing (with the further stipulation that the principle is in that other thing but is not temporal),[59] and in which the world was created? Because a principle is a principle of something else, the solution should

---

sur les Catégories (Leiden: Brill, 1990), pp. 14 and 113–123; L. G. Westernik, *Anonymous Prolegomena to Platonic Philosophy* (Amsterdam, 1962), pp. xxvi–xxvii; D. Gutas, *Avicenna and the Aristotelian Tradition: Introduction to Reading Avicenna's Philosophical Works* (Leiden and New York, 1988), pp. 225—227. This tradition was transmitted to Arabic philosophy and adopted by Alfarabi, Avicenna, and other Arabic authors. See *ibid*., pp. 227–230. It is possible that Maimonides was acquainted with this tradition and considered obscurity to be a method of concealing esoteric doctrines that he attributes to the Bible. However, Maimonides does not understand the method of obfuscation in the same way Alfarabi and Avicenna did. For Alfarabi and Avicenna method of obfuscation see *ibid*., pp. 228–229 and 308.

56 As noted, the specific referent of a word that indicates a class of objects is determined by the context and the semantic axis of the text. I think that the context of the story of creation implies the elimination of the possibility of a principle that exists simultaneously with that whose principle it is. The principle in which the world was created should exist in the thing whose principle it is.

57 Maimonides is referring to *Guide* II.13, where he uses the same expression, "does not have a temporal beginning" (p. 197/p. 282).

58 See "Interpretative Riddles," where I discuss the literary genre of the riddle and compare it to another type of "interpretative riddle" in Maimonides' *Guide*—an interpretative riddle on some biblical stories, as found in the Midrash. I illustrate this type of "interpretative riddle" by Maimonides' interpretation of the creation of man and by his interpretation of the *naḥash* (serpent) in the story of the Garden of Eden. It is important to note that the interpretation of *bereshit* is a direct commentary on the biblical text and is not mediated by a midrash. Maimonides himself offers the hints that compose the interpretative riddle.

59 A "negative" element that restricts the possible answers to the riddle is characteristic of its literary genre.

also identify that something, of which the specific member of the class *reshit* mentioned in the Creation story is the principle. Only readers who are familiar with Aristotelian philosophy can solve the interpretative riddle. They can look there for a principle that exists within that whose principal it is and that suits the context of the story of creation. In addition, this principle is not temporal. Maimonides does not specify which work of Aristotle should be consulted, as he did in his esoteric interpretation of "firmament" and "the water which were above the firmament."

The medieval commentators Efodi and Crescas suggested an answer based on Aristotle's theory of time. They proposed to identify *reshit* with the "now," which is not a part of time but rather a point that has no duration and is analogous to a point on a line. Just as the point is the cause of the line, the "now" is the cause of time. The "now" is "in" time in a certain way, because it is its beginning. Its priority is causal, not temporal.[60] Hence the "now" is the principle, the *reshit*, and the thing whose principle it is is time.

We have seen that Maimonides' biblical exegesis is grounded on three assumptions. The first is that in his age the masses can understand the idea of an incorporeal God. Hence it is necessary to show them that certain biblical terms also have an incorporeal meaning that should be applied to God. The second assumption is that the Torah is an educational myth. Hence its external meaning conforms to the mental capacity of the masses, while its inner meaning is suited to the grasp of the intellectual elite and teaches philosophical doctrines. The third assumption is that the Torah contains esoteric teaching that should be withheld from the masses and conveyed to the deserving alone. On the basis of these assumptions Maimonides offers three types of biblical interpretations: exoteric ones meant for part of the masses as well as for "perplexed" intellectuals. These deal with words that are likely to corporealize God and with some of the divine revelations. There are also exoteric philosophical interpretations meant exclusively for the intellectual elite, as well as esoteric philosophical interpretations meant for both the "perplexed"

60 Nevertheless, this interpretation poses a dual problem: first, because the "now" has no duration, it is not clear how it is possible to create something "in" it; second, according to Aristotle, the "now" is the limit between the past and the future; hence there is time before every "now" and time cannot have a beginning. If Maimonides is alluding here to the "now" we must admit that he has already anticipated Gersonides' claim that there is a "now" that is the beginning of the future but is not the end of the past. See *The Wars of the Lord*, VI.6.12, pp. 286–288 (Leipzig ed.), pp. 359–363 (Feldman's tr.). See also Narboni's criticism of the interpretation in his commentary on the *Guide*, p. 39.

and the intellectual elite. These interpretations must be concealed from the masses because they are liable to damage their faith. Maimonides uses two types of esoteric method, "soft" and "hard," which differ in the type of allusions they use. "Soft" esoteric interpretations tell readers which Aristotelian text can help them identify the objects intended by the Bible. "Hard" esoteric interpretations, which are more common in the *Guide*, employ various allusive methods. Here we have seen an application of one of them, the interpretative riddle.

Abraham Bar Ḥiyya's Interpretation of the Story of the Creation of Man and the Story of the Garden of Eden[1]

Abraham Bar Ḥiyya (Barcelona, 1065-ca. 1136) is not usually enumerated among the exegetes of the Bible in the usual sense of the word. He did not write an organized commentary to the Bible or to any of its books. Rather, his interpretations of individual verses or complete sections of the Torah are brought in support of philosophical and theological ideas to which he adheres, by way of biblical exegesis.

I. The Context of His Interpretation of the Story of the Garden of Eden

Bar Ḥiyya's interpretation of the story of the creation of man and the story of the Garden of Eden is presented in the Third Part of his book, *Sefer Megillat ha-Megalleh*[2] (written between 1120 and 1129).[3] *Sefer Megillat ha-Megalleh* is an eschatological book, whose main concern is with the calculation of the Eschaton, which Bar Ḥiyya fixed between the years 1136 and 1440, by means of calculations based upon the Jewish tradition and astrological data.

In order to provide a basis for his eschatological calculations, Bar Ḥiyya develops a historiography based upon the idea of a parallel between the Six Days of Creation and the periods into which human history is divided or, to use his language, "the days of the world" (*yemoth ha-ʿolam*). At the end of human history will come the Redemption, parallel to the Shabbat

1 The first part of the translation of this article is based upon a longer version than that printed in Hebrew and which I had in manuscript form.

2 Partial interpretations of the story of the Creation of Man are also found in *Hegyon ha-Nefesh ha-ʿAṣuvah*, I. pp, 53, 54, 55/ pp. 50, 51, 52. References are first to the Hebrew text: Abraham Bar-Hayya, *Hegyon ha-Nephesch ha-ʿAṣuvah*, edited with introduction and notes by Geoffrey Wigoder (Jerusalem, 1971); followed, after the semicolon, by the English translation: *The Meditation of the Sad Soul by Abraham Bar Hayya*; translated [from the Hebrew] and with an introduction by Geoffrey Wigoder (London, 1969). The present article relates only to *Sefer Megillat ha-Megalleh*.

3 See Julius Guttman, "Introduction," in *Sefer Megillat ha-Megalleh*, ed. A. Poznanski (Berlin, 1924; photo reprint: Jerusalem, 1968), p. x (Hebrew).

day. According to another view, at the time of the Redemption the Resurrection of the Dead will occur, and those dead who will arise to renewed life will then live eternally in this world, in which there will be introduced certain "innovations," such that it will become a "new world."

His interpretation of the story of the Garden of Eden is intended to provide a basis, by means of biblical interpretation, of his view concerning the Resurrection of the Dead. Bar Ḥiyya proves therein that, according to the Bible, already at the beginning of human history there existed a state in which the human body was not vulnerable to the influence of his material environment and that therefore Adam was able to live eternally in his body. Such a situation will recur in the future, at the end of human history, and those who will be resurrected at the time of the Redemption will continue to live forever, without suffering any pain or disease.

Sefer Megillat ha-Megalleh, like Bar Ḥiyya's other books, is addressed to a very specific readership—to the Jews of southern France and those of Christian Spain during his period—and it answers their needs in the theological, philosophical and scientific realms. The discussion of the Resurrection of the Dead is specifically directed to them. According to Bar Ḥiyya, the faith in the Resurrection is one of the basic principles of Judaism, and one who denies it is excluded from the community of Israel.[4] He accepts the view of R. Saʿadiah Gaon, according to whom the Resurrection of the Dead is mentioned in the Bible. In his opinion, Ezekiel 36:12-14 clearly states that, at the time of the Redemption, the Resurrection of the Dead will occur. Even though, according to Bar Ḥiyya's opinion, R. Saʿadiah Gaon proved this matter adequately, he felt the need to return and to strengthen his argument by means of additional textual proofs because, thus he claims, certain Jewish thinkers in southern France and in Christian Spain who lived during this period questioned it. Their argument, as presented by Bar Ḥiyya, is that if there will indeed be a Resurrection of the Dead, this will occur on the Great Day of Judgment and that thereafter human beings will no longer exist in this world. Members of these circles proposed two arguments in support of their view:

(a) An argument from common sense, based upon everyday experience—namely, that it is not possible that a person who has already died will return to live again in this world in a different manner than that

4 See *Sefer Megillat ha-Megalleh*, III, p. 49 (all quotations from *Sefer Megillat ha-Megalleh* are according to the above- mentioned edition, n. 3).

in which he lives today. That is, it is inconceivable that a person lives in this world and nevertheless not be subject to harm, not suffer pain, not become ill, and not die a second time. It follows from this that it is illogical that the dead will rise to life anew at the time of the Redemption and thereafter continue to live eternally in this world.

(b) A claim based upon interpretation of the biblical text—there is no religious obligation to believe in the Resurrection of the Dead. The Torah, which is the authoritative guide to the ethical–religious behavior of every Jew, on the one hand, and to the beliefs and opinions which obligate him, on the other, does not at all mention the belief in the Resurrection of the Dead nor even allude to it. On this point, Bar Ḥiyya's contemporaries polemicized with the interpretations given by R. Saʿadiah Gaon to certain biblical verses in his book *Sefer ha-Emunot ve-ha-Deʿot*, Part Seven. According to them, those verses which Saʿadiah Gaon cites as teaching the Resurrection[5] "are said by way of metaphor, in order to amplify the matter of the future redemption of Israel" (p. 48). They do not in fact refer to the resurrection of individual human beings, but rather to a national resurrection: "The kingdom of Israel shall return to life and be resurrected and awaken; after it had been weakened and died, it will live again and awaken like a dead man who has emerged from his grave, or one sleeping who rises from his sleep" (*ibid.*).[6]

Bar Ḥiyya wrote the Third Part of *Sefer Megillat ha-Megalleh* as a response to his contemporaries. He confronts both of the arguments that they raised. Regarding the argument from Scripture, he responds by rejecting an allegorical interpretation of those verses which they cited, on the one hand, and by noting additional verses in the Bible alluding to the Resurrection which are not subject to an allegorical interpretation of

5 Isa. 26:14, 29. These verses are brought by R. Saʿadiah Gaon, *Sefer ha-Emunot ve-ha-Deʿot*, VII. 4, in the translation by Judah Ibn Tibbon. The third verse is Isa 27:13, which I did not find either in Ibn Tibbon's translation or in the second edition of Part Seven, translated by Y. Qāfiḥ, *Sefer ha-Nivḥar ba-Emunot u-va-Deʿot* (Jerusalem, 1970).

6 Such an argument was already raised during the period of R. Saʿadiah Gaon. In the second edition of Part Seven of *Sefer ha-Nivḥar ba-Emunot u-va-Deʿot*, Ch. 1, R. Saʿadiah Gaon says: "And I have seen some people in the nation who explain every verse in which mention is made of the Resurrection of the Dead at the time of the Redemption as referring to the restoration of sovereignty and the renascence of the nation" (p. 219). In the first version of Part Seven, as translated by Ibn Tibbon, R. Saʿadiah Gaon presents this approach as a possible interpretation of the verses, and not as an interpretation given by a number of his contemporaries: "Perhaps it is possible to think other views regarding these verses, such that the matter of the resurrection of the dead would refer to the revival of the kings and the restoration of the monarchy"—*Sefer ha-Emunot ve-ha-Deʿot*, trans. Judah Ibn Tibbon (Josefop, 1878; photo ed. Jerusalem, 1962).

the kind that his contemporaries gave to the other verses, on the other hand.[7] Hence, the Bible requires belief in the Resurrection of the Dead.

Bar Ḥiyya answers the argument from common sense by noting the limitations of knowledge. In his opinion, knowledge obtained by means of revelation is superior to that attained by reason in terms of its scope: there are issues with which the human intellect, including science and philosophy, is unable to deal. According to what he writes in the Second Part of *Sefer Megillat ha-Megalleh*, they may only be answered "from the Torah, from the Holy Scriptures, and from the words of our Rabbis of blessed memory, who have a tradition received from the Holy Spirit" (p. 14). Among these issues, which Bar Ḥiyya enumerates in the Second Part of his book, are the question of the number of days of the world, and therefore the manner of calculation of the End.[8] According to his statement in the Third Part of the book, this holds true for the Resurrection of the Dead as well.[9] Human beings' knowledge of the order of the world is not complete: they only know a part thereof, that which is given to them through everyday experience. From this partial knowledge of the order of the world, they are unable to judge the order as a whole. Hence, they cannot prove the possibility of the Resurrection of the Dead at the time of the Redemption through purely rational means, but must learn these things from the biblical stories. Nevertheless, Bar Ḥiyya thinks that science and philosophy contain elements on whose basis it should be possible to explain the Resurrection of the Dead. The physician Galen (second century CE)[10] and the philosopher Aristotle were very close to proving the idea of Resurrection of the Dead in a manner similar to that understood by Bar Ḥiyya. Bar Ḥiyya claims that,[11] if they would have had

7 Ezek. 37:12-14; Dan. 12:2. These verses are also cited by R. Sa'adiah Gaon in *Sefer ha-Emunot ve-ha-De'ot*, VII. 4.

8 See II, pp. 14, 39.

9 See ibid, III, pp. 50-51.

10 On Galen, and Bar Ḥiyya's reliance upon him, see below in the chapters "Adam's Immortality" and "The Denial of Eternal Life."

11 According to Bar Ḥiyya, Aristotle was close to the idea of Resurrection when he claimed that: "all of the forms and the souls will devolve and return to the world in the future" (III, p. 50). However, according to Bar Ḥiyya he does not think that they return to their original matter, whereas the idea of Resurrection is based upon the belief that souls shall return to their original matter. The above passage does not appear in Aristotle's *De generatione et corruptione* to which Bar Ḥiyya refers the reader here. It may be that this is the interpretation of Bar Ḥiyya or of someone from whom he learned these matters of *De generatione et corruptione* II.11; cf. on this matter J. Guttman, "Introduction." in *Sefer Megillat ha-Megalleh*" (above, n. 3), who argues that Bar Ḥiyya "was mistaken in his understanding of Aristotle, for those forms of generation and corruption which perpetually revolve are not for Aristotle individual

further, super-rational knowledge, if they would have believed in the Torah and accepted the concept of God as having a will, they would have been able to develop their systems and to have established on its basis the idea of the Resurrection of the Dead. This view enables Bar Ḥiyya to use philosophical and physiological doctrines which were accepted in his day, the Platonic–Aristotelian doctrine of the soul, and elements taken from Galen's physiology, to interpret the story of the creation of man and that of the Garden of Eden, and to go beyond them to find a basis for grounding the idea of the Resurrection of the Dead.

The interpretation of the story of the creation of man and that of the Garden of Eden serves as an answer to the claims made by his contemporaries on two levels: on the level of biblical exegesis and on the scientific and philosophical level. Bar Ḥiyya proves thereby that, according to the Bible, already at the beginning of human history, there existed a situation in which the human body was not vulnerable to the influence of its material environment; hence, it was possible at that time for human beings to live eternally within their bodies too. This situation will return in the future, at the end of the "days of the world" (i.e., of human history): those human beings who will rise from the dead at the time of the Redemption, in the days of Messiah, will continue to live forever and ever without suffering any kind of pain or disease. Part of his interpretation was based upon the semantic–scientific axis, whereby Bar Ḥiyya demonstrates that the Bible was also compatible with scientific explanations that were accepted in his period.

II. Bar Ḥiyya's Method of Bible Interpretation

Abraham Bar Ḥiyya deals only slightly with the theory of biblical exegesis and does not present his method of interpreting the Bible in a systematic or clear way. His method must be inferred primarily from his interpretations of biblical texts. It is nevertheless possible to find here and there in his writings formulations of several general principles of biblical exegesis.

Bar Ḥiyya's basic approach to the interpretation of the Bible is quite clear: he does not think that the biblical texts have one exclusive meaning, which it is incumbent upon the exegete to discover, through which one may see the *truth* of these texts. He openly accepts the view of the

---

entities like an individual human soul, but rather the species of the things which always exist and which move from one individual to another" (xvii-xviii).

Rabbinic Sages according to which "There are seventy faces to the Torah," and he believes that it is possible to simultaneously interpret the biblical texts in different ways, all of which will have the same truth value.[12] In order to ground his approach, he relies upon a well-known text from B. Sanhedrin 34a: "And this is what our Rabbis of blessed memory said: 'One Scripture has several different explanations, but one explanation does not go upon several scriptural passages,'" to which he adds, "And they expounded it, saying, 'Are not my words like fire, says the Lord, and like a hammer that breaks the rock?' [Jer. 23:29]. Just as the hammer divides into several sparks, so does one verse divide into several reasons...."[13]

Regarding the field of significance of the biblical texts, Bar Ḥiyya thinks that a true or correct interpretation thereof can be that which is suitable to wisdom (i.e. philosophy) and science; that is to say, to the philosophical and scientific doctrines which were accepted in his day. While such an interpretation is only one possible interpretation out of many and not the exclusive truth of the text, its conformity with philosophy and science in itself serves as a criteria for the correctness of a possible interpretation of a given biblical text. This criteria is in term subject to an additional criterion—namely, the rules of grammar of the Hebrew language. A possible correct interpretation will thus be one that is suitable to philosophy and science and "which does not depart from the practice of the language"[14] (*Hegyon ha-Nefesh ha-ʿAṣuvah*, p. 43; p. 45). Thus, the rules of the language therefore determine the limits of the interpretation according to the philosophical–scientific semantic axis. However, one must remember that there may be additional interpretations of the Bible, and even of those same texts themselves, on the basis

12 It is important to note that Bar Ḥiyya, unlike Maimonides after him, does not think that certain sections of the Bible are written in the form of "parables"—that is, as texts having two levels of meanings, an "apparent" level and a "hidden" level, and that their "true" philosophical meaning is to be found on their hidden level. Maimonides' esoteric approach was completely alien to him. According to Bar Ḥiyya, the biblical text has only one level of meaning, but this level may be interpreted simultaneously in a number of different ways.

13 *Sefer Megillat ha-Megalleh*, III, pp. 74-75. The formula in B. Sanhedrin 34a is: "Abbaya said: Scripture states, 'God has spoken once, and I have heard twice, for there is strength to God' (Ps. 62:12). One Scriptural verse goes out to several meanings, but one meaning does not come from several Scriptural verses. In the school of R. Ishmael they taught: 'and like a hammer smashing the rock' (Jer. 23:29). Just as a hammer divides into several sparks, so does one Scripture divide into several interpretations."

14 The rule that the interpretation of Scripture must fit the customary use among people who speak the language in which it is written was already proposed by R. Saʿadiah Gaon. See his Commentary on the Book of Job, *Iyov, ʿim Targum u-Perush Rabbenu Saadyah ben Yosef*, translated into Hebrew, elucidated and redacted by Yosef Qāfiḥ (Jerusalem, 1973), p. 20.

of other semantic axes, all of which will have the same truth value.

It should be noted here that even though Bar Ḥiyya accepts the possibility of interpreting the biblical texts "according to the opinion of the "speculative thinkers" (*Ḥakhmei ha-Meḥqar*) it follows from his words that such an interpretation is only possible when there is general agreement among all of the "sages of the nations" regarding the question at hand.[15] In addition, as rational knowledge is limited, there are truths within the theoretical realm, as well as rules of right conduct which are only subject to apprehension by means of prophecy.[16] It is therefore possible to find them in the Torah, which is the expression of prophetic apprehension, through interpretation of its text.

In dealing with the question of the calculation of the Eschaton by interpretation of the Account of Creation, Bar Ḥiyya relates explicitly to the interpretations given by the Sages to the Bible. In his opinion, one may give a new interpretation to biblical texts which has no support in the Talmudic and Midrashic literature, so long as such an interpretation does not contradict the interpretation given by the Sages.[17]

Regarding the language of the Bible, Bar Ḥiyya mentions the well-known phenomenon of the existence of equivocal words in language, a phenomenon that exists in all languages, including the Hebrew language: "But you should know that most words in Hebrew, and in other languages, are used equivocally, in many meanings" (*Hegyon ha-Nefesh ha-ʿAṣuvah*, I, p. 42; p. 44). While Maimonides makes use of equivocal terms in order to identify the significance of a word in that biblical verse which it comes to explain, Bar Ḥiyya makes use of the same phenomenon in order to construct differing interpretations of biblical texts, at times even of the very same biblical text, on the basis of the various meanings of the same word. As we shall see, Bar Ḥiyya interprets two equivocal words in the story of the Garden of Eden—the nouns *daʿat* ("knowledge") and *ʿeṣ* ("tree")—making use of their different meanings in interpreting different aspects of the story.

However, as we have said, his main way in interpreting the Bible is to be inferred from his interpretations as such—a point to which I shall

15 See, e.g., *Sefer Megillat ha-Megalleh*, I, pp. 5, 10.

16 See especially *Sefer Megillat ha-Megalleh*, I, p. 13; and *Hegyon ha-Nefesh ha-ʿAṣuvah*, I, pp. 47; 50-51; and cf. *Sefer Megillat ha Megalleh*, II, pp. 14, 39; and III, p. 51.

17 See *Sefer Megillat ha-Megalleh*, III, p. 74. The things are said there regarding the concrete question: calculation of the End by means of the interpretation of the Account of Creation, and not in general.

return later on in this article. Here I shall only say that Bar Ḥiyya has great linguistic sensitivity and creates his interpretations on the basis of subtle distinctions in the biblical style. His basic assumption is that every word in the Bible and every stylistic change in the biblical descriptions is of significance and importance for understanding the various aspects of the biblical stories, and he bases central ideas in his interpretation upon them. Words which are seemingly synonymous or which seem intended merely to serve literary purposes, such as the various verbs used to describe the creation of man, are not such, but each is of significance in its own right. He constructs a central part of his approach to the interpretation of the creation of man based on the different meanings of these verbs. The duplication of words in the story of the Garden of Eden, such as *ʾakhol toʾkhel* ("you shall surely eat") or *mot tamut* ("you shall surely die') does not come, according to his interpretation, simply for emphasis or for aesthetic purposes, but rather carries meaning: each word in the doubled word-pair has a different significance. He bases central ideas in his interpretation of the story of the Garden of Eden on the different meanings of the words in these pairs. Bar Ḥiyya also pays attention to the cases of the verbs which appear in the story of the Creation of Man and the story of the Garden of Eden, attaching special interpretations to the use of these verbs in the past tense and their use in the future tense. Finally, it should be noted that, alongside his interpretation of the central verbs and nouns in the story of the Creation of Man and that of the Garden of Eden, Bar Ḥiyya also interprets the prefixed prepositions, *beit* and *kaf* in the biblical text, making the interpretation of the text in which they appear dependent thereupon.

III. The Story of the Creation of Man

1. The Explanation for the Existence of Two Different Stories of the Creation of Man in the Book of Genesis

The Interpretation of the Verbs in the Story of the Creation of Man

In his interpretation of the story of the creation of man, Abraham Bar Ḥiyya particularly emphasizes the verbs: in his opinion, the verbs in the story carry the framework of meaning, whereas the nouns "fill it in" with contents. A simple reading of the story of man's creation reveals that the Bible uses various different verbs here to indicate the act of creation. In

Genesis 1:26, there appears the verb *ʿaśoh*: "Let us make man" (*naʿaśeh adam*); in 1:27, the verb used is *baraʾ*, "to create" ("and God created man"); while in Genesis 2:7, the Bible uses yet another verb, *yaṣor*, "to form" ("then the Lord God formed man..."). In Genesis 5:1, in which an abbreviated version of the creation of man appears, two of these verbs there appear one after another—"create" and "make"—as follows: "This is the book of the generations of man (Adam); on the day that God *created* man, He *made* him in the likeness of God." One may of course explain this by saying that the use of different verbs to indicate the creation of man is intended to serve an aesthetic function: to vary and enrich the story from a linguistic viewpoint. However, such an answer would not be suitable to the exegetical mentality of Abraham Bar Ḥiyya. Like the Rabbinic Sages before him, Bar Ḥiyya assumes that every stylistic change in the Bible has a peculiar significance of its own. Hence, he refuses to see the various verbs relating to the Creation as mere synonyms, but must seek the specific significance of each one.

The verb-pair, "create" and "make" (*baroʾ* /*ʿaśoh*), is of particular interest to Bar Ḥiyya. He gives them significance on the semantic–philosophical axis—that is: on the basis of a cosmogony with a severely neo-Platonic bent incorporating numerous Aristotelian elements. According to the cosmogony which he adopts, all things existed "in potentia" in the Divine thought before the Creation of the world, i.e., before the Six Days of Creation. They therefore preceded "by a natural precedence" their existence outside of the Divine thought. "Thereafter," they were placed "in potentia" outside of the Divine thought moving from potentiality to actuality via a temporal process. Outside of the Divine thought, the existence of the things "in potentia" preceded their existence "in actuality" by "precedence in time."[18] According to Bar Ḥiyya's interpretation, the verbs *baroʾ* and *ʿaśoh* indicate the coming into being of things in each of their two types of existence outside of the Divine thought: *baroʾ*, "to create," indicates its being placed "in potentia" in the world, while *ʿaśoh*, "to make," indicates its actualization.[19] The existence of a thing "in potentia" is an incomplete form of existence,[20] while existing "in actuality" is a per-

18 See *Sefer Megillat ha-Megalleh*, I, pp. 8-10.

19 "And we have found it written, that if it mentions the existence of things in potentia so as to be actualized, this is called creation (*beriʾah*), and their actualization is called formation (*yeṣirah*) or making (*ʿaśśiyah*)" (*Sefer Megillat ha-Megalleh*, II, p. 15).

20 "Creation, whose significance is that a thing exists in potential or is incomplete" (*ibid.*, III, p. 55).

fect and full existence. Hence the verb "to create" indicates not only the placing of a given thing "in potentia," but also the incomplete aspect of its existence.[21] By contrast, the verb *ʿaśoh*, "to make," not only indicates the bringing of this thing from potentiality to actuality, but also the perfection of its existence, its entelechy. The description of the creation of man in the Bible thus corresponds to its philosophical description: each one of the verbs of creation relating to man indicates a different stage of creation and a different aspect of man's perfection.

This interpretation of the verbs "create" and "make" (*baroʾ* and *ʿaśoh*) enabled Bar Ḥiyya to answer an exegetical question that engaged many biblical commentators, regarding the seeming redundant nature of the description of the creation of man: namely, why does the Bible contain two successive descriptions of the creation of man, in Genesis 1 and in Genesis 2? Through his interpretation of the verbs "create" and "make," Bar Ḥiyya is able to answer that Genesis 1 and 2 in fact tell a single story: the description of the creation of man in Genesis 2 is simply the continuation and completion of that in Chapter 1, and the Bible is not guilty of "redundancy."

Bar Ḥiyya's interpretation of the verbs *baroʾ* and *ʿaśoh* ("create" and "make") is rooted in Aristotle's explanation of the relation between the practical intellect and action. According to his book, *On the Soul*, III.10 433a 16-18, it is the function of the practical intellect to seek and to find the means of realizing an end external to itself. The practical intellect finds these means through analysis of the end; it then conducts a regression, working backwards from the end to the means needed to attain it. These means are in turn organized as means and intermediate ends; the final step in this process of regression, the final step in the thinking of the practical intellect, serves as the starting point for the practical action that realizes its end. The order of action is thus the opposite of the order of thinking. The action thus follows the sequence of means in reverse order until it realizes the final end.[22] The end, which had been the starting point for the thinking of the practical intellect, is thus the final

---

21 This interpretation enables Bar Ḥiyya to interpret in a coherent manner the astonishing fact that the word "and He created" is used regarding the great sea monsters: "And it is said concerning them, 'and He created' (*va-yivra*') and not 'and He made,' because their portion in life is not a complete one, but their vitality is a force of vitality that is not complete, because they have no lungs with which to breathe, and they do not have the power to live outside of the water like other living things" (*ibid.*, III, p. 53).

22 See also *Nicomachean Ethics* III.5. 1112b 24; and *Metaphysics* VII.7. 1032b 6-30; and cf. *Sefer Megillat ha-Megalleh*, I, p. 8, lines 24-28.

step in the practical process, the final step of the actions themselves. This Aristotelian principle, regarding the inverse relation between the order of thought and the ontological order, may also be formulated by saying that that which is first in thought—the end—is last in order of coming into being, in the process of realizing the end. Bar Ḥiyya makes use of this final formulation of the Aristotelian principle in order to construct the framework for his interpretation of the creation of man.

"Let us make man" (Gen. 1:26) thus refers to the Divine thought that preceded the creation of man. The end of the creation of man first emerged in the Divine thought as a complete entity, realized in actuality. Hence Scripture uses here the verb "make," meaning to turn from potential to actual. "Let us make" must thus be understood as: Let us turn from potential to actual, let us pose man into a state of perfection:

> And it says, "Let us make..." rather than "Let us create" or "Let us form," to make it known that the thought and its completion will be in the completion of the forming of man and his existence. And nothing is called complete and made except through completion of the thought that comes about in its making... And it says at the beginning of [His] thought "Let us make," and did not mention man's coming into existence until the end of the act of making, as is the way of all thoughts, for it is well known that that which is at the beginning of the thought is the end of the deed, as is explained in many places. (III, p. 52)

The interpretation of the verbs *baro*ʾ and ʿ*aśoh*, and the use of the Aristotelian principle—which was given the well-known Hebrew formulation, "The end of the deed is the beginning of thought" in the poem *Lekhah Dodi* by the prominent Kabbalistic poet Shlomo ha-Levi Alkabetz (sixteenth century)—creates a tension between the two poles in the story of the Creation of man: man's state as "potential," incomplete, and his state of standing in actuality, as complete. This framework, according to Bar Ḥiyya's interpretation, is "filled in" by the nouns of the story and they give it its contents. They explain the nature of the state in which man was still "potential" and that respect in which he was incomplete, and the nature of the complete man, man in actuality, or what perfects or completes man. Likewise, the interpretation of the nouns *ṣelem* ("image"), *demut* ("likeness"), and *nishmat ḥayyim* ("the breath of life") is also conducted by Bar Ḥiyya on the basis of this philosophical–semantic axis or, to be more precise: on the basis of a psychology which uses both Platonic and Aristotelian elements.

The Interpretation of the word, ṣelem ("image")

Bar Ḥiyya bases his interpretation of the word *ṣelem* ("image") upon a scientific–philological method. Here he does not make use of the semantic–philosophic axis to deduce the meaning of the word, but rather seeks its meaning in the "biblical lexicon" and on the basis of the natural–semantic axis. He finds a verse in which, in his opinion, the meaning of the word *ṣelem* may clearly be inferred from the context, and determines on that basis its meaning in the story of the creation of man. In 1 Samuel 6:11, we find the expression *ṣalmei teḥoreihem*, "the images of their emerods." According to Bar Ḥiyya, it is completely clear that this expression refers to "the bodies of their emerods and their physical being alone, for the images of the emerods which they made had nothing in common with the matter of the emerods except for their external form alone" (p. 52).[23] An "image" is thus "the body of a living being and its material embodiment, and it is not associated with any other power of the body nor any of its qualities" (*ibid.*). Man's creation in the Divine image therefore refers to the creation of his body, to the creation of the physical form of the human being.

After establishing the significance of the word *ṣelem* on the basis of the biblical lexicon, Bar Ḥiyya expands its significance further on in his interpretation of the story of the creation of man, on the basis of the

---

23 It is interesting that Maimonides brings the very same example in interpreting the word *ṣelem* ("image") in the *Guide of the Perplexed* I.1. This example, specifically, causes him to hesitate, or seemingly to hesitate, in interpreting the word *ṣelem*. At first he says "For what was intended by them was the notion of warding off the harm caused by the *emerods* and not the shape of the *emerods*," (Pines, p. 22) in keeping with the view that *ṣelem* refers to the natural form or substance of a thing. But then he says, "If, however, there should be no doubt concerning the expressions *the images of your emerods* and *images* being used in order to denote shape and configuration..." (*ibid.*). That is, the word "image" in the phrase "the image of their *emerods*" is nevertheless a physical form. "If, however, there should be no doubt" indicates that this latter interpretation is the accepted interpretation for "image of their *emerods*" and Maimonides is "forced," at least to all appearances, to accept it.

For a discussion of Maimonides' interpretation of the noun *ṣelem* and his interpretation of *ṣalmei teḥoreihem* ("the image of their emerods"), see Klein-Braslavy, *Adam Stories*, pp. 18-22; Z. Harvey, "How to Begin to Learn the *Guide of the Perplexed* I.1," *Da'at* 21 (1988), pp. 5-23, at pp. 6-13 (Hebrew); H. Kasher, "On the Forms of the 'Images' (Further Notes to *Guide* I.1)," *Da'at* 53 (2004), pp. 31-42 (Hebrew).

semantic–philosophical axis. Here it is applied, not only to the human body, but also to man's two lower souls: the appetitive soul, which he identifies with the vegetative soul,[24] and the animal soul, as well as to its qualities: reproduction, which characterizes the vegetative soul, and "its domination over the beasts and the animals," characteristic of the animal soul.[25]

Thus, coupled with his interpretation of the verbs *'aśoh* ("to make") and *baro'* ("create"), we now have a coherent understanding of the first part of Genesis 1:26 and of Genesis 1:27: "Let us make man in our image" refers to the Divine thought, the plan for the creation of man's body and of his non-rational souls connected with the body. "And God created man in His own image" refers to the realization of this part of the Divine plan—the placing of man's body and his two lower souls outside of the Divine thought. The creation of man "in the image" is thus the placing of man "in potentia" alone, as an incomplete human being, for he does not yet have the rational soul which is his form.

The Interpretation of ki-demutenu ("in Our Likeness")

The verb *na' aśeh* ("let us make") indicates the Divine intention of creating man *in his perfection*. Thus, verse 26 speaks of this perfected man. The word *ṣelem*, "image," refers to man's body and to his non-rational souls. According to the exegetical logic here, "in our likeness" must refer

---

24 This identification is one of the manifestations of the mixture of neo-Platonic and Aristotelian elements in his psychology. This may be found as well among two other thinkers of Bar Ḥiyya's period: Joseph Ibn Ṣaddiq and Abraham Ibn Ezra. The identification of the Platonic appetitive soul with the vegetative soul was already made by Galen—see A-Ed. Chaignet *Histoire de la psychologie des grecs* (Paris, 1887-93), III, p. 360. It appears in Joseph Ibn Ṣaddiq, *Sefer ha-'Olam ha-Qatan*, p. 25/p.82 and in Abraham Ibn Ezra, *Commentary on Eccles*. 7:3, in *Yesod* Mora', p. 7 and other places. I cite the Hebrew text of *Sefer ha 'Olam ha-Qatan* in Saul Horovitz critical edition (Breslau, 1903) followed by a slash the English translation of Jacob Haberman in *The Microcosm of Joseph ibn Ṣaddiq* /Hebrew text critically edited by Saul Horovitz and provided with an English translation, introduction, and notes by Jacob Haberman (Madison [N.J.: Fairleigh Dickinson University Press, 2003).

25 The attribution of the quality of rulership over animals to the animal soul is evidently an echo of the confusion between the qualities of the Platonic power of anger and the Aristotelian animal soul. Compare Ibn Ezra, *Commentary on Eccles*. 7:3, which attributes to the animal soul the ability of walking from one place to another (Aristotelian) and rulership (Platonic).

Continuing his commentary, on p. 58 Bar Ḥiyya presents another interpretation in which he shows that it is possible to derive from the story of the creation of man the creation of each of the three powers of the human soul separately, in ascending order. By means of this interpretation he limits the meaning of the word "image" to the appetitive and vegetative soul of man, reserving the animal, living soul for the word *va-yiṣer* ("and He formed"). Gen. 2:7: "And He breathed with his nostrils the breath of life," according to this interpretation also indicates the creation of the "thinking and rational [*dabranit*] soul."

to the *neshamah*, the rational soul of man. This conclusion, which necessarily follows from the interpretation given to the verb "let us make," is reinforced by Bar Ḥiyya's interpretation of the phrase "in our likeness" on the basis of the semantic–philosophical axis. "In our likeness" refers to the resemblance between man and God and the angels. According to his doctrine of the soul, man is similar to God and to the angels in the qualities of his "reflective [*hogah*] and rational [*dabranit*]" soul: i.e., wisdom and rulership;[26] that is to say, through his knowledge of science and philosophy and his dominion over the other animals. It follows from this that "in our likeness" refers to the human's rational soul.

Verse 26 thus speaks about the Divine plan for the creation of man in his perfection as a creature with a body, two non-rational souls, and a rational soul. Verse 27, the story of the creation of man on the sixth day, by contrast, speaks of the creation of man "in potentia," of the making of his body, of his vegetative soul and animal soul, but not of his creation in his perfected form. The completion of man's creation is only related in Genesis. 2:7: "And He breathed into his nostrils the breath of life, and man became a living being." Bar Ḥiyya interprets this verse as follows:

> This is to teach you that man does not come into being and that his form is not complete except in his rational soul (*neshamah*), and with it there is completed the pure thought. And it says at the beginning of His thought "let us make," but it does not mention coming into existence except at the end of the act, as is the manner of all thoughts. For it is well known that that which is at the beginning in thought is last in act. (III, p. 52)

Bar Ḥiyya understands "breath of life" (*nishmat ḥayyim)* as "soul of life" and hence as the rational soul, with whose creation that creation of man is completed as it had initially arisen in the Divine thought.

According to Bar Ḥiyya's interpretation, the story of the creation reflects through its style and in its very structure the Platonic distinction between the non-rational souls or powers of the non-rational soul,

26 Compare R. Saʿadiah Gaon, *Commentary on the Torah*, at Gen. 1:26, "in our image and as our likeness - ruler" (p. 12). I cite R. Saʿadiah Gaon's *Commentary* from *Perush Rabbenu* Saʿadiah *Gaon ʿal ha-Torah* , edited, translated and with Introduction and Notes by Yoseph Qāfiḥ (Jerusalem, 1963).

and the rational soul or the rational power of the soul. The body and the non-rational souls are indicated by the word *ṣelem* ("image") in verse 26, whereas the rational soul is indicated by a separate word, "in our likeness" (*ki-demutenu*). In order to emphasize this distinction even further, the story of the Creation describes the creation of each of these aspects in a separate story. The description of the creation of the body and of the non-rational souls, in which man is similar to those animals that are immediately beneath him in the scale of nature, appears in Genesis 1, in the account of the sixth day of Creation. On the other hand, the description of the creation of the rational soul, by which man is distinguished from the other denizens of this lower world, but is similar to the creatures of the supernal world—i.e., to the angels and even to God—appears in Genesis 2. The rational soul alone is eternal, whereas the body and the two lower souls cease to exist with the cessation of the life of the body, like the souls of animals.[27] The similarity between *ṣelem* ("image") and the creatures of the lower world thus derives from the fact that the *ṣelem* is mortal, whereas *nishmat ḥayyim* ("the soul of life") is by its nature eternal:

> The rational soul (*neshamah*), of man is in itself a living creature in the definition of its form, and in its essential formation, and death does not pertain to it at all; but the body is dead when the *ruaḥ* (the spirit) by which the rational soul (*neshamah*) breathed within it, departs the body. (p. 59)[28]

There is thus a complete correspondence between philosophical "speculation" and the Torah in terms of their respective doctrines of the nature of man.

The Interpretation of "Male and Female He created them"

From Bar Ḥiyya's words that, "nothing was created on the sixth day of Creation but their bodily powers (*koḥotehem ha-ṣalmaniyot*; p. 55), one might understand that on the sixth day there was only created the human body (or the human body and humans' lower powers of the soul), whereas

---

27 This view has a basis in Aristotelian thought. See for example, *On the Soul*, 408b 18-29; 413b 24-27.

28 In opposition to the view expressed here, in the Fourth Part of his book (p. 109) Bar Ḥiyya speaks on the possibility of the destruction of the souls of the evildoers and the nations of the world.

man's creation was only completed after the sixth day. And indeed, such an interpretation is mentioned by Bar Ḥiyya in his interpretation of the second half of Genesis 1:27, "male and female He created them." This part of the verse tells us the order of creation of Adam and Eve: first Adam was created, and thereafter Eve. This prompts the question: when was Adam created, and when was Eve created? Bar Ḥiyya proposes two answers to this question. The first is parallel to the explanation of the creation of the bodily powers of man and of his rational soul, as mentioned earlier: "The creation of Eve too was not completed on the sixth day" (p. 55); while the second answer rules out the former possibility:

> Or if it was completed on the sixth day; *and that is the truth, for on the sixth day Creation was completed* [emphasis mine], its completion is not mentioned in the account of that particular day, in order to inform us of the dignity of man. For he is not at all similar to any of the other creatures living on the earth except in the form of his body, and he is considered and counted among the creatures of this world in the qualities of his body, but is considered among the creatures of the upper world and the angels in respect to the qualities of his soul and his divine rational soul (*nishmato ha-elohit*). (*ibid.*)

One may infer from this that man was created in his perfection on the sixth day of Creation and that the story of his creation in Genesis. 2:7 is part of the account of the sixth day of Creation.[29] Thus, the distinction between the two stories is merely a literary device intended to emphasize the uniqueness of man by distinguishing between the description of that which is common to him and to the lower world, and the description of

29 In the *Guide of the Perplexed* II.30 Maimonides says regarding Gen. 2:3-4, "Now all the Sages... are unanimous in thinking that all this story occurred on Friday" (Pines, p. 355), referring perhaps to the *Pesiqta de-Rav Kahana* which states: "In the first hour [the creation of man] occurred in the Divine thought; in the second [hour] He took counsel with the ministering angels; in the third He gathered together his dust; in the fourth He kneaded him; in the fifth He formed him; in the sixth He placed him as a form upon his legs; in the seventh He placed in him a soul; in the eighth He placed him in the Garden of Eden; in the ninth He commanded him; in the tenth he [Adam] violated His commandment; in the eleventh he was judged; in the twelfth he left silently before the Holy One blessed be He." Bar Ḥiyya may also have had this midrash in mind, but he does not explicitly state that the story of the Garden of Eden occurred on the sixth day of Creation.

that which is unique to him and which is held in common with the upper world, thereby pointing out his difference from the creatures of the lower world and his similarity to those of the upper world in the qualities of his rational soul.

The Interpretation of Genesis 1:28

God's blessing to Adam and to Eve in Genesis 1:28—"Be fruitful and multiply, and fill the earth and subdue it; and have dominion over the fish of the sea and over the birds of the air and over every living thing that moves upon the earth"—strengthens the general tendency expressed in the separation between the description of the human body and its non-rational souls from that of the creation of his "soul of life" (*nishmat ḥayyim*). In the account of this creation, too, Scripture does not mention anything except for his lower soul qualities: fruitfulness and proliferation is a quality of the appetitive soul, identified with the vegetative soul, while domination over other living creatures belongs to the qualities of the animal soul.[30] This blessing does not mention any qualities of the reflective soul (*nafsho ha-hogah*), "such as wisdom, understanding, fear of Heaven and observance of the commandments, by whose means man acquires the life of the World to Come" (III, p. 55).[31]

30 Here there is a contradiction within Bar Ḥiyya's words. On the preceding page, he argues that rulership in the sense of "ruling and dominating the creatures of the earth" is among the qualities of the soul in which man was similar to the Creator. Likewise in *Hegyon ha-Nefesh*, (II, pp. 57-58; 60-61), Bar Ḥiyya states that dominion over animals is unique to man. This is also the opinion of R. Saʿadiah Gaon, *Sefer ha-Emunot ve-ha-Deʿot*, IV.1 (p. 151). I quote R. Saʿadiah's *Sefer ha-Emunot ve-ha-Deʿot* from *Sefer ha-Nivḥar ba-Emunot u-va-Deʿot le-Rabbenu Saʿadyah ben Yosef Fioyomi ztz"l*, text and translation... Y. Qāfiḥ (Jerusalem: Sura, 1970).

31 Bar Ḥiyya sees in the *neshamah* or the rational soul not only a tool for acquiring knowledge, but also a religious tool—it is responsible for fear of God and for observance of the commandments (cf. *ibid.*, III, p. 58). This derives from his view that only the rational soul has choice and that therefore it alone is able to receive commandments, to obey them or to violate them. See *Hegyon ha-Nefesh ha ʿAṣuvah*, II, pp. 62, 65; and *Sefer Megillat ha-Megalleh*, III, p. 73; and in the present paper, in the chapter, "The Interpretation of the Tree of Knowledge and the Sin of Adam and Eve."

2. Interpretations of the Corporeality of God in the Story of the Creation of Man

The interpretation of "in our image" and establishing the idea of human uniqueness

Another exegetical problem that engages all exegetes of the Bible, including Bar Ḥiyya, is that of the corporealization of God. Genesis 1:26-27 are among the most anthropomorphic verses in the entire Bible. A literal reading of these verses would seem to imply that man is similar to God in that he is made according to the Divine model, from which it follows that God has a physical form, similar to that of the human being. Many commentators try to limit the degree of corporealization of God alluded to by the noun "image" (*ṣelem*) to similarity to human beings on the spiritual level alone, asserting that the word "image" does not refer to a physical image; hence its use does not imply physical corporealization of God. Rather, it merely indicates a similarity between the qualities of the human soul and those of God.

As we have seen, Bar Ḥiyya interprets the word *ṣelem* in Genesis 1 as referring to the human body and the two lower souls that reside therein. Hence he confronts with all severity the question: does a physical corporealization of God exist in the story of the creation of man? He resolves this problem by means of a philological discussion of the preposition *beit*, and the pronominal suffix in the word "in our image."

According to Bar Ḥiyya, the letter *beit* in the word *be-ṣalmenu*, "in our image," is to be interpreted in accordance with "the first rule among the rules of the *beit*."[32] Hence, "Let us make man in our image" does not mean that man is shaped according to the Divine model, the image of God and/or of the angels, but rather that man is made "with" "our image." One might still ask the question: to what does the preposition *beit* in "in our image," refer? Bar Ḥiyya explains: "In the image which we have made or will make. This is similar to a man who makes a form or image, calling it 'my form' or 'my image'—that which I have made" (III, p. 52). The pronominal suffix indicates that the "image" was made by the one speaking, and only in this sense may one say that it is his. Thus, "Let

32 A full discussion of the various significances of the preposition *beit* appears in the First Part of *Sefer Megillat ha-Megalleh*, I, 6-7. Bar Ḥiyya takes note there of two basic meanings or "two rules" of *beit*: *beit* in the sense of "with," and *beit* in the sense of "within," each one of which is divided into secondary meanings. For purposes of our subject, he details there specifically those of "the second rule."

us make man in our image" means: Let us make man with the image that we have made. These words are intended, according to Bar Ḥiyya, to emphasize the fact that man was created by God in a direct and unmediated act of creation: "And its meaning is, Let us make the image of man with our hands or with our speech and not by any other means" (*ibid.*). "Let us make" means that we and no one else shall make man with his image—that is, with his body, his appetitive soul and his animal soul.

Bar Ḥiyya does not explain the use of the plural form in the phrase "let us make" (*na'aśeh*) and in "our image" (*ṣalmenu*); his paraphrase here, "with our hands," is also rather surprising, as the latter word belongs to that group of words bearing a corporealizing significance and is likely to be understood as alluding to an anthropomorphic understanding of God and/or the angels—certainly not something consciously intended by Bar Ḥiyya.

We have seen that, according to Bar Ḥiyya's interpretation, the story of the creation of man, by its style and by its very structure, emphasizes the basic idea of the theory of man which he adopted, according to which there is a complete difference between the manner in which the human rational soul exists and that of the body. Whereas the rational soul is eternal *by its very nature*, the body dies when the "soul of life" departs it. True, according to Bar Ḥiyya's interpretation Adam, the first man, differed from all other human beings who lived or will live after him until the time of the Redemption, in that he was eternal in his body and not only in his rational soul. Thanks to this interpretation, he was able to claim that this original state will return at the end of human history: after the Resurrection of the Dead at the time of the Redemption, man will once again be immortal in body too.

Bar Ḥiyya anchors this idea, among other things, in his interpretation of the word "with our image" (*be-ṣalmenu*). His interpretation of this word not only excludes that interpretation which anthropomorphizes God, but also provides a basis for the idea of the uniqueness of man as against all other denizens of this lower world:

> Scripture had to mention the image of man in order to inform us that, even regarding man's body, none of the other things in the [lower] world were given permission to benefit from his creation in the way that He gave permission to all the other created things on the earth to benefit any other thing. (*ibid.*)

Whereas all other inhabitants of the lower world were created indirectly, by means of an intermediary—the fish and other sea creatures were created by the intermediacy of the water; the land beasts, the animals (according to Gen. 1:20, 24), and the birds (according to Gen. 2:19) were created by the intermediacy of the earth—*even man's body*, in which he is similar to the creatures of the lower world, was created directly by God.[33] Bar Ḥiyya explains this as follows:

> So that it not occur in the heart of anybody nor in their thoughts that there is anything in the world which had the power to assist in the creation of the human image, they should know and acknowledge that regarding the creation of man the Holy One blessed be He, by His holy word and pure thought, fashioned his image (*heṣlim ʾet ṣalmo*) and put sinews on his body, as it is written, "Let us make man in Our image," which testifies to the image and the body being the work of God (III, p. 54).[34]

The emphasis upon the profound difference between the manner of creation of man's body and that of all the other creatures in the lower world prepares the ground for his claim that, therefore, man can be eternal even in his body.

Further on in his commentary, Bar Ḥiyya reinforces the idea that man differs from all the other creatures of this lower world even in his body, by explaining that this difference is rooted, not only in the *manner* of man's creation, but also in the *material* from which his body was made: God chose and selected the dust from which He formed man. Bar Ḥiyya infers this idea from the stylistic difference between the depiction of the creation of man from the earth and the creation of the other creatures from the earth. Concerning man it says: "and the Lord God formed man of dust from the ground" (Gen. 2:7)—that is, from dust that was "chosen and known" (III, p. 60), whereas regarding the other living creatures it

33 Only the *bodies* of the creatures of this lower world were created by the earth or by the water; their vital spirit (i.e., their animal soul) was given them by God. See III, p. 53.

34 The idea of the direct creation also appears in *Sefer Megillat ha-Megalleh*, III, p. 51. Here Bar Ḥiyya shows that man is similar in the manner of his creation to the creatures of the upper world, which were also created in a direct manner, unlike the creatures of the lower world, which were created in a mediated fashion. In *Hegyon ha-Nefesh*, I, pp. 50-51, 54, he sees the direct creation of Adam as a sign of his dignity.

states "and the Lord God formed out of the ground" (Gen. 2:19)—that is "without choosing and selecting" (*ibid.*). Bar Ḥiyya concludes from this that Genesis 2:7 is intended

> To make clear to you and to make close to your thought that the Holy One blessed be He Himself selected the best and selected dust from which to form man, because that dust was distinct from the earth from which the other animals were made, in order that this selected and chosen dust might be recognized and known in the future, that at the time of the Resurrection of the Dead it will be clothed by the same form and rational soul (*neshamah*) by which it was clothed previously." (*ibid.*)

The Interpretation of "In His Image" and "In the Image of God He created Him"

A similar exegetical problem to that found in verse 26 with regard to the word "in our image" (*be-ṣalmenu*) is presented by the word "in His image" (*be-ṣalmo*) in verse 27, and by the phrase "in the image of God created He him." The possessive pronoun in "in His image" (*be-ṣalmenu*), and the conjunction of "God" to "in His image" seemingly indicate that man was created in the image of God, thereby implying the corporealization of God. Bar Ḥiyya solves this problem by explaining that the possessive pronoun in the word "in *his* image" refers to man and not to God. God created man *in the image of man*. The letter *beit* ("in") in the phrase "in his image" is thus to be understood as it was in the phrase *be-ṣalmenu* ("in our image")—i.e., "with"; that is, God created man with "his bodily powers, which pertain to matter and the body" (III, p. 55). In interpreting the second half of verse 27, Bar Ḥiyya uses a different punctuation than that generally accepted for this verse. He reads: "in the image, God created him" (i.e., with a comma after the word "image"). Hence, one ought to understand the sentence as "coming to inform us that the Holy One blessed be He fashioned his image (i.e., body), and not by any other thing" (*ibid.*). This part of the verse thus reiterates the idea of direct creation, already expressed in verse 26. But whereas verse 26 only speaks of the Divine intention of creating the *image* of man by means of direct creation, verse 27 speaks of the execution of this plan.

The Interpretation of "As Our Likeness"

The problem of corporealization of God is likewise raised by the word "as our likeness" (*ki-demutenu*). As we have seen, Bar Ḥiyya interprets "in our likeness" as referring to the rational soul of the human being, in whose qualities man resembles God, rather than to his physical form. There thus remains a certain resemblance in the spiritual realm between man and God—a resemblance that Bar Ḥiyya tries to reduce insofar as possible. His interpretation of "as our likeness" is based upon a linguistic discussion along the semantic–philosophical axis. According to him, the *kaf* of comparison (i.e., the Hebrew preposition parallel to "as" or "like" denoting similarity between things), *ke* ("like") indicates "the dominance of one thing over another" (III, p. 54). True, according to the theories of poetics accepted in his day, "it is well known that the object of the simile is not fully identical to the simile in every respect, nor is the power of the one like the other" (*ibid.*). Thus, there is not a complete identity between the simile and the intended object of the simile. We therefore need to understand that there is no full resemblance between God and the rational soul of the human being in terms of His qualities of wisdom and rulership and there remains an enormous gap between them. Bar Ḥiyya does not elaborate as to the nature and significance of this gap.

Bar Ḥiyya tries to overcome the problem raised by the similarity or resemblance of God to man suggested by the word "in our likeness" in an additional way: by explaining the significance of the *kaf* of comparison in the biblical lexicon. He notes a number of verses in which the Bible uses the *kaf* of comparison to describe a particular matter in poetic language, whereas other verses describe the very same subject in a prosaic manner. He observes that in poetic language, the *kaf* of comparison is used to indicate the resemblance between two things, albeit by way of hyperbole, when it wishes to emphasize a particular subject.[35] It follows from this that in Genesis 1:26 as well, the use of the *kaf* of comparison should be

35 As an example, Bar Ḥiyya cites the Divine promises to Abraham and to Jacob, in which he states regarding their seed that they shall be "like the stars of the heavens and like the sands which is upon the shores of the sea" (Gen. 22:17); "like the dust of the earth" (Gen. 28:14) and "like the sand of the sea" (Gen. 32:13). He thinks that the parallel to these is in the census of the Israelites in the book of Numbers (1:18 and 3:15) according to which the counting of the children of Israel was not completed, as neither the women nor the Levites were included in the census of the Israelites, nor were the males between the ages of one month to twenty years. God's words in his promise to the patriarchs was only intended to indicate that the number of the children of Israel would be so very great that it could not be completed—and this was said by way of hyperbole, using the "*kaf* of comparison" (III, p. 54).

seen as a form of hyperbole; there is no real resemblance between the qualities of God and those of man's rational soul. Again, Bar Ḥiyya does not pose the question as to the nature and the limits of the similarity between God and man's rational soul according to this interpretation.[36]

3. *The Interpretation of Genesis 5:1*

When the Bible summarizes the description of the creation of man in Genesis 5:1, it includes in one verse that which had previously been described in two different chapters, saying "This is the book of the generations of man; on the day that the Lord God created man, He made him in the likeness of God." The verbs "create" and "make" appear one after another in this verse. Thus, its meaning is that "[God] created him first *in potentia* and thereafter realized him in actuality" (II, p. 15). The completion of man, his "realization in actuality," was performed by breathing into him his rational soul [*neshamah*], his "reflective [*hogah*] and rational [*dabranit*] soul", as indicated by the verb "likeness." "He made him in the likeness of God" is understood by Bar Ḥiyya as: "The Holy One blessed be He breathed a pure "soul of life" [*nishmat ḥayyim*] into Adam, and in that soul [*neshamah*] he was similar to the angels, as is written, 'He made him in the likeness of God'" (III, p. 72). Thus, Bar Ḥiyya understands the word *Elohim* (usually translated as "God") as referring to the angels. Man was made in the likeness of the angels, who are creatures of the upper world. As we have seen in Genesis 1:26 as well, the word *ki-demutenu,* "in our likeness," refers to the rational soul of man. There is, however, a stylistic difference between these two verses: in Genesis 1:26, it states *ki-demutenu*, "as our likeness," while in Genesis 5:1 it states *bidemut elohim*, "in the likeness of God [or, 'the angels']." This stylistic difference is explained by Bar Ḥiyya by saying, By [using] the letter *beit* ("in"), rather than the letter *kaf* ("like"), as was said at the time of his creation, "in our image, as our likeness," because it is used here to explain the matter by which the making of man was completed and the definition of his form was determined, and this was the soul [*neshamah*] that was breathed into him in which he is similar to the angels, and which distinguishes between him and the other animals—that is to say, in those qualities in which he is similar to God, by which his making was completed. (III, p. 62)

---

36 Bar Ḥiyya does not develop any discussion of the theory of the Divine attributes, and hence does not undertake any comparison between God's qualities and those of human beings.

Bar Ḥiyya evidently understands here that the letter *beit* in the word "in [His] likeness" is similar to the *beit* of "in our image"—i.e., "with" his likeness. That is to say, God created man together with his rational soul, which is his form.

4. The Story of the Creation of Man as the Story of Human History

The interpretation of the story of the creation of man which we have just surveyed is built upon the *a priori* assumption that Genesis 1 is an *historical story*: it relates the creation of Adam and the structure of his soul, emphasizing the Platonic distinction between the non-rational souls and his rational soul. However, Bar Ḥiyya also suggests an additional possible interpretation of Genesis 1:26. This verse speaks, not of Adam the first man, but of humankind as a whole. Its purpose is "to inform us that all those generations which were to be created in potentia and to be realized in practice, from the Six Days of Creation until the end of the world as a whole, were in [God's] holy thought, arose and were present in potentia before the Omnipresent" (III, p. 54). The completion spoken of in verse 26 and alluded to by the verb "let us make" (*na'aśeh*) is thus the completion of the creation of all generations of the human race who will come into existence until the end of human history. By this interpretation, Bar Ḥiyya is not reinterpreting the phrase "in our image and in our likeness." It is possible that this interpretation alludes to the fact that the distinction made between the rational part of man and his irrational part is a component of the structure of the human being in general, the structure of all human beings of all future generations; hence, one ought to add to this interpretation the interpretation of the phrase "in our image, as our likeness" as was given previously. If this is indeed Bar Ḥiyya's line of thought, then he already saw the story of the creation of man, even before Maimonides, as a philosophical anthropology.

The interpretation which we have presented now for Genesis 1:26 is derived by Bar Ḥiyya from a *stylistic peculiarity* of this verse. At the beginning of the verse, it states of Adam, in the singular, "let us make *man*" (*adam*), whereas at the end of the verse it states in the plural, "and *they* shall have dominion over the fish of the sea..." As one of Bar Ḥiyya's *a priori* assumptions in his interpretation of the Bible is that the interpretation must conform to the laws of the Hebrew language, one must understand the word *adam* ("Adam" or "man") at the beginning of the story as alluding, not to one individual, but to many human beings. It follows from this that the verse refers to all those human beings whose existence will be realized throughout the course of human history. It should be reiterated here that Abraham Bar Ḥiyya accepts the possibility of a number of simultaneously correct interpretations of the same verse. Hence this interpretation does not exclude the first interpretation of the story of the creation of Adam, according to which one is speaking of one man, Adam, notwithstanding that this interpretation leaves unexplained the stylistic peculiarity that served as the pretext for this latter interpretation. Bar Ḥiyya does not seek a consistent and full interpretation at all costs. He uses various elements of the verses which he interprets, each time in accordance with the immediate exegetical need, in order to find additional meanings of the same text.

5. Adam's Immortality

Bar Ḥiyya's aim, in his interpretation of the story of the creation of man and that of the Garden of Eden, was, as we said, to reinforce by means of the biblical text, the belief in the Resurrection of the Dead at the time of the Redemption. The interpretation of the creation of man just surveyed paves the way. According to this interpretation, man was created out of two heterogeneous elements—the body and those souls connected thereto, and the rational soul. Man's rational soul is immortal by its very nature, whereas his body differs from the bodies of all other creatures of the lower world which it resembles in the manner of its creation—the body of man alone was created directly by God, and God even carefully chose the material for his creation.

The central idea of his interpretation is grounded by Bar Ḥiyya specifically on a verse that at first glance seems unfruitful from an exegetical viewpoint—namely, Genesis 1:29, God's blessing to Adam and Eve: "And God said, behold, I have given you every plant yielding seed which is upon the face of all the earth, and every tree with seed in its fruit; you shall have them for food." He interprets this verse simultaneously on the semantic–philosophical axis and the semantic–eschatological axis.

In his interpretation of the latter part of verse 26, Bar Ḥiyya observes that the Aristotelian principle, "the beginning of thought is the end of deed" (III, p. 52) relates not only to the completion of the creation of Adam the first man and the giving of his rational soul, which is his form, to his body, but also the completion of the creation of all of those future generations whose existence arose in the Divine thought. His interpretation of verse 29 is, in effect, the continuation of this interpretation. Verse 29 tells us of the end of the Divine thought which, in accordance with the above-mentioned Aristotelian principle, was the beginning of action: "And its end is that it shall be within his body, and his soul lives and exists in this world, and it will not experience death" (III, p. 55). That is to say: upon his creation, man will be eternal, not only in his soul but also in his body. Since Bar Ḥiyya assumes here the semantic–eschatological axis, he interprets the verse as coming to teach that "This thought will be completed and realized within him [within man] also in the Future to Come" (*ibid.*). It may be that Bar Ḥiyya interprets things here in a somewhat different manner, and that the word "its end" means, not the final end of the thought, but the end of the "beginning" of the thought—that is, the end of the idea of its end: the ultimate end of the future generations of human beings is that there will be human beings who will be resurrected in the time of the Messiah and no longer die. He therefore says that "this thought will be completed and fulfilled within him in the future." That is to say: the "beginning" of thought will be "the end of the deed."

In his interpretation of verse 29, Bar Ḥiyya relies upon a *stylistic change* in the description of the seed-bearing vegetation in Genesis 1. In verse 11, the seed-bearing plants are characterized by the expressions, *mazri*ʿ*a zera*ʿ ("yielding seed"), and *asher zar*ʿ*o bo* ("in which is their seed"); it goes on to speak of "plants yielding seed," and "fruit trees bearing fruit in which is their seed." In verse 29, by contrast, they are characterized by the phrase, *zore*ʿ*a zera*ʿ—literally, "which sows seed." It states there, "every plant which sows seed... and every tree with seed in its fruit." Moreover, the context in which these two descriptions appear is likewise different: verse 11 speaks of the *creation* of the vegetation whereas verse 29 speaks about the use to which man will put these plants—namely, to eat them. Therefore, Bar Ḥiyya explains that the description of the types of vegetation in verse 11 is based upon their botanical classification—the creation of each group of seed-bearing plants is described there. "Yielding seed" means "that this type of vegetation releases its seed and sows it and it does not renew its seed from within" (III, p. 56), whereas, "with fruit in its seed" refers to those "whose seed is a generation that comes out of itself" (*ibid.*). In verse 29, the text does not repeat the characterization of the vegetation according to their manner of reproduction, but rather explains what happens to them when man eats them. The phrase, "yielding seed," comes to tell us "that it replaces in the body that which is missing in its matter and its form, like a man who sows seed to acquire seed that is like it" (III, p. 55). Or, "that it itself [i.e., the vegetation or tree that is eaten] is transformed and changes the form of the organ that derives benefit from it" (III, p. 56). The description of vegetation in verse 29 likewise teaches us a lesson in human physiology: "that his food [i.e., that of man] replaces the absence of that which exchanges itself everyday in his body, so that he is not beset by either weakness or old age" (III, p. 55).

His interpretation of the phrase "yielding seed" is based upon a physiological theory promulgated by the second-century physician Galen, which he adapts to his own needs. At the beginning of the third section of *Sefer Megillat ha-Megalleh*, Bar Ḥiyya quotes a work of Galen which is not extant.[37] In this work Galen objects to the claim of "one of the sages among the physicians" according to which one may be saved from death from old age by the science of medicine and the proper conduct of the body, particularly by correct nutrition. Galen ridicules the words of that physician, arguing that they derive from his lack of knowledge of the functioning of the human body and the cause of human mortality. He explains that natural death of human beings is caused by the drying out of the moistures of his body as a result of their being warmed by the natural inner heat of the body, on the one hand, and of the air surrounding it, on the other. Since the moistures are that which connect the organs of the human body, their loss causes the degeneration of these organs. This process of loss of moistures is a constant and gradual one,

37 On this matter see J. Guttmann, "Ueber Abraham bar Chijjas Buch der Enthüllung," *MGWJ* 47 (1903), p. 547 and n. 1 there. Compare Avicenna, *Canon*, Vol. I, p. 149: "The body exists so long as it exists, not because its primal natural moistness [is capable] of resisting in a continuous way to that the increasing heat and the heat of its body—which is of its very nature and is created by its motions— will dissolve it, for the opposition of the natural moisture is too weak to attain this. Rather, it exists by the fact that there is exchange of that which dissolves from it, and this is the food... when the drying out is completed, the heat is extinguished and natural death occurs..." (p. 100, n. 102). And cf. Avicenna, *Canon*, I, p. 148: "One of the two kinds of blemish is the dissolving of the moisture from which it is created, and this happens gradually" (see *ibid.*, n. 100). And cf. *ibid.*, p. 149: "And each of the two [that is; the dissolving of the moisture and the decay of the moisture] happens for external reasons, such as the air that dissolves and causes decay, and internal reasons such as the natural warmth in us that dissolves our moisture, and the alien heat created within us from our food and other things that decay" (see *ibid.*, n. 101). I have quoted Avicenna's *Canon* according to Prof. Gotthold Eliakim Weil's notes in his edition of *Maimonides über die Lebensdauer* translated into Hebrew and updated by Michael Schwarz: *Maimonides' Response Regarding the Spam of Life* (Tel Aviv: Papyrus, 1979). The notes do not state the edition from which the *Canon* is quoted.

which can only be partially corrected by proper nutrition. The food which we introduce into our bodies is transformed into the various kinds of moisture that have been lost from each of the organs of the body, and in this manner the unity of the human body is preserved. According to Galen, a special power of the soul known as *the force of transformation* (*ha-koaḥ ha-memir*) is responsible for this process of exchange. However, this force cannot completely compensate for the body's loss of moistures. At times it transforms foods which are harmful to the organs, and at other times it changes less than is needed to replace that which has been lost. Hence, a constant process of deterioration and decay occurs within the human being—that is, the process of aging that concludes in inevitable death—over the course of his lifetime. Medicine may assist the power of transformation and prevent some of the illnesses of the body that are caused by harmful processes of transformation, but it cannot completely prevent the process of deterioration in general, and hence is unable to prevent the death of man from old age. Bar Ḥiyya quotes Galen who says:

> If man were able to restore to his body the moisture that had been lost, in proper form and quantity, no more and no less [than had been lost], man would not die... But at this time, when the transformative force does not have this power, but at times it adds and at other times it loses without proper measure, his words [i.e., those of the physician whom Galen was criticizing] are nothing but vanity. (III, p. 60).[38]

At the end of his quotation from Galen, Bar Ḥiyya comments: "And now you may see from them, that if the Holy One blessed be He were to force the transformative power in the human being and give them the full proper force, man would be immortal in this world" (*ibid.*). With these words, Bar Ḥiyya prepares the ground for his interpretation of Genesis 1:29 and of the story of the Garden of Eden.

The idea expressed in verse 29, according to Bar Ḥiyya's interpretation, is that man was originally created as immortal, and that he will once again be so at the End of Days, upon the Resurrection of the Dead, which

38 For more general things said by Galen regarding this question and parallels in medieval Jewish philosophy, see J. Guttmann, "Introduction," in *Sefer Megillat ha-Megalleh*, p. xviii.

will occur upon the coming of the Messiah. He bases this idea upon the *tenses of the verbs* used in this verse. At the beginning of the verse, it states in the past tense, "Behold, I have given you"; thus, it is speaking here of "an act which has passed, or which was performed immediately when all this was placed before them and given into their hands in the verse of blessing by which they were blessed..." (III, p. 56). The end of the verse, however, is couched in the future tense, "you *shall have them* for food." If the end of the verse referred to the same past event, it should also have been couched in the past tense or the present tense: "And it could have said, 'I have given you to eat' or 'you have it for food,' from which we would have understand that this was their food from the time of their creation" (*ibid.*). The use of the future tense is therefore used to signify, in Bar Ḥiyya's view, "that He promises concerning this thing for the future that is to come," and this future spoken of is the End of Days.

Bar Ḥiyya confirms this interpretation by means of the similarity in contents that exists between the following verse, verse 30, which continues the subject matter of verse 29, and the vision of the End of Days in Isaiah. Verse 30 reads, "And to every beast of the earth, and to every bird of the air, and to everything that creeps on the earth, everything that has the breath of life, I have given every green plant for food." Here too, Bar Ḥiyya understands "to eat" as in verse 29, "shall be for food," from which it follows that in the End of Days the beasts of the earth and the birds of the sky will be vegetarian. And indeed, this description corresponds to that of the End of Days in Isaiah 11:7: "The cow and the bear shall graze together...the lion shall eat straw like the ox." It follows from this that verses 29-30 likewise speak of the End of Days, when the wild beasts shall all be vegetarian. Bar Ḥiyya infers the situation of man from the expression "yielding seed" in verse 29: "And at that time the Holy One blessed be He will strengthen the transformative force within man, so that he will transform his food and concoct it and here will remain no waste matter nor any dregs, but it will restore it to the form of the lost thing of each organ and in its proper measure, no less and no more" (III, p. 56).[39]

39 In his commentary on the Torah (p. 93), Abravanel explains the cause of aging and death in a similar way to Bar Ḥiyya. However, he interprets the function of the Tree of Life in a different manner than does Bar Ḥiyya. In his opinion, the Tree of Life was intended to cause complete transformation of food directly into the organs of the body which enjoy it and hence causes longevity and perpetuate life. For Bar Ḥiyya's view of the Tree of Life see below, in the section "The Interpretation of the Tree of Life."

This situation of immortality was already the lot of the first man [Adam], as indicated by the verb, "I have given," phrased in the past tense: "And concerning this matter, such was the power of the first man before he sinned" *(ibid.)*. The first man lost his immortality because of the sin he committed in the Garden of Eden; however, it will be restored to him at the end of human history, at the End of Days. This explanation requires that Bar Ḥiyya expand his exegesis so as to include therein his interpretation of the story of the Garden of Eden, in order to explain how humanity lost its ability to live forever.

On this point, we ought to point out that Bar Ḥiyya explains human immortality, not as a "miracle" violating the laws of nature to be brought about at the End of Days, but rather as a "miracle " or wondrous phenomenon based upon the laws of nature themselves, and explainable by physiological theories that were accepted in his day. God did not and will not change the nature of the human body at all; in the eschatological future, He will simply strengthen an already existing force within him, thereby man will be granted eternal life. In practice, Bar Ḥiyya applies here his basic outlook regarding the relationship between revelation and intellect. As we have seen, Bar Ḥiyya thinks that man is incapable of fully understanding the order of the universe on the basis of his intellect and his everyday experience alone, but requires revelation in order to complete his knowledge. The Bible tells us that the hypothetical situation spoken of by Galen in fact took place at the beginning of human history and will again exist at its End, in accordance with a known and fixed Divine plan that was known from the outset. The wise men of science and of medicine, who only had experience of a part of human history—namely, the situation of humanity after the sin of the Garden of Eden and before the Resurrection of the Dead—would be unable to imagine the possibility of human immortality, and therefore the people of southern France and Christian Spain, who followed in their wake during the period of Bar Ḥiyya, denied the Resurrection of the Dead at the time of the Redemption.

IV. The Interpretation of the Story of the Garden of Eden

Bar Ḥiyya's interpretation of the story of the Garden of Eden follows exegetical lines similar to those characteristic of his interpretation of the story of creation of man: like that of the creation of man, the story of the Garden of Eden is one that concerns an historical event: the story of the sin of Adam and of Eve at the beginning of human history. However, it is also the story of the human being in general, his ethical–religious behavior and his reward in the World to Come.

1. The Story of the Garden of Eden as the Story of an Historical Event

The Tree of Knowledge and the Sin of Adam and Eve

One of the central problems engaging commentators on the story of the Garden of Eden is the lack of consistency in the description of the two trees upon which man's fate is dependent: the Tree of Life and the Tree of Knowledge. Genesis 2:9 refers to two special trees which grow in the center of the Garden, the Tree of Life and the Tree of Knowledge. However, in verses 16-17 of that chapter only the Tree of Knowledge is mentioned, and it alone serves to test man. Likewise in Chapter 3, with the exception of verses 22 and 24, it speaks only of the Tree of Knowledge. The Tree of Life, which plays no particular role in the story to this point, reappears in verses 22 and 24, where its appearance elicits some surprise: according to Genesis 2:17, the only tree from which man was not allowed to eat was the Tree of Knowledge, whereas according to what it is stated in 3:22, 24, God is apprehensive that man will also eat of the Tree of Life. Are we to understand from this that prior to his sin Adam was allowed to eat from the Tree of Life, and that only thereafter God did not wish this to happen?[40]

Bar Ḥiyya answers this complex of exegetical problems by implementing his basic exegetical assumption, according to which the story of the Garden of Eden occurs on two levels of meaning. The story of the eating of the Tree of Knowledge is understood as the story of an historical event—the sin of Adam and Eve; while everything pertaining to the Tree of Life relates to human destiny in general and is a chapter in his anthropological doctrine.

There is also a whole series of exegetical problems regarding the func-

---

40 On the exegetical problems entailed in this story, see J. Skinner, *The International Critical Commentary: A Critical and Exegetical Commentary on Genesis* (Edinburgh, 1930), pp. 52-53. Modern biblical critics attempt to resolve these exegetical problems by claiming that the Garden of Eden story in its extant form is a later redaction combining two originally different stories. In one of them there is only mentioned the Tree of Knowledge, and in the second the Tree of Life is also mentioned. The dominant story in the extant text is the former one. See *ibid.*, p. 53.

tion of the Tree of Knowledge in the story of the Garden of Eden. The "knowledge of good and evil" is understood by the majority of exegetes as ethical distinction or judgment. The most widely-accepted interpretation of this "knowledge" claims that the Tree of Knowledge enables man to acquire ethical discernment. However, such an interpretation raises two difficult problems: 1) If the eating of the Tree of Knowledge provides man with ethical discernment, why did God prohibit Adam from eating from it? Why did God wish to withhold from man the capability of ethical discernment? 2) Did not the very fact of the prohibition against eating from the Tree of Knowledge itself assume that man already had ethical discernment? Otherwise, how is it possible to give a commandment to one who does not yet discern between good and evil, between that which is proper to do and that which it is improper to do? And if indeed it is known that man had ethical discernment before he was commanded not to eat from the Tree of Knowledge, one might ask: what was eating from the Tree of Knowledge likely to give him?

The exegetical difficulties become even greater further along in the story: God explains to Adam that eating from the Tree of Knowledge will bring those eating there a degree of resemblance to God—at least according to the most widespread interpretation of "the Tree of Knowledge of Good and Evil"—in the sense of resembling God in His capability of ethical discernment: "you shall be like God, knowing good and evil" (Gen. 3:5). God is thus represented as one who wishes to withhold from man the capacity for ethical discernment so that he will not resemble Him. And indeed, according to Genesis 3, Adam and Eve did not die immediately upon eating from the Tree of Knowledge as they had previously been told by the serpent, but rather acquired the cognition of shame because of their nakedness. At this point one may well ask the question: what is one to make of their acquisition of this new knowledge? Is one to see it as the beginning or symbol of a new manner of perceiving the world? Or is it perhaps, to the contrary, an unimportant, disappointing piece of information which did not answer the anticipations of the two when they ate of the Tree of Knowledge? They did not acquire knowledge which would bring them closer to resemblance to God, but simply shame regarding their own nakedness. The conclusion of the story would seem to confirm the words of the serpent: "And the Lord God said: Behold, the man has become like one of us, knowing good and evil; now, lest he put forth his hand and take also from the Tree of Life, and eat, and live forever" (Gen. 3:22). The serpent was right: humankind had acquired ethical discernment and thereby came to resemble God in His ethical qualities, but he was not yet similar to Him in terms of being immortal. God is afraid lest man also acquire eternal life and resemble Him in that, and therefore expels Adam from the Garden of Eden.[41]

This complex set of problems is resolved by Bar Ḥiyya with the help of a number of exegetical principles. The most interesting of these is his interpretation of the word "knowledge" (*da'at*), which appears a number of times in the Garden of Eden story. According to Bar Ḥiyya, knowledge is an equivocal word, with two basic meanings: on the one hand, bodily affectibility, sensation, impression—or, in his language, *ḥashasha;* and, on the other hand, "knowledge and understanding." On the basis of these two meanings of the word *da'at*, the phrase *da'at tov ve-ra'*, "knowledge of good and evil," may refer to the sensation of good and bad things, or the ethical discrimination between good and evil and knowledge of the good and bad things which will occur in the future.

Bar Ḥiyya reinforces the first interpretation of the word *da'at*, knowledge, by use of the biblical lexicon. He finds the word *da'at* used in the sense of bodily affectibility, sensation or feeling in Judges 8:16, where it states about Gideon, in his battle at Sukkot, "And he taught (*va-yoda'*) [by the briers and thorns of the desert] the men of Sukkot." Bar Ḥiyya interprets thusly: Gideon caused the people of Sukkot to feel the blows and stings of the thorns and thistles. Thus, the Bible itself uses the verb *yado'a* in the sense of feeling and the receiving of sensation by means of the body. Bar Ḥiyya does not need to confirm the second meaning of the word *da'at,* as its use in the sense of knowledge is the common dictionary meaning of the word *da'at*, and it is also the interpretation given by "the ancient ones" to the word *da'at* in the expression *'eṣ ha-da'at tov ve-ra'*, "the Tree of Knowledge." As we shall see below, Bar Ḥiyya distinguishes between these two meanings of "knowledge of good and evil": ethical knowledge, which is the significance accepted by the commentators; and knowledge of the good and evil things which will happen to human beings in the future. This meaning is derived by Bar Ḥiyya in the course of his interpretation from the context of the words "knowledge of good and evil."

The actions of things on the human body are opposing and their

41 See Skinner's book (above, n. 40), pp. 95-97.

results may be good or bad, such as health or sickness, life or death, and so on. In Genesis 1:9, the word *da'at* bears, according to Bar Ḥiyya's interpretation, the sense of bodily affectibility, and the Tree of Knowledge is a tree that causes the one eating it to be affected *in his body* by things external to himself. Bar Ḥiyya emphasizes the negative effects: it enables the body to be injured, to be subject to bad effects, including death. Thus, God's warning to Adam that he will die if he eats of the Tree of Knowledge is correct, for man will then be susceptible to death as one of the forms of bodily evil existing in the world: "And the Tree of Knowledge of Good and Evil is the tree, which one who obtains it and is connected thereto, understands and is concerned about all the different changes which come about in the world—namely, good and evil, life and death, and similar things" (p. 61). This explanation of the Tree of Knowledge resolves the question as to how God could impose a commandment upon man before he had ethical discernment, and why God wished to withhold from man the capability of ethical discernment whereby he would come to resemble Him. According to this interpretation of Bar Ḥiyya, the Tree of Knowledge did not give those who ate of its fruit ethical discernment, but something else entirely: physical vulnerability to evil.

According to Bar Ḥiyya's theory of the soul, ethical discernment is performed by the "reflective and rational (*dabranit*) soul." Therefore, man's creation in his perfection, as a creature with a "soul of life" (*nishmat ḥayyim*), i.e., a rational soul, is simultaneously identified with his creation as one having ethical discernment: "and you cannot say that Adam did not know the difference between good and evil, for the Holy One blessed be He breathed into him the "soul of life," thereby completing his form, and through it he reflects and thinks (*hogeh u-medaber*) and is distinct from the animals and the beasts, and is similar to the angels" (*ibid.*). The resemblance to the angels lies in his ability for ethical discernment, but not in his sensation of good and evil, which assumes the existence of the body. It was only regarding this resemblance that the verse in Genesis 3:22 states: "Behold, the man has become like one of us, knowing good and evil." Similarly the fact that God warned Adam against eating of the Tree of Knowledge indicates that he already had ethical discernment, for it is not plausible that He would impose upon man commandments or proscriptions if he did not already possess that ability:

> And if he did not recognize the difference between good and evil, he would not be fit to receive such a proscription nor a commandment for which he would be punished or deserve merit [if he performed it], until He can say to him "Eat" or "Do not eat." For the Holy One blessed be He does not warn or command or punish or dispense merit except to those who have discernment and understand the difference between good and evil, and this matter is clear and known to every man, and there is no need to elaborate upon it (*ibid.*).[42]

The interpretation of Eve's sin is based upon the assertion that the serpent deliberately exploited the ambiguity of the term *daʿat* ("knowledge") when he tempted her and misled her, as well as upon the interpretation of the meaning of the word *naḥash*, "serpent." The noun "serpent" (*naḥash*) is a symbolic term, indicative of the nature of the serpent's activity, which involved misguiding and leading astray. However, Bar Ḥiyya explains the precise significance of this name in two different ways: in one place he explains that the word *naḥash* is derived from the verb *le-naḥesh*, "to divine," in the sense of "to know in advance the bad and good things that shall take place in the future:" and concerning this he was named *naḥash* (Serpent) in that he led the woman astray, by engaging her in soothsaying and divination" (p. 62). Bar Ḥiyya thus interprets *daʿat* in the sense of prior knowledge of the good and bad things that will occur in the future. According to the tempting words of the serpent, it is this knowledge which Adam and Eve will acquire by eating from the Tree of Knowledge.

The second explanation of the term *naḥash* is presented by Bar Ḥiyya at a later stage of his interpretation of the story of the sin of Adam in the Garden of Eden. In interpreting Genesis 3:1, "And the serpent was clever" he writes: "And his cleverness was derived from his name. His name was *naḥash*, and he advised to speculate [*naḥesh*] concerning the words of God" (p. 65). The word is thus derived, according to this interpretation, from *le-naḥesh* in the sense of "to conjecture, to specu-

---

42 R. Saʿadiah Gaon already felt this problem when he translated Gen. 3:5: "knowing good and evil *better*" (*Torah Commentary*, p. 15)—that is to say, even prior to their sin Adam and Eve had some sort of ethical discernment.

late." The serpent advised the woman to attempt to understand the true meaning of God's words.[43]

These two explanations of the meaning of the word *naḥash*, "serpent," do not contradict one another and may be sustained simultaneously. The serpent's cleverness lay in the advice he gave the woman to re-examine the Divine prohibition not to eat of the Tree of Knowledge and to see whether she properly understood its significance. Together with Eve, the serpent reconstructs the words of the Divine warning, saying to her, "Did not God say, 'You shall not eat of any of the trees of the garden...'" (Gen. 3:1). The woman, being tempted, repeats the Divine prohibition, but her words are slightly different from those originally said by God. Bar Ḥiyya, following the Sages,[44] attributes importance to these linguistic differences, explaining each of the stylistic differences as carrying a particular significance. The differences in wording reflect Eve's understanding of God's words. The basic idea underlying this comment is that Eve is extremely precise in her expression. In Genesis 2:15 it says: "of every tree of the Garden you may surely eat (*'akhol to'khel*)"; while Eve said, "of the fruit of the trees of the Garden we may eat." The variation in her formulation is based on what is written in Genesis 1:29, which specifies the kinds of trees from which Adam was to eat—fruit trees bearing seed. She says, "of the fruit of the tree which is in the midst of the Garden." She does not use the phrase, "the Tree of Knowledge," as according to her understanding "the Tree of Knowledge" is not the name of the tree. The word "knowledge" brought in conjunction with "tree" is only intended to indicate that it is forbidden to touch this tree. Eve thus understood knowledge in the sense of sensation, bodily affectibility, a meaning which Bar Ḥiyya expands here to include "touching." She therefore translates

---

43 Bar Ḥiyya thus anticipated Maimonides' interpretation of the noun *naḥash* on the basis of its etymology, real or imagined. There is, however, a significant difference between Bar Ḥiyya's interpretation and that of Maimonides. Maimonides see the serpent as an allegorical figure, whose meaning is indicated by the noun *naḥash*, whereas Bar Ḥiyya uses the etymological method to explain the nature of the serpent's seductive activity, rather than to identify the figure of the serpent in the story of the Garden per se. He does not engage at all in interpreting the figure of the serpent. Thus, whereas Maimonides does not explain the significance of the noun *naḥash* and only makes use of the etymological method as a hint towards identifying this figure, leaving the actual identification to the reader who "is wise and understands by himself," Bar Ḥiyya explains in both of his commentaries the meaning of the serpent's seductive activity on the basis of etymology. For Maimonides' interpretation of the figure of the serpent, see (in this volume) "Interpretative Riddles in Maimonides' *Guide of the Perplexed*," pp. 155-157.

44 See B. Sanhedrin 29a. I wish to thank the translator of this article, Yehonatan Chipman, for this reference.

"knowledge" as "you shall not touch it" (p. 65). At an earlier stage of his interpretation, Bar Ḥiyya explains that Eve understood "knowledge" as "knowledge of the body, which is sensation and touching" (p. 62). Hence she was strict with herself and said, not only that it was forbidden to eat of the tree, but that even to touch it was forbidden.

The serpent seduced Eve by interpreting God's admonition in a different way than she does. First of all, he explains to her that she had in fact not understood God's words because she misunderstood the key word *daʿat*, "knowledge." The word *daʿat* as used by God in His admonition means knowledge "of that which shall occur in the future, for good and for evil" (*ibid.*), and does not relate to sensation or touching, as had been understood by Eve. Therefore the serpent says, "and you shall be like God, knowing good and evil," in the sense of "knowing what will occur in the future for good and for evil," (*ibid.*), by means of soothsaying and divination.

In addition, the serpent explains to Eve that she erred in her understanding of God's words, "you shall surely die (*mot tamut*)." Eve, in reconstructing or repeating God's words, says "lest you die" rather than "you shall surely die," as in God's original words. The serpent understands that Eve thereby expresses her apprehension of the punishment of death, because she understands death as punishment for transgression. To this, the serpent answers that "you shall not surely die"—that is to say: "Your death shall not be death as a consequence of punishment, but rather death as is the way of all living creatures, and because of death man will have need of you, and the death of which He spoke is not punishment for the eating" (p. 66). There is thus no connection between eating from the Tree of Knowledge and death. Man is mortal, like all other creatures, and therefore the woman was created so that she might bear offspring and allow the continuity of the human race. This last argument is the serpent's strongest one of all, for he speaks to the woman and points out that her very existence proves the correctness of his interpretation of God's words. God did not want man to know in advance those things that would happen in the future, both good and bad, and therefore prohibited his eating of the Tree of Knowledge. Eve, tempted by the serpent's explanation, again looks at the tree and sees that it is similar in appearance to all the other trees of the garden, and that it is "pleasant in appearance and good to eat," just like the other trees of the garden, concerning which it says in Genesis 2:9, "every tree that is pleasant to the sight and good for food." She concludes from this that the serpent's advice is sound: "and the tree was desirable to acquire knowledge." "Tree" (*'eṣ*), according to Bar Ḥiyya's interpretation, is an equivocal term. It may indicate a particular type of vegetation, but it may also allude to "advice" (*'eṣah*), as derived from the root *'uṣ*. In the second half of the verse the word *'eṣ* appears in its second meaning, that of advice or consul, for if it did not have a different meaning than it did at the beginning of the verse there would have been no need to repeat it; one could have sufficed by alluding to it with a pronoun, saying "and *it* was desirable, to acquire knowledge." The counsel of the serpent which was given to Eve, was that it was "desirable to acquire knowledge." *Le-haskil*, "to acquire knowledge," is understood by Bar Ḥiyya as referring to the acquisition of practical knowledge rather than theoretical knowledge; to understand the good and evil that are likely to come to Adam and to Eve from those things that surround them. Such understanding is acquired by astrology and divination: "Experience (*nisayon*)[45] and divination are useful for acquiring knowledge and to understand every thing." (p. 66)

The sin of Eve, according to Bar Ḥiyya, was performed "by error and in transgression" (p. 62): "In error," because the serpent misled her and caused her to interpret God's warning incorrectly; "in transgression," because even if she understood the prohibition incorrectly and thought that eating of the Tree of Knowledge would not cause her to die, she ought to have listened to the Divine order as such. Eve's sin was therefore a transgression of God's command.

The result of eating of the Tree of Knowledge was "and they knew that they were naked" (Gen. 3:7). This indicates that the first interpretation given by Eve to the word *da'at* ("knowledge") was correct, and that God's words meant that eating of the Tree of Knowledge would make Adam and Eve vulnerable in their bodies to various things in the physical world that surround them. Bar Ḥiyya interprets "And they knew" in this verse as meaning "they felt." Adam and Eve felt that they were naked when they felt the harm caused them by the currents of air upon their naked bodies. They did not acquire any new knowledge, ethical knowledge or knowledge of the future. In order to protect themselves from harm, evidently

45 "Test" (*nisayon*) is understood here in an astrological sense. See Israel Efrat, "Philosophical Terminology in the Writings of R. Abraham Bar Ḥiyya Ha-Nasi'," in his *Jewish Philosophy in the Middle Ages: Terms and Concepts* (Tel Aviv, 1969), p. 163 (Hebrew).

from the cold, they sewed themselves garments from fig leaves. Thus, Bar Ḥiyya completely excludes the element of shame from the story. He strengthens his own interpretation by the claim that, if "and they knew" in this verse had the meaning of "they understood," then Scripture ought to have said, "and they saw that they were naked" (p. 66), because "understanding of nakedness is through the sight of the eyes" (*ibid.*).

One still needs to ask the question: How is one to understand what is said in Genesis 3:22, "Behold, the man has become [lit., "was"] like one of us, knowing good and evil." Bar Ḥiyya answers this by means of a grammatical analysis: the word *hayah* ("was") appears in the verse in the past tense, from which it follows that these words refer to the situation of Adam and Eve prior to the eating of the Tree of Knowledge and not thereafter. Man was created with ethical discernment, and as such is similar to the angels: "Originally, *before he went astray*, man was like one of the angels, to know good and evil" (p. 66).

Adam and Eve's Punishment—the Denial of Eternal Life

In punishment for their sin, Adam and Eve were denied eternal life. From Bar Ḥiyya's words, the impression gained is that he understands human history in general, and thus also the biography of Adam and Eve, in a deterministic fashion: sin and the punishment thereof were known to God in advance and were determined by Him as part of the general Divine plan for the world.

According to Bar Ḥiyya the repetition of the verb *akhol* in "you shall surely eat" (*ʾakhol toʾkhel*) in Genesis 2:16 alludes to two acts of eating from the trees of the garden, to be performed at two different times: *ʾakhol* (the infinitive of the verb "to eat") alludes to Adam and Eve's *immediate eating* from the Tree of Knowledge, performed "in error and transgression," from which ensued the punishment "you shall surely die." By contrast, *toʾkhel* (the same verb in the future tense) indicates the eating from the Tree of Life in the future—that is to say, the survival of the soul of the righteous man in the World to Come. From this interpretation one gains the impression that eating from the Tree of Knowledge, in opposition to the divine commandment, was at least known to God from the outset.

The words "You shall surely die (*mot tamut*)," in God's warning, may be interpreted in two ways: a) as the natural consequence of eating of the Tree of Knowledge and not punishment for it. Just as a person who touches fire is burned because it is the natural property of fire to burn one who touches it, similarly one who eats of the Tree of Knowledge will die because such is the natural quality of this tree, i.e., to cause death to one who eats of its fruit. It was in this sense that Eve understood God's warning, according to Bar Ḥiyya's interpretation, when she interpreted *daʿat* as the effects on the body by good and evil. Thus, the serpent did not properly understand her words, "lest you die," when he interpreted them as expressing apprehension of a death penalty; b) death is in fact a punishment for eating of the Tree of Knowledge. Death is not a natural consequence of the eating, as the Tree of Knowledge has no harmful characteristics whatsoever. Death was imposed upon man by God because he had violated His commandment. Adam "was punished with death because he violated the command of the Omnipresent" (p. 62). Regarding this interpretation, Bar Ḥiyya says: "And this is the truth, and for that reason Scripture repeated the verb *mot tamut* ('you shall surely die"). The serpent's tempting words are thus incorrect: man is not mortal by his very creation like the other animals in this lower world; he was created as capable of living forever even in his body, as Bar Ḥiyya explains in his interpretation of Genesis 1:29. But this ability was denied him as a punishment for his violation of God's commandment.[46]

The impression that Bar Ḥiyya accepts a deterministic view of human destiny is strengthened when we read his explanation of the creation of Eve: "And when the Holy One blessed be He said, 'You shall surely die,' and Adam was punished with death [i.e. mortality], He immediately said, 'It is not good for man to be alone,' *because death had been decreed upon him*; and if he will be alone and die, then the memory of man will be erased from the world..." (p. 63). Since "you shall eat" already includes within it the certainty that man will sin, and "you shall surely die" the certainty that he will be punished by death, that is, by the denial of eternal life, God must create Eve as "a helpmate to him": "That she may help him to bear offspring that will persist in the world, corresponding to himself" (*ibid.*). The eternity of the species therefore comes about instead of the eternity of the individual. Hence, the serpent was right when he said to

46 The duplication in the phrase *mot tamut* ("you shall surely die") alludes, according to Abraham Bar Ḥiyya, to two levels of punishment: *mot*—"on the punishment for the transgression in which all of creation was eradicated" (p. 62)—i.e., the punishment of the generation of the Flood. According to his interpretation, the Flood came because of the sin of Adam, and the curse, "the earth shall be cursed because of you" (Gen. 3:17) refers to it (*Sefer Megillat ha-Megalleh,* II, pp. 24-25). *Tamut*—referring to death, which is decreed upon all living things to this day" (p. 62); that is, that man's being mortal is a result of the sin.

Eve: "and because of death man will have need of you" (p. 66); however, Bar Ḥiyya explains this fact in a different manner than did the serpent. Woman was not created because man was mortal from the moment of his creation, but because God knew in advance that he would sin and be punished by the denial of eternal life.

The act of sin is explained by Bar Ḥiyya in accordance with the same line of reasoning. He argues that the serpent tempted the woman and not the man, "because the corruption that appeared before the Almighty by which the two of them would go astray, caused the woman to come into the world, and as a result it was caused that this sin would come about through her" (p. 65).

One must therefore understand that, according to Bar Ḥiyya, there was a Divine plan determined in advance: man was intended to sin and to be punished for his sin with the denial of eternal life, and therefore the woman was created initially in order to facilitate the continuity of the human species. In a deliberate, symbolic manner, in that her very existence was a result of the sin, Eve was also the cause of the sin. Even though the course of events was determined in advance, the status of the sin and its punishment is not nullified: eating from the Tree of Knowledge is a *transgression* of God's command, even though it was a transgression that was known to God in advance, and even determined by Him; and the nullification of eternal life was a *punishment* for this transgression, even though this punishment was known and predetermined by God. The sin and its punishment were both necessary links in the deterministic chain of events.

Bar Ḥiyya derives his explanation of the denial to man of eternal life from his interpretation of Genesis 2:21: "and He took one of his ribs," interpreted in terms of the semantic–scientific–philosophical axis. Here, Bar Ḥiyya returns to an idea that he had already developed in his interpretation of Genesis 1:29, influenced by Galen's physiology, according to which the vegetable food eaten by Adam was immediately transformed upon being eaten, in a complete way, to those parts of his body which had deteriorated due to the evaporation of their moistures. In this manner, both aging and death from old age were prevented. While in his previous presentations of this viewpoint, Bar Ḥiyya only spoke of one force being responsible for this process, the force of transformation, here he distinguishes between two forces: "the force of transformation" (*koaḥ ha-hamarah*) and "the formative force" (*koaḥ ha-meṣayer*). The transformative force, "which transforms the form of the food, but cannot assimilate it to that thing which is lacking from the body" (p. 64), and the formative force "which would change the food in his body into the form of that thing which deteriorates in each and every organ" (*ibid.*). According to what Bar Ḥiyya says further on in his interpretation here, it becomes clear that he sees these two forces as two levels of the same force: the force of transformation in its most complete state, when it is strengthened, is able to bring about the complete transformation of food into the forms of those organs which are lacking, and then it is identical to "the formative force." But when the "the formative force" is weakened, "naught remains of this force except the force of transformation" (*ibid.*).[47]

Ṣelaʿ (usually translated as "rib" or "side") in Genesis 2:21 is explained by Bar Ḥiyya as a metaphor created by way of analogy. The formative force is one of the four forces that sustain the body, that is, one of the four forces of the nourishing force in the vegetative soul. Its relation to the body is like that of the rib or central beam of a building—from which it is possible to refer to it as "the central beam of the body," by way of analogy. Thus, "and He took one of his ribs [sides]," means that He took one of the forces that sustains the body, the formative force. According to this interpretation, Adam already had a formative force. He was able to transform his food into the forms of those organs in his body which were deteriorated, in a complete manner, and therefore he did not age and could anticipate eternal life. Upon the creation of the woman, this force was taken from him and given to her. "And He closed flesh beneath her," is interpreted by Bar Ḥiyya as meaning that man received the power of fertility instead of the formative force that had been removed from

47 Joseph Ibn Ṣaddiq (*Sefer ha-ʿOlam ha-Qatan*, pp. 25-26/pp. 82-83) provides a clearer depiction of these two forces and of their mutual relationships. According to Ibn Ṣaddiq's description, the formative force is the first power of the vegetative soul that develops within man. It is present within him from the moment the seed of the male and the ovule of the female join [i.e., conception], its function being to fashion the form of the fetus's organs until their completion. The augmentative force develops the various organs, whose form has already been fashioned by the formative force, and causes them to grow. The nutritive force helps both of these primary forces. It itself acts by means of four forces: the attractive force, the maintaining force, the digestive and transformative force, and the excretory force. Ibn Ṣaddiq defines the changing force (*ha-koaḥ ha-meshaneh*) by saying "it assimilates the food to the individual nourished by it, transforming it to suit its nature" (p. 19/p.75) This force is thus similar to the "transformative force" mentioned by Bar Ḥiyya. It seems that Bar Ḥiyya attributes to the formative force in Adam the ability to accomplish complete transformation of food rather than the function of fashioning the organs of the fetus. In his opinion, after this force had been removed from Adam, there only remained within him the transformative force, which is one of the nutritive forces within the vegetable soul, whose transformative ability is incomplete.

him. According to the biblical lexicon, the word *baśar*, "flesh," also has the meaning of "seed" (*zeraʿ*). Thus the verses, "but you are my bone and flesh" (*'akh ʿaṣmi u-veśari 'atah;* Gen. 29:12) or "his flesh runs (*rakh beśaro*) with his discharge" (Lev. 15:3) indicate that the "organs of generation in man are called flesh." Thus, in Genesis 2:21, the word "flesh" appears, according to Bar Ḥiyya's interpretation, in the sense of seed.

"And the Lord God took the rib/side which He had taken from the man and made it [lit, "built it"] into a woman" (Gen. 2:22) refers to the function of the formative force, which had been taken from the man and given to the woman. The verse says, "and He built up" (*va-yiven*) and not "He formed (*va-yeṣer*)" or "He made (*va-yaʿaś*)," because the formative force that had been taken from Adam does not act within the woman in the same way as it had previously acted within the man, and does not transform her food into the forms of her deteriorated organs in a complete way, but rather operates upon the fetus within her womb. The life of the fetus in its mother's womb is conducted according to the same principle used to explain Adam's immortality: the blood received by the fetus is its food; it is exactly enough to be turned into parts of its body, just as Adam's food was transformed in a complete manner into those organs of his body which had been deteriorated. The blood contains neither lack nor excess; therefore the fetus, according to Bar Ḥiyya, does not have any discharges or waste matter. The process of transformation of the blood into the organs of the fetal body is performed by the "formative force" which the woman received from the man, and which acts within the fetus so long as it is inside its mother's womb. Upon leaving the womb, it is left only with the force of transformation, whose power of transformation is imperfect; therefore man is condemned to old age and to death from old age. The formative force whose activity we are able to observe today, after the sin of the Garden of Eden, is a transformed version of the formative force that existed in Adam, in which the capacity for "personal" eternal life is transmuted into the internal life of the species through its activity upon the fetus.

The Serpent's Punishment

The punishment given to the serpent was based upon the principle of measure for measure: the serpent had "lowered" the meaning of his name, *naḥash*, which had been derived from the word *le-naḥesh*, "to conjecture, to speculate" in the sense of the ability "to conjecture" and "to know the future with the help of various signs." "But he derived from his name his misleading advice" (p. 66), which was, on the one hand, to attempt to understand God's words in a different manner and, on the other, to engage in divination and astrology, in order to know the good and bad things that would happen in the future.[48] Hence he was punished by a lowering of his stature. Bar Ḥiyya accepts the view of the Sages in B. Sotah 9b concerning the primordial serpent: "I have said that he shall walk with upright posture, and now he shall crawl on his belly." However, he explains this on the basis of his interpretation of the sin of the Garden of Eden. The serpent had thought that "Divination can discover the essence of all things." Therefore, based on the principle of measure for measure, he was made to crawl upon the "essence" of the lower world, namely, upon the earth—"For the dust and the earth are the root and matter from which were formed the bodies of this world. From the dust was formed man, and from the earth the other living creatures" (*ibid.*)—as well as to eat from that "essence": "you shall eat dust" (Gen. 3:14). God's latter words are interpreted by Bar Ḥiyya in an ironical way: "Come, conjecture regarding the dust, whether you can understand with your divination powers the difference between the dust from which Adam was formed, and the earth from which were formed the other creatures of the earth along with the vegetation of the earth." That is to say: see whether your powers of divination have indeed led you to an understanding of the structure of the world, whether you can distinguish between the choice dust from which man was formed, and the ordinary dust from which the other living creatures were formed. "All the days of your life" (Gen. 3:14) also refers to the days of the Messiah. Then, too, according to Isaiah's vision of the End of Days, "dust shall be the serpent's food" (Isa. 65:25)—the serpent will continue to eat dust.

2. The Story of the Garden of Eden as a Chapter in Ethical Theory and in the Theory of Recompense

At the beginning of his interpretation of the story of the Garden of Eden, Bar Ḥiyya declares that this story is an interpretation "of the history of the world in a different manner and regarding other matters" (p. 60) than that of "the formation of man." He refers here to an interpretation

48 Bar Ḥiyya does not explain how he understands the connection between eating from the Tree of Knowledge and soothsaying and divination.

which sees the story of the Garden of Eden as a story of humankind in general, and of his ethical–religious behavior in particular.

Interpretation of the verbs that indicate Adam's entering into the Garden of Eden

In Chapter 2 of Genesis, three different verbs are used to indicate Adam's entering the Garden of Eden. In verse 8 it says: "and the Lord God planted a garden in Eden, in the east, and He put there (*va-yaśem*) the man whom He had formed," while in verse 15, there appear two other verbs: "And the Lord God took (*va-yikaḥ*) the man, and placed him (*va-yaniḥehu*) in the Garden of Eden, to work it and to keep it." Had Scripture simply wished to describe Adam's entering into the Garden of Eden, it could have sufficed with the first verb alone: *va-yaśem*, "and He placed." As it makes use of three different verbs, we must assume that each one of them has a special meaning. Bar Ḥiyya thus interprets these three verbs as intended to indicate three different states of man generally in the Garden of Eden, relating to the history of the human species and not to Adam alone.

The methodology which he uses is a homiletical one. That is to say: he does not rely upon the biblical lexicon, nor upon the common usage of the Hebrew language, nor upon the biblical–philosophical lexicon. The interpretation of these three verbs is determined on the basis of the assumption which he accepted *ab initio* regarding the area of significance of these verbs, and for their interpretation he also makes use of the associations which they elicited to other biblical verses. Thus, *va-yaśem* ("and He put") refers to Adam, and describes the situation of Adam in the Garden of Eden immediately after his creation. Adam was intended at this point to be immortal, as has already been demonstrated by Bar Ḥiyya in his interpretation of the story of the creation of man: *va-yikaḥ* ("and He took") refers to the expulsion of Adam from the Garden of Eden as punishment for his sin. Bar Ḥiyya relies here upon a linguistic association: the verb l*akoaḥ*, "to take," also appears in the description of the sin of Eve in Genesis 3:6: "and she took (*va-tikaḥ*) of its fruit and she ate." It follows from this that in Genesis 2:15 as well the verb *lakoaḥ* alludes to the stage of sin in the course of human events. "And He put him" (*va-yaniḥehu*) indicates the calm of the soul of the righteous in the Garden of Eden after the death of the body and prior to the Resurrection of the Dead. Bar Ḥiyya bases this interpretation upon the meaning of the verb *nuaḥ*, "to rest," hence he understands the verb *va-yaniḥehu* as "He placed him to rest." The soul finds rest in the Garden of Eden after the death of the body; therefore the verb *va-yaniḥehu* ("and He placed him to rest") refers to this state of man. The central idea expressed in the interpretation of these three verbs is implied specifically in his interpretation of the last verb, "and He placed him to rest." This verb indicates that certain individuals within the human species, which had lived previously in the Garden of Eden and was intended to live there eternally, in both body and soul, but was expelled from there because of its sin, may return to the Garden of Eden in their souls alone after the death of their bodies, and remain there until the Resurrection of the Dead. The verbs, "to till it (*le-ʿovdah*, lit., to work it) and to keep it (*le-shomrah*)," complete the idea implicit in the verb *va-yaniḥehu*. They are intended to indicate "two matters regarding which the righteous inherit the life of the World to Come" (p. 61): "To till it (*le- ʿovdah*)—refers to the service of Torah (*ʿavodat ha-Torah*) and fear of Heaven by which he merits to the life of the World to Come" (*ibid.*). That is to say: by what does the righteous man earn life of the World to Come? By his service of God and by his fear of God. "'And to keep it' (*le-shomrah*)—that this privilege is kept for him (*shmurah lo*) until he ascends from his grave and will live together with the living in the world of the Messiah" (*ibid.*). The existence of the soul distinct from the body in the Garden of Eden is only a temporary state, an intermediate stage between the individual's death and his resurrection in the days of Messiah, when the soul will again be connected to the body and the two of them together will enjoy eternal life.

The Interpretation of the Tree of Life

Bar Ḥiyya's interpretation of the Tree of Life fits well into this interpretation of the verbs indicating Adam's entering into the Garden of Eden. The Tree of Life, according to Bar Ḥiyya's interpretation, is none other than the Torah. Like many other commentators, Bar Ḥiyya relies here upon Proverbs 3:18: "It is a tree of life to those that take hold of it." The Tree of Life is "the tree in which are found life and understanding and wisdom and light and all good qualities, and it does not have any quality which is not good and praiseworthy. And one who merits to this tree merits to the level of the supernal world and the angels" (p. 61). According to the theory of the soul adopted by Bar Ḥiyya, the human soul (*neshamah*) is the soul (*nefesh*) "through which man is able to understand words of wisdom and the fear of God and occupation with matters of Torah and the commandments which lead to the life of the World to Come" (p. 58). According to his interpretations of "in our likeness" (Gen. 1:26) and "in the likeness of God" (Gen. 5:1), and according to his theory of the soul, those good qualities in which man resembles the creatures of the supernal world are the qualities of his soul of life, the qualities of the rational soul alone. "The Tree of Life," the Torah, is thus the means given into man's hands so that he may acquire the qualities of the rational soul, so as to resemble the beings of the upper world, and thereby enjoy the life of the World to Come. Namely, that his soul returns to the Garden of Eden after the death of his body, and remains there until the Resurrection of the Dead.

This interpretation of the Tree of Life allows Bar Ḥiyya to resolve one of the exegetical problems mentioned earlier: namely, was Adam also proscribed from eating from the Tree of Life? According to Bar Ḥiyya's interpretation, Adam was allowed to eat of the Tree of Life, for it was said, "from *every* tree of the Garden you may surely eat," from which one may understand that "he was promised and allowed to eat from the Tree of Life, because the Tree of Life was among the trees of the garden, of which it was said, 'from every tree of the Garden...'" (*ibid.*). However, this permissible eating refers to eating in the future world: after the expulsion from the Garden of Eden and after the giving of the Torah, on "the third day" of the days of the world. For "two days, the first day and the second day, the inhabitants of the world were not fit to have the Torah given to them because of the sin of Adam, until this sin was atoned for at the time of the Flood at the end of the second day, and it was suitable that the Torah descends upon the earth on the third day" (p. 24). Humankind's punishment was not only the loss of eternal life on the part of Adam and of the generations which came after him, but also that "because of the sin of Adam, the Flood came to the world, for it says regarding the sin of Adam, 'the ground shall be cursed because of you' (Gen. 3:17)" (*ibid.*). This curse refers to the Flood, for when the Torah interprets the significance of the name of Noah, it states: "This one shall bring us relief [lit., comfort us] from our work and from the toil of our hands, *out of the ground which the Lord has cursed*" (Gen. 5:29). That relief which came about through Noah was the nullification of the edict of the Flood, for in Genesis 8:21, following the Flood, God says: "I will never again *curse the ground* because of man." With the cancellation of the edict of the Flood, man was given the means to return to the Garden of Eden from which he had been expelled, he was given the Torah, and he was allowed to eat from the Tree of Life.

This interpretation, according to which permission to eat from the Tree of Life is set in the eschatological future, is established by Bar Ḥiyya in two ways: a) On the basis of the exegetical assumption that there is nothing extraneous in the Bible, the duplication of the words *ʾakhol toʾkhel* ("you shall surely eat") must be of significance. Therefore, Bar Ḥiyya interprets "to eat" (*ʾakhol*) as referring to "the Tree of Knowledge, from which you shall eat immediately" (p. 62)—that is to say, the sin of Adam and Eve. But the word *toʾkhel* ("you shall eat") refers to "the Tree of Life, from which he shall eat in the future" (*ibid.*). That is to say: it alludes to the fulfillment of the Torah after it will be given to the people of Israel. This interpretation is reinforced by a linguistic analysis: "you shall eat" is couched in the future tense. b) From an examination of the linguistic usages in the Bible, Bar Ḥiyya discovers that the verb *va-yeṣav* ("and He commanded"), accompanied by the preposition *ʿal*, "upon," always appears prior to a negative commandment, whereas when accompanied by the preposition *et*, it indicates a positive commandment. In verse 16 it says, *va-yeṣav ʿal*, "and He commanded [the man, lit., upon man]...," from which it follows that the commandment referred to there is a negative one.[49] Thus, the sentence, "from every tree of the garden you shall surely eat" does not include any commandment, and therefore should be read as a parenthetical remark containing a promise for the future: that is, in the future, following the giving of the Torah, the people of Israel will be able to merit the life of the World to Come by fulfilling the Torah and its miṣvot.

The Expulsion from the Garden of Eden

The interpretation of the expulsion from the Garden of Eden complements the interpretation of the Tree of Life, on the one hand, and answers an exegetical problem that arises from the story of the Garden of Eden, on the other.

In Chapter 3 of Genesis, two different versions are given of the ex-

49 This interpretation is repeated by Abraham Ibn Ezra in the Second Recension of his *Commentary on Genesis*: "Every commandment which is followed by *ʿal* ("upon") is a negative commandment as in, 'and I shall command the clouds not to rain upon it' (Isa. 5:6)" (p. 150). The reference to the *Commentary on Genesis* is to Abraham Ibn Ezra, *Perush ha-Torah*, edited by Asher Weiser, vol. 1 (Jerusalem: Mossad ha-Rav Kook, 1976).

pulsion of Adam from the Garden of Eden. In verse 23 it says: "And the Lord God sent him forth (*va-yeshalḥehu*) from the Garden of Eden, to till the ground from which he was taken," whereas verse 24 states: "And He expelled (*va-yegaresh*) the man; and He placed at the east of the Garden of Eden the cherubim and a flaming sword which turned every way, to guard the way to the Tree of Life." Modern Bible critics see the existence of these two versions as further evidence of the later redaction of the story on the basis of two sources, in only one of which the Tree of Life is mentioned. Verses 22 and 24 belong, in their opinion, to a narrative which also speaks about the Tree of Life, whereas verse 23 is evidently the original sequel to verse 19 in that story in which the Tree of Knowledge alone is mentioned. The problem of the existence of these two versions of the sending of Adam away from the Garden of Eden is resolved by Bar Ḥiyya in a manner similar to his solution of the problem of inconsistency in the descriptions of the functions of these two trees—the Tree of Life and the Tree of Knowledge: namely, by presenting different semantic axes for each one of the versions. According to his interpretation, verse 23 speaks of the destiny of man's *soul*, whereas verse 24 speaks of the destiny of his *body*.

Bar Ḥiyya bases his interpretation on a linguistic analysis. The verb *shalaḥ* is an equivocal word. It can indicate the sending of someone as an emissary, or it may refer to the removal of somebody, his being sent away. Bar Ḥiyya shows that when the verb *shalaḥ* appears in the Bible in the sense of sending away or distancing, it is always accompanied by the preposition *et,* as in the verse, "you shall surely send away the mother" (*shaleḥ teshalaḥ et ha'em*; Deut. 22:7). However, when it appears in the sense of sending a messenger, Scripture does not add the preposition *et.* Thus in Genesis 3:24 we read, "and the Lord God sent him (*va-yeshalḥehu*)," without the addition of the word *et*. Hence, one must understand the meaning of the word *shalaḥ* in this verse in the sense of "to send"—that is, "that He made him a messenger in order that he might return" (p. 67). The one sent on a mission, according to Bar Ḥiyya's interpretation, is the soul of man, his rational soul. He finds support for this interpretation in the fact that the use of the pronoun rather than the use of the name "Adam" is found earlier in the Bible, in the description of man's creation in Genesis 2:7. It says there, "and He breathed into his nostrils the soul [or: breath] of life," there too referring to the soul. It follows from this that the phrase, "and He sent him" likewise refers to the soul. The mission of the soul is "to work [or: till] the earth" which, as Bar Ḥiyya has already explained in his interpretation of Genesis 2:15, refers to "the service of the Torah and the fear of God by means of which he merits the life of the World to Come" (p. 61). Through his performance of the miṣvot, the righteous man merits to return to the Garden of Eden, which is the World to Come.[50] To this, Bar Ḥiyya adds: "'And He sent him' in the Holy Scriptures—he comes to the world for a matter of dignity" (p. 67). He bases his exegetical argument on the use of the verb *shilaḥ* in 2 Samuel 3:24, 1 Kings 20:34, and Jeremiah 40:5. The "sending" in Genesis 3:23 is thus a sending of man's soul "with honor, that it may return, but the body is that which is expelled" (p. 68).[51]

The first half of verse 24 speaks of the destiny of man's *body*. Bar Ḥiyya infers this from the appearance of the noun *adam*, "man," after the verb, instead of adding the pronoun to the verb itself. It states here, "and He expelled the man." And indeed, in the description of the creation of man, the noun *adam* is used whenever it refers to man's body alone. Thus, in Genesis 1:27 it says, "And God created man" which, as we have seen, is interpreted by Bar Ḥiyya as referring to the creation of the human body and his lower soul–powers, which constitute his "image." Concerning the body of man it says "and He expelled him" rather than "He sent him," so as to make it clear that one is speaking here only of the *removal* of man's body from the Garden of Eden and not of his being sent as a messenger who shall return. Man will never return in his body to the Garden of Eden.

The second half of verse 24 is associated by Bar Ḥiyya with his interpretation of the Tree of Life and to verse 23, which he understands as alluding to the destiny of members of the human race in the future: "And He placed east of the Garden of Eden the cherubim, and the fiery sword which turned every way, to guard the way to the Tree of Life." The cherubim allude to "the Torah which was given between the cherubim" (*ibid.*).

50 Bar Ḥiyya's solution is the opposite of that of the modern commentators. He associates verse 23 with the story of the Tree of Life, whereas they connect it with the story of the Tree of Knowledge, and verse 24 to that of the Tree of Knowledge. However, Bar Ḥiyya also attributes the second half of verse 24 to the story of the Tree of Life.

51 This view is brought by Ibn-Ezra in his commentary to Gen. 3:23 in the name of "a great Spanish sage," to which he is opposed, as has already been noted by Julius Guttmann in his introduction to *Sefer Megillat ha-Megalleh*, p. xxii. D. Kaufmann was mistaken when he identified the "great Spanish sage" with Solomon Ibn Gabirol. (See D. Kaufmann, "Solomon Ibn Gabirol's Allegorical–Philosophical Interpretation." In his *Meḥkarim ba-Sifrut ha-ʿIvrit* [Jerusalem, 1965], p. 131, n. 26 [Hebrew]).

Bar Ḥiyya evidently envisions here the description of the Tabernacle in Exodus 25. The word *kedem* (which we have translated here as "East") is interpreted by him, as in the word *kadimah*, to mean "before." The Torah precedes the Garden of Eden on the path of the righteous soul towards the life of the World to Come: when a human being engages in Torah, his soul merits to the Garden of Eden. The word "sword" (*ḥerev*) likewise has a hidden meaning and is not to be understood in its literal sense. We are told of the existence of this hidden meaning by the Bible itself, through its preceding the word *ḥerev* ("sword") by the word *lahat* ("fiery"). *Lahat* is understood by Bar Ḥiyya as derived from the word *lahatehem* (Exod. 7:11), i.e. their magical tricks; hence it alludes to something hidden. Bar Ḥiyya sees the word *lahat* as a directive given us by the biblical text itself for the reading of the word that follows. The word *lahat* instructs us to seek some hidden meaning in the word "sword" (*ḥerev*).[52] According to Bar Ḥiyya's interpretation, the word "sword" alludes to the various types of deaths of human beings. The "sword" is an instrument used for killing in war; therefore, this word refers to death by stabbing. *Ḥerev*, in the *qal* verbal construction, is an equivocal word. One of its meanings is "dry," while another is "destroyed" or "eradicated." From each of these meanings, Bar Ḥiyya infers a different type of death. *Ḥerev* in the sense of dryness indicates death from old age, which is caused, following Galen's doctrine, which he accepted, from the drying out of the body's vital fluids. *Ḥerev* in the sense of destruction or eradication indicates "death in youth, which is similar to destruction; for the death of young people who have not filled out their days is a destruction of the world" (*ibid.*). *Mithapekhet* ("revolving" or "rotating") refers to the "sword"—that is, the various types of death that "turn for the good" in the case of the righteous, whose souls return to the Garden of Eden. The "path of the Tree of Life" is thus the path of the Torah. If one observes the ways of the Torah and fulfills its commandments, miṣvot, his soul shall return to the Garden of Eden after his death.

Thus, even though at first glance it would appear that Abraham Bar

52 In my book, *Maimonides' Interpretation of the Story of the Creation* (Jerusalem, 1978; 2nd ed., 1987), pp. 102-103, I demonstrated that Maimonides also speaks of the existence of a kind of "meta-language" in the Torah. He interprets the verb *kara'* ("to call out") as a directive given by the text to understand one of the two objects of this verb as an equivocal noun, whose meaning when alongside *kara'* is different from its meaning earlier in the same text. See also (in this volume) "The Interpretation of the Second Day of Creation": The Interpretation of the Verb *Va-yiqra*," pp. 27-28. Bar Ḥiyya thus anticipated Maimonides in noting that the Bible contains directives for its own interpretation.

Ḥiyya's interpretation of the story of the creation of man and that of the Garden of Eden is a fragmentary one, jumping from one semantic axis to another, a closer and more exact reading reveals that it contains a great deal of internal logic. Unlike modern Bible scholars, Bar Ḥiyya assumes that these narratives have a number of different semantic axes: they do not only revolve around an event that took place at the beginning of human history, but point towards the overall course of human history, emphasizing its point of conclusion in the Resurrection of the Dead to occur at the time of Redemption. These two stories also entail a dimension that transcends time: they explain a number of basic features of human psychology and religious ethics. In all areas of this interpretation, Bar Ḥiyya assumes that biblical expressions are subject to interpretation in accordance with a philosophical–scientific semantic axis. Having established these *a priori* assumptions, his commentary is quite consistent and complete, and he succeeds in overcoming most of the exegetical difficulties over which biblical researchers have deliberated through our own time.

Bibliography

Works by Maimonides

Mishnah ʿim Perush Rabbenu Moshe ben Maimon (Commentary on the Mishnah). Original Arabic text and Hebrew translation by Yoseph Qāfiḥ (Jerusalem: Mossad ha-Rav Kook, 1963-68).

Dalālat al- ḥāʾirīn (The Guide of the Perplexed). Original Arabic text redacted by Shlomoh Munk and edited with variant readings by Y. Joel (Jerusalem, 1930-31).

Epistle of Resurrection. In *Moshe ben Maimon, Iggerot*, edited by Mordecai D. Rabinovich (Jerusalem, 1970).

Epistle to Yemen. In *Epistles of Maimonides: Crisis and Leadership*, texts translated and noted by Abraham Halkin; discussed by David Hartman (Philadelphia: Jewish Publication Society of America, 1985), pp. 91-131.

Iggerot ha-Rambam, edited by David H. Baneth (Jerusalem: Mekitze Nirdamim, 1946)

Iggerot, Sheʾelot u-Teshuvot. Arabic text and Hebrew translation with notes by Yoseph Qāfiḥ (Jerusalem: Mossad ha-Rav Kook, 1972).

Introduction to Pereq Ḥeleq. In *Haqdamot le-Perush ha-Mishnah*, edited with notes by Mordecai D. Rabinovich (Jerusalem: Mossad ha-Rav Kook, 1961).

Le Guide des Égarés: traité de théologie et de philosophie/ par Moïse ben Maimon dit Maïmonide, traduit pour la première fois sur l'original Arabe et accompagnié de notes critiques, littéraires et explicatives par Shlomoh Munk, nouvelle edition, 3 vols (Paris, G. P: Maisonneuve, 1960).

Maimonides' Commentary on the Mishnah, Tractate Sanhedrin. Translated into English with introduction and notes by Fred Rosner; foreword by Aaron D. Twerski (New York: Sepher-Hermon Press, 1981).

Maimonides' response to R. Ḥasdai ha-Levi. In *Koveṣ Teshuvot ha-Rambam ve-Iggerotav* (Leipzig: A. Lichtenberg 1859), pp. 23a-24b.

Iggeret ʾel R. Ḥasdai ha-Levi le-Alexandriya (*Maimonides' response to R.*

Ḥasdai ha-Levi). In *Letters and Essays of Moses Maimonides*. Arabic text and Hebrew translation, edited and translated by Isaac Shailat (Maaleh Adumim: Ma'aliyot Press, 1988] vol. 2, pp. 677-684).

Mishneh Torah (*The code of Maimonides*), *Sefer ha-Mada*ʿ, edited by Mordecai D. Rabinovich, commentary by Samuel T. Rubinstein (Jerusalem: Mossad ha-Rav Kook, 1958).

Moreh ha-Nevukhim (*Dalālat al- ḥāʾirīn*). Original Arabic text and Hebrew translation by Yoseph Qāfiḥ. 3 vols (Jerusalem: Mossad ha-Rav Kook, 1972).

Sefer Moreh ha-Nevukhim. Translated into Hebrew by Samuel Ibn Tibbon with four commentaries: Efodi, Shem Tov, Crescas and Abravanel, edited by I. Goldman (Warsaw 1861, repr. Jerusalem 1960).

Moreh Nevukhim le-Rabbenu Moshe ben Maimon. Translated, with notes, addenda and indexes, by Michael Schwarz (Tel Aviv: Tel Aviv University Press, 2002).

Pirqei Moshe (*Medical Aphorisms of Moses*), edited by Suessmann Muntner (Jerusalem: Mossad ha-Rav Kook, 1957).

Sefer Moreh ha-Nevukhim...Translated into Hebrew by Samuel Ibn Tibbon, edited by Yehuda Even-Shemuel with *Perush ha-millot ha-Zarot* by Samuel Ibn Tibbon (Jerusalem: Mossad ha-Rav Kook, 1981).

The Guide of the Perplexed. Translated from the Arabic, introduction and notes by Shlomoh Pines (Chicago: Chicago University Press, 1963).

Maimonides' Response Regarding the Spam of Life published in the Arabic original with German translation and Introduction, discussion and notes by Prof. Gotthold Eliakim Weil, the Arabic text translated into Hebrew, with Hebrew translation of the Introduction, discussion and notes and with the notes updated, by Michael Schwarz (Tel Aviv: Papirus, 1979).

Other Works Cited

Primary Sources

Abravanel, Isaac. *Perush ʿal ha-Torah (Commentary on the Torah)* (Jerusalem: Benei Arabel, 1964).

———. *Sefer Shamayim Ḥadashim*, edited by B. Heidenheim. (Rodelheim, 1828; repr. Jerusalem, 1966).

———. *Perush* le-Moreh Nevukhim (Commentary on the *Guide of the Perplexed*). In *Sefer Moreh Nevukhim*, translated into Hebrew by Samuel Ibn Tibbon with four commentaries: Efodi, Shem Tov, Crescas and Abravanel, edited by I. Goldman (Warsaw, 1861, repr. Jerusalem, 1960).

Al-Farabi. *Al-Farabi's Commentary and Short Treatise on Aristotle's De Interpretatione*, translated with introduction and notes by. F. W. Zimmermann (London: Oxford University Press, 1981).

———. *Al-Farabi on the Perfect State...* a revised text with introduction, translation and commentary by Richard Walzer (Oxford: Clarendon Press, 1985).

Babylonian Talmud (Vilna-Romm, 1880-86).

Bar Ḥiyya, Abraham. *Sefer Megillat ha-Megalleh von Abraham bar Chija... ed.* Aldolf Poznanski (Berlin, 1924; photo reprint: Jerusalem, 1968)

———. Abraham Bar-Hayya, *Hegyon ha-Nephesch ha-ʿaṣuvah*, edited with introduction and notes by Geoffrey Wigoder (Jerusalem, 1971)

———. *The Meditation of the Sad Soul by Abraham Bar Hayya*; translated [from the Hebrew] and with an introduction by Geoffrey Wigoder (London, 1969).

Baḥya Ibn Paquda. *The Book of Direction to the Duties of the Heart*. Arabic text with Hebrew translation, edited and translated by Yoseph Qāfiḥ (Jerusalem: Akiva-Joseph, 1973).

Crescas, Asher. *Perush le-Moreh Nevukhim (Commentary on the Guide of the Perplexed)*, in *Sefer Moreh Nevukhim*, translated into Hebrew by Samuel Ibn Tibbon with four commentaries: Efodi, Shem Tov, Crescas and Abravanel, edited by I. Goldman (Warsaw, 1861, repr. Jerusalem, 1960).

Efodi (Profiat Duran). *Perush le-Moreh Nevukhim* (*Commentary on the Guide of the Perplexed*). In *Sefer Moreh Nevukhim*, translated into Hebrew by Samuel Ibn Tibbon with four commentaries: Efodi, Shem Tov, Crescas and Abravanel, edited by I. Goldman (Warsaw, 1861, repr. Jerusalem, 1960).

Genesis Rabbah. Edited by J. Theodor and H. Albeck, 2nd ed. 2 vols (Jerusalem: Wahrmann Books, 1965).

Halevi, Judah. *Sefer ha-Kuzari*. Translated into Hebrew by Samuel Ibn Tibbon. edited by A. Ṣifroni (Tel Aviv: Maḥbaroth le-Sifrut, 1964).

Ibn Ezra, Abraham. *Perush ha-Torah*, edited by Asher Weiser. 3 vols (Jerusalem: Mossad ha-Rav Kook, 1976).

———. *Yesod Mora'*. In *Kitvei R. Abraham Ibn Ezra*, vol 2 (Jerusalem: Maqor, 1970).

Ibn Kaspi, Joseph. *Maskiyot Kesef*. In *Sheloshah Qadmonei Mefrashei ha-Moreh* (Jerusalem, 1961: facsimile edition of Salomo Werbluner , ed. Frankfurt am Main, 1848).

Ibn *Ṣaddiq*, Joseph. *Sefer ha-ʿOlam ha-Qatan*. Text critically edited by Saul Horovitz (Breslau, 1903).

———. *The Microcosm of Joseph ibn Saddiq*/Hebrew text critically edited by Saul Horovitz and provided with an English translation, introduction, and notes by Jacob Haberman (Madison [N.J.: Fairleigh Dickinson University Press, 2003).

Levi ben Gershom (Gersonides). *Milhamot ha-Shem* (Leipzig, 1866).

———. Levi ben Gershom (Gersonides)*The Wars of the Lord*, 3 vols., translated with an Introduction and notes by Seymour Feldman. Vol. 3 (Philadelphia: Jewish publication Society of America, 1984-1999).

———. *Ḥamishah Ḥumshei Torah ʿim Beʾur Rabbenu Levi ben Gershom: Bereshit* (*Rabbinic Pentateuch with Commentary on the Torah by R. Levi ben Gerson (Gersonides,* 1288–1344*): Genesis,* edited from mss. and provided with introduction and notes by Baruch Braner and Eli Freiman, (2nd ed, Jerusalem: Maaliyot, 1993).

Midrash Leqaḥ Tov, edited by Shlomo Buber (Vilna, 1884)

Midrash Tanḥuma, edited by Shlomo Buber (Vilna,1885).

Narboni, Moses. *Be'ur le-Sefer Moreh Nevukhim,(Commnetary on The Guide of the Perplexed)*, edited by Jacob Goldenthal (Vienna, 1852).

Rashi. *Commentary on the Torah*. In *Miqra'ot gedolot* (New York: Pardes, 1961).

Sa'adiah Gaon. *Perush Rabbenu Sa'adiah Gaon 'al ha-Torah*, edited, translated and with Introduction and Notes by Yoseph Qāfiḥ (Jerusalem, 1963).

———. *Sefer ha-Emunot ve-ha-De'ot*. Trans. Judah Ibn Tibbon (Josefop, 1878; photo ed. Jerusalem, 1962).

———. *Sefer ha-Nivḥar ba-Emunot u-va--De'ot* . Translated by Yoseph Qāfiḥ, (Jerusalem, 1970).

———. *Iyov, 'im Targum u-Perush Rabbenu Saadyah ben Yosef* (Commentary on the Book of Job.). Translated into Hebrew, elucidated and redacted by Yoseph Qāfiḥ (Jerusalem, 1973)

Shem-Tov ben Yoseph. *Perush le-Moreh Nevukhim* (Commentary on the *Guide of the Perplexed*). In *Sefer Moreh Nevukhim*, translated into Hebrew by Samuel Ibn Tibbon with four commentaries: Efodi, Shem-Tov, Crescas and Abravanel, edited by I. Goldman (Warsaw, 1861, repr. Jerusalem, 1960).

Simplicius of Cilcia. *Commentaire sur les Catégories*. Traduction commentée sous la direction de Ilsetraut Hadot (Leiden: Brill, 1990).

Secondary Sources

Altmann, Alexander. "Das Verhältnis Maimunis zu der jüdischen Mystik," *MGWJ* 80 (1936), pp. 305-30.

———. "The Ladder of Ascension." In A. Altman, *Studies in Philosophy and Religious Mysticism* (London, 1969), pp. 1-32.

———. "Maimonides' 'Four Perfections'," *Israel Oriental Studies* 2 (1972), pp. 15-24.

Amir, Yehoshua. "Ha-allegoriyah shel Philon be-yaḥasah la-allegoriyah ha-homerit," *Eshkolot* 6 (1971), pp. 35-45 (Hebrew).

Berman, Lawrence V. *Ibn Bajja and Maimonides—A Chapter in the History of Political Philosophy*, Ph.D. Dissertation (Jerusalem, 1959) (Hebrew).

———. "Maimonides on the Fall of Man," *AJS Review* 5 (1980), pp. 1-16.

———. "Maimonides on Political Leadership," in *Kinship and Consent: the Jewish Political Tradition and its Contemporary Uses*, edited by Daniel J. Elazar (Jerusalem: Rubin Mass, 1991), pp. 135-144) (Hebrew).

———. "The Political Interpretation of the Maxim: The Purpose of Philosophy is the Imitation of God," *Studia Islamica* 15 (1961), pp. 53-61.

Buffière, Felix. *Les mythes d'Homère et la pensée grecque* (Paris, 1956).

Chaignet, A- Ed. *Histoire de la psychologie des grecs* (Paris: Hachette, 1887-93).

Davidson, Herbert. "Maimonides' Secret Position on Creation." In *Studies in Medieval Jewish History and Literature*, edited by Isador Twersky (Cambridge Mass.: Harvard University Press, 1979), pp. 16-40.

Diamond, James Arthur. *Maimonides and the Hermeneutics of Concealment: Deciphering Scripture and Midrash in the Guide of the Perplexed* (Albany: State University of New York Press, 2002).

Efrat, Yisrael. "Philosophical Terminology in the Writings of R. Abraham Bar Ḥiyya Ha-Nasi'. " In *Jewish Philosophy in the Middle Ages: Terms and Concepts* (Tel Aviv, 1969) (Hebrew).

The Encyclopedia of Language and Linguistics. Edited by R. E. Ashen et al. vol. 3 (Oxford; New York: Pergamon Press, 1994).

Fletcher, Angus. "Allegory." In *Dictionary of the History of Ideas*, edited by Philip Wiener (New York, 1973).
Frazer, James George. *Folklore in the Old Testament: Studies in Comparative Religion, Legend and Law* (London: Macmillan, 1923).

Georges, Robert A. and Dundes, Alan. "Toward a Structural Definition of the Riddle," *Journal of American Folklore* 76 (1963), pp. 111-118.
Glücker, John. "Modality in Maimonides' *Guide of the Perplexed*," *Iyyun* 10 (1959), pp. 177-91 (Hebrew).
Goldman, Eliezer. "The Special Labor in Attaining Truths," *Shenaton Bar-Ilan* 6 (1968), pp. 309-312 (repr. in E. Goldman *Expositions and Inquiries – Jewish Thought in Past and Present*, edited by A. Sagi and D. Stattman, Jerusalem, 1996) (Hebrew).
Gutas, Dimitri. *Avicenna and the Aristotelian Tradition: Introduction to Reading Avicenna's Philosophical Works* (Leiden and New York: Brill, 1988).
Guttman, Julius. "Introduction." In *Sefer Megillat ha-Megalleh von Abraham bar Chija...* ed. Aldolf Poznanski (Berlin, 1924; photo reprint: Jerusalem, 1968) (Hebrew).
———. "Ueber Abraham bar Chijjas Buch der Enthüllung," *MGWJ* 47 (1903), pp. 446-468; 545-569.

Hadot, Ilsetraut. *Commentaire sur les Catégories/ Simplicius*. Traduction commentée sous la direction de Ilsetraut Hadot (Leiden: Brill, 1990).
Harvey, Warren Zev. "Averroes and Maimonides on the Obligation of Philosophic Contemplation (*I'tibār*)," *Tarbiṣ* 58 (1989), pp. 75-83 (Hebrew).
———. "Political Philosophy and Halakhah in Maimonides – Appendix: The Perfection of Man and the Political Imitation of God," *Bina* 3 (1994), pp. 58-59.
———. "How to Begin to Learn the *Guide of the Perplexed* I.1," *Da'at* 21 (1988), pp. 5-23 (Hebrew).
Heinemann, Isaac. "Abravanel's Lehre vom Niedergang der Menschheit," *MGWJ* 82 (1938), pp. 381-400.

Ivry, Alfred. "Maimonides on Possibility." In *Mystics, Philosophers and Politicians*, edited by J. Reinharz and D. Swetschinski (Durham, N.C.:

University Press, 1982), pp. 67-84.

Kaivola-Bregenhoj, Annikki. *Riddles: Perspectives on the Use Function and Change in a Folklore Genre* (Helsinki: Finnish Literature Society, 2001).

Kasher, Hannah. "Maimonides' Interpretation of the Story of the Cleft of the Rock," *Da'at* 35 (1995), pp. 29-66 (Hebrew).

——— . "On the Forms of the 'Images' (Further Notes to *Guide* I.1)," *Da'at* 53 (2004), pp. 31-42 (Hebrew).

Klein-Braslavy, Sara. *Maimonides' Interpretation of the Story of Creation* (Jerusalem: Ha- Ḥevrah le-Ḥeqer ha-Miqra', 1979, 2nd edition with corrections and additions, Jerusalem: Reuben Mass, 1987) (Hebrew).

——— . "The Flourishing Era of Jewish Exegesis in Spain: The philosophical Exegesis (Solomon Ibn Gabirol, Bahya Ben Joseph, Judah Halevi and Moses Ben Maimon/ Maimonides/ Rambam')," in M. Saebø , (ed.), *Hebrew Bible / Old Testament - The History of Its Interpretation*, vol. I part 2 - The Middle Ages, (Vandenhoeck & Ruprecht, Göttingen, 2000), pp. 302-320.

——— . "Bible Commentary." In Ken Seeskin, (ed.), *The Cambridge Companion to Maimonides* (Cambridge: Cambridge University Press, 2005), pp. 245-272.

——— . *King Solomon and Philosophical Esotericism in the Thought of Maimonides* (Jerusalem: Magnes Press, 1996 repr. 2008) (Hebrew).

——— . *Maimonides' Interpretation of the Adam Stories in Genesis* (Jerusalem: Reuben Mass, 1986) (Hebrew).

——— . "Maimonides' Interpretation of the Verb *bara'* and the Creation of the World," *Da'at* , 16 (1986), pp. 39-55 (Hebrew).

Kongais-Maranda, Elli. "Theory and Praxis of Riddle Analysis," *Journal of American Folklore 84* (1971), pp. 51-61.

Kreisel, Howard. *Maimonides' Political Thought – Studies in Ethics. Law and the Human Ideal* (Albany: State University of New York Press, 1999).

Lettinck, Paul. *Aristotle's Meteorology and its Reception in the Arabic World* (Leiden– Boston: Brill, 1999).

Nuriel, Avraham. "'The Torah Speaks in the Language of Human Beings' in the *Guide of the Perplexed.* " In *Religion and Language*, edited by M.

Hallamish and A. Kasher. (Tel Aviv, 1981), pp. 93-99 [repr. in Nuriel, Avraham. *Concealed and Revealed in Medieval Jewish Philosophy* (Jerusalem, 2000), pp. 93-99] (Hebrew).

———. "The Question of a Created or Primordial World in the Philosophy of Maimonides," *Tarbiṣ* 33 (1964), pp. 372-87 (Hebrew).

——— . "Le-berur musag ha-Satan be-Moreh Nevukhim: ṣiyünim shonim shel ha-Satan," *Jerusalem Studies in Jewish Thought* V (1986), pp. 83-91 (Hebrew).

Pagis, Dan. "Toward a Theory of the Literary Riddle." In Galit Hasan-Rokem and David Shulman (eds.), *Untying the Knot: On Riddles and Other Enigmatic Modes* (New-York: Oxford University Press, 1996), pp. 81-108.

Petraitis, Casimir. *The Arabic Version of Aristotle's Meteorology*, a critical edition with introduction and Greek-Arabic glossaries [by] Casimir Petraitis (Beyrouth: Dare el-Machreq, 1967).

Pines, Shlomo. "Lecture on Maimonides' *Guide of the Perplexed.*" Published from Pines' manuscript by S. Stroumsa and W. Z. Harvey, *Iyyun* 47 (1998), pp. 115-128 (Hebrew).

———. "Translator's Introduction - The Philosophical Sources of the *Guide of the Perplexed.*" In *The Guide of the Perplexed Moses Maimonides* translated with an introduction and notes by Shlomo Pines (Chicago: Chicago University Press, 1963), pp. lvii-cxxxiv

Ravitzky, Israel. "The Question of a Created or Primordial World in the Philosophy of Maimonides," *Tarbiṣ* 35 (1965-66), pp. 333-48 (Hebrew).

Regev, Shaul. "The Vision of the Nobles of the Children of Israel (Exod. 24:9-11) in Medieval Jewish Philosophy," *Jerusalem Studies in Jewish Thought* 4, nos. 3/4 (1985), pp. 281-302 (Hebrew).

Ricœur Paul. "Qu'est-ce qu'un Texte. " In *Hermeneutik und Dialektik*, II. Edited by R. Bubner, Konard Cramer, Reiner Wiehl (Tübingen: J. C.V. Mohr [P. Siebeck], 1970), pp. 181-200.

———. "Sur l'exégèse de Genèse 1,1-2,4a." In *Exégèse et Herméneutique* (Paris: editions du Seuil, 1971), pp. 67-84.

Rivlin, Joseph Joel. "Perush R. Saʿadiah Gaon la-Torah." In *Sefer ha-Yovel li-Khvod Y. N. L. Epstein* (Jerusalem, 1950), pp. 133-160 (Hebrew).

Robinson, James T. "Some Remarks on the Source of Maimonides' Plato

in *Guide of the Perplexed* I, 17," *Zutot* 3 (2003), pp. 49-57.
Rosenberg, Shalom. "On the Interpretation of the Bible in the *Guide*," *Jerusalem Studies in Jewish Thought* 1/1 (1981), pp. 85-157 (Hebrew).

Schwarz, Michael. *Maimonides' Response Regarding the Spam of Life* (Tel Aviv: Papyrus, 1979 (Hebrew).
Steinschneider, Moritz. *Die hebräischen Übsersetzungen des Mittelalters* (Berlin, 1893; repr. 1956).
Strauss, Leo. "How to Begin to Study the *Guide of the Perplexed*." In *The Guide of the Perplexed*, translated by Shlomo Pines (Chicago: Chicago University Press. 1963), pp. xi-lvi.

Tate, J. "Cornutus and the Poets," *Classical Quarterly* 23 (1929), pp. 41-45.
———. "On the History of Allegorism," *Classical Quarterly* 28 (1934), pp. 105-111.

Westernik, Leendert Gerrit. *Anonymous Prolegomena to Platonic Philosophy*, introduction, text. translation and indices by L. G. Westernik (Amsterdam, 1962).
Whitman, Jon. *Allegory: The Dynamics of an Ancient and Medieval Technique* (Cambridge Mass.: Harvard University Press, 1987).
———. "Allegory." In The *New Princeton Encyclopedia of Poetry and Poetics*, edited by A. Preminger and T. V. F. Brogan (Princeton, N.J.: Princeton University Press, 1993), pp. 3–4.
Weil, Gotthold Eliakim. *Maimonides über die Lebensdauer*, translated into Hebrew and updated by Michael Schwarz: *Maimonides' Response Regarding the Spam of Life* (Tel Aviv: Papyrus, 1979).
Wolfson, Harry A. "The Kalam Problem of Nonexistence and Sa'adiah's Second Theory of Creation." In *Studies in the History of Philosophy and Religion*, I. Twersky and G. H. Williams (eds.), vol. 2 (Cambridge Mass.: Harvard University Press, 1977), pp. 338-358.

Index of Topics and Names

Abraham (the patriarch), 13, 95 n. 10
Abraham Bar Ḥiyya, **221-272**
Abravanel, Isaac, 31 n. 15, 35, 45 n. 33, 54 n. 18, 111 n. 33, 112 n. 35, 189 n. 21, 214, 249 n. 39
Account of the Beginning, 8, 9, 24, 49, 51, 53, 85, 90, 102, 111, 126, 164, 185, 186, 200, 206, 207, 208, 211, 213, 217
Account of the Chariot, 8, 9, 51, 53, 96, 125, 126, 164, 166, 167, 168, 170, 185, 200, 201, 206
Adam, 11, 13, 66, 68, 71, 78, 79, 80-85, 103 n. 20, 222, 229, 236 n. 29, 239, 244-245, 251-256, 260-267, 269, 270
Adam and Eve, 12, 13, 81 n. 10, 84, **147-150**, 151, 155, 236, 237, 245, 251, 252, 255, 258, 259, 268
Adams' sons, 21, 72, 80, **82-83**, 84, 85, 207
Aggadic expansion, 12, 13, 93, 95, 97, 98, 99, 101, 102, 104, 146
Akiva, 32-33, 35, 36, 167, 174, 211 n. 34, 214
Alexander of Aphrodisia, 76
Alfarabi, 8, 123, 133, 135, 138 n. 22, 163, 196, 187 n. 7, 198, 200, 218 n. 55
Altmann, Alexander, 113, 119 n. 48
Allegory, 136, 145, 147, 156, 157 n. 19, 158, 165
  See also Parable
  midrashic allegories, 146, 147, 158, 160
  of "a woman of virtue," 12, 125, **141-142**
  of the creation of man, 12, 147, **149-150**
  of the Garden of Eden, 12, 13, 58, 68, 147
  of the "married harlot," 12, 14, 125, **134-140**, **205-206**, 208
  of the second type, **134-135,** 190 n. 22
  of the Serpent, 12
  of the Serpent-Samael in *Pirqei de-Rabbi Eliezer* **151-154**
  Solomon's. *See* Parable
  types of prophetic allegories, 90, 134
  See also Interpretation, allegorical
Amphibolous terms, 7
Angel/angels, 24, 59, 92, 93, 97, 98, 99-102, 104, 105, 107, 109, 111, 113-116, 117, 121, 127 n. 6, 153 n. 14, 156, 234, 235, 236, 238, 243, 254, 259, 266

Angel of death, 152-153
Anthropology, 79, 80, 81, 83, 85, 90, 137, 139, 142, 143, 149, 201, 206, 244
Aristotle, 46, 110, 129, 131, 210, 216 n. 50, 217 n. 55, 219, 224, 230
  Meteorology, 10, 29, 31, 33, 34, 35, 46, 48, 49 n. 37, 214-215
  Physics, 48
  physics. *See* Aristotelian physics
Aristotelian, 213, 220, 229. 231. 232, 233 nn. 24-25, 235 n. 27, 245, 246
  anthropology, 149, 206
  astronomy, 210
  logic, 13
  metaphysics, 164, 201, 209
  philosophy, 8, 9, 13, 28, 68, 100, 109, 127, 138 n. 22, 147, 148, 149, 163, 164, 198, 201, 207, 210, 213, 218, 219
  physics, 46, 48, 76, 78, 101, 125, 129, 133, 143, 149, 164, 200, 201, 208, 210, 212, 213, 215, 271 n. 52
  psychology, 140, 154, 158
Aśoh, **25-27**, 32, 229, 230, 231, 233, 234, 239, 244, 263
Avicenna, 8, 29 n. 13, 112 n. 35, 163, 218 n. 55, 247 n. 37

Baḥya Ibn Paquda, 178 n. 15
*Bara*ʾ, *baro*ʾ, 11, 22, 25, **71-75**, 78, 80, 86, 215, 229, 230, 231, 233
Ben-Zoma, 175
Bereshit, 14, 215, 217 n. 54, 218 n. 58
Berman, L.V., 63 n. 42, 118 n. 47

Chapter headings, 9, 153, 167, 170 n. 8, 201, 202 n. 16
Cleft of the Rock. *See* revelation, Cleft of the Rock
Creation, 22, 26, 33, 39, 40, 41, 42, 44, 72, 73, 215, 229 nn. 19-20, 246
  creatio ex-nihilo, 11, 71-74, 76-79, 85 n. 17
  first day of, 22 n. 2
  of Eve, 84, 236, 260, 262
  of man, 15, 21, 52, 60, 80, 85, 95-96 n. 14, 97, 207, 212 n. 33, 218, 221, 225, **228-250**, 254
  of the angels, 24
  of the firmament, 44, 47
  of the sea, 31
  of the world, 9, 11, 21, 22, 42, **71-78**, 79, 81, 83, 86, 186, 200, 207, 229
  Plato's position, 11, 71, 72, 74, 79
  second day of, 10, **21-50**
  six days, 21, 71-72, 81, 221, 229, 244
  sixth day, 81, 234-236
  story of, 10, 14, 15, 21-29, 33 n. 18, 43, 44, 49, 50, 72, 73, 76, 78, 79, 80, 91, 109, 110, 195, 207, 208, 209, 213, 215, 217, 218 n. 56, 219, 236
  third day of, 30, 50

Crescas, Asher, 49 n. 37, 111 n. 33, 121 n. 50, 215, 219

Davidson, Herbert A., 71 n. 3, 77, 85 n. 17
Derivative
  terms, 7, 128, 129, 154
  meaning, 126, 127, 128, 129, 133, 154, 157, 200 n. 11
Disciple. *See* Reader, disciple
Divine science. *See* Metaphysics
Dundes, Alan. *See* Georges

Earth, 22, 24, 25, 28 n. 12, 33, 34, 35, 37, 45, 46, 48, 49, 72, 73, 86, 96-98, 103, 105, 107, 108, 111, 211, 212, 240, 241, 264, 270
element, 96, 101-102, 109 n. 32, 209
  equivocal term, 31, 208
Educational myth, 8, 135, 196, 197 n. 7, 198, 200, 201, 219
Efrat, Israel, 258 n. 45
Elisha ben Abuyah, 174, 175, 177, 182
Elohim (the term), 59-65, 72, 81, 243
End of Days, 15, 224, 248, 249, 250, 264
Equivocal terms, nouns, words 7, 10-12, 13, 14, 23, 26, 28, 30, 31, 36, 37, 38, 48, 51, 53, 59, 60, 61, 63 n. 42, 65, 68, 72, 73, 74, 79, 80, 81, 84 n. 14, 93, 101, 104, 106, 107, 110, 113, 114, 115, 116, 125, 126, 128, 154, 160, 177, 198, 199, 202, 204, 208, 227, 253, 258, 269, 271
  explanation, 72, 73, 74, 75, 78
  terms based on etymology, 13, 155
  See also Interpretation, etymological interpretation of names
Esoteric, 9, 10, 321, 126, 135, 146, 153, 160, 163, 195, 197, 198, 200, 201, 206, 211
  biblical texts, 95, 201, 203, 206, 211, 213, 214
  doctrines, 13, 125, 135, 163, 164, 165, 166, 173 n. 11, 175, 201, 218
  literature, 8, 9, 195
  matters, 167, 197, 205
  sciences, 90, 186
  teaching, 12, 89, 164, 167, 185, 197, 200, 208, 217, 219
  See also Method, esoteric; interpretation, esoteric
Esotericism, 13, 135, 186, 200, 206
Esotericist, 74, 77, 78, 79, 85
Eve, 13, 84, 85, 150, 151, 154, 155, 156, 236, 255, 256, 257, 258, 260, 261, 265
  See also Adam and Eve
Ezekiel, 58 n. 29, 92 n. 7, 198 n. 8
  See also Vision, Ezekiel's vision of the chariot

Galen, 15, 57 n. 27, 224, 225, 233 n. 24, 247, 248, 250, 261, 271
Garden of Eden, 9, 11, 12, 13, 14, 15, 21, **51-69**, 72, **80-82**, 83,

84, 85, 97, 103, 147, 150-160, 172, 207, 21 n. 33, 218 n. 58, 221, 225, 227, 236 n. 29, 245, 248, **250-272**
Georges, Robert A., 146
Gersonides, 7, 85, 213 n. 38, 216 n. 50, 219 n. 60
God
apprehension of, 12, 13, 112, 113, 117, 122, 123, 126, **183-194**, 197
apprehension of His attributes, 118-120, 204-205
God called, *See* Metalanguage, *Va-yiqra'*
incorporeal, 195-199, 202
Good and Evil, 60, 62-64, 252-255, 257-260
Guttmann, Julius, 247 n. 37, 248 n. 38, 270 n. 51

Ḥasdai ha-Levi, 89 n. 1
He Called. *See Va-yiqra'*
Heaven, 10, 22-28, 37, 39, 41, 46, 47, 72, 73, 77, 86, 103, 104, 106, 107, 108, 109, 110, 151, 152, 199, 208, 209, 210, 211, 214, 216 n. 47
Heinemann, Isaak, 65 n. 45
Hesiod, 146
Homer, 146
Hidden level, 27, 28, 44, 46, 79, 91 n. 5, 95, 98, 100, 103, 110, 122, 123, 226 n. 123
See also Meaning, hidden meaning
Hint, 10, 28, 33, 66, 67, 68, 80, 96, 97, 98, 101, 105, 147, 151-155, 157, 158, 160, 164, 198 n. 8, 201, 203, 211, 214, 215, 217, 218, 256 n. 43
equation hint, 152, 153, 150

Ibn Bajja, 8
Ibn Kaspi, Joseph, 90 n. 3,
Ibn Ezra, Abraham, 7, 92 n. 8, 233 n. 24, 268 n. 49
Ibn Tibbon, Judah, 223 nn. 5-6
Ibn Tibbon, Samuel, 22, 29 n. 13, 59 n. 33, 108 n. 29, 113 n. 37, 117 n. 44, 151 n. 1
Ibn Ṣaddiq, Joseph, 233 n. 24, 262 n. 47
Imagination, 46, 62, 140-141 n. 28, 152-155, 158 n. 21, 159, 175, 180, 181 n. 18, 182, 210
Immortality, 14, **245-250**
Intellectual elite, 14, 125, 136, 183, 198, 200, 208, 219, 220
Interpretation
allegorical, 11, 146
by means of Midrash, 12, 66, 89, **91-109, 112-116, 121-123**, **147-160**, 172, 180, 211, 218 n. 58
esoteric, 12, 14, 21 n. 1, 22, 125, 145, 147, 201, 202, 203, 204, 207, 213, 214, 215, 219, 220
etymological interpretation of names, 13, 155-160, 216 n. 50, 256 n. 43.
See also Method, etymological method
exoteric, 14, 125, 126, 133, 195, 198, **199-213**, 214 n.

40, 219
midrashic interpretation, 91, 92, 93, 103, 123, 211
by structure of relation, 12, 125, 130, 131, 142, 143, 160 n. 31
See also Meaning, structure of
Interpretative riddle, 12-13, 14, 95-101, **145-160**, 218-220

Jeremiah, 92
Job (the book of) 58, 67, 151, 152, 153, 187

Kalam, 76
Kaufmann, David, 270 n. 51
Kreisel, Howard, 196 n. 4

Law, 8, 42, 54, 77, 83, 198, 200, 205 n. 21
Levi ben Greshom. *See* Gersonides
Lexicographical chapters, 106 n. 27, 107 n. 28, 176, 179, 198 n. 8, 199

Ma'aseh Bereshit, 166, 167, 172
See also Account of the Beginning
Ma'aseh Merkavah, 165, 169, 171, 172, 173, 177, 183
See also Account of the Chariot
Mal'akh. *See* Angel
Man (*'ish*) (the term), 120, 128, 132, **133**, 139, 140, 156
Mashal. *See* Parable; Allegory
Masses, 8, 9, 14, 40, 47, 125, 126, 135, 136, 183, 195. 196, 197, 198, 199, 200, 203, 204, 205, 207, 208, 210, 214, 215, 219, 220
See also multitude; vulgar
Meaning
Borrowed/derivative, 93, 107, 116, 117, 126, 127, 128, 129, 133, 154
hidden 8, 45 n. 34, 47, 48, 60, 145, 154, 158, 160, 271
external, 47, 48, 55, 134, 136, 137, 149, 154, 206, 219
figurative, 126, 128, 130, 131 n. 15, 154
inner/internal, 47, 60 n. 37, 134, 136, 137, 138, 149, 154, 206, 211, 213, 219,
literal, 28, 45, 55, 56, 60, 60 n. 37, 91, 103, 108, 134, 136, 138, 139, 141
philosophical, 14, 131, 149, 154, 163, 164, 167, 199, 209, 213
structure of, 128, 130, 133
Metalanguage, 10, 28, 208, 271 n. 52
Va-yavdel, 25, **27**, 29, 214 n. 40
Va-yiqra', 10, 25, **27-28**, 30, 31, 37, 38, 208, 209
Metaphor, 27, 92, 127, 153, 223, 262
of the "Married harlot," 12, 14, 125, 126, 129. **130-133**, 135-140, 142, 143, 205, 209
of the "woman of virtue," 125 n. 1, 141-143
of honey, 176, 177
Metaphysics, 7, 9, 24, 53, 118,

125, 164, 165, 166, 167, 173, 174, 183, 184, 185, 186, 187, 188, 193, 197, 200, 201
Method, 21, 22, 28, 51, 68, 76, 131, 145, 147, 204
"connect its chapters one with another," 10, 21, 59, 69, 100, 108, 153
esoteric, 12, 14, 125, 201, 202, 205, 207, 214, 220
esoteric methods of transmission, 9, 14, 125, 173, 201, 207, 215, 217
etymological, 156, 158, 159, 160, 256
See also Interpretation, etymological interpretation of names
obscurity, 217 n. 55
of apprehension, 166, 189 n. 23
of interpretation, 8, 10, 11, 15, 22, 134, 156, 158, 189, 225, 232
of scattering, 14, 21 n. 1, 147, 152, 201, 202
See also Interpretative riddle
Midrash/Midrashim, 12, 13, 55, 64, 66, 84, 91, 92, 93, 95, 97, 98, 99, 100, 103-106, 109, 113-116, 121, 123, 148-160, 163, 168 n. 3, 164, 168, 172, 180, 211, 218 n. 58, 227, 236
See also Interpretation, Interpretation by means of midrash; Interpretation, midrashic; Reader, of the midrashim; Riddles, midrashic
Miracle, 250
Montague, Richard, 127 n. 5
Moses, 13, 14, 39, 40, 43, 83, 104, 111, 115, 118-123, 181, 191, 202, 204-205
Multitude, 8, 39, 45 n. 33, 52, 53, 58 n. 28, 74, 75, 77, 79, 81, 83 n. 14, 183, 196, 197, 200, 201, 209, 210, 213, 214
See also Vulgar
Munk, Shlomo, 29 n. 13, 46 n. 35, 113 n. 37, 151 n. 11
mysteries of the Torah 8, 12, 51, 66, 74, 89, 90, 102, 111, 164, 183, 197, 200 n. 13, 215

Naḥash, 13, 82, 155, 156, 157, 159, 218 n. 58, 255, 256, 263
See also Serpent
Narboni, Moses , 23, 24, 35, 36, 158 nn. 21, 22, 159, 219 n. 60
Natural science. *See* physics

Onqelos, 59 n. 33, 212

Pagis, Dan, 145 n. 2
Parable/ parables 7, 12, 13, 14, 27, 29, 51, 53, 58 nn. 28-29, 68, 90, 207, 226 n. 12
See also Allegory
biblical parable 91, 104 105
kinds of, 90
See also Allegory, of the second type; types of prophetic allegories
Maimonides', 189
of Adam's sons, 82, 83, 85 n. 18

of apples of gold in a silver setting, 27-28
of the first type, 90, 104, 106
of the slothful, **190-192**
of Jacob's Dream of the Ladder in *Guide* I.15, **103-142**
of Jacob's Dream of the Ladder in *Guide* II.10, 90, 91 92, **95-102**
of Jacob's Dream of the Ladder in the midrash, 92
of the "married harlot." *See* allegory of the "married harlot"
of the ruler's palace, 66-67
of the second type. *See* allegories of the second type
"Parable and riddle," 164, 168, 185, 207
Prophetic parable 91-92, 94, 95, 96
Solomon's 130, 168, 169, 170 n. 8, 175-178, 182, 189, 190, 191
Theory of 90, 91, 104, 106
Perplexity, 51, 52, 53, 56, 57, 58 n. 29, 61, 65, 67, 198, 199, 200, 201, 213
Perplexed man/ people, 54, 55, 56, 57, 65, 77, 198, 199, 200, 201, 219
Petraitis, C., 29 n. 13
Physics, 7, 9, 12, 24, 29, 46, 48, 53, 55, 76, 78, 85, 90, 101, 102, 112, 118, 119, 125, 143, 149, 164, 167, 185, 186, 188, 200, 201, 208, 210, 212, 213, 215, 217 n. 52
See also Account of the Beginning
Pines, Shlomo, 29 n. 13, 54 nn. 13.16.17, 55 n. 24, 59 n. 33, 108 n. 29, 113 n. 37, 117 nn. 44-45, 134 n. 17, 151 n. 11, 185, 196
Plato, 149. *See also* Creation, Plato's position
platonic psychology, 225, 232, 233 nn.24-25, 234, 244
Profiat Duran (Efodi), 37, 111 n. 33, 159 n. 28, 185
Prophecy, 12, 13, 89, 90, 91, 94, 117, 119 n. 48, 121, 126, 179, 181 n. 18, 200 n. 13, 227
books of 7, 12, 13, 51, 53, 60, 170 n. 5, 207
Prophet, 90, 91, 92 n. 6, 94, 95, 113, 114-116, 117, 118, 119, 121, 122, 123, 156, 157, 168, 181, 204, 205
Prophetic
dream, 90. 112 n. 35, 122
parable, 91, 105
vision, 90-91, 94, 97, 99, 100, 112 n. 35
Proverbs, 58 n. 29, 130, 190, 192
Providence, 13, 119, 122, 197, 200 n. 13, 215

Qāfih, Yoseph, 22, 29 n. 13

Reader
disciple (of Maimonides), 11, 52, 54, 58, 60 n. 35, 64, 65, 66, 83 n. 14, 172, 174, 175, 179, 190 n. 22

of Bar Ḥiyya's *Megillat ha-Megalleh,* 222, 224 n. 11
of the Bible, 28, 44-46, 48, 51, 54-56, 58
of the *Guide*, 8, 9, 10, 11, 13, 14, 29, 32, 51, 52, 54-69, 75, 77, 89 n. 1, 100, 102, 108, 110, 116, 117, 125, 127, 134, 136, 145-160, 178, 188, 190, 198-203, 205, 206, 208, 210, 213-216, 218-220, 256 n. 43
of *Hilkhot Yesodei ha-Torah*, 9
"the man busy with sciences" (the objector), 54-59, 62, 64-68
of the midrashim, 45-48, 55, 56-58 ,68
of riddles, 147
of Solomon's books, 13, 123
perplexed reader 8, 9, 14, 55, 213
Redemption, 221-225, 239, 245, 250, 272
Reshit, 127 n. 61, **215-219**
Resurrection of the Dead, 15, 222-225, 239, 241, 245, 248, 250, 265, 266, 267, 272
Revelation
in the Cleft of the Rock, 14, 40, 43, **118-123**, **202-205**
in the burning bush, 181, 191
Riddle, 95, 97, 100, 145 n. 3, **146-147**, 148-160
literary, 12, 58 n. 29, 145, 152
folk, 145
midrashic, 148, 150, 155, 157, 159
oppositional, 149
Robinson, James, 129 n. 8
Rosenberg, Shalom, 112 n. 35

Sa'adiah Gaon, 7, 45 n. 33, 73, 214, 216 n. 47, 222, 223, 224 n. 7, 226 n. 14, 234 n. 26, 237 n. 42
Sages (of the Mishnah, the Talmud and the midrashim), 9, 29 n. 13, 32, 35, 37, 38, 39, 45, 50, 55, 56, 58, 64, 66, 81, 84, 91 n. 4, 97, 100, 102, 109, 110, 115, 122, 151, 153, 157, 159 n. 29, 160, 163, 164, 165, 166, 167, 168, 169, 170, 171, 172, 173, 174, 175, 177, 178, 181, 182, 183, 184, 185, 186, 191, 195, 196, 201 n. 15, 207, 210 n. 30, 211, 212, 214 n. 40, 226, 227, 229, 236 n. 29, 256, 264
Sammael, 13, **150-159**
Satan, **151-153**, 155, 159 n. 29
Schwarz, Michael, 18, 29 n. 13, 56 n. 26, 58 n. 29, 108 n. 29, 113 n. 37, 117 n. 45, 151 n. 11, 247 n. 37
Serpent, 12, 13, 95 n. 14, 97, 147, **150-160**, 218 n. 58, 252, 253, 256, 257, 258, 260, 261, 263-264
Shailat, Isaac, 89 n. 1
Shamayim. *See* Heaven
Shem Tov ben Joseph Shem Tov, 35, 36, 111 n. 33, 113 n. 38, 121 n. 50, 159 n. 28, 217 n. 54
Shlomo ha-Levi Alkabetz, 231

Song of Songs, 58 n. 29
Solomon (King), 13, 14, 58 n. 29, 130-133, 135-138, 140, 141, 143, 156, **163-194,** 205, 206
Somekh, Sasson, 55 n. 25
Sphere, spheres, 7, 12, 22, 23, 24, 33, 37, 38, 42, 44, 46, 77, 90, 96, 101, 102, 106, 109, 110, 111, 112, 118, 119, 208, 209, 210, 212, 213
Soul
  animal, 96, 140, 192, 233, 234, 237, 239, 240 n. 33
  appetitive. *See* vegetative
  faculties of the soul, 68, 140, 148, 153 n. 14, 155, 159
  force/ power of transformation, 248, 261-263
  formative force (*koaḥ ha-meṣayer*), 248, 249, 261-263
  lower souls. *See* non-rational souls
  non-rational souls, 233, 234, 235, 236, 237, 238, 244
  of life (*nishmat ḥayyim*), 232, 234, 237, 239, 243, 254, 267, 268, 269
  perfection of, 54, 56
  rational, 96, 233-237, 239, 241-245, 254, 267, 269
  vegetative, 96, 140, 233, 234, 237, 239, 262
Steinschneider, Moritz, 29 n. 29

Talmud, 9, 152, 163, 166, 167, 169, 170, 172, 173, 175, 180, 181, 227
talmudic dictum, 196 n. 3, 197 n. 7
Talmudic Sages, 84, 157, 163, 165, 168, 169, 172, 175
Theodor, Jehuda , 91 n. 4

Vision
  Ezekiel's vision of the chariot, 24 n. 7, 96, 102, 112 n. 35
  Isaiah's, 249
  Michaia's, 199-200 n. 11
  of Jacobs' ladder, 95, 96, 105, 111
  of the nobles of the children of Israel, 182
  Moses', 181
  prophetic, 91-92, 94, 97, 99, 100, 112 n. 35, 156
  Zechariah's vision of the chariot, 95
Vulgar, 23, 44, 45, 47, 207, 210, 213, 214, 215
  See also multitude; masses

Woman, 149, 150, 156, 256, 257, 261, 262, 263
  See also Eve; Adam and Eve
  the term (*ʾishah*), 12, 125, **126-129**, 130, 131, 132, 133, 140 n. 26, 142-143, 160 n. 31
  See also Allegory, Allegory of "a woman of virtue;" of the "married harlot;" Metaphor,

Metaphor of "a woman of virtue;" of the "married harlot"

Yaḥyā ibn al-Biṭriq, 29 n. 13

Zechariah, 92 n. 7, 95, 96

Index of Sources and Citations

Bible

Genesis
1, 43, 80, 230, 235, 244, 246
1:1-2:4, 72
1:1- 2:6, 21
1-5, 11, 16, 78, 79, 80, 84, 85
1:1, 11, 14, 22, 24, 37, 71, 72, 73, 74, 78, 86, 109, 127, 208, 127, 211, 216 n. 151, 217
1:1-2, 21
1:2, 29, 30, 209
1:4, 27
1:5, 28
1:6, 31
1:7, 14, 213, 214 n. 40
1: 6-8, 22, 24, 25, 45 n. 33
1:7, 14, 27, 29, 30, 32
1:8, 24, 28, 37, 208 n. 25
1:9, 254
1:10, 28, 30, 31, 208, 209
1:11-12, 211
1:14, 24, 27, 38
1:15, 24, 38
1:17, 23, 24, 38, 209, 214
1:18, 27
1:20, 24, 38, 240
1:24, 240
1:26, 130 n. 12, 148, 197, 229, 231, 233, 242, 243, 244, 267
1:26-27, 21, 60, 61, 80, 238
1:27, 84, 229, 233, 236, 270
1:28, 137
1:29, 245, 246, 248-249, 256, 260, 261
1:31, 42, 43, 118
2, 66, 230, 235, 265
2-3, 72, 80, 84
2:1-3, 22
2:3-4, 236 n. 29
2:4-3:24, 21
2:5, 212
2:6, 211, 212
2:7, 21, 229, 233, 234, 236, 249, 241, 269
2:9, 251, 257
2:15, 256, 265, 279
2:16, 259
2:17, 251
2:19, 240
2:21, 261, 262
2:22, 251, 263
2:23-24, 148 n. 9
2:24, 251
3, 252, 268
3:1, 255, 256
3:5, 59, 60, 61, 62, 64, 65, 81, 82, 255 n. 42
3:6, 81 n. 10, 265
3:7, 64, 81 n. 10, 258
3:17, 260 n. 46
3:14, 264
3:17, 267
3:18-19, 67
3:20, 156
3:22, 259, 254

3:23, 279
3:24, 269
4, 72, 82, 85
4-5, 80
4:1-15, 21
5, 82, 83 n. 14
5:1, 229, 243-244, 267
5:2, 84
5:3, 82
5:29, 267
8:21, 267
13:16, 95 n. 10, 129
22:17, 242 n. 35
28, 89
28:12, 92, 93, 97, 103
28:12-13, 12, 96
28:13, 107
28:14, 94, 242 n. 35
29:12, 263
32:13, 242 n. 35
57:4, 151 n. 12,

Exodus
3:6, 181, 191
7:11, 271
19, 121
19:2, 104
19:20, 103
24:9-11, 180
24:11, 182
25, 271
26:3, 128
31:18, 26
33, 40
34, 40
33-34, 121
33:13, 120
33:14, 203 n. 18
33:13-20, 14
33:18, 203 n. 18
33:19, 43, 118
33:20, 14, 203 n. 18, 204, 205
33:21-23, 14, 202
33:23, 122
34:6, 203 n. 18
34:6-7, 14, 40, 119, 204, 205

Numbers
1:18, 242 n. 35
3:15, 242 n. 35
12:3, 181
12:8, 181, 191
20:16, 114, 115

Deuteronomy
4:1, 104
22:7, 269
32:4, 43
33:26, 23, 109, 209
33:26, 27, 111, 112 n. 35

Judges
2:1, 114, 115
2:1-4, 115
8:16, 253

1 Samuel
3:24, 270
6:11, 232

2 Samuel
23:20, 58 n. 29

1 Kings
20:34, 270
22:19, 199

Isaiah
5:6, 368 n. 49
11:7, 249
21:14, 169 n. 4
26:14, 223 n. 5
26:29, 223 n. 5
27:13, 223 n. 5
44:13, 211
55:1, 169 n. 4
65:25, 264
66:1, 23

Jeremiah
9:23, 121 n. 51
23:29, 226
46:27, 93

Ezekiel
1:26, 198
36:12, 222
37, 58 n. 29

Haggai
1:1, 115
1:13, 104, 115

Psalms
2:4, 23
8:4, 26
19:2, 24
33:6, 26, 27
49:13, 66, 68, 103 n. 20
62:12, 226 n. 13
68:5, 109, 111, 112 n. 35
78:32, 92
101:7, 32
107:24, 26
123:1, 2

Proverbs
2:2-5, 187
2:4, 187, 188
3:18, 266
3:32, 193
5:16, 168
5:17, 169, 170
6:26, 125, 130, 133, 136, 137, 149-150, 205
7, 125, 134, 135, 136
7:6-21, 14, 135, 136, 150, 205
7:24-25, 135, 136
11:13, 172
19:20, 188, 189
21:25, 190, 191
21: 25-26, 192, 193
23:9, 171, 172
25:11, 27, 58 n. 28, 137
25:16, 175, 177, 178
25:27, 176, 177, 178
27:26, 166, 167, 169, 170
31:3, 192, 193
31:10, 138, 141
31:10-31, 125, 141
31:11-31 141

Job
14:28, 66
14:20, 66, 67
28, 187
28:12, 187, 188

Ecclesiastes
4:17, 178, 182, 189
7, 184
7:16, 178
7:24, 184, 186, 187, 188
10:2, 159

10:10, 188, 189

Song of Songs
4:11, 166, 167, 170, 171, 177

Daniel
10:6, 99

2 Chronicles
36:16, 115

Rabbinic

Mishnah

Ḥagigah
2.1, 9, 167, 170 nn. 8, 9, 183, 206

Babylonian Talmud

Berakhot
7a, 181
18b, 58 n. 29
31a, 39 n. 27, 195 n. 1

ʿErubin
18b, 82

Taʿanit
7a, 165, 169, 170

Ḥagigah
Chap. 2 (*Ein Dorshin*), 163, 165, 168, 172, 173, 175, 177, 181, 183
12a, 167
12b, 109, 110, 111, 112 n. 35, 211 n. 35
13a, 9, 166, 167, 172, 201
14b, 32, 167, 174
15a, 175 n. 12

Kiddushin
17b, 39 n. 27

Baba Qama
60b, 58 n. 29

Baba Meṣiʿa
31b, 39 n. 27, 195 n. 1

Baba Batra
15a, 58 n. 29
16a, 152

Sanhedrin
29a, 256
34a, 226,
35b, 103 n. 20
38 b. 66 n. 46
89b, 151 n. 12

Ḥullin
91b 98, 99, 100

Midrash

Genesis Rabbah
1.14, 211 n. 34
4.1, 32
4.2, 35, 37, 214 n. 40
4.7, 50
8.1, 13, 84, 148

9.5, 43 n. 31
11.2, 103 n. 20
11.5, 66 n. 46
11. 2, 103 n. 20
12.6, 66 n. 46, 103 n. 20
13.1, 21
16.1, 103 n. 20
21.14, 103 n. 20
40.9, 95
68.2, 98, 99, 103, 105, 113, 121
68.12, 98
68.13, 92 n. 8, 95
69.5, 95

Exodus Rabbah
3.1, 181 n.17

Leviticus Rabbah
1.1, 114, 115
20.1, 181 n. 17

Numbers Rabbah
2.25, 181 n. 17
16.1, 114

Deuteronomy Rabbah
5.3, 109 n. 31

Canticles Rabbah
168 n. 3

Ecclesiastes Rabbah
168 n. 3
1.1, 156

Leqaḥ Tov
103 n. 21

Pirqei de-Rabbi Eliezer
4.1, 98
Chap. 13, 13, 150
Chap. 18, 109 n. 31, 111 n. 34, 112 n. 35

Tanḥuma
Vayeṣe, 92, 97, 98, 103 n. 20
Sheḥ, 114 n. 40, 116 n. 42

Sifrei
Vaetḥanan, 116 n. 43

Pesiqta de Rav Kahana 92, 236 n. 29

Pesiqta Rabbati, 98, 103 n. 20, 109 n. 31

Philosophy

Abraham Bar Ḥiyya
Hegyon ha-Nefesh ha-ʿAṣuvah, 221 n. 2, 226, 227, 237, 240 n. 33
Megillat ha-Megalleh, 15, **221-272**

Abravanel, Isaac
Be'ur le-Sefer Moreh Nevukhim, 35, 54 n. 18, 111 n. 33, 189 n. 21
Commentary on the Torah (*Perush ha-Torah*), 31 n. 15, 35, 45 n. 33, 85 n. 15, 214, 249 n. 39
Sefer Shamayim Ḥadashim, 112 n. 35

Alfarabi
Commentary and Short Treatise on Aristotle's De Interpretatione,

138 n. 22
Summery of Sophistical Refutations, 129, 133
The Perfect State
10.6, 159 nn. 24, 26

Aristotle
Categories 12, 14ᵃ25ff, 216 n. 50
De Interpretatione, I, 16ᵃ3–8, 138 n. 22
Metaphysics
IV, 1, 216 n. 50
VII.7. 1032b 6-30, 230 n. 22
Meteorology
I.3.4.9, 34
I.9, 346b25-30, 35
II.2, 354b, 24-32, 31 n. 15
II.2-3, 354b 32–355b 20, 31 n. 15
II.3, 357 b17—21; 358a 5-27, 31 n. 15
IV.6, 383a 5-10, 35
Nicomachean Ethics
III.5. 1112b24, 230 n. 22
On the Heavens
II.9, 210 n. 28
Physics
I.9 192ᵃ22–23, 129, 133
IV. 7–9, 210 n. 29
Rhetoric
III.2, 146 n. 6

Baḥya Ibn Paquda
Duties of the Heart
VIII.3, 178 n. 15

Crescas, Asher
Perush le-Moreh Nevukhim, 49 n. 39, 215 n. 43

Gersonides
Commentary on Genesis, 85, 216, n. 50
The Wars of the Lord
VI.2.2, 216 n. 50
VI.2.7, 213 n. 38
VI.6.12, 219 n. 60

Ibn Kaspi, Joseph
Maskiyot Kesef, 90 n. 3

Ibn Ezra, Abraham
Commentary on Genesis, 92 n. 8, 216 n. 51, 268 n. 49, 270 n. 51
Commentary on Ecclesiastes, 233 nn. 24, 25
Yesod Mora', 233 n. 24

Ibn Ṣaddiq, Joseph
Sefer ha-ʿOlam ha-Qatan, 233 n. 24, 262 n. 47

Judah Halevi
Kuzari
2:2, 204 n. 19

Maimonides
Commentary on the Mishnah
Introduction, 170-171
Ḥagigah 2.1, 170 nn. 8, 9
Epistle of Resurrection, 195 n. 2
Epistle to Yemen, 94
Hilkhot Yesodei ha-Tora
2.12, 167, 177, 192
4.13, 167, 174
7.3, 12, 89, 90 n. 2, **91-95**
Hilkhot Deʿot
1.4, 194 n. 26

1.6, 194 n. 26
3.2, 177
4.19, 192 n. 25, 193
Laws Concerning Marriage
chap. 21, 138 n. 24
Guide of the Perplexed
Epistle Dedicatory, 52, 60 n. 35, 65 n. 44
Instruction with Respect to this Treatise, 10, 21, 51, 59, 69, 145, 153, 202
Introduction, 7, 8, 10, 11, 13, 21 n. 1, 27, 28, 45 n. 34, 48 n. 36, 51, 54, 55 n. 23, 57, 60, 65 n. 44, 74, 90, 103, 104-105, 108, 125, 130, 134, 137, 138, 139, 141, 145, 150, 153, 170 n. 5, 184, 185, 186, 192, 193, 198, 199, 201, 205, 206, 217
Introduction to II, 78, 140 n. 27, 152 n. 14, 159 n. 25
Introduction to II (in II.2), 7-8, 206 n. 23
Introduction to III, 8
I, 126, 129
I.1, 60, 80, 81, 130 n. 12, 198 n. 8, 232
I.2, 11, **51-69**, 80, 81, 82, 84 n. 14, 13
I.3, 181
I.4, 126 n. 14, 178-179, 200 n. 11, 202 n. 17, 203 n. 18, 209 n. 27
I.5, 178, 179, 180-182, 184, 188 n. 20, 190, 191, 194
I.6, **125-129**, 131, 133
I.7, 82, 83 n. 14, 84 n. 14, 107 n. 28, 116 n. 43, 126 n. 4
I.8, 116, 122, 199 n. 10, 202 n. 17, 203 n. 18, 209 n. 26, 210 n. 32
I.9, 23, 200 n. 9, 209 n. 27
I.10, 101, 113, 116
I.11, 23
I.14, 79, 81, 126, 200 n. 9, 209 n. 27
I.15, 122, 89, 90, **103-123**, 127 n. 6, 202 n. 17, 203 n. 18
I.16, 222, 127, 202 n. 17, 203 n. 18, 216 n. 52
I.17, 129 n. 8, 149
I.18, 178
I.21, 202 n. 17, 203 n. 18
I.26, 195 n. 2, 197 n. 6
I.29, 195 n. 2, 197 n. 6
I.30, **176-177**
I.31-32, 173
I.32, 75, **173-176,** 177, 178, 179, 180, 182, 190-192
I.31-34, 173, 179
I.33-34, 173, 195 n. 2, 197
I.33, 182-183
I.34, 177, 179, **182-194**
I.35, 52, 90, 196, 198, 199 n. 9, 200 n. 13, 215
I.37, 202 n. 17, 203 n. 18
I.38, 122, 202 n. 17, 203 n. 18
I.42, 191
I.47, 195 n. 2
I.50, 138 n. 22
I.51-53, 204
I.50-60, 52
I.54, 14, 40, 43, **118-122**, **204-205**
I.58, 23
I.64, 202 n. 17, 203 n. 18

I.65, 25
I.66, 25, 27
I.67, 25
I.70, 23, 55, 108-110, 111, 154
I.71, 75
I.72, 101, 102
I.73, 210 n. 31
II.1, 111, 112 n. 35, 152 n. 14, 159 n. 24
II.2, 206
II.4, 110-11, 112 n. 35, 152 n. 14
II.5, 24
II.6, 60, 101, 113, 114, 127 n. 6
II.7, 78, 101
II.8, 210 nn. 28, 30
II.9-24, 78, 153 n. 14
II.10, 12, 89, 90, **95-102**, 103, 109
II.12, 152, 153 n. 14
II.13, 11, 72-73, 218 n. 57
II.14, 76 n. 7
II.17, 76 n. 7, 78
II.18, 76 n. 7
II.19, 76
II, 19-24, 77, 78
II.20, 76
II.22, 76
II.24, 77, 210 n. 29
II.25, 74
II.29, 29, 152 n. 14, 157 n. 18, 201 n. 15, 206
II.30, 10, 11, 12, 13, 14, **21-50**, 52, 58, 64-65, 66, 68, 72, 74, 80, 81, 82, 83 n. 14, 84, 85, 109, 110, 127 n. 6, **147-160**, 169 n. 4, 172, **208-219**, 236 n. 29
II.36, 141 n. 28
II.37, 152 n. 14
II.38, 152 n. 14
II.43, 156 n. 17
II.45, 130
III.2, 24
III.4, 23
III.7 24
III.8, 60 n. 36, 125, 129, 130, **131-132**, 136-142, 192, 193, 205
III.10, 38, 43, 74,
III.11, 43 n. 31
III.12, 140, 141 n. 28, 194 n. 24
III.13, 38, 39, 41, 42, 49, 50
III.15, 78
III.19, 57 n. 27
III.22, 151 n. 14, 159 n. 29
III.25, 38, 41, 42
III.27, 200 n. 12
III.50, 83
III.51, 52, 66-67
III.54, 65 n. 44, 170 n. 6, 184, 187, 189
Introduction to Pereq Ḥeleq, 45, 48, 56, 58, 68, 168, 195 n. 2
Pirqei Moshe, 57 n. 27

Narboni, Moses
Be'ur le-Sefer Moreh Nevukhim, 35, 36, 158 n. 21

Profiat Duran (Efodi)
Perush le-Moreh Nevukhim, 37, 111 n. 33, 158 n. 21

Rashi
Commentary on Genesis 1:1, 216-217 n. 51

Sa'adiah Gaon
Commentary on the Book of Job, 226 n. 14
Commentary on the Torah, 216 n. 47, 234 n. 26, 255 n. 42
Sefer ha-Emunot ve-ha-De'ot
IV.1, 237 n. 30
VII, 223
VII.4, 224 n. 7

Shem Tov ben Joseph Shem Tov
Perush le-Moreh Nevukhim, 35, 36, 111 n. 33, 113 n. 38

Also published by Academic Studies Press in 2011

MODERN JEWISH THINKERS

From Mendelssohn to Rosenzweig

Gershon Greenberg

496 pages

Cloth 978-1-936235-31-5

$65.00 / £44.25

Paper 978-1-936235-46-9

$33.00 / £22.50

Historical conditions at the end of the eighteenth century opened an arena between the formerly autonomous Jewish community and the Christian world, which yielded new departure points for philosophy, including revelation and philosophical reason, dialectically considered; rationalism as intellection and advancing consciousness, heteronomous revelation, historicity, and universal morality. In *Modern Jewish Thinkers*, Greenberg restructures the history of modern Jewish thought comprehensively, providing first-time English translations of Reggio, Krokhmal, Maimon, Samuel Hirsch, Formstecher, Steinheim, Ascher, Einhorn, Samuel David Luzzatto and Hermann Cohen. The availability of these sources fills a gap in the field and stimulates new directions for teaching and scholarly research in modern Jewish thought, going beyond Spinoza and Mendelssohn at one end, and to popular 20th century figures on the other.

Gershon Greenberg (PhD Columbia University) works at American University in Washington, DC, in the fields of Holocaust religious thought, America-Holy Land, and nineteenth-century German-Jewish thought, and has taught in the departments of Jewish thought at Israel's major universities.

"By making available well-chosen, well-introduced and clearly translated texts by so many nineteenth-century thinkers hitherto unavailable in English, Gershon Greenberg's Modern Jewish Thinkers *will change the way the subject is taught. We can now put in students' hands a single volume that will guide us through the labyrinthine twists and turns of Jewish philosophy from Mendelssohn to the interwar period. This is a major achievement and a major event for the classroom!"*

—David Sorkin, Professor of Jewish Studies, University of Wisconsin-Madison

"Modern Jewish Thinkers *is a quintessential anthology, literally a "gathering of flowers" from the garden of modern Jewish thought. Greenberg has selected and translated from German and Hebrew an array of the most seminal texts, hitherto largely unavailable in English, which exemplify various trajectories of Jewish theological encounter with the challenge of modern philosophical culture. This richly annotated source book will surely be indispensable for scholars and students alike."*

—Paul Mendes-Flohr, University of Chicago

SEX REWARDED, SEX PUNISHED

A Study of the Status "Female Slave" in Early Jewish Law

Diane Kriger

424 pages

Cloth 978-1-934843-48-2

$48.00 / £32.75

A masterful intersection of Bible Studies, Gender Studies, and Rabbinic law, Diane Kriger explores the laws pertaining to female slaves in Jewish law. Comparing Biblical strictures with later Rabbinic interpretations as well as contemporary Greco-Roman and Babylonian codes of law, Kriger establishes a framework whereby a woman's sexual identity also indicates her legal status. With sensitivity to the nuances in both ancient laws and ancient languages, Kriger adds greatly to our understanding of gender, slave status, and the matrilineal principle of descent in the Ancient Near East.

Diane Kriger (PhD University of Toronto), a lawyer by training, had a strong interest in the classics, ancient languages and Talmudic studies. Dr. Kriger wrote or contributed to several articles on slavery and the status of women in ancient Judaism and in the surrounding societies. In 1997-1998, she co-founded and served as associate editor of Women in Judaism: A Multidisciplinary Journal, an academic journal published electronically. Dr. Kriger edited texts and articles on biblical studies, and — most recently — she edited a new Siddur for Holy Blossom Temple in Toronto. Dr. Kriger died in December 2008.

"Diane Kriger's scholarship was meticulous and perceptive. Her unique academic background in both law and the ancient Near East provided her with unparalleled means to understand the alwa and the position of slave women in ancient Israel. Her work not only fills a vital space for studies in ancient Jewish law, but also has a place in the interpretation of modern Jewish law."
—Jennifer Hellum, Department of Classics and Ancient History, University of Auckland

SORROW AND DISTRESS IN THE TALMUD

Shulamit Valler
312 pages
Cloth 978-1-936235-36-0
$59.00 / £40.25

Both the Babylonian Talmud and the Jerusalem Talmud depict a wide range of sorrowful situations tied to every level of society and to the complexities of human behavior and the human condition. The causes and expressions of sorrow amongst the Sages, however, are different from their counterparts amongst common people or women, with descriptions varying between the Babylonian and the Jerusalem Talmud. In *Sorrow and Distress in the Talmud*, Valler explores more than 50 stories from both the Babylonian and the Jerusalem Talmuds, focusing on these issues.

Shulamit Valler (PhD Jewish Theological Seminary) is a professor of Talmud and Chair of the Jewish History department at the University of Haifa. Her numerous publications include *Women and Womanhood in the Babylonian Talmud* (1999) and *Massekhet Sukkah — a Feminist Commentary on the Babylonian Talmud* (2009).

THE TWILIGHT OF REASON

Benjamin, Adorno, Horkheimer and Levinas Tested by the Catastrophe
Orietta Ombrosi
200 pages
Cloth 978-1-936235-75-9
$65.00 / £44.25

"Think of the disaster" is the first injunction of thought when faced with the disaster that struck European Jews during the Shoah. Thinking of the disaster means understanding why the Shoah was able to occur in civilized Europe, moulded by humane reason and the values of progress and enlightenment. It means thinking of a possibility for philosophy's future.

Walter Benjamin, who wrestled with these problems ahead of time, Theodor Adorno, Max Horkheimer and Emmanuel Levinas had the courage, the strength and the perception – and sometimes simply the desperation – to think about what had happened. Moved by indignation and the desire to testify, they felt the urgent need to address the cries of agony of Auschwitz's victims in their thinking.

Orietta Ombrosi (PhD University of Paris X-Nanterre) is assistant professor of moral philosophy at the Sapienza, University of Rome. She is the author of *Le crépuscule de la raison. Benjamin, Adorno, Horkheimer et Levinas à l'épreuve de la Catastrophe*, (2007) and *L'umano ritrovato. Saggio su Emmanuel Levinas* (2010), and the editor of *Tra Torah e Sophia. Orizzonti e frontiere della filosofia ebraica* (2011).

WITHOUT RED STRINGS OR HOLY WATER

Maimonides' *Mishneh Torah*

H. Norman Strickman
170 pages
Cloth 978-1-936235-48-3
$48.00 / £32.75

Maimonides was one of the greatest Jewish personalities of the Middle Ages: a halakhist par excellence, a great philosopher, a political leader of his community, and a guardian of Jewish rights. In 1180 CE, Maimonides composed his Halakhic magnum opus, the *Mishneh Torah*, which can be described without exaggeration as the greatest code of Jewish law to be composed in the post-Talmudic era, unique in scope, originality and language. In addition to dealing with an immense variety of Jewish law, from the laws of Sabbath and festival observances, dietary regulations, and relations between the sexes to the sacrificial system, the construction of the Temple, and the making of priestly garments, the *Mishneh Torah* represents Maimonides' conception of Judaism. Maimonides held that the version of Judaism believed in and practiced by many pious Jews of his generation had been infected with pagan notions. In the *Mishneh Torah*, he aimed at cleansing Judaism from these non-Jewish practices and beliefs and impressing upon readers that Jewish law and ritual are free from irrational and superstitious practices. *Without Red Strings or Holy Water* explores Maimonides' views regarding God, the commandments, astrology, medicine, the evil eye, amulets, magic, theurgic practices, omens, communicating with the dead, the messianic era, midrashic literature, and the oral law. *Without Red Strings or Holy Water* will be of interest to all who are interested in the intellectual history of Judaism.

H. Norman Strickman (PhD Dropsie University) is a rabbi at Marine Park Jewish Center and a professor of Judaic Studies at Touro College in New York.

www.ingramcontent.com/pod-product-compliance
Lightning Source LLC
Jackson TN
JSHW060718090725
87332JS00004B/153
* 9 7 8 1 9 3 6 2 3 5 2 8 5 *